ENTERPRISE SYSTEMS

Backup and Recovery

A CORPORATE INSURANCE POLICY

ENTERPRISE SYSTEMS Backup and Recovery

A CORPORATE INSURANCE POLICY

Preston de Guise

CRC Press
Taylor & Francis Group
Boca Raton London New York

CRC Press is an imprint of the
Taylor & Francis Group, an **informa** business
AN AUERBACH BOOK

Auerbach Publications
Taylor & Francis Group
6000 Broken Sound Parkway NW, Suite 300
Boca Raton, FL 33487-2742

Printed in the United States of America on acid-free paper
10 9 8 7 6 5 4 3 2 1

International Standard Book Number-13: 978-1-4200-7639-4 (Softcover)

Library of Congress Cataloging-in-Publication Data

De Guise, Preston.
Enterprise systems backup and recovery : a corporate insurance policy / Preston de Guise.
p. cm.
Includes bibliographical references and index.
ISBN 978-1-4200-7639-4 (hardback : alk. paper)
1. Electronic data processing--Backup processing alternatives. 2. Data recovery (Computer science)
I. Title.

QA76.9.B32D45 2008
005.8'6--dc22 2008026402

Visit the Taylor & Francis Web site at
http://www.taylorandfrancis.com

and the Auerbach Web site at
http://www.auerbach-publications.com

Dedication

For Darren

Contents

Preface

One of the least attractive things about backup is that we always hope we don't need it. That is, in an ideal world where nothing ever goes wrong (intentional or otherwise), it would be an unnecessary activity.

A great many psychological studies have been conducted where aversion therapy can be used to train people to associate unpleasant feelings with a task or action that they may otherwise enjoy or at least view with neutrality. Part of the reason why many people dislike backups is that often when we need to use a backup, it is because something bad has happened.

A well-budgeted, well-designed backup system, however, does not have to be painful or unpleasant to use. Such a system only comes about when several key factors coalesce. These are (in no particular order) business involvement, IT acceptance, best practice designs, enterprise software, and reliable hardware.

As a backup consultant — whether architecting, implementing, or supporting solutions — I get to see the consequences of an insufficiently synergistic approach to back up systems periodically. If IT staff don't accept their role in backups, the environment becomes a mess. If bleeding edge or overly complex designs are put in place, it's like trying to keep a house of cards upright in a storm. The same occurs for the reverse: trying to shoe-horn poorly designed or ill-fitting software or insufficiently robust hardware into an enterprise solution just causes unnecessary angst. Perhaps the least understood of the components, and the one that invariably causes the worst headaches, is business involvement.

When I first started working as a data protection consultant, I had what could only be described as an epiphany. Backups are not an IT function — they are a business function. Like the proverbial tip of an iceberg, the actual copying of data from online media to another type of media should represent just a fraction of the overall activities. Without business involvement — the stating of requirements, the allocation of budget, the establishment of service level agreements, and the oversight of testing, just to name a few — it's entirely reasonable to say that there is no backup system.

Data growth is continuing at a rapid pace. Individual home users now have more storage on their desktop than many businesses did across all their servers ten years ago. For businesses, the growth has been just as high, if not higher. Disk is cheap, or relatively so, and the march towards mass online storage has been accompanied by the need to achieve faster and more efficient backup.

Contributing to what is sometimes referred to as the "data glut" has been an increasing awareness in government and other regulatory bodies that corporate data — those binary 1s and 0s that previously seemed so intangible and irrelevant — forms a critical component of the history of a business. Where once a court might demand paper copies of information, it's now recognized that considerable amounts of a company's activities occur purely within an electronic realm. Thus, with information necessary for discovery (confirming compliance to statutory obligations) existing in electronic form only, laws have been introduced in many countries requiring businesses to protect their data properly and have it readily accessible.

The net result of all this is that backup is not going away. Companies are increasingly working at making their own individual "data glut" more manageable through such technologies as single instance storage, true archiving, hierarchical storage management and deduplication, but one fact remains throughout all this — data must still be protected.

With regulatory requirements for data protection becoming more commonplace, and the world economy requiring electronic interaction, the role of backup as a business rather than an IT function has never been more pronounced.

It's an exciting time to be in the data protection arena.

Acknowledgments

This book would not have seen the light of day were it not for the support and feedback from colleagues and friends who helped along the way. My profound thanks particularly go to Siobhán Ellis, Maree Grant, Brian Norris, Carolina Chavez, and Dan Frith. I'm also very grateful to John Wyzalek and the team at Taylor and Francis for working with me to bring this book to publication.

I also owe much to the original system administration team I worked with — Dave, Andrew, Scott, John, and Jason — because the first main activity I was entrusted with when I joined the team was backups. One could say that was the job that led to my ongoing interest in the field of data protection. (I didn't enjoy being the "backup boy" to start with, but it started feeling good after that first successful recovery at 3 a.m.)

My partner, Darren, deserves recognition for always providing moral support and being a sounding board, not to mention opening my eyes to another realm of desktop productivity I'd previously dismissed.

Taking the long-term view, my parents Lynne and Peter deserve special thanks: from the day the first computer entered our household, it was clear I'd found a career. They supported my interest in computers right from the very start, which culminated in their sacrificing much to put me through university, something for which I can never fully repay them.

There is a very special group of people that deserve ongoing thanks — not just from me, but also from the businesses they work at, from the smallest companies to the largest enterprises. They are the people who are tasked with data protection — whether it be a formal part of their job or an unacknowledged activity they do of their own accord — people who are responsible for looking after data at a company, helping to keep that company running. It's an oft-times thankless task, so I take this space to thank those who look after data, and in doing so, look after the jobs of their colleagues.

Finally, my thanks go to all those involved in the development and support of backup products, who invest time, money, and professionalism into making products we all rely on to maintain a functioning economy.

Acknowledgment

Chapter 1

Introduction

1.1 Who Should Use This Book?

Hundreds of years ago, primitive villagers would stand at the mouth of a volcano and throw an unfortunate individual into its gaping maw as a sacrifice. In return for this sacrifice, they felt they could be assured of anything they requested, such as a safe pregnancy for the chief's wife, a bountiful harvest, a decisive victory in a war against another tribe (which presumably had no volcano to throw anyone into), and protection from bad things.

Some companies treat a backup system like those villagers did the volcano. They sacrifice tapes to the backup system in the hopes that it guarantees protection. However, when treated this way, backups offer about as much protection as the volcano that receives the sacrifice.

Backups are often seen as a guarantee of protection, even when they are not treated or configured correctly. In particular, there is a common misconception that if something called "backup software" is installed, then a backup system is in place. However, a backup system is considerably more than just backup software.

Within a corporate environment there are no other applications that will have such a deep and comprehensive reach into regular systems as backups do. Backup and recovery systems, when implemented correctly, touch just about every system in an environment. For this reason, they need to be treated with respect and understanding. Nothing else in an environment will be as critical to the ongoing safe access of data as a backup system, and simultaneously, little else in an environment will be so sensitive to issues.

Many companies have become blasé about backups, and as a result they often accept second-rate, poorly functioning systems as "the best we can manage." Alternatively, they might properly install and configure a backup system, and then fail to maintain it. If something goes wrong and data can't be restored, the failure is blamed on the backup system — erroneously in many cases.

The goal of this book is to help any company develop a better backup system. To do this, what is needed most is knowledge. Specifically, we need to understand

- What features and functionality should be expected in a backup environment?
- What terminology and concepts are unique to backup software, and what can be related to other areas?

- How can a backup system be monitored successfully? (This is more than just "what constitutes success?")
- How can the performance of a backup system be improved?
- What features are just "window dressing," and should be ignored as irrelevant?

By knowing all of the above, it will be possible to use backup systems as an insurance policy against failure, rather than as a volcano requiring periodic sacrifices.

There are a multitude of reasons why backups are performed, but the real, single reason is for recovery. If something goes wrong and data is lost, an organization must be able to use the backup system to get that data back.

A common misconception is that only a few people in an organization need to have any involvement with backups; this couldn't be further from the truth. Just as backup systems reach into almost all IT systems, so should the knowledge of backups reach into a plethora of positions within an organization. Following is just a very small list of roles that need to have some understanding of backups. Depending on the role, this may require a simple understanding of backups, or a complete understanding of how backups have been implemented within an organization:

- System and backup administrators
- Application administrators
- Operators
- Help-desk staff
- Key system users
- Technical team leaders
- Middle management
- Upper management
- CIO, CEO, and company board

This is not to say that everyone in the environment must be an expert on every possible aspect of backups and the deployed backup environment — indeed, this would be unnecessary and wasteful. However, everyone in the list needs to know something. To demonstrate this, the following is a quick set of examples, covering only a brief selection of the responsibilities for each role:

- System and backup administrators need to know everything about the backup system, and should understand backup concepts sufficiently so that they can judge the backup system against industry best practices.
- Application administrators need to know how to work with the backup system, and how the backup system interacts with their applications.
- Operators need to know how to monitor backups, change media, perform recoveries, and facilitate ad-hoc backups.
- Help-desk staff need to know how to initiate and monitor user data recoveries.
- Key system users need to know how the backups interact with their systems and what limitations may be imposed.
- Technical team leaders and middle management need to know how the backup environment has been designed, how it is currently functioning, and how to escalate issues.
- Upper management need to know (in very broad terms) how the system is designed, and how to ask the right questions to do spot-checks on the status of the backup system.

- The CIO, CEO, and company board all need to know that the backup system(s) is(are) functioning and protecting the company.

Everyone has some form of ownership/responsibility with the backup solution. To be certain, if data can't be recovered, an upper-level manager might be able to dismiss a system or backup administrator for not protecting data properly (or at all). However, it might be the CEO who is charged with contempt of court and ordered to spend a year in jail, or it might be the company shareholders who express their wrath after the company is fined $10,000,000 for failing to meet statutory regulations regarding the protection of data. Everyone really does have a part to play.

A common saying is "the buck stops here." In the field of backups, "here" is "everywhere." There might be key decision makers and policy makers, but backup is one area where nobody in a company can say, "I thought it was his problem," or "She's in charge, not me."

So, to get back to our original question — who should use this book? The answer is everyone. Regardless of whether you are a key user, an operator, an administrator, a CEO, CIO, or CFO, everyone needs to know enough about backups so that they can fulfill their role.

1.2 Concepts

1.2.1 What Is a Backup?

Perhaps some might think this is a rhetorical question.

One of the more traditional responses to this question is "a backup is a copy of data." The general problem with most definitions of "backup," including this common response, is the failure to mention the actual reason why backups are made: recovery.

Backups require a healthy dose of paranoia and therefore no matter how much they are automated, they still have to be monitored to make sure they succeed. They have to be tested periodically to ensure that components that were working weeks or months ago still work now. They usually involve the highest number of removable parts (i.e., the individual pieces of media themselves) and are, for many organizations, one of the least correctly funded parts of the IT environment. Being responsible for backups can also be one of the most thankless tasks in an environment, as for many organizations they are not considered until something fails — i.e., the only time the backup administrator gets attention is when there are problems. Therefore, even backup consultants might say that "backups are a pain."

With all this in mind, backups obviously aren't made just for the fun of it. A worthwhile definition of a backup should also include the reason for the backups, and therefore we will use the following definition for the rest of this book:

> A backup is a copy of any data that can be used to restore the data as/when required to its original form. That is, a backup is a valid copy of data, files, applications, or operating systems that can be used for the purposes of recovery.

By using a definition of backups that includes the purpose of the backup — that being recovery — we force attention not only onto backups, but such critical activities as recovery, recovery testing, archival, disaster recovery, and disaster recovery testing. Too often, consideration of "backup systems" neglects these critical activities until they are required!

The purpose of backup systems should be entirely self-evident. Unfortunately this is frequently not so. For instance, a known ploy of outsourcing firms is to have Service Level Agreements (SLAs) that focus only on backup requirements, rather than recoveries. While it's certainly the case that recovery targets can only be accurately set when created on a per-system basis, this deliberate obfuscation of the purpose of the backup system can only create trouble for the company whose data is (or is not) being protected.

The problem with so many supposed "backup systems" in enterprises today is that they are put in as an afterthought. Entire systems will be installed without any backup planning, and when it is finally considered, there is either insufficient interest or insufficient budget to install an acceptable backup solution. A system with, say, 100 GB of storage might have a DDS-5 tape drive attached to it just before it becomes "production ready." In short, this has no testing, no capacity planning, and no chance of working acceptably. As default storage capacities on systems continue to grow by orders of magnitude, this problem only continues to grow with the industry.

Unfortunately, once one or two of these "not quite barely good enough" systems slip into an environment, it sets a precedent that can be difficult and perhaps costly to break. However, what should be seen is that the cost exists only at the initial capital investment, and in fact the cost from not changing to a properly designed enterprise backup system could be disastrous.

It should be understood that ongoing spending on a backup system mostly falls into operational expenditure rather than being a continuous exercise in capital investment. That is, each deployed enterprise backup system will have an initial investment followed by periodic expenditure. For smaller organizations, this differentiation may not make much of a difference, but for larger organizations, this can make a considerable improvement in how budget is allocated.

In reality, the backups themselves have a life span that exceeds that of the system(s) they are protecting, something that is not necessarily considered as part of the planning process of a system. For instance, we can describe the life span of a production server on the basis of how (and when) backups are performed over its entire life cycle. This might resemble the following:

1. Installation
   A. Pre-purchase
      i. The existing backup system is considered in the context of the new system being purchased — that is, a verification of backup infrastructure capacity in relation to the proposed new system is performed, and the backup system is expanded if necessary to meet capacity requirements
      ii. If expansion of the backup system is required, the requisite components/features should be purchased now
   B. Installation
      i. New system is received and has the appropriate operating system install, patching, and security options installed
      ii. Backup software is installed on the host, and first backup is taken
   C. Recovery testing (files)
      i. If this is the first install of this type of operating system, a complete disaster recovery test should be performed
      ii. System has appropriate applications/software installed
      iii. Backup is taken
   D. Recovery testing (base applications)
      i. Once recovery testing has completed successfully, the system/backup administrators should hand the system over to the developers

2. Development cycle
   A. Repeat
      i. Daily development
      ii. Daily backups, appropriate to the type of development occurring; these backups may be different than the backups that the final system will receive in full production (e.g., databases may be initially backed up cold rather than hot; where this is the case, it must be clearly noted)
   B. If the intended production backup mechanism is different than the development/test backup mechanism, the production backup mechanism should be implemented at the end of the development cycle, with suitable testing to confirm successful operations; only the production backup mechanism should be used from this time (if any expansion of the backup system was required, it now should be in place)
   C. If this is a new system or application, then during the development phase at least one bare metal recovery test (complete system recovery from a fresh operating system install) should take place to ensure that applications and procedures being developed are recoverable
3. Test cycle
   A. End user testing with daily backups
   B. Confirmation that each of the following recovery tests have been performed successfully, with their processes clearly (and correctly) documented
      i. Cold, offline backups
      ii. Standard hot backups
      iii. Bare metal recoveries (i.e., disaster recovery testing)
   C. An authorized manager should sign off any decision not to conduct these tests (e.g., tests might be skipped due to the system being essentially the same as another previously deployed system; however, this should still be acknowledged)
4. Production operations
   A. Following successful completion of steps (1) through (3), the system can be designated as production-ready
   B. Production cycle
      i. Daily use
      ii. Daily backups
      iii. Monthly/yearly (or other periodic) backups as required
      iv. Periodic file, directory, and application recovery testing
      v. Occasional bare metal recovery/disaster recovery testing (typically, this would occur after significant changes to the system such as major operating system upgrades, etc.; this may only need to be done on a per-system type basis)*
      vi. Archival operations as required
      vii. After designated periods of time, or the purchase of new backup technologies, monthly/yearly/archival backups should be relocated to new backup media
      viii. After designated periods of time, older media should be destroyed once they are past their retention time, and either media integrity cannot be guaranteed or the media technology is no longer to be used
      ix. After designated periods of time, when legal requirements necessitate the destruction of old data, backups should be reviewed to delete data that is not to be retained;

* Not for every machine, but for each "type" — e.g., Windows file servers. Unix mail servers, etc.

if this is not possible due to other data on media which must be kept, that data which is to be kept should be relocated to allow the destruction of media

5. Post-production
   A. System is decommissioned, with all applications shut-down and no data access occurring
   B. Multiple final copies of the system are generated through cold, complete offline backups
   C. Documentation is generated for a recovery of the system from its final decommissioning backup, and stored with the final backups generated; this documentation should include details of the backup software that needs to be used for recovery — in essence, the documentation should be written as if it were for a "green" site with no assumed knowledge of the backup software
   D. Additional cold, offline backups should be generated with "common" tools such as native OS backup tools or open source backup tools, so that very long-term recovery is not dependant on a single product
   E. System is redesigned for another purpose (potentially starting the process again) or retired
   F. After designated periods of time, or having moved to new tape technologies, decommissioning backups, and monthly/yearly/archival backups should be relocated to new media or destroyed as appropriate

What this should demonstrate is that backups for a system may start weeks or sometimes even months before end users first touch the system (depending on the length of the development and test cycles), and will continue to be maintained in some fashion possibly for years after users have ceased using the system. (Of course it is likely that few, if any, of the backups taken during the early phases of development will require any form of long-term retention, and typically most pre-production backups are deleted before a system enters production.)

This level of planning is rarely seen in organizations, usually due to a misunderstanding of the purpose of backups. Too many companies focus on backups as if they themselves are the end requirement — an ongoing budgetary black hole whose results (the backup media) are rarely needed.

Instead, we need to remain focused at all times on the real definition for backups — that being something that facilitates recoveries. Indeed, considering the most severe of circumstances, we can define the purpose of backups as follows:

> Backups are performed to allow a company to continue to operate, rather than going out of business, in the event of a failure occurring.

Maintainers of backup systems often face a persistent struggle for budget, compared to the budget allocation processes for other departments within an organization — even in comparison to procurement within other sections of an IT department. When considering the purpose of backups, this is not sensible; from a corporate continuance perspective, to give short shrift to the backup budget is potentially disastrous.

It is commonly the case that people only know about their system administrators when something goes awry. The best system administrators are therefore often seen as the ones whom end users don't know. Similarly, in an optimum operating environment where no problems occur, few people will know of the backup administrator, yet that doesn't mitigate the need for backups.

One might compare such situations with the "year 2000 problem." The post-Y2K wrap-up was perhaps one of the best examples of illogical thinking the IT world has ever seen. A great many commentators (primarily journalists but also some management in various companies) felt that because nothing catastrophic had happened, Y2K had never actually been a threat — therefore the money spent to resolve the problem had been completely wasted. (This would be somewhat akin to someone refueling their car because the warning light comes on, and then deciding that, because the car doesn't stop running, they hadn't really needed to refuel at all.)

1.2.2 Think Insurance

Over time some companies that experience limited numbers of failures reduce the available budget for backups, considering them unnecessary. (Regardless of whether this is a literal reduction or simply a failure to grow the backup system to meet demands, the end result is the same.) Those same businesses, however, would never decide to cease taking regular insurance just because no claims had been lodged over a period of time.

There is no difference between backups and insurance. Similar to insurance policies, backup systems are an investment that would be preferable to avoid needing to collect on. For instance, most people who own a home carry some form of home and contents insurance policy from year to year. Every year they hope that they don't have to make a claim, as making a claim invariably means that something bad has happened — something they'd rather have avoided. Not having needed to make a claim is hardly justification for not renewing the policy each year though. It is the same for backups — a company should have backups running every day on systems, and every day where the backups aren't required should be considered a good day, not one where money has been wasted.

Ultimately, backups become an accepted component in a company when management and users stop thinking of them as an end in themselves or a "bottomless pit" cost center, but instead consider them to be a form of insurance the company needs if it's going to survive system failures.

1.2.3 Information Lifecycle Protection (ILP)

A lot has been said in the media in the last few years about information lifecycle management, or ILM. This is erroneously considered to be the part of the role of a backup product, even by backup product vendors, who should know better! In actual fact, ILM and backups really have nothing in common except that both relate to information.

There are two very different streams for interaction with information in a corporate environment — management and protection. Although some might argue that protection could be classified as part of management, it is more accurate to say that ILM and ILP are sibling activities. Information lifecycle management refers to:

- Creating, updating, and deleting content
- Relocating content as storage and access requirements change
- Indexing of content
- Auditing of content

On the other hand, information lifecycle protection refers to:

- Ensuring content is available
- Ensuring content does not become damaged due to system, application, or user error

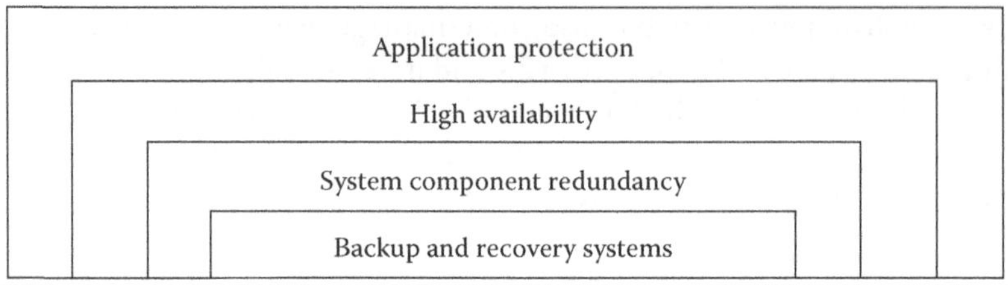

Figure 1.1 Information life cycle protection tiers

- Ensuring that content can be restored in the event of loss or corruption, for its designated useful/required life span

Drilling further on protection, we can explain each component as:

- Availability — any form of high-availability system (e.g., clusters, RAID, multisite synchronous replication, etc.)
- Protection from damage — virus scanning, auto-save in applications, etc.
- Restoration — retrieval of information from backups in the event of information loss or destruction

Instead of erroneously lumping backup and recovery systems into ILM, we can therefore consider backup and recovery systems to be a core component of a shadow activity to ILM — information lifecycle protection, or ILP. Figure 1.1 represents it another way:

- We first rely on applications to protect us from information loss. This may include the obvious options such as virus scanning, but also covers less-considered areas as application and operating system race condition avoidance.
- At a lower level, we rely on high availability.
- As a final fall-back, we rely on systems redundancy to avoid data loss.
- In the event of data loss, we rely on our backup/recovery systems to restore information.

1.3 Backups Versus Fault Tolerance

Fault tolerance is the industry catch-all term to describe systems, applications, and configurations that can survive the failure of components with no noticeable (or accepted degraded) impact on users. Different systems and environments provide reasonably varied levels of fault tolerance. The following are examples of fault tolerance:

- Hardware redundancy, including
  - RAID (redundant array of inexpensive disks): With the aim being that any individual filesystem can survive the failure of at least one disk, or possibly more, depending on the configuration used
  - Multiple NICs (network interface cards): If a NIC, switch port, or even a switch fails, the host can remain connected to the network in a reduced form
  - Hot-swappable memory, CPUs, peripherals: New components can be added to replace failed components without having to take the system down for maintenance

  - Redundant data paths: If a particular channel to data fails, another channel can be used to access the same data; in particular this is often a required feature of SAN implementations, and is best achieved through multiple interface cards at the array and the host, connected via different switches that are independent of one another
- Array-to-array volume replication, which may be synchronous or asynchronous
- Clustering
  - LAN clustering, where another system continues to provide application/data access even when the first system fails
  - WAN clustering, where another site (or campus) can continue operations even if the primary site fails, offering the same services as the original site
- Volume management software, providing soft-RAID: This often provides greater flexibility than hardware RAID, but usually with reduced performance due to the need to leverage primary processor time; this allows companies to achieve some level of redundancy without necessarily spending a considerable amount of money on disk storage
- Data/application replication: For poor bandwidth environments or systems that do not support active clustering, data/application replication allows for faster restoration of services at another location if the primary site goes down
- Snapshots: For systems that must have minimum data loss and minimum recovery time, snapshots may allow administrators to roll back to earlier versions of filesystems made available either in an ad-hoc fashion (e.g., before maintenance) or at predetermined times throughout the day (e.g., hourly).

To have a system that delivers 100 percent agreed (negotiated) uptime, several of these options may be required. However, none of them (nor all of them combined) can provide sufficient protection to negate the need to perform backups.

Similarly, backups do not exist to provide fault tolerance — merely fault recovery. They represent a lower tier of service delivery that encompasses such areas as controlled environments and appropriate work procedures.

What can be said, however, is that fault tolerance — clusters, RAID, etc. — cannot provide the level of availability they promise without an appropriate backup system to cope with an unexpected failure. There are no options, therefore, of deploying a fault-tolerant system without backups. Fault tolerance and backups are in effect complimentary medicines or synergistic processes for a corporate environment.

If deployed correctly, increasingly sophisticated (and costly) types of fault tolerance can provide various levels of protection from failures such as:

- Destructive viruses
- Human error causing data loss or corruption
- Catastrophic hardware failure
- Malicious damage

However, as the following factors are increased, the cost of implementing and maintaining fault-tolerant systems increases substantially (in some cases, nigh on exponentially):

- Severity (degree) of any individual failure
- The complexity of the failure (i.e., the number of simultaneous failures tolerated)
- The longevity of the protection provided in the event of a failure

Uninterruptible power supplies represent a simple yet elegant example of rising fault-tolerance costs. A UPS for a single system that provides enough power to allow the system to shut down safely in the event of power loss is relatively cheap. However, as the number of systems grows, providing power merely to allow the controlled shut-down of potentially hundreds of systems, switches, storage arrays, tape libraries, etc., quickly becomes extremely expensive. Even greater cost is incurred if ongoing power must be provided (e.g., requiring diesel power generators to keep a computer room running).

Unfortunately, some companies do happen to assume that fault-tolerant systems remove the need for backups. Some vendors (or perhaps more appropriately, some inexperienced staff at some vendors) will even try to sell fault-tolerant systems as a means of avoiding backups. "Our disk systems are so robust they'll never need to be backed up" is the sort statement commonly attributed to vendors who have a poor grasp of ILP.

There is a saying in system administration — "nothing corrupts faster than a mirror." This is a warning to the uninformed — a mirror (or rather, any form of redundant disks) cannot protect against data corruption. If one side of a mirror is corrupted, the other side is also corrupted — instantly. A mirror, for instance, does not protect the system from a user accidentally erasing a whole directory, a single file, or even a single character in a single file.

The same can equally be said about clusters. Clusters typically will either share a common disk (in which case the data is corrupted regardless of what server is failed-over to), or will replicate data between each other; in either case, "nothing corrupts faster than a cluster."

Similarly, data replication (i.e., keeping multiple copies of data, in theory, across the entire planet) does not provide the same level of protection against corruption as backups do. This is equally true of snapshots. Even if data replication or snapshots between sites occurs only once every 24 hours, and therefore wouldn't be instantly corrupted due to a mistake at one site, it is usually only possible to roll back a limited number of versions of the data. This is usually measured in days, not weeks, months, or years. After all, not all corruption is instantly noticeable. Some corruption may take an extended period of time to notice, particularly if data is only being accessed infrequently. Site/data replication and filesystem/volume snapshots will not protect indefinitely, and rarely provide protection from long-term data corruption.

Array manufacturers of course would offer to sell sufficient disk to provide months of snapshot capabilities, but this would come with potentially significant performance issues over time, even if it were an economically viable option.

Thousands of more examples could be raised, but the same point remains regardless — no matter what is done with systems, no matter what steps are taken to avoid hardware failure, data or site loss, the simple truth remains that backups must be made.

1.4 Risk Versus Cost

No company, regardless of size, financial backing, or employee knowledge, can completely eliminate risk from their information technology environment. Even if one were to use the entire budget for a company for five years exclusively on fault tolerance, high availability, and backups, it would still not be possible to provide a 100 percent guarantee that:

- Systems will never fail.
- Data will never be lost.
- Backups will never be needed or, if needed, will meet all conceivable contingencies.

For example, the following sorts of scenarios are unlikely to be catered for by even the largest of organizations:

- Worldwide thermonuclear war resulting in a catastrophic disruption to society
- Planet-killer asteroid hitting Earth
- Runaway nanotechnology experiment destroying all matter

Indeed, it could be argued that if any of these sorts of scenarios occurred, most staff would justifiably have more pressing concerns than whether data is sufficiently protected or can be recovered.

An almost endless number of extreme-catastrophe scenarios can be given. However, what this serves to highlight is that, for any particular system, an organization needs to make a "risk versus cost" decision on how it is protected — whether via backups only, or fault tolerance, high-availability configurations, and backups. In extreme scenarios, companies must also consider the potential human aspect of the disaster — will staff even care?

Bringing ourselves back to smaller and more approachable situations, we can obviously see that the level of investment and protection will be entirely dependent on the criticality of the systems.

The "risk versus cost" approach is simple. For every system in an environment, the organization must decide the following:

- The risks
  - Technical: What is the risk of this system failing?
  - Commercial: What is the risk to the business of an unprotected failure?
- The costs
  - Technical: What is the cost in time of this system failing?
  - Commercial: What is the cost of a loss of data on this system?
  - Fiscal: What is the cost of the desired level of protection to avoid this scenario?

Note that two very distinct types of risk must be evaluated — the technical risk of failure as well as the commercial risk. Too often, one risk is understood, but the other is not. For example, the IT department may understand that there is a 5 percent risk of the system failing at any time (i.e., it has 95-percent availability), but the business as a whole may not have an appreciation of the risk to company operations if a failure occurs. There is a similar delineation regarding cost, with the three varieties — technical, commercial, and fiscal — all needing to be understood.

These five questions form the crux of any decision on how systems are to be protected. For example, consider an end user's desktop computer. Many organizations might establish the following policies in relation to desktop computers:

- As personal computers don't have the same level of redundancy as servers, and users are known to do "silly" things, the risk of the PC failing is deemed "medium."
- The cost of the system failing is minimal — one user not having a workstation does not affect the bottom line of the company.
- IT policies state that all users should store their data on the fileserver, so the cost of data loss should be quite low because there should be no business data stored on the desktop.
- As there are tens of thousands of end users in the company, the risk to the business of an individual user's PC suffering an unprotected failure is deemed "low."

This might appear to be an acceptable analysis, and in many organizations may be sufficient. However, consider an example of how this scenario might play out:

- The corporate lawyer uses a PC.
- The lawyer has "lost" the drive mapping to the file server recently, and has logged a call with the help desk to restore it. Normal attempts to remap the drive share have failed, and the help desk has not been able to send someone to fix it yet, as it's a busy time and there's a backlog of support issues to be dealt with.
- Needing to continue to work, the lawyer has had others e-mail documents that need action and has stored them on the local PC to make revisions.
- Revisions are made and stored locally.
- Hard drive in PC fails.
- Business is found to be in contempt of court because urgently needed legal documentation could not be delivered due to hard drive failure, with the judge considering "my hard drive crashed" as the corporate equivalent of "the dog ate my homework."

This might appear to be an exceptional set of circumstances, but it highlights the need to ensure that if a decision is made not to back up a particular machine, operational policies must be designed to mitigate that risk. For example, in this case rather than merely having a stated policy, if the IT department had actually set system permissions to deny local storage, the help desk would have had to action the service request sooner. This would have meant that a hard-drive crash on the PC, while inconvenient, would not have resulted in data loss. (Alternatively, it could be argued that with the policy of "no local storage," a failure to connect to the network drive share should have been treated as a higher priority issue by the help desk staff. We should remember, though, that technical staff frequently assign priorities to issues based on the level of urgency conveyed by the user, even though users may not understand or appreciate the nature and urgency of the problem.)

Another issue that this scenario demonstrates is the notion of cascading failures. That is, a single failure may not actually result in data loss, but may result in an increased risk of data loss. RAID systems demonstrate this on an ongoing basis; in a standard mirroring arrangement, the failure of a single disk does not present a problem, but it does mean that a second failure prior to mirror reconstruction represents a much larger risk. In the same way that chess players must think multiple moves ahead in the game to achieve victory, companies need to consider, or at least acknowledge, the risk that cascading failures may occur.

Examining an alternate situation, laptops are often recognized as having important data on them, yet many businesses take the attitude that they are "too difficult" to back up, and therefore users are encouraged instead to make their own backups using CD/DVD burning, or to ensure they copy files across to the server whenever they are connected to the network. In this scenario, and all other scenarios where user intervention is chosen over backup automation, it is necessary to remember the following rule: any form of user-initiated backup is doomed to failure.

This is typically not due to any bad decisions on the part of the users. Rather, it recognizes that users have their own jobs and their own work responsibilities. When discussing this with end users, it is very usual to hear that they're not interested in extending their responsibilities to include work that they consider to be the domain of the IT department. "Doomed" is therefore an apt description.

The failure to calculate "risk versus cost" correctly does not occur only at the desktop and laptop levels. Businesses can make biased decisions that (1) do not reflect the importance of a system,

(2) misjudge effort involved in restoration activities for unprotected systems, or (3) do not cater for required policies as a result of the decisions. Following are typical examples of potentially faulty decisions:

- Server x does y, and any other server can do that.
- Server x doesn't need its operating system backed up, as it's just a generic OS install.
- We don't need to back up x because it's replicated from another location.
- We have a standard build for servers of type x, so we can quickly recreate it.

Depending on the type of server or function, sometimes these decisions can be correct. More often than not, however, such decisions are flawed. For instance, if a server receives data replicated from another server (such as a Web server in a demilitarized zone [DMZ] receiving updates from the production environment), it may seem that it doesn't require backups. However, consider that any individual server consists of data, applications, and operating system. Thus, although it may be the case that a decision can be made not to back up the data, this may not necessarily mean that the rest of the host can remain unprotected. Assuming such a system fails, the process of recreating the server may be as follows:

1. Source new hardware
2. Re-install operating system
3. Patch operating system
4. Create user accounts
5. Perform security hardening
6. Install and patch applications
7. Fully re-sync data
8. Reinstate automated data replication

In this example, we have at least eight distinct steps involved in the installation, and only the final two steps deals with the replicated data. In the above example, steps 3–6 could conceivably be skipped by (1) having backups and (2) installing the backup software as part of the operating system install. As such, it could be argued that "this server receives replicated data" is an insufficient justification in itself for choosing not to back up the sample host. Finally, it should also be noted that if the time taken to replicate the data fully again greatly exceeds the time taken to restore the data, or introduces noticeable impact on the production host owning the data, the decision is even more flawed.

Proxy servers provide an example of hosts that are not routinely backed up, but should be. The data on a proxy server, after all, comes from machines on the Internet, and is only a local cache for performance reasons. However, there is a tangible cost, both in time and money, of repopulating a corporate proxy server by user downloads:

- User wait times incurred as users must retrieve a completely fresh copy of all previously cached content
- Bandwidth utilization costs from the company's ISP as a result of there being no cached data

Finally, consider automated processes for standard system builds. These are often seen as a way of eliminating backups for systems that provide services, but store no user data. Although this may be the case from time to time, they don't necessarily address the following:

- Will any patches need to be installed after the OS rebuild?
- Do any user accounts need to be recreated?
- Do any additional applications need to be installed?
- Does the system need to be reattached to a domain or other master security environment?
- Are there any service customizations (e.g., share configurations, etc.) to be performed?
- Are there any unique soft identifier tags associated with the host (e.g., hostid, machine SID, etc.) that need to be reset if rebuilt from scratch?

If the answer to any of these questions is "yes," it may mean that backing up the host would be a good idea. This is particularly the case if there is no clear procedure for customizing a host once it has had an OS installed.

There is no perfect methodology for deciding whether a particular type of host or system should receive backups. Equally, however, no organization should have a blanket, immutable requirement not to back up certain types of servers; there will always be extraordinary cases even for servers that might otherwise appear not to need backups.

A simple rule of thumb to use when determining what should or shouldn't be backed up is the following: if it takes more than 15 minutes to perform customizations to a system after the base operating system has been installed, and those customizations can't be done by any random team member without referring to written instructions (i.e., they are not "industry best practices" for a particular operating system), then the system should be backed up.

However, more generically, the following rule should be considered whenever a risk versus cost decision is made regarding backups for any individual machine:

> It is always better to back up a little more than necessary than not to back up enough, and be unable to complete a recovery.

1.5 Dispelling Myths

This book should help to dispel several myths associated with backups. Some of these are humorous, some are causes for concern, and some are outright dangerous.

1.5.1 Myth: Tape Is Going to Die Within a Few Years, and We'll All Be Backing Up to Cheap Disk

Myth criticality: Humorous — This claim is made almost every quarter, usually by IT journalists who have just attended the launch of a new backup-to-disk or data-replication product. Tape remains, and will continue to do so for a considerable time, the cheapest mechanism for offline, offsite data protection.

This is not to say that at some point, a technology will be introduced that will supplant tape. For instance, if some form of ultra-dense, low-priced flash memory storage were to be developed, this might fit the bill. However, until such time as the price per GB of such technology comes within 10 percent of the price per GB of tape, and the speed is comparable or better, tape will reign supreme.

Even if tape is replaced, the industry will be dealing with tape remnants possibly for decades to come.

1.5.2 Myth: Commercial Backup Software Is Not as "Trustworthy" as Operating System Invoked Tools

Myth criticality: Humorous — Although this may seem a glib response, backup software vendors would no longer be in operation if their products were not trustworthy. Furthermore, operating system backup tools have no more claim to reliability than commercial tools.

1.5.3 Myth: Commercial Backup Software Is Not as Efficient as Customized Backup Scripts Written by a Good System Administrator with Local Environment Knowledge

Myth criticality: Cause for concern — In 2004, one commercial backup vendor published its "speed record," backing up over 10 TB per hour of real customer data, with a sustained file-level backup throughput of 2.6 GB/s. It is reasonably safe to assume that few, if any, system administrator-developed scripts have been able to achieve backup performance approaching this scale.

1.5.4 Myth: The Use of Commercial Backup Software Would Require Staff Training

Myth criticality: Cause for concern — Companies must recognize the need to train staff in the tools they use (whether that training is formal or informal), and because it is foundation software to the rest of the organization, the correct use of backup software must be taught to necessary staff.

1.5.5 Myth: Commercial Backup Software Offers No Tangible Improvements over Regular Operating System Backups

Myth criticality: Cause for concern — Other than the potential for high-performance backups previously stated, backup software offers a multitude of benefits over regular operating system backups including, but not limited to:

- High-speed restores by using only the media absolutely required, with fast positioning to required data
- Indices for easy recovery browsing, as opposed to "guessing" the media required
- Library/device management
- Bare metal recovery tools (mileage will vary depending on the product)
- Centralized protection and management in a heterogeneous environment

1.5.6 Myth: Deploying Commercial Backup Software Requires Budgeting for Additional Yearly Maintenance Fees

Myth criticality: Cause for concern — This means that the business doesn't see backup as insurance, and possibly sees it as a function solely belonging to IT. Budget for the backup environment should be drawn from all aspects of the business, not just IT.

1.5.7 Myth: Backup Is a Waste of Money

Myth criticality: Dangerous — For the most part, this myth holds little sway anymore, though some "old guard" may still feel this is true. Although it is true that, if scoped or implemented incorrectly, backup systems can cost more money than necessary and may not provide correct protection, it is very dangerous to categorize all backups as a waste of money on the basis of one or more flawed implementations.

1.5.8 Myth: It Is Cheaper and More Appropriate to Develop In-House Backup Systems Than to Deploy Commercial Backup Systems

Myth criticality: Dangerous — Backup systems are a core application, and little to no business justification exists to develop backup software "in-house" rather than purchasing commercial software. The same companies that would have staff develop backup software in-house would not typically support any of the following:

- Writing a relational database from scratch rather than deploying an off-the-shelf product that is tried and tested
- Writing a word-processor from scratch because the corporate word processor runs slower than a plaintext editor
- Writing an operating system because the operating system vendor of choice recently decided to start charging on a per-seat basis for their licenses
- Writing their own clustering software because a vendor "couldn't possibly understand" the high-availability requirements of the company

1.5.9 Myth: If a Department Can't Fund Backups for Its Systems, They Don't Get Backed Up

Myth criticality: Dangerous — Companies, particularly larger ones, often employ cross-charging, where various departments charge each other for the activities they perform. However, even in environments where cross-charging is aggressively pursued, there remain some shared resources that should not be cross-charged. Like insurance policies, for many companies backup should fall into this category.

Where backup must be cross-charged, what should be the case is that no budget is allocated without consideration of backup costs. That is, any new system acquisition or, more broadly, corporate change or development must factor in any costs associated with backing up the back-end systems that facilitate those changes.

In short, this attitude indicates a fatal flaw in company attitude towards backup.

1.6 The Top Ten Rules

Much of the rest of this book is devoted to recommending best practices in a backup environment. Whether planning a new backup environment, implementing changes to an existing environment, or simply using a current system, there are ten critical rules that should be considered to be set in stone, and followed at all times:

1. Think insurance.
2. Backup to recover.
3. Trust empirical evidence only, do not make assumptions.
4. Leading edge is OK; however, bleeding edge is not.
5. Document systems.
6. Backup is not archive.
7. Fault tolerance and high availability do not supplant backup.
8. Backup is a corporate activity, not an IT activity.
9. Test, test, test.
10. Backup and recovery systems must evolve with the company.

As we progress, the reasons for these rules should become quite clear.

1.7 Online Resources

Further resources, including sample procedures and forms cited in this book, may be found at the accompanying Web site: http://www.enterprisesystemsbackup.com.

Chapter 2

Human and Technical Layers

2.1 Introduction

An enterprise data protection system is more than just a collection of machines and media. The people that interact with the environment play a vital role, and understanding where the backup system fits within the environment is critical.

2.2 Human Layers: Roles and Responsibilities

2.2.1 Overview

Far too few people understand that they have a role to play in backup and recovery systems. If someone is asked what his or her role is, and responds with any of the following, then it is likely they don't have an adequate appreciation of data protection in a corporate environment:

- "I'm too senior to worry about backups."
- "They're not my concern."
- "My system administrators handle that."
- "Another system administrator handles that."
- "I just handle the operating system, the application people handle the rest."
- "I just handle the application, the system administrators handle the rest."
- "I just change the tapes."
- "I'm the senior system administrator — the junior administrator handles backups."
- "We don't need to do backups."
- "I assume the IT staff handle the backups."

It is useful to evaluate a company hierarchy from the perspective of backups, i.e., to consider the roles at various levels of an organization, and what involvement the people who fill those roles should have with the backup system. Although this break-down wouldn't necessarily be applied as part of an official job description for many of the roles, it helps to reinforce that backups form a core component that starts at the lowest rung in IT and extends right through to the board or the CEO.

This hierarchy can be broken down broadly into three groups: technical staff, management, and end users.

2.2.2 Technical Staff

We start our review of backup responsibilities with the people who should have the most day-to-day involvement in a backup system — the IT staff. Although we'll also cover the responsibilities of management and end-users in the backup environment, it is undisputedly the case that as the custodians of the systems, IT staff must accept responsibility for backups in the environment, or else systems will not be properly protected and may not be recoverable.

2.2.2.1 Operators

An operator does not just "change tapes." Indeed, it is preferable to install a backup solution that requires minimal human intervention for media changing. However, an operator should be capable of:

- Diagnosing common problems (such as error messages that indicate hosts were offline during a backup, etc.)
- Restarting backups if necessary
- Starting ad-hoc backups as requested by users and system/application administrators
- Performing ad-hoc restores as requested by users and system/application administrators
- Understanding the importance of correct media handling
- Having a sufficient understanding of the types of backups performed so as to know what backups should be running, and when
- Understanding the maintenance windows that may be part of a backup system, and how other system maintenance functions may interact/interfere with the backup system
- Being able to liaise with the company's offsite media management services to ensure the timely return of media
- Having access to corporate policies regarding who can request the recovery of what component

This clearly creates an implication that the operators should have access to documentation relating to the backup software, and furthermore should receive training and updated procedures whenever a new process is implemented.

2.2.2.2 Help Desk Staff

Where an organization employs both help desk staff and operations staff, it is usually the case that operations staff are responsible for the server-related components of the backup system, while help desk staff are responsible for the user-related components of the backup system. In this case, a help desk staff member will need to be capable of:

- Diagnosing common problems in ad-hoc backup and recovery operations
- Having a basic understanding of the backup schedules and maintenance windows to know when restores can and can't be accommodated
- Understanding media recall procedures
- Understanding formal procedures in relation to recovery requests
- Having access to corporate policies regarding who can request the recovery of what component

In general, help desk staff should be able to assume that the backup system is operational unless otherwise advised by other staff members.

2.2.2.3 Backup Administrators

Typically, backup environments are administered by one of two different groups — backup administrators or system administrators. If an organization has dedicated backup administrators, they will obviously have the core responsibility for the system. In this case, backup administrators will need to be able to:

- Perform all operator tasks with the system
- Perform all help desk tasks associated with the system
- Explain the overall backup configuration in detail
- Clearly diagnose what types of recovery may be required, and explain those to management/end users
- Teach use of the system to any other group of personnel, regardless of whether that group is technical, management, or users
- Provide and maintain details of daily backup success/failure states
- Provide and maintain capacity/trending information to management, tracking the ability of the environment to meet the ongoing needs of the business
- Liaise with management in planning improvements, infrastructure changes, etc., and being aware in advance of changes that may impact the backup system; i.e., a backup administrator should be a member of the change management team for a company
- Maintain backup systems documentation
- Conduct backup and recovery tests
- Provide regular updates during critical recoveries (even if those updates are to say "everything is going OK")

Additionally, backup administrators should never assume anything about the backup system, i.e., they should rely on empirical evidence. (To put it another way, if a backup administrator wants to assume something about the backup system, the administrator should assume failure rather than success.)

If the organization has no dedicated backup administrators, then it is usually the case that essential administration of the backup system will fall to the system administrators. If this is so, system administrators should be able to perform not only all of the activities outlined in the following section, but all of the above steps as well.

2.2.2.4 System Administrators

Of the two different types of system administration groups in IT departments, the best type is one where everyone knows at least a little bit about all the systems, and all the work that everyone else does. This is a knowledge-sharing group. Another type of system administration group is where everyone does their own thing. Knowledge sharing is at a minimum level and a question from a user about a particular system gets the response, "System X? See Z about that." This is a person-centric group.

To be fair, person-centric groups don't get started at the desire of the team members. They spring from long periods of insufficient resourcing, which eliminates the chance to find time for information sharing. (Indeed, taking the time required for information sharing may even be actively discouraged by management as being "unproductive.") After a while such habits become ingrained, so even when there is free time available it is used for activities other than knowledge sharing.

For any system administered by the group he or she belongs to, a system administrator should be able to:

- Initiate ad-hoc backups as required using well-documented procedures
- Perform an operating system recovery using well-documented procedures
- Perform (possibly with the assistance of application administrators) an application/data recovery using well-documented procedures
- Perform all these steps in isolation from other team members; no procedure should be dependent on the presence of particular staff members
- Provide regular updates during recoveries even if those updates are to say "everything is going OK"

Note that in each operational activity I recommend that staff be able to perform steps according to well-documented procedures. This is not meant to imply that systems will be so complex that procedures are required at all times. However, it does discourage situations where "meat memory" is the only place where operational procedures are stored. It will be noted throughout this book that documentation is a strongly recommended activity. In short, although activities may appear to be straightforward when first taught, or after a full night's sleep, a lack of documented procedures becomes a hindrance when activities are being completed for the first time by new staff, or by staff who have not performed the activity for a lengthy period, or have been up and working for 24 or more hours.

Additionally, system administrators should never assume anything about the backups.

All system administration teams should ultimately be allowed (and required) to move into a knowledge-centric system, and backups are a key example of where this is most important.

2.2.2.5 Application Administrators

For the purposes of this book, an application administrator is classed as anyone employed for the primary purpose of installing, configuring, and maintaining a complex application. For example, this might cover such systems as Oracle®, SAP, Microsoft® Exchange, IBM® Lotus Notes, or Novell® GroupWise. Within the backup environment, an application administrator should be able to:

- Communicate all special backup and recovery requirements to the system/backup administrators, never assuming that those administrators will already know of such requirements
- Be able to provide clear, accurate, and testable recovery documentation to system/backup administrators
- Alert administrators to any configuration changes
- Understand the backup schedules and configuration in place for the systems their applications run on as well as for their applications
- Be involved in recovery testing
- Start and stop the application reliably — this is required for disaster recovery and cold-backup scenarios

Additionally, application administrators should never assume anything about the backups of their systems.

It is very important that the application and system administrators share information freely about the systems they administer to avoid any "knowledge disconnect" — where one person knows critical information about a system or application, but does not think to pass it on to another person who needs to be aware of it — something to be avoided at all times in a backup and recovery environment.

2.2.3 Management

Despite any protestations otherwise, managers do have a responsibility to play when it comes to backup and recovery systems. While it is unlikely to be as "hands on" as the responsibilities of the IT staff, it exists nevertheless, and a properly functioning backup system can only be achieved when both management and IT staff fulfill their roles synergistically.

2.2.3.1 Local Management and Team Leaders

A person in local management, such as a production systems manager, manager of information systems, or team leader, should be able to:

- Clearly communicate business requirements with backup, system, and application administrators
- Be prepared to listen to and accept technically required modifications suggested by backup, system and application administrators, and be prepared to champion those modifications to more senior management
- Be able to liaise between technical staff and more senior management to determine acceptable risk mitigation plans or, where budget is not available for preferred systems protection, acknowledgments of known risks
- Be able to explain (in broad terms) the structure of the backup system to key customers and to upper management
- Be able to change tapes
- Have procedures available to work with the offsite media management services, i.e., know how to send media offsite and recall them
- Be able to act as a buffer between those performing a recovery and everyone else in a time of crisis

- Be responsible for managing the development and maintenance of the disaster recovery plans
- Never assume anything about the backups

You may wonder why this level of management should not be able to assume that backups are working unless otherwise notified. Management at this level are at the coalface of the backup system, so to speak, and as such need more detailed involvement in its day-to-day workings. Such managers should have access to, and check on a daily basis, a dashboard view of the status of the backup system, its successes, failures, and capacity trending. Managers who do not have access to this information are at risk of being unable to report issues or status confidently and accurately to more senior management.

> **Shrapnel Recoveries.** The role of a manager as a buffer during recoveries cannot be overemphasized. From an organizational or personnel perspective, two diametrically opposed approaches to recoveries exist: the "calm" approach and the "shrapnel" approach.
>
> The "calm" approach is where a consistent flow of communications occurs at all levels, allowing everyone to have a finger on the pulse of the recovery and be aware of its current status. This also requires trust between IT staff, users, and management. That is, if the person conducting the recovery says that a step will take two hours, they should be trusted to issue an update if further delays become apparent.
>
> The "shrapnel" approach is where the staff performing the recovery get interrupted frequently for status updates or potentially heated discussions with key users, application administrators, or management demanding explanations of why the system or data hasn't been recovered yet. (That is, particular staff "fly apart" and others get hit by the shrapnel.) This creates a very disruptive and stressful scenario for everyone.
>
> One way to deal with the shrapnel recovery approach is to keep the person performing the recovery "logically isolated" from shrapnel employees. The team leader should instead act as a buffer, intercepting incoming calls and ensuring that staff working on the recovery can continue to do so without interruption, or with only valid interruptions.
>
> The role of management is to discourage the "shrapnel" approach to recoveries strongly or, failing that, protect the staff performing the recovery so they can get the work done. People are more prone to make mistakes if they are angry, upset, or tired, and allowing others to interfere with work neither speeds up the recovery nor increases its accuracy.

Lower management (team leaders and one-up leaders) should also be able to change tapes and request tapes. In a late-night or weekend recovery scenario where two staff are available — the system/backup administrator and a manager — the goal of the manager should be to facilitate the recovery through administrative/operator functions.

Involvement at this level from lower management has its advantage when it comes to any debriefing/analysis meetings regarding a critical recovery. Having been on-hand, a manager has more of a feel for the flow of the operation, and can participate in continuous improvement of the systems and operations. By being involved in the recovery, a manager can start to see where processes might be improved, or where resources might be better allocated, and perhaps in larger examples, even where budgetary requests might be better justified.

Reciprocally, managers involved in the recovery process are also in a far better position to make suggestions to backup, system, and application administrators as to how processes need to be improved, or where processes appear to have gone wrong. Constructive feedback from management is usually far more graciously accepted by technical staff where management have been involved in the activity, even peripherally.

2.2.3.2 Upper Management

Upper management should

- Be able to explain, in broad terms, the big-picture view of the backup configuration
- Strongly discourage shrapnel recoveries
- Understand the difference between a business requirement and its technical implementation
- Strongly discourage both domain disputes and knowledge disconnects
- Understand and be able to explain to financial controllers and the board/CEO the role of backup and recovery systems as an insurance policy
- Periodically (and randomly) request details of the backup status
- Plan disaster recovery testing scenarios

Upper-level/senior management should be able to assume that, by and large, backups are functional. This of course should only be after receiving enough empirical evidence to justify that assumption.

When upper management request details of the backup status, they should also seek reasons behind failures. This doesn't mean that large amounts of time should be taken preparing formal written reports; verbal or concise e-mail reports should be more than sufficient. If backups failed, follow-up status requests should be made one or two days after to confirm it was a random occurrence and not an ongoing problem. Obviously, if there are still failures after a few status requests, a more formal analysis, and perhaps even an escalation to the support vendor(s), will be needed.

When it comes to planning disaster recovery testing, upper management should aim to have spare hardware/equipment available so that as much as possible can be achieved during business hours. After all, staff have lives and families, and (by and large) would prefer to spend their after-work hours doing their own thing rather than performing tests. Obviously, not all equipment can be duplicated for testing purposes for most organizations, so occasionally tests may have to be done on production equipment. Keeping these tests to a minimum can help to keep staff happy and productive.

There are also strong financial and business justifications for performing tests on dedicated test or spare hardware. What happens if a test fails on production equipment? For instance, if a test is scheduled to run on a Sunday afternoon, but catastrophically fails and requires a 48-hour recovery to be performed, what will be the impact to the business while operations are restored?

2.2.3.3 The Board and the CEO

In several countries, legislation is being introduced, or has already been introduced, making board members and directors personally responsible in the event of a company failing to meet minimum IT requirements in relation to records retention. The implications of this should raise the profile of the backup environment in every company. Any board member, and even the CEO should therefore:

- Be confident in asserting that the company has an appropriate data recovery strategy in place (or failing that, be able to explain what steps are being taken to rectify the situation)
- Stamp out empire building that might interfere with the recoverability of business systems
- Approve legitimate requests for the backup environment by upper management
- Routinely ask about backup status — again, although such management should be able to assume that such systems are operating smoothly unless told otherwise, spot-checks are still appropriate, and should not be seen as time consuming
- Personally thank staff members who recover critical corporate systems

Is the last point important? If a few technical people in a company bring a system back up after a disaster, then to some degree (and for a short while at least), the well-being of the company is owed to staff who did the recovery. As such, they deserve the thanks of senior management no less than a sales person who won a huge contract, or the legal team who brokered a large acquisition, etc. Consultants often hear ad-hoc rumblings from IT staff, not because they necessarily perceive their job as having too much work, but because it often seems to become a thankless task with little regard to the personal sacrifice involved.

If management feel that a recovery has taken too long, it is important not to bemoan the amount of time it took. Staff members still need to be acknowledged as having got the data back. Then feedback can be asked for as to what might be done to make the recovery easier or faster should it be required again. Such staff will have the most constructive feedback about what processes could be improved either to speed up the recovery or avoid the need to do it at all. This may of course involve budgetary requests. Some processes can't be improved and some failures can't be avoided without spending money. It is important to remember that as the number of layers increase between technical staff and the highest management, the chance of required systems not being implemented due to perceived cost and bottom-line improvement also increase. By speaking to the staff responsible for day-to-day corporate information insurance, senior management are able to cut through any artificial obstacles.

2.2.4 Users

2.2.4.1 Key Users

Key users exist somewhere between system/application administrators and end users for a particular system. These are people who know — as a result of length of service at the company or technical/field skills — the ins and outs of a particular system as well as any user could be expected to know, and can liaise with system and application administrators over faults, system planning, or operational changes. They may even come from a technical background that allows them to understand the systems in a vein similar to application or system administrators. These users fulfill two key functions when it comes to backup and recovery systems:

- Providing input on when backups should run, and the maximum impact they can make to the usability of a system
- Mentoring or coaching regular end users in what can and cannot be expected of backups for the system

2.2.4.2 End Users

Although it goes without saying that, on a day-to-day basis, end users should have little to no involvement with backups for the systems they access within an organization, they do need to fulfill some functions with respect to backups:

- Be able to articulate clearly (using either formal request templates when available, or precise informal requests) what they need recovered, when it needs to be recovered by, when it was deleted (or at least, when it was last used), and where it should be recovered to
- Do not assume that the backup system is a blank check for improper systems usage; knowing that backups are performed on a system does not reduce in any way the requirements for responsible access to systems
- Do not treat a backup system as an archive system; i.e., if quotas are in place, using backups to delete older files that are still needed, with the express intent to request a recovery for those files later, is irresponsible

2.2.5 Domain Disputes

One of the more common issues that create significant friction in organizations is task delineation. Application administrators may feel that system administrators encroach on their domain, and will vigorously attempt to prevent this. System administrators may similarly feel overridden when application administrators state the system-level requirements of a particular application. Consultants who are brought in to work on backup environments (or for that matter, any part of an IT system) often cite domain disputes as one of the primary interruptions to their work.

Domain disputes have no place in backups. (In fact, they have no place in organizations, but we're focusing on the backup domain at the moment.) The failure that usually causes domain disputes between system and application administrators is usually a four-part one whereby:

- System administrators may fail to communicate why they are looking at application-level administration.
- Application administrators may assume that system administrators are blocking activities rather than facilitating them.
- Application administrators and system administrators might assume that neither understand enough about the others' domain.
- Management may either actively encourage or at best ignore these disputes and misunderstandings.

(There are certainly times where domain disputes are justified based on the action of one or the other team. Regardless, these disputes mark an organization that cannot properly communicate or act synergistically.)

There is an easy solution to domain disputes. A system administrator is charged with a duty of care — that being to ensure systems and their services/data remain available to users in a working state. This will encroach on every domain associated with the system. Similarly, we can assert that an application administrator is charged with a duty of care over the application he or she administers, and therefore will need to be assured that adequate procedures are in place to ensure the ability to back up and recover the application. This will necessitate a periodic review of procedures with system administrators.

In many organizations some form of domain encroachment is essential to the stable running of systems. For instance, in organizations where system administrators are on-call 24/7, yet application administrators/key users aren't, it is essential that those who are not providing 24/7 support for systems hand over all required details on recovery and access to systems while they are not available. In the same way that a recovery of a system should not be delayed or halted by one particular system administrator being unavailable, it should not be delayed or halted by the unavailability either of key users or application administrators.

There is nothing wrong with declaring that particular key users or application administrators must be involved in recoveries. However, the obvious requirement to this is that such staff must also be available 24/7, or must hand over all instructions relating to their duties during a recovery if they cannot be available 24/7.

2.3 Technical Layers

2.3.1 Introduction

Having examined the personnel aspect of backup and recovery systems, you must next understand the way in which protection systems interact with the rest of the IT environment. This interaction occurs in two distinct areas:

- When evaluating the IT environment as a whole, backup and recovery systems represent their own technical service layer in the same way that processing (server) layers and client access do.
- When zooming into an individual system, backup and recovery software exists at a specific location in the system component layers, simultaneously dependent on the lower system component layers while providing protection against the failure of any particular layer.

2.3.2 Technical Service Layers

Within every organization, the technical infrastructure can be said to exist at multiple layers. These layers may represent wholly separate classes of infrastructure, or may be logical groups of similar components. Each layer has its own function and interacts in its own way with the various other components and layers of the organization. A simple diagram showing various technical service layers may be found in Figure 2.1. In a simple breakdown we can envisage at least six layers, which are outlined in the following sections.

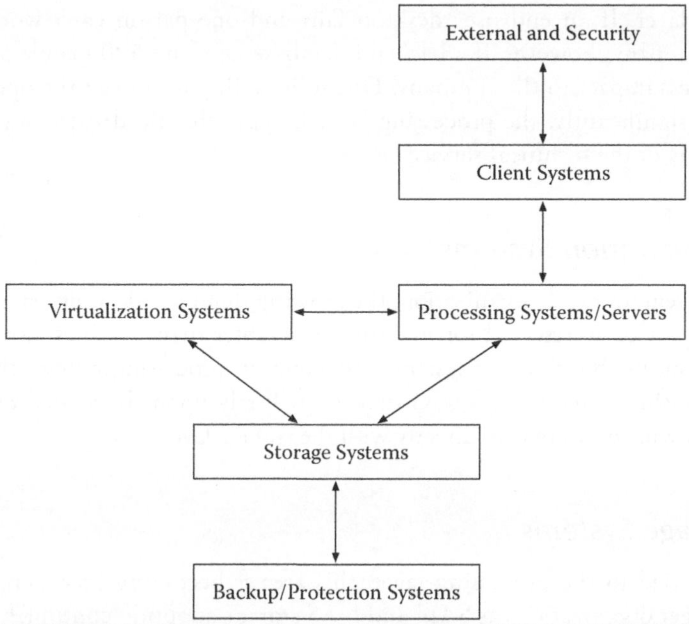

Figure 2.1 Technical service layers

2.3.2.1 *External and Security*

This is the outer, protective layer of the IT systems for a company. It represents those components of the environment that are designed to protect the rest of the environment from intrusion or malicious damage. This would include such components as firewalls, mail relay SPAM and virus filters, content-filtering proxies, and so on. Although security administration will have representatives from other administrative personnel, it may also combine direct involvement from management, legal, and human resource roles.

2.3.2.2 *Client Systems*

This comprises the end users of the environment and the systems they use to gain access to the corporate IT infrastructure — i.e., their desktops, laptops, thin clients, and so on. Although one of the most visible aspects of an organization, it is one of the aspects that typically has the most loose and permissive service level agreements. This can be a boon to administrators, but may be a source of frustration to users when things go wrong. A common misconception when SLAs are defined is that if a user's client machine is in some way damaged, it is not a high cost and the user may have to wait a while for repairs. At the bottom line, however, this equates to a decision that it is OK for the company to pay people to do nothing for an extended period of time. When viewed in this light, such poor SLAs rarely seem to make sense.

2.3.2.3 *Processing Systems/Servers*

This could also be referred to as the server layer. The bulk of background processing and application serving occurs at this layer, and although it may not be as visible to end users, it is a very business-critical layer. If an end user desktop fails and one person can't work, that's a loss of income to the company; however, if a backend database fails and 500 people can't work, that's a significant business impact to the company. Due to its ability to impact the operational activities of the company significantly, the processing layer is typically afforded the most protection and redundancy of any of the technical service layers.

2.3.2.4 Virtualization Systems

Although not present for every organization, the growing trend in mid-range systems virtualization has seen a layer previously reserved for mainframes re-enter many business environments. When used, virtualization sits above storage systems and alongside processing systems that are not virtualized. Those processing systems that are virtualized will rely upon the virtualization systems, and those that are not will communicate directly with the storage layer.

2.3.2.5 Storage Systems

Once intimately tied to the processing layer, this area is becoming increasingly divorced from processing in larger organizations as SAN and NAS storage adoption continues to take off, and in many organizations, outpace the use of DAS. For a company to get the most of centralized storage systems, the systems need to be maintained separately from the various administration groups in control of the processing layer. This results in a separate storage provisioning group that is responsible for providing capacity (at the appropriate performance) to the various processing groups. The administration of this storage can see a very different skill set requirement from that of a typical system or application administrator, further highlighting the differences between the layers.

2.3.2.6 Backup/Protection Systems

Regardless of whether backups are maintained by a particular processing group or not, backups are always a layer unto themselves. Backup and recovery systems should be deployed to protect all other layers in the operations of an organization. As mentioned previously, backup and recovery systems touch more IT systems than just about any other service, and thus need to be maintained as a critical system with clear definitions of the roles of the staff involved.

2.3.3 Service Component Layers

Within any individual system there will be a layering of components that are dealt with. We can describe a simple system component layer as shown in Figure 2.2. That is, the end user is the final, visible layer of a host, but only represents a portion of the actual full content and scope of the host. The end user interfaces with applications, which rely on application services. The application services in turn depend on the operation system, which relies on the hardware, power, and network connectivity to be stable. (We will ignore systems without network connectivity, as they are rare in full corporate environments.)

For the end user to be able to work, the applications must work as expected, and for the applications to work as expected, the application services must work as expected. For the application services to work as expected, the operating system must work as expected, and for the

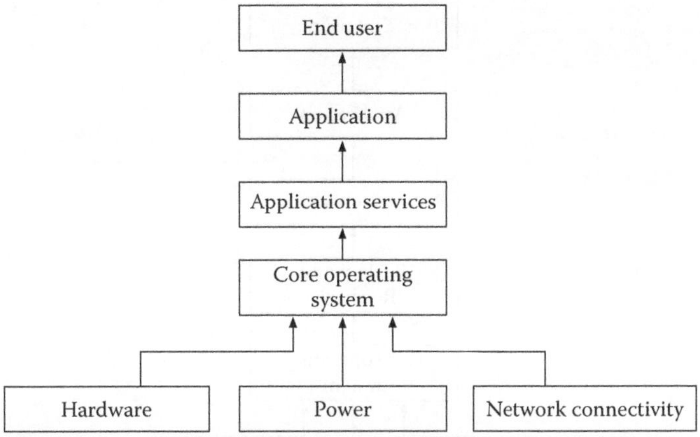

Figure 2.2 Simple system component layer diagram

operating system to work as expected, the hardware, power, and network connectivity must work as expected.

In this sense, the IT environment is quite fragile — each layer depends heavily on the successful functioning of lower layers, and only when all layers are functioning correctly do we have a working system.

Slotting backup services in, we can say that for the backup services to operate successfully, the operating system and all lower dependencies must be working as expected. Failure of any of these lower components will typically result in a failure of the backup software. While the backup software may be required to assist with operating system recovery, it can only do so to the point that the operating system and hardware can be made operational again. By inserting backup services between the operating system and application services layers, we indicate that for everything from the application services and above to function correctly, those components need properly functioning backups, and have therefore determined the correct position in the system layering, and shown in Figure 2.3.

Having placed backup services at their functional layer, we can move on to describe that their purpose is to provide recovery from failure of any layer (including their own) in a system. However, their successful operation typically depends on a properly functioning operating system and the underlying hardware.

This is not to say that a backup system can't be used to recover hosts from operating system or hardware failure, but what I am trying to highlight is that it is only possible to back up and recover hosts successfully while hardware and operating systems are functioning. The implication therefore is that in a disaster recovery situation the first task is typically to get the hardware and operating system functional before trying to perform a recovery. It should be noted that there are bare metal recovery tools available for particular platforms — bare metal refers to recovering without there being an operating system present. This may typically involve booting from a CD/DVD or tape and starting the recovery agent. Such products enjoy varied success and are highly specific to individual platforms, usually with specific requirements as to what can and can't be done. However, we can say even these products rely on an operating system of sorts as all applications must run on top of an operating system, even if that operating system is a primitive, read-only environment stored on CD/DVD or tape.

When considering operating system changes, consider that the backup software at a fundamental layer needs to understand the basic principles of the operating system being used. Upgrading

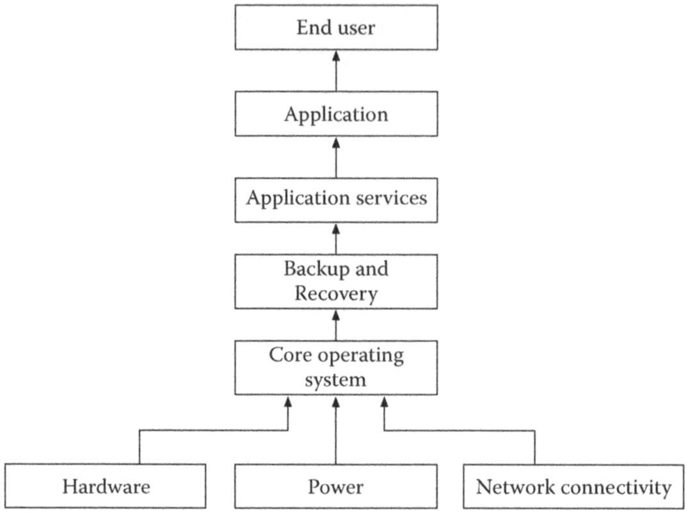

Figure 2.3 System component layers including backup and recovery software

to the latest and greatest version of a vendor's operating system may bring additional operational benefits, but what happens if the version of the operating system isn't supported by the backup product? What if the operating system vendor has implemented a new API for high-speed access to the filesystem, and the backup product hasn't yet been configured to work with that API, so its performance considerably decreases? What if the operating system vendor has added new access control lists (ACLs), which the backup product can't read, and thus can't backup the file? Or worse, depending on the data sensitivity involved, the backup product backs up the file, but allows the wrong people to restore it, or the wrong people to access it after restoring it?

Similarly with the application services layer, and particularly with databases, upgrading a database without confirming compatibility may result in a situation where database backups fail completely. Some database vendors have made reasonably large changes to their backup API in minor version releases of their software, which in turn causes interface problems to backup software.

The key lesson to consider is that once a backup and recovery system has been implemented into an environment, consideration of it must become a core factor of the change control for the environment. Ideally, change control procedures should reference the backup product, and prompt the person proposing a change to confirm that either the backup product in use is compatible or that a version upgrade must also be done on the backup product to accommodate the proposed operating system or application upgrade. If there are no known versions of the backup product compatible with the proposed operating system or application version upgrade, the upgrade should be put on hold while discussions are held with the vendors, or until workaround or alternative backup and recovery solutions can be determined.

Chapter 3

Backup and Recovery Concepts

3.1 Introduction

Backups and backup software can be grouped into a series of categories, and in this chapter we'll examine those groupings. Many functions can be present in backup and recovery software, and the presence (or non-presence) of those functions will have a significant impact on the usefulness of a product to an organization. What is important to keep in mind is that not all the functionality provided may be required for any given solution, so any choice in backup products should be made based on availability of required functions, not just a line-by-line functionality comparison between product data sheets.

Of course, in an ideal world certain features and functions should be present in all products as a logical result of being offered as a data protection product. Sadly, this is not the case when we move from an ideal world to the real world. Core protection functionality — such as adequate protection of the backup server itself so that disaster recoveries are possible — can be found in very restricted or reduced form in some of the world's most popular backup software, further proving that the most popular isn't necessarily the best. This is not only a serious failing on behalf of the manufacturers, but should also serve as a reminder that it is important to know enough to:

- Ask the right questions
- See past glitzy interfaces to core functionality
- Focus on protection functionality above and beyond all other considerations when examining either new backup software or an existing environment

3.2 Host Nomenclature

When discussing a backup environment, the following terms are used to describe the hosts within the environment:

Server: The backup server, or "master" server, which is responsible for scheduling of backups, configuration, management of media and backup indices, etc.

Client: Any host that is protected by the backup server. This will typically include many or all of the machines that would be referred to as "servers" by normal classification — e.g., fileservers, mail servers, database servers, etc. These are all "clients" to the backup server.

Media server or storage node: A machine that exists between the client and server that can perform backup and recovery operations for itself or other hosts, as directed by the backup server (this type of host will be discussed in greater detail later in the book).

3.3 Backup Topology

When considering backup topology, there are two broad categories of backup environments that can be designed — centralized and decentralized. In general, a centralized backup environment implies the use of a solid workgroup-class or enterprise-class product, whereas a decentralized backup environment may imply either "home-grown" or poorly fit solutions. For data centers, consider only centralized backup management. For satellite offices, workgroup products may be appropriate, but there is still considerable merit in the consolidated control that only a centralized backup product can offer.

3.3.1 Decentralized Backups

A decentralized environment is where each host backs up its own data to backup devices (usually tape) that are directly attached to it. If a commercial backup product is involved, then typically each host (or server) within the environment is its own "master server," being entirely self-contained and separate from the rest of the environment for backup. This is a backup model that is often most found in small to mid-sized organizations that have grown from just one or two servers into sometimes as many as 30 to 50 servers. In these environments backups are often considered as an afterthought following system purchase, resulting in the perceived need for standalone tape drives attached to each system.

Few, if any, enterprises with more than one host to be backed up in one location stand to benefit from decentralized backups.

A decentralized backup may resemble the configuration shown in Figure 3.1. In reality, decentralized backups are not appropriate for consideration in most organizations as they place a higher (and unnecessary) workload on system administrators and operators, and may result in data loss due to a higher need for manual intervention on tape drives, tape changers, configuration, and systems maintenance. They can also result in significantly higher units of media being required.

Advantages of decentralized backups

- Fewer hosts will have recovery dependencies.
- Each individual host may (allegedly) have a simpler configuration (this is debatable).

Disadvantages of decentralized backups

- The need for a tape drive (or drives) per host quickly increases the price of the solution, and can result in a situation whereby lower-cost and less-efficient backup devices are used to keep costs down.
- The environment introduces an artificial need for tape operators as the number of hosts or the amount of data increases; this also impacts on the delivery of recovery services.

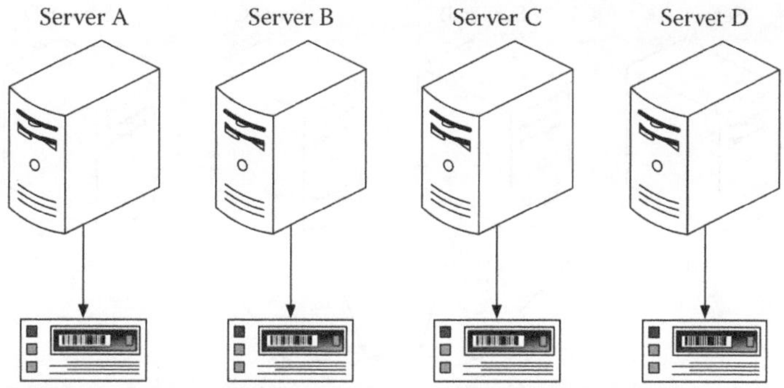

Figure 3.1 Decentralized backup architecture

- Although any individual host may have a configuration that appears simpler, maintaining all the various configurations becomes more complex.
- No centralized reporting functionality.
- No centralized management and configuration functionality; e.g., if a decision is made to change full backups from, say, Friday night to Saturday night, this will need to be changed on every backup server as opposed to a single backup server.
- More difficult to provide recovery services to end users or help desk staff, as tapes still need to be changed to facilitate recoveries, etc.
- If using commercial backup products, the per-server cost typically increases faster than simply adding more clients, or seats, to an existing centralized backup system.
- As more master servers are deployed, the chances are increased that multiple different backup products will be deployed due to perceived individual license costs; this makes the environment more difficult to maintain for administrators who must be conversant with multiple products.

3.3.2 Centralized Backups

In a centralized backup environment, multiple hosts back up either to a single "master" server, or a single "master" server and one or more "slave" servers. (These "slave servers" are referred to by the two leading backup products in the market as "storage nodes" and "media servers," and these terms are used interchangeably throughout the book.) While traditionally this implies a backup across the network, other methods of implementing centralized backups (discussed later) can significantly reduce or even completely eliminate backup data flowing across the network.

A sample centralized backup environment might resemble the configuration shown in Figure 3.2, in which a single server is responsible for backups, with a small tape library attached. All other hosts in the environment provide their data to the backup server, which is in turn responsible for writing it out to and retrieving from tape. This is a very simple example of a centralized backup environment, but it serves to highlight the general layout.

Advantages of centralized backups

- With centralization, tape/media libraries can be used more readily, which reduces the need for operators, allows recoveries to be initiated faster due to more media being immediately available, and allows for lower hardware costs; e.g., a single 180-slot tape

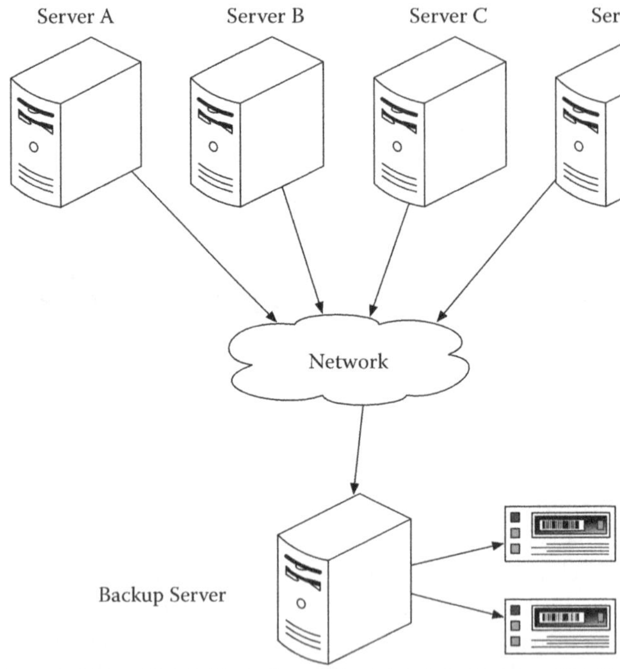

Figure 3.2 Centralized backup architecture

library and its ancillary connectivity components will be considerably cheaper than, say, 10 × 20 slot libraries and their ancillary connectivity components.
- Overall configuration of the backup environment becomes easier, as all aspects of the environment are controlled from a single source.
- Protection of the backup environment itself becomes easier in a centralized environment than in a decentralized environment.
- Consolidated reporting is significantly easier, which in turn allows for other services, such as trending, capacity analysis, and volume-based billing.
- In larger enterprises, centralized backups allow for the hiring of dedicated backup administrators, who can reduce the workload of the system administration teams; with dedicated staff, more time is available to keep backup services running reliably and efficiently (this also helps to consolidate services across platforms, rather than solutions being developed for each platform or location within an organization).
- Recovery services can be farmed out either to help desk staff or even end users in some cases, as media-changing should not be required for most recoveries.
- Licensing costs should decrease in comparison to decentralized commercial backup products, as a single master license and multiple client connection licenses will cost less than a series of master server licenses.

Disadvantages of centralized backups
- Implementing a centralized backup environment typically requires a larger capital investment to kick-start the process.

It should be clear that centralized backup environments are far more appropriate in corporations than decentralized environments, even given the initial cost in setting up the environment;

centralized environments ultimately scale far more efficiently than decentralized environments due to the reduced incremental cost (both fiscal and administrative) for adding new clients to an existing environment rather than creating new environments.

3.4 Backup Levels

Depending on which backup product is used, a variety of backup levels will be supported. The backup level controls or sets the number of files or the amount of data that gets backed up as part of any particular operation.

Note that although there are industry standard names to most levels, some backup products choose to present contrary naming standards. The most common deviations from the norm are provided in this book where appropriate for reference purposes.

3.4.1 Full Level

A full backup is quite simply a backup of everything selectable, regardless of when it has changed. Unless special "directives" or "rules" have been established to block the backup of particular files or systems, a full backup should see the transfer of all data from a host to the backup media. Full backups provide the simplest recovery mechanism for businesses, as a recovery operation is a single consolidated read from the source medium, without need to use multiple sources generated at different dates/times.

While almost all organizations use full backups as part of their backup schedules, they are only applicable on a daily basis for organizations where all of the following are true:

- Either 24/7 availability is not a requirement, or system availability is not affected as a consequence of backups.
- A complete backup takes a minimum amount of media.
- Backup/system administrators may not be available on a daily basis, and therefore a primary goal is to reduce to a bare minimum the amount of media required to complete a restore.

Obviously, a key requirement for full backups is that the backup window needs to be large enough to accommodate a complete read of all data on a system every night. While this may be acceptable to smaller organizations, they can typically represent a considerable overhead on the amount of media used as the number of systems — or the amount of data on each system — grows over time. As the amount of data for an organization grows, or the required backup window shrinks, full backups become less of an option on a daily basis, and typically become only one part of the overall backup schedule/calendar.

Advantages of full backups

- Recovery from a full backup involves a single, consolidated read from one backup "set."
- Typically, no dependencies exist between one backup and the next — the loss of a single day's backup, for instance, does not affect the recoverability of other backups.

Disadvantages of full backups

- Without mitigating activities such as snapshots, the backup window is the largest for all types of backup levels; where the backup window requires an application or database outage, this also implies the longest system downtime during the backup process.
- Uses the maximum amount of media per backup, and therefore costs the most.
- Full backups can take considerably longer to run than other backup levels.

3.4.2 Incremental Level

An incremental backup targets only those files or items that have changed since the last backup (regardless of what level it was). This often results in considerably smaller backups, and can also typically result in a much smaller backup window, although there are some notable exceptions.

For many workgroup and non-commercial backup products, incremental backups are only possible at the filesystem level — that is, a fileserver or user's desktop machine can have an incremental backup, but databases cannot. Backup products that fall into the enterprise classification (depending on the capabilities of the various databases used) will also offer incremental database backups. In these cases the space savings can be even more impressive than incremental backups of filesystems. A 2 TB Oracle® database may only have, say, a 5 percent change during the day, but in either a full database backup regime or an incremental backup level, the entire 2 TB needs to be backed up every day. With incremental database backups, the amount backed up is typically only a small percentage more than the actual amount of changed data in the database.

For most organizations, incremental backups form a fundamental part of a weekly backup regime, whereby a full backup is done once a week, and incrementals are done for the rest of the time. For example, in many organizations (assuming backups start in the evening rather than the early hours of the morning), this might mean a backup schedule as shown in Table 3.1. In this schedule, a full backup is run on a Friday night (to give a maximum time to complete), with incremental backups run on all other days in the week. This ensures that a minimum backup window is used during peak activity times, with a longer backup window only being used during non-peak activity times.

Over the course of a week, this style of backup might be represented as shown in Figure 3.3. That is, after the full backup, each daily backup stores only those files that have changed since the backups from the previous day. Such a backup policy typically makes for short, small backups.

> At many companies, the people responsible for backups (or backup budgets) state that they don't have many users accessing their systems on a weekend, and therefore have no need to run incremental backups during that time. This is usually a false economy.
>
> If there are only a few users accessing the system, then for most systems there are few changes and those changes will typically be small. If that is the case — that the

Table 3.1 Standard Incremental Backup Schedule

Friday	*Saturday*	*Sunday*	*Monday*	*Tuesday*	*Wednesday*	*Thursday*
Full	Incremental	Incremental	Incremental	Incremental	Incremental	Incremental

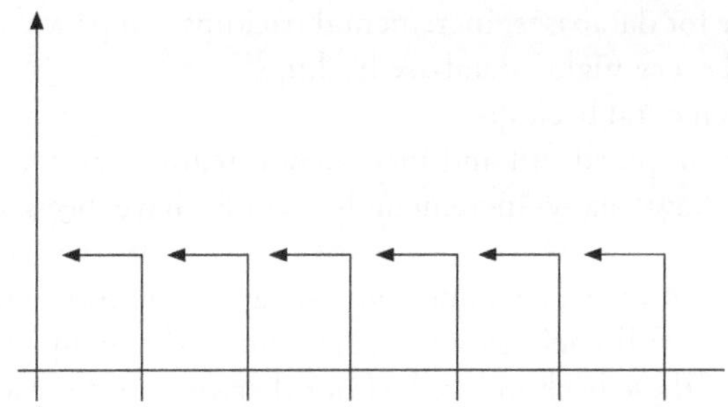

Figure 3.3 Incremental backups

changes are few and small — then the material cost of actually running an incremental backup during this time is negligible.

However, consider the cost of, say, having a system crash after the Finance Department has worked all weekend to close out the books for the month or end of financial year. The cost of all the lost data and time required to re-enter the data will easily exceed the occasional extra cost for media.

One of the most important rules to remember in backups is that it is always better to back up a little more than not enough. Therefore, all but the simplest of businesses should plan to run incremental backups on the weekend and other non-working days.

Alternatively, consider the following rule — rather than having a policy of not performing incremental backups on non-work days, have a policy that incremental backups will be performed unless sufficient reason can be shown otherwise.

Although incremental backups represent a window-shrinking mechanism and can reduce the overall amount of media used in a backup on a nightly basis, they also take more effort and time to use in a complete system or filesystem recovery. Therefore organizations must be careful to implement a backup environment where incrementals do not present a significant detriment to recovery performance. (For example, only doing a full backup once a month, and potentially needing to recover from it and 30 incremental backups, all from tape, is not necessarily a good idea.) That being said, most organizations will use incremental backups with little impact.

Advantages of incremental backups

- Less backup media is used per backup job, as only those files that have changed are backed up. By implication, a backup regime combining full and incremental backups will typically use considerably less media than a backup regime where only full backups are performed.
- The backup window can be considerably shorter for a full backup. Where outages are required for the backup to be properly processed, this usually reduces the size of the outage window.

- When available for databases, incremental backups can provide considerable cost reductions over "full every night" database backups.

Disadvantages of incremental backups

- Recoveries from a mixed full and incremental regime can require more media changes depending on how many incremental backups have been done since the last full backup.
- Complete recoveries have dependencies — e.g., a complete system recovery cannot be done without the full backups and all incremental backups between the full and the failure. If any of these backups are lost or otherwise fail to read from, the recovery cannot be 100 percent complete. (It should be noted that not all products perform adequate backup dependency checking, and can actually delete fulls on which incrementals still rely.)*

3.4.3 Differential Level

A differential backup is one where a series of changes are backed up, possibly covering several days worth of changes. This "rolls up" multiple changes into a single backup job. (When tape libraries were rare, this backup level was seen as an important feature to avoid a large number of manual tape changes for recoveries.)

Two types of differential backups may be found in backup products — simple differential and multi-leveled differential. A simple differential level merely backs up all changes that have occurred since the most recent full, regardless of what backups have occurred in between.

Some backup products instead offer multi-leveled differential backups, which have grown out of traditional UNIX backup tools such as dump and restore. We will examine multi-layered differential backups after discussing simple differential backups, as they are a logical extension of the simple style.

It should be noted that although differential backups are very commonplace at the operating-system level for most backup products, their support in databases is limited and may work quite differently than what is expected. For example, some databases treat incremental and differential backups quite the same, with the exception that differentials might delete transaction logs. It is therefore important when deploying differential backups for databases that a comprehensive review of the impact of differential backups is performed before they are relied on for recovery.

3.4.3.1 Simple Differential Backups

To evaluate how differential backups might work within an environment, consider the sample backup schedule shown in Table 3.2, which would work as follows:

On Friday, a full backup is done.

For Saturday through Monday, incremental backups are done. That is, the incremental backup on Saturday backs up all files that have changed since the full on Friday. The incremental

* Within Veritas NetBackup, incremental backups are known as "differential incremental" backups. The rationale for such a decision appears to be that the backup consists of the filesystem "differences" each day; hence "differential incremental." For users of backup products with more-conventional naming standards, this can appear unnecessarily complex.

Table 3.2 Sample Simple Differential Backup Schedule in Weekly Backups

Friday	*Saturday*	*Sunday*	*Monday*	*Tuesday*	*Wednesday*	*Thursday*
Full	Incremental	Incremental	Incremental	Differential	Incremental	Incremental

backup on Sunday backs up all the files that have changed since the incremental on Saturday, and so on.

On Tuesday, a differential backup is performed. This backs up all files that have changed since the full on Friday. This means that a recovery on Wednesday should only require media from the full and differential backups, skipping the Saturday/Sunday/Monday incremental backups.

On Wednesday, an incremental backup is performed, backing up all files that have changed since the Tuesday differential.

On Thursday, an incremental backup is performed, backing up files that have changed since the Wednesday incremental.

This might be represented as shown in Figure 3.4.

Differential backups were considered vital when autochangers were cost prohibitive, as they reduced the amount of media that might be required for a recovery. Similarly, they are seen as useful in organizations where autochangers remain cost prohibitive, or where the system administrators are also the operators. Thus, it was and in some organizations still is common to see backup schedules as shown in Table 3.3. The rationale for this schedule is that a recovery on any given day will only need the media written to from the full backup and the most recent differential backup, using the following schedule:

Full backup on Friday

The differential on Saturday backs up all files that have changed since the Friday full

The differential on Sunday backs up all files that have changed since the Friday full

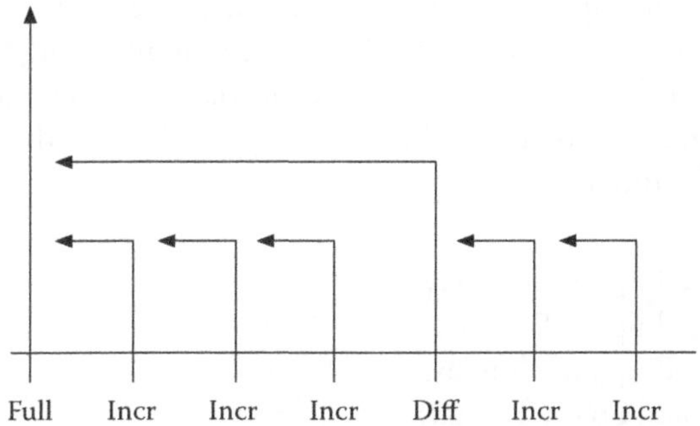

Figure 3.4 Full, incremental, and differential backups

Table 3.3 Sample Backup Schedule With Full and Differential Backups Only

Friday	*Saturday*	*Sunday*	*Monday*	*Tuesday*	*Wednesday*	*Thursday*
Full	Diff	Diff	Diff	Diff	Diff	Diff

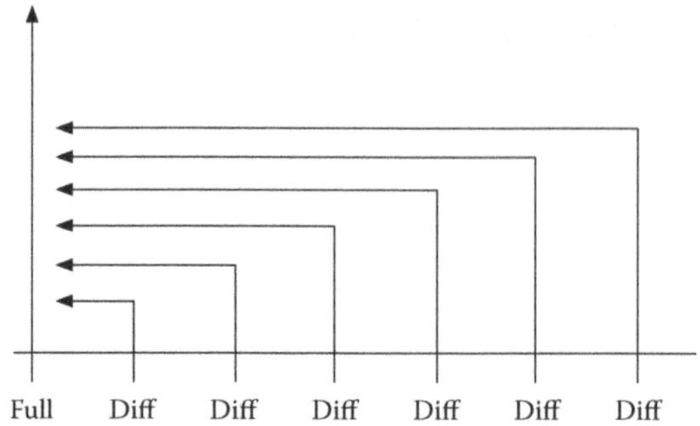

Figure 3.5 Full and differential backups only

The differential on Monday backs up all files that have changed since the Friday full, and so on through to the differential on Thursday, which again backs up all files that have changed since the Friday full

This can be represented as shown in Figure 3.5.

Some assume that differential backups automatically mean less backup media are used than a simple full + incremental recovery, but this is not guaranteed to be the case. In particular, on systems where there is a larger percentage change that is spread throughout a higher percentage of files on the filesystem, it is possible to result in a recovery where more media is used for recovery from differentials than would be required for incremental recoveries.

Consider a system with 200 Gb of total used space where the daily change is 15 percent, which represents 30 Gb per night. Using LTO Ultrium 1 tapes, each night's incrementals would fit easily onto a tape. (Following best practices, the nightly backups would remain in the library, with copies sent offsite regardless of whether differential or incremental backups are being used.) We'll assume that the full backup occurs on a Friday night, and this will consume the same number of tapes regardless of which backup level is used for the rest of the week.

However, taking a worst-case scenario, we'll assume that all the files that change on a nightly basis are different from those that change the previous day. For incremental backups this makes no difference — approximately 30 Gb will be backed up per day. For differential backups, though, this makes a considerable difference:

30 GB would be backed up on Saturday.
60 GB would be backed up on Sunday.
90 GB would be backed up on Monday.
120 GB would be backed up on Tuesday.
150 GB would be backed up on Wednesday.
180 GB would be backed up on Thursday.

Therefore, over the course of a week, incremental backups have used 6 × 30 GB = 180 GB, whereas differential backups have consumed 630 GB. Using LTO Ultrium 1 cartridges that fit 100 GB native to a tape (assuming no compression), the incremental backups will require two cartridges, whereas the differential backups will require seven cartridges.

Table 3.4 Monthly Backup Schedule Integrating Full, Differential, and Incremental Backups

Sunday	*Monday*	*Tuesday*	*Wednesday*	*Thursday*	*Friday*	*Saturday*
1/Full	2/Incr	3/Incr	4/Incr	5/Incr	6/Incr	7/Incr
8/Diff	9/Incr	10/Incr	11/Incr	12/Incr	13/Incr	14/Incr
15/Diff	16/Incr	17/Incr	18/Incr	19/Incr	20/Incr	21/Incr
22/Diff	23/Incr	24/Incr	25/Incr	26/Incr	27/Incr	28/Incr
29/Diff	30/Incr	31/Incr				

This is, of course, a worst-case scenario, and some may dismiss it as being irrelevant, although such situations have been observed in the past and do not require the "100 percent of changed files are new files" scenario we've used to perform the exercise. Before deploying differential backups, it is always worthwhile to run comparisons on various percentage changes to determine what situations will and won't work for a particular environment. It should be understood that differential backups are not the "silver bullet" they are often claimed to be, and can introduce additional media requirements that are onerous.

Although the usefulness of differentials in a weekly backup cycle decreases, particularly as media capacity is increased and tape autochangers are introduced into an environment, differentials can still play a very useful component in schedules where full backups are performed less frequently, such as monthly. For example, a backup schedule might resemble the configuration shown in Table 3.4. In this case, a full backup is performed on the first Sunday of the month, with differential backups done on all other Sundays in the month, and incremental backups are done on all other days of the week. In this scenario, full backups are only performed once per month, but with differentials performed weekly, the maximum number of backups required for a complete system recovery will be one full backup, one differential backup, and six incremental backups. That is, a full system recovery will never need more than the full backup from the start of the month, the differential backup at the start of the relevant week, and the incremental backups performed during the week.

If a policy were used whereby full backups were done on the first of the month, and incrementals for the rest of the month, a complete system recovery might see as many as 31 backups required. If each of those backups must be sourced from different media, this would significantly hamper the speed of the recovery.*

Advantages of differential backups
- Recoveries require fewer "backup sets"
- Provide better recovery options when full backups are run rarely (e.g., only monthly)

Disadvantages of differential backups
- Depending on the daily change delta for a filesystem, the amount of media required for a differential schedule may exceed the amount of media required for incremental backups for the same period

* Some backup products, such as Veritas NetBackup, refer to differential backups as "cumulative incremental" backups. The rationale for such a decision appears to be that the backup consists of the various incremental changes that have occurred to the filesystem, "accumulated" into a single backup. Users of backup products with more-traditional nomenclature will find this naming strategy unnecessarily complex, if not confusing.

 - While almost universally supported for filesystem backups, differential backups have mixed support for non-filesystem data protection, such as database and mail server backups

3.4.3.2 Multi-Layered Differential Levels

Multi-layered differential backups are a logical extension to the simple differential backup level. This still keeps with the differential concept, but extends it to allow multiple levels interfacing with one another in a way that is similar to how simple differential backups interact with full backups.

Multi-layered differential backups grew out of tools such as UNIX dump and restore, but have been incorporated into some commercial backup products. These tools provided nine differential backup levels (numbered 1–9) rather than a single differential backup level. In this style of backup, any differential level *x* backs up all files that have changed since the last full or lower-numbered differential level (whichever was the more recent).

Table 3.5 represents a simple multi-layered differential backup strategy, with the following schedule:

- A full backup is performed on Friday.
- The incremental on Saturday backs up all files that have changed since Friday.
- The Level-5 differential on Sunday backs up all files that have changed since Friday.
- The incremental on Monday backs up all files that have changed since Sunday.
- The Level-7 differential on Tuesday backs up all files that have changed since Sunday.
- The incremental on Wednesday backs up all files that have changed since Tuesday.
- The Level-3 differential on Thursday backs up all files that have changed since Friday.

This example (represented in Figure 3.6) would typically be an overly complicated backup, but suits our purposes to explain how multi-layered differential backups interact with each other.

Table 3.5 Sample Multi-Layered Differential Backups (weekly)

Friday	*Saturday*	*Sunday*	*Monday*	*Tuesday*	*Wednesday*	*Thursday*
Full	Incremental	Level 5	Incremental	Level 7	Incremental	Level 3

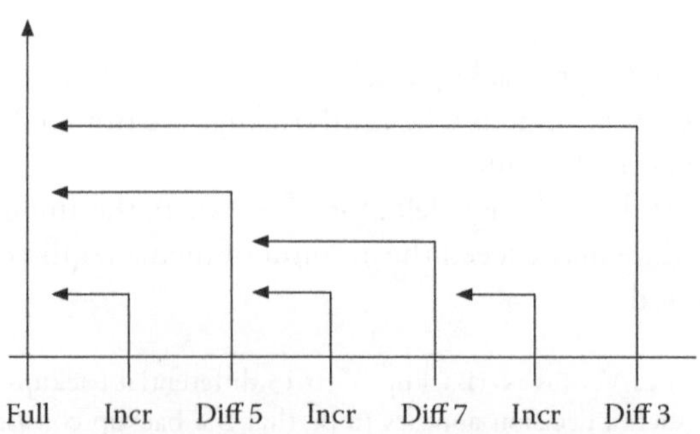

Figure 3.6 Pictorial representation of multi-layered differential backups

Even more so than simple differential backups, multi-layered differential backups are most applicable to schedules where full backups are performed infrequently. An example of this might be backing up archive servers. An archive server, for the purposes of this discussion, would be a host where the following types of data are stored on it:

- Infrequently accessed documents
- Completed projects
- Images and copies of CD-ROMs and DVD-ROMs
- Operating system images
- Vendor patches

This data should still be backed up, as it represents a significant impact to have to recreate it manually. However, once placed on the system, files rarely change and the cost of doing a full backup every week is prohibitive. A differential backup strategy such as that shown in Table 3.4 might be appropriate, but may still result in too many full backups being done.

Note that many organizations choose not to perform daily incremental backups of archive servers, instead relying on end-of-week backups only. This should be seen as a dangerous option, particularly when archive servers are frequently (and undesirably) designed with less redundancy than other fileservers. Archive servers — particularly those used to store customer or corporate data rather than just ease-of-access software and operating system images — need to be backed up on a daily basis to protect any new changes. This should, of course, represent a trivially small percentage of the overall system size. If this is not done, data may still be lost — and in fact may be lost permanently. If users or processes automatically move rather than copy data to the archive server, then a subsequent failure of the archive server may represent a loss of the only online copy of the data. If no access attempt is made of the data on the archive server for some considerable time after archive, then it may only be noticed as missing "too late" for recovery from the backups of the original host of the data.

Another common rationale for not backing up archive servers works along the lines of "that just holds live system images — if it goes down before the weekly backup, we'll just regenerate the images." At this point a failure of an archive server would create the need for a new production systems outage, not to mention additional afterhours work for staff.

In such cases, a quarterly backup strategy may be more appropriate. This is where a full backup is performed only once every quarter. With full backups only quarterly, there is an obvious need to balance carefully the need to minimize the number of backups that must be used for recovery, while simultaneously avoiding a situation where differential backups consume so much space that they represent an exorbitant media cost to the system. Such a scenario may resemble Table 3.6, in which a full backup is performed on the first Sunday of the first month. Incrementals are

Table 3.6 Quarterly Backup Schedule, Month 1

Sunday	*Monday*	*Tuesday*	*Wednesday*	*Thursday*	*Friday*	*Saturday*
1/Full	2/Incr	3/Incr	4/Incr	5/Incr	6/Incr	7/Incr
7/Level 5	9/Incr	10/Incr	11/Incr	12/Incr	13/Incr	14/Incr
15/Level 5	16/Incr	17/Incr	18/Incr	19/Incr	20/Incr	21/Incr
22/Level 5	23/Incr	24/Incr	25/Incr	26/Incr	27/Incr	28/Incr
29/Level 5	30/Incr	31/Incr				

Table 3.7 Quarterly Backup Schedule, Month 2

Sunday	*Monday*	*Tuesday*	*Wednesday*	*Thursday*	*Friday*	*Saturday*
			1/Incr	2/Incr	3/Incr	4/Incr
5/Level 3	6/Incr	7/Incr	8/Incr	9/Incr	10/Incr	11/Incr
12/Level 5	13/Incr	14/Incr	15/Incr	16/Incr	17/Incr	18/Incr
19/Level 5	20/Incr	21/Incr	22/Incr	23/Incr	24/Incr	25/Incr
26/Level 5	27/Incr	28/Incr	29/Incr	30/Incr		

performed Monday through Saturday, and level-5 backups are performed for the other Sundays in the month. As we can see at this point, there is little difference in the implementation of the first month than what we would find implemented for a simple differential monthly schedule.

In the second month (Table 3.7), a level-3 differential backup is performed on the first Sunday of the month. Incrementals are performed for Monday through Saturday, and level-5 backups are done for the rest of the Sundays in the month.

At this point we have a change in what the level-5 backups refer to. In the first month, they backed up all changes that had occurred since the full at the start of the month. However, in the second month, they backup all changes that have occurred since the level-3 differential performed at the start of the month. This helps us to place some restraints on media usage for the differential backups.

Our third month repeats the second month in structure (Table 3.8).

Thus completes a quarterly backup schedule, with the next month having the next full backup performed (Table 3.9). Any particular recovery in the quarter will need at most:

Table 3.8 Quarterly Backup Schedule, Month 3

Sunday	*Monday*	*Tuesday*	*Wednesday*	*Thursday*	*Friday*	*Saturday*
					1/Incr	2/Incr
3/Level 3	4/Incr	5/Incr	6/Incr	7/Incr	8/Incr	9/Incr
10/Level 5	11/Incr	12/Incr	13/Incr	14/Incr	15/Incr	16/Incr
17/Level 5	18/Incr	19/Incr	20/Incr	21/Incr	22/Incr	23/Incr
24/Level 5	25/Incr	26/Incr	27/Incr	28/Incr	29/Incr	30/Incr
31/Level 5						

Table 3.9 Quarterly Backup Schedule, Next Full Backup

Sunday	*Monday*	*Tuesday*	*Wednesday*	*Thursday*	*Friday*	*Saturday*
	1/Incr	2/Incr	3/Incr	4/Incr	5/Incr	6/Incr
7/Full	8/Incr	9/Incr	10/Incr	11/Incr	12/Incr	13/Incr
14/Level 5	15/Incr	16/Incr	17/Incr	18/Incr	19/Incr	20/Incr
21/Level 5	22/Incr	23/Incr	24/Incr	25/Incr	26/Incr	27/Incr
28/Level 5	29/Incr	30/Incr				

- The media used for the full backup
- The media used for the most recent level-3 backup (if one has been performed)
- The media used for the most recent level-5 backup (if there has been one performed following the full or level 3)
- Incremental backups written since the last full or differential backup

For servers that are too large — or take too long — for frequent full backups, this schedule can often be appropriate. By combining full backups, incremental backups, and multiple differential levels, a somewhat delicate balance can be achieved between media usage for backups and media usage for recoveries.

The pros and cons of multi-layered differential backups essentially mirror those for simple differential backups. Although they may appear a little more complex than simple differential backups, they can be ideal for environments that require less-frequent full backups.

3.4.4 Consolidated Level

Few backup products actually offer consolidated backups (otherwise known as "synthetic full backups"), and typically those that do offer them have restrictions on how (and where) they may be used.

A consolidated backup is a mechanism of never (or very rarely) performing full backups, while always having a full backup to recover from. This sounds illogical, but consolidated backups are designed for systems where the cost in time of a full backup is too high, but recovery from a large number of incremental or differential backups is too time consuming.

Consolidated backups typically use the following strategy:

1. A full backup is done on system commissioning or during extremely infrequent downtime.
2. For a set period of time, incremental/differential backups are performed.
3. After that set period has elapsed, a consolidation is performed, whereby the full backup and the previously executed incremental/differential backups are merged into a new full backup. This may or may not include simultaneously merging an incremental from the system.
4. Repeat steps 2 and 3 for the life span of the system.

Advantages of consolidated backups
- Eliminate the need to perform multiple full backups over the life span of the system.
- Allow for recovery from recent full regardless of how long it has been since an actual full backup has been performed.
- Useful for backing up remote offices over slow links to a central location if the first full backup can be performed in the central location.

Disadvantages of consolidated backups
- Not supported by all backup products.
- Even backup products that support consolidated/synthetic full backups will typically have limited support, and may only provide support for flat filesystem backups. Databases and special system components may still require more conventional backup approaches.

- May create a single point of failure. Rather than being able to recover from a previous full backup if the most recent full backup has some type of error (logical or physical), no or only extremely limited recovery options may be possible.

3.4.5 Manual Backups

Although not technically a backup level, it is often worth differentiating whether a backup product supports manual backups. These are ad-hoc backups that are initiated by an administrator or end user rather than scheduled from the backup software.

Manual backups offer an additional level of protection and allow for user-extension to the backup product, catering for applications and scenarios that the backup vendor was either unable to anticipate or unwilling to support directly.

If manual backups are supported, they should be discouraged except under the following circumstances: (1) completely ad-hoc operations (e.g., a system administrator backing up a few key files before making a change to the system); and (2) to extend the backup system for a particular site requirement (e.g., using manual backups to protect a database for which there is no module/plug-in available for the backup product).

Manual backups can represent significant administrator overhead. Consider, for instance, a backup environment with 300 hosts. If those 300 hosts each run manual backups at a local administrator-designated time, then there is no easy way to disable those backups for scheduled maintenance. Moreover, such a strategy prevents the backup administrator(s) from being able to anticipate and plan for resource usage at specific times during a backup window.

Advantages of manual backups
- Allows for ad-hoc backups to be run on an as-required backup, without scheduling
- Allows for extension of the backup system beyond the design of the backup software vendor

Disadvantages of manual backups
- If misused, may result in resource contention on the backup server
- May create administrative overheads if used regularly, or outside of regular centralized backup scheduling

3.4.6 Skipping Backups

Most backups require consideration not only of when they will be active, but also when they will be inactive. For instance, an end-of-month backup typically runs one day in an entire month, and doesn't do anything for the rest of the time. There are typically three different ways that backup products can handle this:

1. Not support it, requiring administrator intervention to disable and re-enable backup jobs at appropriate times.
2. Utilize "windows," which specify times or dates when a particular backup can run.
3. Utilize some form of a "skip" level, which allows a schedule to be enabled permanently, but doing nothing when required.

Any backup product that doesn't support some form of skipping is obviously not worth considering in an enterprise environment. True enterprise backup products, however, will typically fall either into category 2 or category 3 in the above list.

In essence, regardless of how this form of scheduling is achieved, the net result is an important factor in enterprise backups: the ability to define "set and forget" schedules that do not require periodic and repetitive administrator intervention to function correctly.

In addition to allowing for scheduled non-backup periods, an enterprise backup product also needs to be able to allow easily for the configuration of ad-hoc windows of inactivity, so that non-regular downtime can be catered for. This can allow for backups to be skipped for planned system outages, etc., without resulting in erroneous failure reports from the system.

Advantages of "skip" backup levels/windows

- Allows backup schedules to be completely automated, requiring less administrator intervention.
- Allows non-regular backup downtimes to be scheduled in advance.

Disadvantages of "skip" backup levels/windows

- None. The lack of such a feature should be considered a "fatal flaw" in any backup environment.

3.4.7 Full Once, Incrementals Forever

Technically, this is not a backup level as such, but instead a technique for backups. However, as it is intimately tied to backup levels, it is appropriate to discuss this technique in the current context.

Some backup products offer what is described as a "time-saving" method whereby a single full backup is generated, and from then onwards for the entire life span of a server only incremental backups are performed. This is different than consolidated backups, which actually convert a series of incrementals and fulls into a single new full backup. If backups were to be kept for a year, "full once and incrementals forever" would imply 1 × full backup, and 364 (or 365 for leap years) × incremental backups.

To overcome obvious limitations, companies that offer this type of backup typically offer a "media aggregation" feature whereby, as other backups expire on media, new media is generated to group the incremental backups onto fewer tapes. This is typically performed based on low watermarks being triggered — e.g., with less than 35 percent of the backups on a volume still requiring retention, the system might aggregate the backups requiring retention from that volume and another to form a new volume, allowing the old volumes to be recycled.*

Assuming even a 3:1 media space recovery regime over the course of a year, this still results in a phenomenal amount of media required for a full system recovery. With backups themselves not consolidated, each individual backup on a piece of media will still need to be read through, meaning that there will still be just as many backups to recover from as were performed. Assuming, for instance, that each incremental in the above description goes onto a different piece of media, and that we can constantly achieve a 3:1 media saving using media aggregation, we still might have

* Media aggregation simply reduces the amount of physically separate media required for a recovery. It does not perform any true backup consolidation or synthesis as discussed in section 3.4.4, "Consolidated Level."

364 incremental backups stored on as many as 120 volumes. When viewed from a recovery that is not shortly after implementation, this backup technique appears considerably flawed.

This model is effectively a hedged bet against ever needing to perform a full system recovery. It is true that many organizations typically need to restore only individual files or directories rather than entire filesystems or systems. These organizations usually see "fulls once, incrementals forever" as an acceptable backup policy — until the chips are down and a full system recovery needs to be performed. Ultimately, this form of backup is somewhat of a gimmick, and should be avoided wherever possible, as it strongly violates the principle that backups should provide an easy recovery mechanism.

Advantages of "incrementals forever"

- After the first full backup, the backup window will be considerably smaller for all future backups.
- If a deployed backup product doesn't support consolidated backups, but supports this model, it may allow for a smaller backup window indefinitely, although at a price.

Disadvantages of "incrementals forever"

- Complete system or even complete filesystem recoveries may need to make use of a large number of backup volumes. It is quite easy to see in this scenario that such a system does not factor in the recovery performance hit that can occur from a large incremental-based recovery.
- Having only one full backup is very much a case of "all your recovery eggs in one basket."
- Allowing for media aggregation without disrupting regular backup and recovery operations may require additional backup devices.
- Physical wear-and-tear on media and devices during recoveries may be excessive.

3.5 Data Availability

Depending on the type of backup performed, the availability of data to end users may be affected, or rather the level of data availability required by the organization will make a profound impact on the type of backups that can be performed. In this section, we'll discuss the various types of data availability in backups.

3.5.1 Offline

An offline backup is where the data or system that is backed up is unavailable for other use for the duration of the backup. (In database circles, these types of backups are referred to as cold backups.)

This obviously results in an outage on the data and application(s), which lasts as long as the backup takes to complete. This presents obvious disadvantages to 24/7 businesses that cannot be denied (though in section 3.5.3, "Snapshot Backups," we'll see how offline backups can be simulated while still having highly available data). However, in applications or businesses where 24/7 availability is not required, there are some advantages to offline backups, most typically where there are no dedicated IT staff to perform more complex recoveries that may arise from other forms of backup.

It should be noted that offline backups may actually cause performance problems outside the backup window. Many modern enterprise applications, particularly databases, use sophisticated caching techniques to reduce the amount of IO operations required, with SAP and Oracle being two such applications. As soon as an application is shut down, any cache that it may have been maintaining is typically lost. Indeed, some vendors will strongly recommend against restarting their application frequently for reasons of cache performance alone.

Advantages of offline backups

- Recovery is typically trivial.
- For even complex environments, recoveries can be performed by staff who might not otherwise be system or application administrators if following well-tested instructions.
- In some cases, this can be used to achieve reasonably complex backups with minimum downtime by making use of clusters and shared/snapshot storage. For example, companies have made use of clusters to perform backups of databases without agents for their particular backup product by disconnecting a cluster node and backing it up with an offline copy of the database, without impacting the primary database. (This creates the obvious requirement to have at least a three-node cluster to avoid a scenario whereby availability or performance is compromised for backup.)

Disadvantages of offline backups

- Without snapshots or other expensive techniques, applications that rely on the data are unavailable for the entire duration of the backup.
- Care has to be taken to ensure that all components of the data are unused during backup. For example, if data resides on multiple filesystems, there must be no changes to any of those filesystems during the backup. Not taking this into account is a common mistake for new administrators of backup systems.
- For databases in particular, incremental offline backups are usually not supported — i.e., offline database backups usually force a full backup. If the database is only a few gigabytes in size, this may be OK; however, it quickly becomes impractical as the size of the database increases.
- Over time this model is unlikely to work as the amount of data to be backed up grows. For instance, a small company might be able to back up in offline mode initially, but as systems grow in size, users may find themselves unable to access systems due to backups still being active. (In some cases, this results in situations whereby companies choose to run backups less frequently, which has obvious disadvantages for the recoverability of an environment.)

3.5.2 Online

In an online backup, the data or systems that are being backed up remain completely available for the duration of the backup (in database circles, these are referred to as hot backups). Online backups will typically create a performance hit on systems as they are backed up — i.e., they will remain available to users, but will run slower — whether this is noticed by the end users will have as much to do with the speed of the hosts and storage as with the design of any applications running at the time.

For databases, this performance hit is caused by the requirement to do much greater transactional logging during the backup. Transactional logging is used in circumstances where a possibly inconsistent backup is taken of a database file, but another file generated (and backed up after the database file has been fully backed up) can be used to restore consistency. A discussion (with examples) on how transactional logging might work can be found in appendix A, section A.2 "Transactional Logging."

Regular filesystem backups (say, of an operating system disk, user accounts, and so on) are typically taken on a risk-based approach — i.e., an online backup is performed, but nothing is in place to prevent modifications occurring to the file currently being backed up. That is, it is deemed in most instances an acceptable risk to have this occur.

Most backup products provide some mitigation to the risk involved in online filesystem backups by producing a warning message for any file that changes during a backup. This, of course, is dependent on whether the operating system being backed up allows concurrent access of files while they are open for read/write operations. In cases where filesystems (such as Microsoft's NTFS) allow a file to be kept open locked for exclusive access, "open file agents" have been developed by both backup vendors and third-party vendors. These reside between the operating system and the backup agent to present a cached copy of an open file when the backup agent attempts to open it for reading. (With the introduction of virtual snapshot technology in Windows 2003, the need for third-party open file agents has been greatly reduced on the Windows platform.)

> **Cautions for Backing Up Filesystems That Don't Support Exclusive File Locking.** Administrators of filesystems that don't support exclusive file locking (such as many of the standard UNIX and Linux filesystems) still have to remain cautious when it comes to performing online backups — perhaps even more so than those where an agent is required on filesystems that implement locking. For example, most major database products run on the major UNIX and Linux platforms. For the most part, these systems allow a file to be opened for read/write while another process reads the file.
>
> What needs to be understood clearly is that there is a considerable difference between being able simply to back up a file and being able to back up a file that can be used by the database after it has been restored.
>
> For example, consider an Oracle database running on Solaris using UFS filesystems. A backup agent could walk the filesystem and back up all the Oracle files that contain the database while the database is up and running, without any administrator intervention. However, if those files were restored, and an attempt were made to start Oracle against them, the database would complain of corruption and refuse to start. If needing to perform online backups for databases, always use an agent or other appropriate backup mechanism rather than just relying on being able to read the file(s) associated with the database.

Increasingly as even the most basic of systems become required for 24/7 availability, online backups have been the only option for many companies. Such organizations can no longer afford to shut a machine down for hours for a backup if it means that a customer will refuse to wait. Reporting "the system is currently unavailable" to a customer is now accepted as an informal way of saying "please buy this product or service from a competitor."

As application/data storage requirements continue to increase, the amount of time required for backups has also increased. (Conversely, the amount of time available for recoveries has decreased, but we will discuss that later.)

The unfortunate relationship between offline and online backups is that while an offline backup possibly represents a significant interruption to service delivery, it represents an extremely streamlined recovery. In particular, depending on the application or database being backed up, online database backups designed for no interruptions may require a longer or more complex recovery procedure.

Advantages of online backups
- No outage to end users or customers during the backup process.
- Due to the above, applications that build cache are unaffected by backups.
- Allows for higher availability.

Disadvantages of online backups
- May be more complex to configure and administer.
- For databases, a database administrator may be required as recoveries will not be simple filesystem restores.

3.5.3 Snapshot Backups

A snapshot backup is a "point-in-time" backup that allows immediate recovery of a system to the exact point in time that the backup was initiated. The difference between this and a regular backup is that the snapshot provides the same point-in-time backup for all files, regardless of what time the files are backed up, whereas a conventional hot/online backup will allow the backup of different files at varying times. Snapshots are typically employed in high-availability systems that must be recovered in minimal time, but can either withstand very brief outages or have well-known IO activities during the backup period. For example, a backup might see files saved to tape with the following time frame:

- C:\Data\File1.dat, backed up at 22:30
- C:\Data\File2.dat, backed up at 22:32
- C:\Data\File3.dat, backed up at 22:45

The difference between a snapshot backup and an online backup is whether or not the files can change. In a regular hot/online backup, there is nothing to prevent "File2.dat" from changing during the backup of "File1.dat," or "File1.dat" from changing after it has been backed up but before all other files have been backed up. Using a conventional open file agent, the files may be safely retrieved from a cache, but there will be no consistency between the files (which is vital if the files are, say, part of a database).

In a snapshot backup, however, the filesystem backup is read-only and not updated by any processes. This means that multi-file consistency (indeed, entire filesystem or system consistency) is provided — neither "File1.dat," "File2.dat," nor "File3.dat" in the example above will change in any way whatsoever while the other files are being backed up. It is for this reason that we can say that snapshots provide complete point-in-time recovery capabilities.

Snapshots can be broken down into two sub-categories, based on whether they are hot (online) or cold (offline). A hot snapshot is one where the system is left up and running while the snapshot is taken — i.e., the data in the snapshot was active at the time it was taken. This provides not only for point-in-time recovery, but also allows for it to be done without any outage of the applications during the backup.

A cold snapshot, on the other hand, still requires the shutdown of the application or system. Unlike regular offline backups, however, a cold snapshot backup typically results in an outage of only a few seconds, or at most a few minutes, as opposed to an outage for the entire length of the backup, i.e., the system/application is shut down, a snapshot is generated, the system/application is restarted, and the snapshot is then mounted for backup. With this in mind, some companies choose to use snapshots to achieve cold, offline backups while still keeping the system available for the vast majority of the backup window.

Companies that work in the global marketplace, of course, need to be aware that just because it might be midnight at their data center, it is not midnight everywhere else in the world, and therefore even a five-minute outage may not be acceptable if it impacts customers or business processes in other time zones. Thus even cold snapshots may represent too long an outage.

Snapshot backups increasingly fulfill two different niches within the backup and data protection arena: (1) fast generation of a point-in-time copy of the volumes/filesystems for backup; and (2) provision of multiple "roll-back" points during a small window that traditional backups cannot achieve. For example, snapshots might be taken hourly during business hours. In this sense, snapshots are often seen as a mechanism of meeting SLAs for minimal data loss — something that backups alone may not be able to achieve given a high run frequency and small available window.

A more in-depth overview of the various snapshot techniques available can be found in appendix A, section A.3, "Snapshots."

Advantages of snapshot backups

- Allow the easy acquisition of a point-in-time copy of the system.
- Can allow for faster recoveries — mount the snapshot and copy the required files (for individual file recovery), or roll the snapshot back to perform a complete filesystem recovery.
- Depending on the snapshot technology, multiple snapshots can be performed over a short period of time, which allows systems to meet SLAs for minimal data loss.
- Snapshots may be able to be mounted on alternate hosts, further reducing the load on the client system during the backup process.

Disadvantages of snapshot backups

- Typically require additional volume management software, or intelligent disk arrays.
- Require additional disk space (though not necessarily double the disk space).
- Snapshot disks must be the same speed as original disks. (Companies that do snapshot "on the cheap" by using ATA or SATA arrays to snap fiber arrays quickly find performance while snapshots are active to be unusable.)
- Snapshots either will require a significant performance hit up front to duplicate a volume completely or, if a more-advanced snapshot technique such as copy-on-write is used, will suffer performance issues as the number of snapshots are increased, and the number of writes on the original volume are increased.
- Coordinating snapshots across multiple hosts (e.g., for clustered servers, or multi-tiered database/application servers) can be tricky.

3.6 Data Selection Types

Backup products fall into two main categories — inclusive or exclusive backups. This refers to how data is selected for backup by the backup agent. Ultimately, remembering the rule that it is always better to back up a little more than not enough, exclusive file selection models should always be favored over inclusive file selection models.

3.6.1 Inclusive Backups

An inclusive backup is one where a list is built of the data or filesystems that require backup, and only items that are in the list are selected for backup. Typically, this refers to a specification of the filesystems — for example, on a UNIX system backups might be specified for the following:

- /
- /boot
- /var
- /home

On a Windows system, backups might be specified for the following:

- C:
- D:
- E:

Some organizations prefer this type of backup system under the belief that it allows them greater control regarding what data gets backed up. This is, in almost every case, a misguided belief founded on false economies. Time after time, across almost every company, this policy simply results in data loss.

A common example is "we won't backup the operating system, it can be reinstalled and settings re-applied." In most cases, this is not properly thought through. Take a UNIX environment, in which case the sequence might be the following:

- Reinstall the operating system
- Customize groups and users who can access the system
- Make amendments to such items as the mail delivery system to suit the organization
- Recreate printers
- Reinstall any third-party system administration tools that reside on the operating system area
- Perform any additional security hardening required

Depending on the use of the system, the level of customization may be more or less than the above list, but there will invariably be some activities that are required on the host after the base operating system has been installed. Typically, this level of customization exceeds a short period of time, even for well-documented systems. Windows systems are not exempt, and will have their own issues that sometimes overlap the above list. For example, many products perform "special" backups of key Windows components such as the registry; rather than backing up the base files that comprise the Windows registry hives, it is necessary to export them properly first. These files may therefore not be backed up as part of a "C:\" backup at all, but require an additional special option turned on. A common mistake with inclusive backup policies is to forget about these special components and therefore be unable to perform host disaster recoveries.

As soon as the amount of time taken to customize a machine exceeds a very short period of time, any perceived advantages of not backing up the operating system are lost. If the customization is something that can only be done by a single person in a system administration team, more comprehensive backup/restore scenarios are definitely required.

Taking a worst-case scenario, the operating system area of a machine might represent, say, 4 GB. As the operating system region changes infrequently, the incremental backups on such a system will have almost no impact on tape requirements. It would be reasonable to assume that such an operating system region will have less than 100 MB of changes per day. Plotting a six-week daily backup retention period, with fulls once per week, we could assume that this will require 6 × 4 GB for full backups and 36 × 100 MB for incremental backups.

This equates to a scenario of requiring an extra 28 GB (rounded) of backup capacity over a six-week cycle. Assuming the backup system uses DLT IV tapes with no compression, this means less than one tape, even using a DLT 7000 tape drive. In 2007, a DLT IV tape cost approximately AU$35. Viewed in this light, this represents a somewhat unimpressive "cost saving." In comparison though, assuming a system is used by a small number of users (e.g., ten), and each of those users is paid (on average) $30 per hour, the "cost" of the system needing one hour of customization after install is a minimum of $300. If the activity of those users is required for revenue generation, this cost rapidly increases.

What this example should show is that in the best case, inclusive backups represent a false economy. Saving a few dollars here and there on backup media might improve the bottom line when no recoveries are required, but will be quickly forgotten by upper management when systems cannot be accessed by even a handful of users.

Inclusive backups, however, represent a considerably worse threat than the above — the potential for data loss due to human error. Inclusive backups typically end up in situations where data is stored on filesystems different than what is being backed up, or an explicit list of files and filesystems to back up will miss a particular file that is required for easy (or worse, successful) recovery. A common mistake in inclusive backup systems is where an administrator adds a new filesystem to a host, and then fails to update the backup criteria for the machine.

Inclusive Backups Invite Human Error. A company once had an SAP system whose nightly cold backups had been manually managed via inclusive backups — i.e., each filesystem to be backed up was explicitly listed. During a review it was determined that they had added an additional 2 × 30 GB filesystems containing SAP database files to the host without including these filesystems in the backup. This error was picked up several weeks after the filesystems were added. Although no failure had occurred in this time, the potential for failure was high — the production operations of the entire company had been geared around a total dependency on SAP; thus the complete loss of the SAP system would have resulted in significant productivity outages, data loss, lost work time, etc.

What was worse was that the backup product normally worked using an exclusive file selection mechanism, but had been deliberately shoe-horned into an inclusive backup model.

Based on these reasons and examples, inclusive backup policies or products should be strongly discouraged. Further, products that only offer inclusive backup strategies should be discarded from any consideration when evaluating possible enterprise backup software due to potential for data loss.

Advantages of inclusive backups
- None. There are no features of an inclusive backup system that cannot be provided by an appropriately managed exclusive backup system.

Disadvantages of inclusive backups
- Data loss can occur, resulting in anything from additional work being required to job loss or collapse of a company dependent on a backup system that was not or could not be configured for adequate protection.

3.6.2 Exclusive Backups

Exclusive backups are the exact opposite of inclusive backups — rather than explicitly specifying what should be backed up, only what should not be backed up is explicitly specified. The automated selection of what is to be backed up is typically achieved through specifying a special "global" backup parameter, such as "All" or "ALL_LOCAL_DRIVES" for "All filesystems." While the parameter will vary depending on the backup product, the net result is the same — rather than manually having to specify individual filesystems or drives to be backed up, and adjust settings whenever more filesystems are added, the one parameter should act as a catch-all.

An exclusive backup product will automatically protect all filesystems attached to a client. Typically, this is restricted to filesystems that are "locally" attached to the system — i.e., network attached filesystems are usually not included, due to either licensing or performance requirements. (As SAN storage is seen as locally attached storage, such systems would be included in an automated backup.) Where required, network-attached filesystems can be explicitly added to the backup policy.

Exclusive backup systems are designed using the axiom of "better to back up more, than not enough," and should be favored at all times over inclusive backup systems. In this sense, exclusive backup products have clearly been designed to maximize data protection. A key benefit that exclusive backup systems grant is the reduction in risk for human error when filesystems are added or otherwise changed. The backup system should automatically detect any new filesystems on hosts configured for exclusive backups in the environment, and automatically protect them as part of the next backup. (It should be noted that special backups, such as databases or mail servers, would usually still have to be configured manually, though this will be the same for inclusive backup products as well.)

Users of backup software that works on an inclusive model will usually object to exclusive backups on the grounds of "there are things I just don't want to back up." Again, as per inclusive backups, many arguments towards the non-backup of files or areas of systems may be erroneous, or represent false economies.

A common example of files that companies don't want to back up is found in user multimedia files (such as MP3s). In this case, exclusive backups offer a better mechanism than inclusive backups. Rather than having to specify everything other than multimedia files to be backed up, as one would in an inclusive backup system, the exclusive backup system allows for specific actions (such as skipping files and directories) to be configured based on either nominated directories, or known file names/extensions.

Ultimately, an exclusive backup model is designed to minimize the risk of data loss, as opposed to inclusive backup models, erroneously designed to minimize the amount of backup media to be purchased/used by a company. (We say "erroneously" because the same effect can be achieved, more safely, with an exclusive backup product.) However, any gratitude for savings made on media budget for a year are quickly forgotten when a critical system can't be recovered because files and filesystems were not included in the backup policy (either accidentally or deliberately).

Advantages of exclusive backups
- Maximizes the potential for the backup environment to provide recoverability of data and systems.
- Reduces the risk of human error or forgetfulness resulting in data loss.

Disadvantages of exclusive backups
- Requires additional analysis of each system to confirm what, if anything, may be excluded from the backups. (It should be noted that this would be considered by many to be a standard system-administration function anyway.)

3.7 Backup Retention Strategies

The way in which a backup product handles the retention of backups directly affects how recoveries work, and for how long recoveries can be performed. Because we have stated from the beginning that the purpose of a backup is to allow recoveries to be performed when required, retention strategies have a direct impact on the quality of the backup product. We can classify two types of retention strategies within backup products: the simple model, and the dependency-based retention model. Although it is the more complex one, the dependency model is most appropriate to present first. This is because it is only after the dependency-based retention model is understood that it can be appreciated just how poor and inappropriate the simple model is in a backup environment.

3.7.1 Dependency-Based Retention

This model takes the approach that a specified retention period creates dependencies among the individual backups for true data protection. This creates a situation such as shown in Figure 3.7, which recognizes that the incremental backups do not in themselves offer true recoverability of an entire filesystem — they rely on the full backup that was done before them. In these models, although the full is technically "outside" the retention period, it is not flagged as eligible for removal because there are backups inside the retention period that still require it. Typically, this means that backups only become recyclable after a new sequence exists to "replace" them — for example, a new full backup has occurred, which "breaks" the dependency chain. This is shown in Figure 3.8. This method typically results in more media being required, but the advantage of this

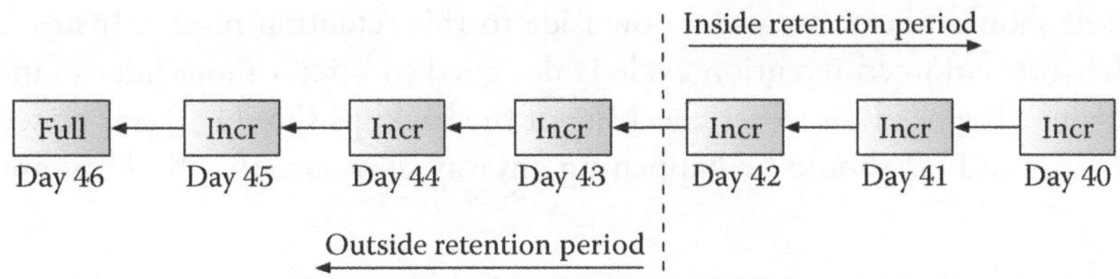

Figure 3.7 Backup retention showing recovery dependencies

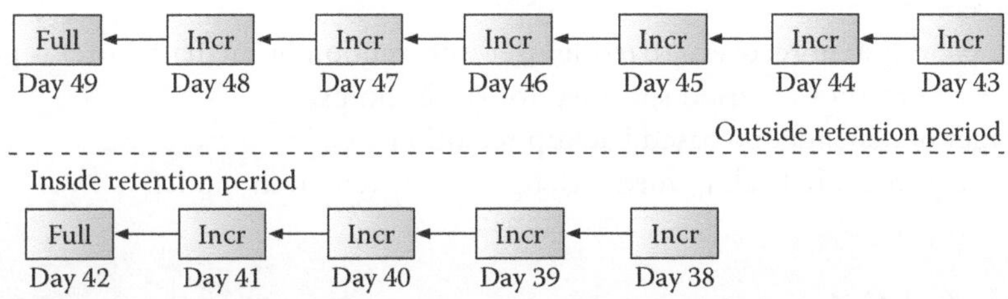

Figure 3.8 Backup retention with successive dependency chains

backup system is that users can be assured they definitely do get their complete specified retention. Let's be clear on this: dependency-based retention models are designed to guarantee that the retention period specified by the administrator of the system is honored.

Another way to think of this form of retention is "complete recovery protection" — the backup product is designed not only simply to allow any individual backup instance to be recovered from, but on the basis that the worst-case scenario (complete system restoration) also needs to be achievable right through to the complete configured retention time. If backups must be preserved for legal or auditing reasons, it may mean that dependency-based retention could be legally required in an environment.

Although full backups are always important, if anything they become more important in a dependency-based retention system. If a full backup — or for that matter, any backup that would terminate/interrupt a dependency chain — fails, then the existing dependency chain must continue to grow. This may in turn result in a dependency chain such as shown in Figure 3.9. In short, if a full fails, the backup product must extend the life span of the previous full and intervening incremental backups to force the integrity of the backup period. Note that in this case we are referring only to a failed full or scheduled full that never ran, rather than a backup that successfully ran, but was subsequently accidentally erased, or was on media that failed.

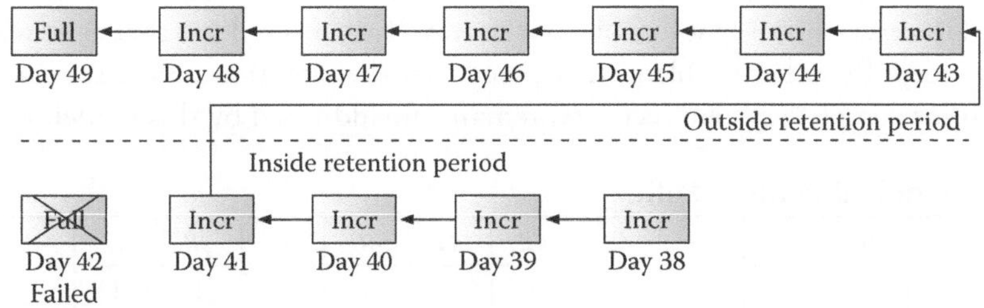

Figure 3.9 Backup dependency chain with failed full backup

This in itself should not be seen as a downside to this retention model. Instead, it should be recognized that this enforced retention cycle is designed to offer a more-honest and robust data protection scheme. The need for closer checking of the backups should (1) not be seen as a higher cost than data loss and (2) should be happening anyway to ensure that backups are operating as expected.

Advantages of dependency-based backup retention

- Backups that are still within their retention time are only removed when the system is certain that there can be no other backups that depend on them for complete system recovery.
- Complete system recovery (barring user intervention or media failure) is guaranteed for the entire retention period specified for the backups.

Disadvantages of dependency-based backup retention

- May require more backup media than a simple retention model.

3.7.2 Simple Model

This is (unfortunately) far too common a model of how recovery from backup is controlled in products. In this situation, the retention time specified for backups is viewed only on the basis of recoverability from an individual set or backup.

Take, for instance, a six-week retention time. This equates to 42 days of backups. Viewing the backups via the retention window allows us to see what happens to backups that move outside their retention time. In the model shown in Table 3.10, all italicized backups would be immediately considered available for removal or recycling — i.e., so long as all backups on media housing these backups are recyclable, the media could be re-used by the backup system.

This is a retention strategy based solely on false economies. If the full backup from day 43 is expunged, this means that the system as a whole cannot be recovered for a full six weeks worth of backups. Instead, only five weeks (assuming all full backups succeed) worth of backups can be recovered using the full system recovery model. Although the incremental backups from days 37–42 could be used to recover individual files, the entire filesystem they provide backups for could not be successfully recovered. This approach in essence hedges its bets on only needing to perform a complete filesystem recovery from the most-recent full backups. However, there are a plethora of recovery scenarios that this fails to address.

Some backup products that provide simplistic retention systems attempt to counter the loss of a full backup (which extends dependency chains in dependency-based products) by forcing the full backup to re-run the next-scheduled backup runtime if it fails. This is intended to offer a counter-solution to the full dependency chain scenario that can be encountered in the dependency chain model. However, this only solves one of the two distinct problems that exist with the simple dependency model. The other problem, that being that the retention period specified by the user is not honored for complete system recovery, remains unaddressed by this model.

Table 3.10 Simple Retention Policy

49	*48*	*47*	*46*	*45*	*44*	*43*	42	41	40	39	38	37	36	35	34
I	*I*	*I*	*I*	*I*	*I*	*F*	I	I	I	I	I	I	F	I	I

Note: I = incremental backup, F = full backup

One of the common and illogical manifestations of this model is an encouragement for the user to see a separation between the full backup that occurs periodically and the incremental backup that occurs nearly everyday. For example, in these types of backup products, users may refer to their "weekly backup set" and their "daily backup set" as being two distinctly different sets. This for the most part tricks the users into believing that there is no relation between, say, a weekly full backup and daily incrementals. Of course, when evaluated from a system protection perspective, such an idea is clearly farcical.

When considering complete data protection, backup products that use this type of retention model should be avoided wherever possible in corporate environments, unless longer retention models are used, and management-signed acceptance of the system restoration risks involved is provided.

Advantages of simplistic backup retention

- None. The perceived media saving is irrelevant when compared to the risk of not being able to recover systems.

Disadvantages of simplistic backup retention

- Does not guarantee full system recovery for the entire retention period specified by the backup administrator.
- Often encourages an artificial separation between full and incremental backups at the cost of system recoverability.

3.7.3 Manual Backups Revisited

Previously, when discussing the various backup levels that may be offered by a backup product, we discussed the notion of manual or ad-hoc backups. For the most part, backup products that calculate retention dependency avoid factoring manual backups into the dependency tree at all — i.e., the dependency tree is typically built on scheduled backups only.

If this sounds odd, consider a couple of scenarios: (1) System administrator does an ad-hoc, client-initiated backup of /opt. Obviously, all files in /opt are backed up. But /opt is normally part of the/(root) filesystem for this particular machine. How should backups for /opt be processed in the dependency tree? (2) System administrator does an ad-hoc, client-initiated backup of C:\, which includes the junction point C:\SAN\DataVolume1. Is this to be seen as a backup of both C:\ and C:\SAN\DataVolume1, or just an "extra large" backup of C:\?

If manual backups were to be counted within dependencies, that process of slotting them in among other backups would at best be very CPU/memory intensive as entire indices are scanned for directory-level comparison within backups on a daily basis, or worse, error prone. Thus, manual backups may be ignored when determining dependency trees.

If planning to work with manual backups, it is necessary to consider what impact this may have on backup dependencies if available in the backup system. That is, will this create dependencies that are difficult for the backup product to resolve, or will the backup product ignore the manual backups that have been performed when performing dependency checks? This should be either documented or readily discoverable by the vendor.

3.8 Recovery Strategies

There are several broad categories in which backup products will offer means to accomplish recoveries. Not all products will support each strategy, so if looking for a new product, it will be necessary to determine which strategies are required the most, and confirm from backup and recovery vendors which strategies are supported by their product.

3.8.1 Recovery Types

By "recovery type" we refer to how the backup product offers to perform a recovery — how files which have been backed up may be selected for recovery, or recovered without selection.

Although we present multiple types here, there are three types that should be considered mandatory for a backup product:

1. Last filesystem view recovery: This presents a view of the filesystem as it was as of the last backup.
2. Point-in-time recovery: Although the last filesystem view is arguably the most-common recovery that administrators and users will require, for many companies a substantial portion of recoveries will need to be of data that was backed up prior to the most-recent backup. This option allows a user to step back through previous versions of the filesystem, allowing not only the selection of what to recover, but when.
3. Non-index recovery: Being able to perform a recovery from an index of files is an obvious requirement, but a less-obvious but still necessary requirement is to be able to recover without those indices if necessary. If there are issues or failures with the index for a backup or client that requires recovery, it may not be acceptable for the business to spend time trying to fix the index. In such cases, it becomes necessary to perform recoveries without the index, and deal with maintenance later.

3.8.1.1 Aggregated Filesystem View

A somewhat opposite intent to the last filesystem view (below) is the less-useful aggregated filesystem view. Not only does the aggregated filesystem view show the filesystem contents as of the last backup, it includes into the view all files from backups between the most-recent full backup and the last run backup.

To understand an aggregated filesystem view, let's consider a backup schedule where the full backup occurs on a Friday evening, and incremental backups are performed Saturday through Thursday evenings. Consider then the following scenario:

- Full backup occurs on Friday.
- On Sunday, the directory "/Users/preston/Archives/Oldest" is deleted by a scheduled job.
- On Monday, the file "/Users/preston/Desktop/expenses.xls" is created.
- On Tuesday, the file "/Users/preston/Desktop/expenses.xls" is deleted.
- On Tuesday, the file "/Users/preston/Desktop/Letter.pages" is created.
- On Wednesday morning, the "/Users" directory is accidentally deleted, and needs to be recovered.

If a recovery agent using an aggregated filesystem view is used to recover on Wednesday morning, it will show both the "/Users/preston/Archives/Oldest" directory as well as the "/Users/preston/Desktop/expenses.xls" file, even though neither of these files existed as of the most-recent backup performed.

Although this model may initially appear to provide a good recovery mechanism, its advantages are outweighed by its disadvantages.

Advantages of aggregated filesystem recovery view

- Presents all files backed up since the last full (typically). This reduces the need to alter the point in time the recovery is browsed for.
- Provides an easy mechanism to recover from successive days worth of accidental or malicious data deletion.

Disadvantages of aggregated filesystem recovery view

- May cause a security failure. If deletion was intentional due to a security consideration, an administrator may not think to repeat the deletion at the conclusion of the recovery, or remember to exclude the file(s) from recovery.
- Some filesystems have significant volumes of data change on a daily basis. In certain circumstances where there has been significant deletion and new data creation, it is possible to enter a recovery situation where the recovery fails due to insufficient space on the filesystem as older, previously deleted files are also recovered.
- If neither of the above two problems occur, the end result is still one that many system administrators may consider to be a "messy" filesystem.
- Users may be confused by previous versions of files and directories.
- Data duplication may occur if between successive backups files and directories have been moved from one part of the filesystem to another.

3.8.1.2 Last Filesystem View

This recovery variant only shows the files that were on the filesystem as of the last backup — i.e., it assumes that deletions that occurred between backups are actually intentional, and the desire is to return the filesystem as close as possible to what it was as of the failure.

In our previous example, we considered the following scenario:

- Full backup occurs on Friday.
- On Sunday, the directory "/Users/preston/Archives/Oldest" is deleted by a scheduled job.
- On Monday, the file "/Users/preston/Desktop/expenses.xls" is created.
- On Tuesday, the file "/Users/preston/Desktop/expenses.xls" is deleted.
- On Tuesday, the file "/Users/preston/Desktop/Letter.pages" is created.
- On Wednesday morning, the "/Users" directory is accidentally deleted, and needs to be recovered.

As discussed previously, the aggregated filesystem view would show those files that had been deleted prior to the Tuesday night backup on Wednesday morning, potentially allowing an administrator to recover a logically inconsistent filesystem or an overfull one.

For the last filesystem view, we literally see only the files present on the filesystem as of the last backup. Assuming a Tuesday night backup, from our previous example, we would not see the following files and directories for a Wednesday morning recovery: /Users/preston/Archives/Oldest (deleted on Sunday), and /Users/preston/Desktop/expenses.xls (deleted on Tuesday).

Advantages of last filesystem recovery view
- Shows the filesystem as of the last backup performed. This allows administrators very quickly to recover system state as of the last backup.
- When attempting to return a filesystem to the most-recent copy of it, this provides the most logically consistent view.

Disadvantages of last filesystem recovery view
- It becomes important to know when data was deleted, to know when to recover it from. Supporting point-in-time recoveries is effectively a mandatory requirement of a backup system that performs last filesystem recovery views.
- May require multiple recoveries if data loss has been gradual.

3.8.1.3 Point-in-Time Recovery

Point-in-time recovery would be required in the following examples:

- User makes significant change to a document that will be too difficult to back out of, hence referring to the previous night's backup will be the more time-effective method of resetting the document.
- Taxation officials request a copy of the finance database from the closure of the previous financial year.
- User working on a document leaves terminal logged on with application running while on vacation for a few days. Unfortunately, during this time the word processor crashed, leaving the document automatically saved with 0 bytes used on disk. When user returns from vacation and discovers the document "empty," a recovery from several days prior is required.
- Database administrator requests a copy of the database from a month ago to be recovered onto another server to complete last month's reporting.

In all of these examples, the goal is not to recover the most-recent files backed up, but files that were backed up at some point in the past.

Point-in-Time Recoveries Prove the Need for Backup Duplication. In a later topic we'll discuss backup duplication, which refers to generating a "backup of backups." Some organizations insist they do not need to perform backup duplication if they back up to a remote site (e.g., tape library in the disaster recovery site attached to the backup server via dark fiber). Point-in-time recoveries clearly shows this to be a false statement. In the event of a loss of the disaster recovery site, although the current production site data is undamaged, all file history has (conceivably) been lost.

Point-in-Time Recoveries Prove That Snapshots Are Not Backups. In a later topic we'll also discuss snapshots and their function in the backup process. Sometimes, over-eager and ill-informed staff at various vendors will tell customers that purchasing an array with snapshot functionality ensures that they'll never need to run another backup. At this point it is neither technically nor financially feasible to retain sufficient snapshots to avoid doing point-in-time recoveries over the entire expected life span of a backup. For instance, most financial data needs to be kept for at least ten years. Although hardware manufacturers would love to sell sufficient disk and performance for retaining ten years of snapshots of a database, significantly less money and headaches will deliver a comprehensive backup solution.

Advantages of point-in-time recoveries
- Allows prior system or data states to be re-established at an appropriate point within the retention period, rather than the most-recent backup, addressing recovery options beyond those necessitated by the immediate reporting of files deleted.
- Facilitates audits and legal/tax obligations in many companies through the recovery of older records.

Disadvantages of point-in-time recoveries
- None. A backup product must support point-in-time recoveries.

3.8.1.4 Destructive Recovery

Although a destructive recovery may sound like a contradiction in terms, what it refers to is completely replacing the contents of a filesystem or system with that being recovered, thereby deleting files or data that were not present at the time of the backup.

There are two types of destructive recovery. The first is where, on a per-file basis, files that were not present at the time of the backup are deleted from the filesystem as the recovery progresses (or the filesystem is formatted first). The second type leverages restoration from block-level backups, rather than file-level backups, to overwrite the entire filesystem completely. (We'll discuss block-level backups at a later point.)

Advantages of destructive recoveries
- If an external agent has introduced corruption to a system, a destructive recovery may be seen as an appropriate mechanism to bring the system back to a usable state.
- When combined with a point-in-time recovery, a destructive recovery may provide increased coherence in the recovered system by removing files from a more-recent time to the recovery.

Disadvantages of destructive recoveries
- If not understood, or used incorrectly, a destructive recovery could result in significant data loss.

3.8.1.5 Non-Index Recovery

So far we've primarily discussed recoveries that are performed via a "browse" of the filesystem or data to be recovered. Across almost all backup products, the indices that must be maintained for a per-file view of the backup can grow to a very large size. Additionally, although backup vendors do their best to protect against such events, there is always some risk that an index for a backup may in some way become corrupt. Also, some backups may be generated with indexing deliberately turned off — for example, a "closure" backup of a fileserver used explicitly for a project might not have indices if it is determined that the only time the data will ever be recovered is in its entirety, rather than requiring individual file recovery.

For these purposes, most backup products offer the ability to perform a recovery of an entire backup without the need to refer to indices. (Although for the most part this will refer to per-filesystem backups, it may encompass a larger target depending on the circumstances.) That is, everything that was stored as part of an individual backup is recovered, regardless of whether the backup can be browsed on a per-file basis.

Sometimes, administrators may even choose to perform such a recovery even when indices are available. This is typically chosen when the most-recent backup is a full, and the "cost" of selecting all files in the index for recovery is high. This cost can be perceived as high when there are a very large number of files on a filesystem. In index-based recoveries, the index must be searched for relevant entries and those entries must be "tagged" for recovery. This obviously requires time, and a tangible data structure must be maintained for holding the details of the files to be recovered. This may not seem terribly relevant if waiting less than ten seconds for file selection to complete, but if millions of files need to be recovered, this may have a significant impact on the recovery time. (Indeed, in some recoveries involving very large numbers of files — say, tens of millions — the file selection time has been known to take longer than the recovery itself!)

Depending on the backup product, non-index recoveries can also be used where there is physical damage to the backup media so as to try to retrieve "as much as possible" of the backup.

Advantages of non-index recoveries

- Can allow for the recovery of data even if the backup product is itself experiencing data loss or corruption.
- Depending on the product, this may facilitate faster recoveries when there are large numbers (e.g., millions) of files to be recovered.
- Depending on the product, this may facilitate recovering data from faulty media, skipping past soft errors.

Disadvantages of non-index recoveries

- May result in additional data being recovered than intended, if not filtered correctly.
- Typically does not aggregate multiple backups; i.e., each non-index recovery needs to be performed as an individual activity. This leaves responsibility for choosing the appropriate files to recover with the user performing the recovery.

3.8.1.6 Incremental Recovery

This refers to a situation whereby the user performing the recovery must manually run a recovery for each backup that has been done since (and including) the last full, i.e., rather than the backup system automatically recovering from only the backup sets that are required, the user is forced to perform (or more likely, observe), a recovery from each set (from oldest to newest). Alternatively, the backup software may "automatically" perform such recoveries.

This may appear to be just a standard recovery, but can be quickly demonstrated as a poor recovery technique. Imagine seven days of backups, and on each day a 2-GB file has changed, and therefore is backed up each time. For a last filesystem recovery, point-in-time recovery, or aggregated recovery, selecting the 2-GB file for recovery would result in only a single instance of the 2-GB file being recovered.

For an incremental recovery, however, each version of the 2-GB file would be recovered, incrementally, starting at the full backup (or the first time it appeared on the filesystem, whichever was more recent). Each copy of the file would be recovered on top of the previous copy of the file, until the required version had been recovered. Thus, when recovering a filesystem from a full backup seven days ago with six incrementals because just for a single 2-GB file we have seen 14 GB of data recovered. Amazingly, there are still backup products that "offer" this particular feature.

Within products that work via a manual incremental recovery, the backup administrator or user performing the recovery typically selects from the available backup sets those that should be recovered from. There may in this situation be the option of drilling down into selected sets to choose which files or data should be recovered from the backup set. Although promoted as a mechanism for maximizing control over the backup product, such selection options invariably demonstrate that the product has been designed with backups, not recoveries in mind.

There are no advantages to a backup product offering an incremental recovery strategy, and the disadvantages are obvious, as stated above. In short, products that default to recoveries or only offer recoveries via this mechanism should be ignored from serious consideration.

3.8.2 Recovery Locality

We refer to recovery locality as where recoveries are initiated from, with respect to the backup server, and the host that owns the data being recovered. Depending on the product in use, there may be several locality options available during a recovery, and this may in turn increase the level of services that can be offered.

3.8.2.1 Local Recovery

A local recovery is one where the client that lost the data initiates the recovery, regardless of its network location and where the data it lost may have been backed up to. This could be considered to be a "pull" recovery — the client "pulls" the files from backup storage.

This is the simplest form of recovery, and allows for the end users or system administrators of individual hosts to have control over the recovery with minimum involvement from the backup administrators or operators.

The ability to perform this type of backup is often seen as a differentiator between workgroup and enterprise backup products, with workgroup products often focusing on the "push" model, where recoveries are initiated by the backup administrator only on the backup server. Note that to support a local recovery strategy properly within an environment — especially if the end users are not privy to the entire backup system — it will be necessary to configure the hardware and storage capacity of the backup environment to have enough media online for the majority of recovery requests, and automatically notify backup administrators and tape operators of the need to locate and load offline media to facilitate the recovery.

Alternatively if one or both of the above cannot be configured, it will be necessary to have an effective communications strategy between users that can perform recoveries on individual systems and backup administrators/operators to ensure that recovery requests do not either (1) tie up the backup system inappropriately or (2) sit waiting for media to be returned for an excessive period of time because no one is aware that media is required.

3.8.2.2 Server-Initiated Recovery

A server-initiated recovery is where the backup server can be used to commence a recovery, with the data either being recovered locally to the backup server or pushed out to a client. Some products will refer to this as a "push" recovery for that reason.

This offers a convenient mechanism for some recoveries, and when it exists as just one among many recovery locality options, should be seen as a benefit in a backup product.

However, products which only offer server-initiated recoveries or provide only the most-comprehensive recovery options for this particular type of recovery may not be the most appropriate, particularly in a large environment. That is, in an enterprise environment, it is important to differentiate between backup administration and recovery operations. There are two distinct reasons for this: (1) those who need to perform recoveries should not need to have access to the backup server(s), and (2) it is unreasonable to expect that a backup administrator should be responsible for the actual running of every recovery within an environment.

3.8.2.3 Directed Recovery

Directed recoveries, otherwise known as remote recoveries, are where the user or administrator (appropriately authorized) can initiate a recovery on one host, and recover the data to another host, which in turn may not be the host that the data was originally backed up from.

A directed recovery features three different types of clients, which may or may not be the same:

1. Control client — the host that the recovery program/process is run from
2. Source client — the host whose data is being recovered
3. Destination client — the host that will receive the recovered data

When a backup product supports directed recoveries, it will typically also support local recoveries in that the source, control, and destination client should be able to be the same host. In a fashion it may also support server-initiated recoveries in that the recovery software on the backup server could act as the control client. Thus, for users coming from workgroup backup products, even if a backup product doesn't cite having "push" or "server-initiated" recoveries, it will be able to perform the same operation if directed, or remote recoveries are supported.

Directed recoveries allow for considerable flexibility in how recoveries are performed, but do require additional security considerations to ensure that the facility isn't abused and data misappropriated.

They can be very useful, however, in help desk and operator-initiated recoveries, as well as the automation of system refreshes (e.g., updating a development system with a copy of the production database once per month). Note that they can also be said to fulfill an important security function; using people who would not normally have access to particular systems can still be charged with responsibility for recovering data back to those systems.

3.8.2.4 Cross-Platform Directed Recovery

Any cross-platform recovery is by necessity a directed recovery. A cross-platform recovery refers to initiating a recovery on one type of host and recovering it to another type of host.

Cross-platform directed recoveries have various levels of functionality depending on the backup software in use and the operating systems involved, and some of this functionality may be restricted by security requirements from various operating system vendors. For instance, consider the recovery of files from an NTFS filesystem that had access control lists (ACLs) preventing anyone other than the CEO from accessing them. Would it be really appropriate in such instances (even if convenient) to allow an administrator on a UNIX system, which does not have the same ACLs, to recover the file?

At the very least, cross-platform-directed recoveries may offer the ability for the control client to be a different operating system to the source and destination. After this option, the ability for the source and destination clients to be different operating systems will be entirely dependent on the operating system compatibility and support offered by the backup vendor. If cross-platform-directed recoveries are important, this should be discussed with the vendor prior to making a purchase, as it is typically an esoteric-enough feature not to be readily documented in marketing material or specification sheets. Even when cross-platform-directed recoveries have been supported by vendors, that support has been known to change radically on a version-by-version basis.

3.9 Client Impact

Backup products and techniques can be differentiated based on the level of impact they have on the performance of the client being backed up, which for the purposes of this section we'll refer to as the owner-host — i.e., the machine that "owns" the data that is being backed up. This allows us to separate data ownership from backup ownership, because depending on the backup model used, the machine that owns the data may not be the machine that hosts the data for the purposes of the backup.

3.9.1 Server-Based Backups

In backup parlance, "server-based backups" refer to backups where data is read directly from the server that owns the data — the owner-host or client of the backup system.

This is the most-common form of backup used in organizations — during the process the owner-host client is responsible for reading its own data and transferring it to the backup server, an intermediary server, or its own backup media if it has been designated to do so. Backups of this kind have the strongest impact on the owner-host — in addition to whatever other processing requirements it has during the backup period, it must also read the data and transfer it to the appropriate host or media.

This is the traditional backup model for both decentralized and centralized-via-network backups. For many organizations, server-based backups will be entirely acceptable, and only when 24/7 availability or 24/7 high performance becomes a key requirement will companies typically need to look beyond server-based backup strategies.

Server-based backups typically create two additional types of load on an owner-host: (1) CPU and network bandwidth for transfer of data from owner-host to the backup server, and (2) disk IO from reading the data.

A common assumption is that server-based backups don't allow for very much in the way of complex options. However, using server-based backup strategies, even very large enterprises can achieve complex backup strategies. For instance, SAN-based dynamic tape allocation is an example of a powerful backup strategy that can be used in server-based backups. In this case, the strain on the network is considerably reduced, but the owner-host of the data will still perform additional processing during backups.

Advantages of server-based backups
- Simplest backup method — easy to understand. There is a 1:1 mapping between the host that owns the data and the host that transfers the data for backup, making the location of data for recovery simple.
- Typically, no extra installation or configuration steps required other than a basic install and setup to run this type of backup.

Disadvantages of server-based backups
- Backup directly impedes the performance of the host that owns the data.
- Any outage required for the backup directly impacts the availability of the data being protected.

3.9.2 Serverless Backups

When discussing server-based backups, we introduced the term "owner-host," which referred to the machine considered to own the data being backed up. For serverless backups, we must also introduce the term "data-provider," which refers to the machine that provides storage for data. In a directly attached storage environment, the owner-host and the data-provider will be the same; however, in a SAN (Storage Area Network) or NAS (Network Attached Storage) environment, the data-provider may be an entirely different machine or device.

In a traditional backup environment, the owner-host is responsible for the backup of its data. This works for most situations, but sometimes this isn't appropriate. This doesn't always work in the following examples:

- Where the data-provider presents data to multiple operating systems, it may not be possible (or safe) for any one operating system to take responsibility of the data.
- Where the owner-host has strict processing availability requirements, it may not be allowed to suffer reduced processing capacity to provide data to the backup process.
- The owner-host may not be able to provide sufficient performance for the backup process, whereas the data-provider may be able to.
- The network link to the owner-host may not be sufficient for a high-speed backup.

We can therefore state that a serverless backup is one where the owner-host suffers minimal impact during the backup process. Note that unlike other descriptions that may have been encountered for serverless backups, we do not claim that a serverless backups eliminates all impact on the owner-host.

Several techniques can be used to achieve serverless backups, including but not limited to the following:

- Within a SAN-based backup environment, volumes may be backed up directly from the array using NDMP (Network Data Management Protocol). This shifts load processing away from the owner-host. (NDMP will be discussed in more detail later.) Alternatively, the SAN may allow for multiple concurrent hosts to access the LUN (volume), with only one copy in read/write mode.

- For NAS devices typically the most-efficient way of completing backups is via NDMP, which shifts load processing away from the hosts that have mounted the data.
- A combination of SAN or NAS and custom software or third-party backup integration might see "snapshots" or "clones" of volumes generated and mounted on another host for the purposes of backup. This can result in not only a serverless backup, but also a LAN-free backup if the backup server or its storage nodes are able to mount the SAN or NAS volumes directly.

Many organizations make the mistake of assuming that serverless backups result in no performance impact for the owner-host. This is a misconception that is somewhat encouraged by backup vendors and array manufacturers. Although the owner-host may no longer suffer significant CPU/network bandwidth impact as a result of the backup, background IO processing may still result in slower IO performance either before, during, or after the backup. Depending on the situation, this may still be noticed by end users.

Serverless backups should not be seen as a silver bullet for backup performance, and any performance improvement delivered will entirely depend on the type of performance issues being experienced. For instance, if the disks or array holding the data being backed up represent the primary bottleneck, switching to serverless backups may result in little improvement in performance.

3.9.2.1 Filesystem/Volume Clones and Snapshots

We define a volume clone as being a complete copy of a volume. This is the equivalent of breaking off a mirror from a RAID-1 unit. For the purposes of discussing clones and snapshots as separate entities, both traditional and fast resynchronization snapshots can be considered a method of cloning, as they result in a complete 1:1 copy of the original volume.

Clones in themselves will not cause an impact during the backup process, but will need to be synchronized either before or after the backup, which will result in additional IO loading. Users may therefore experience noticeable degraded system performance if other IO processing occurs during clone generation.

Comparatively, true snapshots, such as copy-on-write and cache snapshots, will not cause a performance impact on the owner-host either before or after the backup. However, depending on the IO activities taking place on the owner-host during the backup process, and the backup level performed on the snapshot by the backup server, the IO performance of the data-provider for the volume or filesystem may be impeded. This therefore can result in a slight impact on IO operations on the owner-host during the backup.

3.9.2.2 Array Replication

Even complex scenarios such as array replication, where the backup is run from an entirely separate array, fail to protect the owner-host entirely from additional processing. For instance, array replication will result in one of the following:

- If replication is stopped to allow a completely clean mount of the replicated filesystem(s), once the backup is performed from the replica(s), there will be some IO impact following the restart of the replication as it "catches up."
- If replication occurs as synchronous writes, the secondary array acts as a mirror would, and therefore write processing is slowed down to allow more physical copies to be generated of each write.
- If replication is asynchronous, there is always the risk of the write-buffer/cache becoming congested, which will either result in performance degradation immediately or after the buffer congestion has eased (or communications have been restored in the event of a communications loss).

3.9.2.3 Summarizing Serverless Backups

Typically, it should be understood that although serverless backups can significantly reduce the impact of the backup process on an owner-host, the load is not 100 percent mitigated; at some point there must be some additional load either placed directly on or indirectly experienced by the owner-host, either due to true snapshots or through snapshot/clone creation. The goal therefore is primarily to reduce the CPU processing load associated with transferring a backup.

After CPU load and network performance impacts have been mitigated, any additional increase in performance will follow the same rule as high-availability targets — the smaller the IO impact required on the owner-host, the more money will need to be spent. Just like high availability, this will become a case of diminishing gains, and therefore businesses will need to choose the level of IO disruption acceptable based on the amount it will cost them to implement.

Advantages of serverless backups

- Can significantly reduce the load of the owner-host during the backup process.
- Can also be used to achieve LAN-free backups.
- Depending on the type of bottleneck(s) being experienced in a traditional server-based backup, implementing serverless backups can result in a considerably faster backup.
- Can result in a reduction in the number of client licenses required for a backup, particularly in a homogeneous environment (e.g., mount snapshots from 50 machines onto a single host, and back them all up from one location).

Disadvantages of serverless backups

- If using tools provided by the backup software vendor, it typically requires additional licenses and setup. If using "home-grown" utilities, it still requires additional setup.
- Requires a SAN or NAS environment so that multiple hosts can have access to the same volumes or copies of volumes simultaneously. This may also require additional licensed features from the array manufacturers.
- May limit recovery options. (If snapshot or clone backups are performed, it may not be possible to do a "low level" disaster recovery of a machine from a snapshot that was backed up using another host.)
- In particular when snapshots are used, it can result in confusing recoveries. For instance, if the backup server is used to mount snapshot images for backup, but is replaced with a host that has a different server name, users of the system wishing to perform a recovery will need to know when systems were replaced so they can determine which host they need to issue a recovery request for.

3.9.3 Virtual Machine Snapshots

With the growth in popularity of host virtualization in the x86/x64 server market, it is worth evaluating virtual machine backups. An in-depth explanation of how host virtualization works is well beyond the scope of this book, but for those not familiar with it, suffice it to say that host virtualization allows multiple operating systems to run within an "emulation machine server" on a host. The virtual machine server allocates resources (such as CPU, memory, disk, and network) and presents a basic and stable simulated-hardware environment to each virtual machine, and these virtual machines all exist independently of one another. This often provides a significantly faster and more-reliable deployment model, with more stable drivers.

These virtual machines typically reside in one or more "disk containers" on the virtual machine server's filesystem (which for enterprise-class virtualization servers will have been optimized for holding a few very large files).

A growing option when using host virtualization is to snapshot the running virtual machine and back up the disk file(s) associated with that machine rather than installing a traditional backup agent within the guest operating system and performing regular backups.

In theory, this can save considerably on complexity and licensing costs. For instance, if a virtual machine server runs up to ten or twenty virtual machines, and there are databases in each guest operating system, the licensing costs could be very high for individual clients. However, if backed up at the virtual machine server level, each guest operating system is just a flat file, and only one client connection license would be required — for the virtual machine server — rather than one client connection license for each virtual machine. (In particular, given the nature of virtualization, the number of virtual machines running on a virtual machine server can be considerably variable, which makes calculating license costs somewhat of a grey art.)

For example, a virtual machine server may resemble Figure 3.10. In this case there are four virtual machines presented by this virtual machine server, hosts A, B, C, and D. Although individual users of these servers see them as "real" hosts, when viewed at the virtual machine server layer they are in fact just a series of files containing the disks used by the virtual machines and configuration data. Thus, to back up hosts A, B, C, and D, it is possible to back up the filesystem on the virtual machine server. Even with just four virtual machines, there may be considerable license cost savings.

However, this does not happen without administrative or operational impacts. To snapshot a running host reliably, core applications on that host may need to be quiesced temporarily (which at worst means temporarily halting them). This may not be necessary if using traditional hot backups running within the guest operating system. To avoid manually initiated backups, a backup

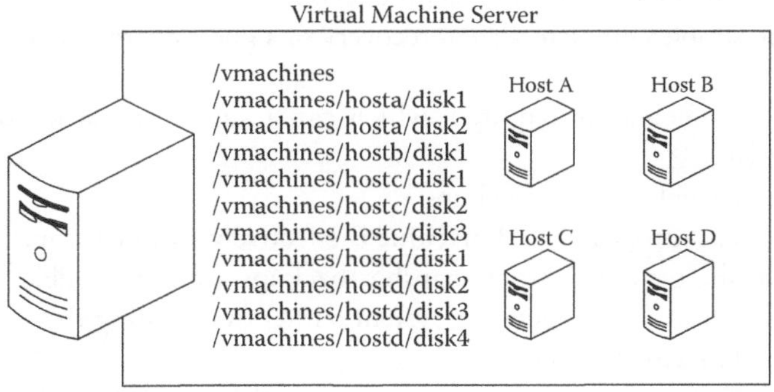

Figure 3.10 Virtual machine server

product will need to support arbitrary command execution prior to the backup. Such an option allows the scripting of operations to be executed to allow the safe backup of the virtual machine files.

Recovering virtual machines that have been backed up in this fashion can be a double-edged sword, as the efficiency depends entirely on the amount of data that needs to be recovered. For instance, complete virtual machine recovery becomes possibly the easiest disaster recovery that can be performed — recover the files associated with the virtual machine, and start the machine. This eliminates any "boot from CD and install drivers," or "install a simple operating system," or "boot from the network and download the SOE," or any of a number of other OS-install bootstrap methods that might be required for traditional complete system recoveries.

On the other hand, restoring individual files or directories becomes complex and wasteful. The snapshot files that contain the guest operating system must be restored to another area on the virtual machine server, and then the guest operating system must be started to retrieve from within it the files it was making use of. This creates two challenges: (1) to recover a single file on a large guest operating system, it may be necessary to restore tens or hundreds of gigabytes of data — i.e., the entire virtual machine; and (2) starting up a secondary copy of a running production system requires the disconnection of network functionality from the just-restored copy before it is started, otherwise conflicts or even data loss may result. To just copy a few files, it may be necessary to disconnect the recovered virtual machine from the network, start it, change its network identity, then restart it connected to the network to transfer the files.

Thus, while virtual machine snapshots have their uses, they should be seen more as adding value to "offline" archival backup processes for virtual hosts, and in general they are of use for total system recovery, as opposed to per-file recovery. In this sense, they are suited for systems with little dynamic data, or systems where partial file recovery is of little or no use, such as Web proxies, firewalls, print servers, and database servers. On the other hand, fileservers would receive little benefit from daily backups of this type.

Recently, virtualization technologies have been expanded and further integrated with backup software to allow the virtual machine server to mount components of its virtual machines for backup purposes. Although this adds some flexibility to the backup process, it is usually somewhat limited in operating system and file ACL support. Further, with added integration to backup products, licensing costs tend to increase again.

Advantages of virtual machine backups

- Reduces licensing costs — multiple virtual machines may be backed up using the one license allocated to the virtual machine server.
- Allows for simple/complete system recovery of a guest operating system with minimum fuss.
- No database agents are required, which can result in an easier-to-configure backup environment.

Disadvantages of virtual machine backups

- Each day's backup of a virtual machine is effectively a full backup.
- Individual file recoveries from snapshot backups are not possible — it is required to recover the entire guest operating system (either over-writing the real one or to another area/virtual machine server).
- Starting a recovered guest requires special considerations to avoid creating a production outage on the real guest machine.

- Only suitable for small/simple virtual machines. Certainly not suitable for systems such as virtual machine fileservers, or virtual machine mail servers. (For example, recovering a 200 GB virtual machine file to retrieve a single 1 KB e-mail would be a time-consuming task.)
- There is always as much free space required on the virtual machine server as the largest virtual machine to receive these backups.

3.10 Database Backups

Backups encompass far more than just filesystem-level protection. For many organizations, the most critical systems and data exist as databases, and in these environments the backup system needs to be designed to protect these applications as much as any of the individual filesystems involved.

Regardless of which backup product is used, there will be up to five different backup methods available. Some of these have already been alluded to in section 3.5, "Data Availability," but we now focus on availability as it applies to database backups.

3.10.1 Cold Backup

This is the most primitive database backup that can be performed. Prior to the backup, the database and its associated processes are shut down to ensure that no updates take place. The backup system then performs a simple filesystem backup of the client, which encompasses all the database files.

This may sound simple enough, but we must consider that this typically requires some scripting around the backup process to ensure the database is shut down prior to backup and started up in time for users to access it when required. For maximum certainty of backup success, the backup product should be used to shut down the database using a "pre-backup" script, and should also restart the database following the completion of the backup. (In such configurations it is also common to have a monitoring process that can abort the backup if it takes too long, so that users may access the system by a specified time.)

If the shutdown and startup sequences are not handled properly, and the database is shut down after the backup starts, or is restarted while the backup is still running, one of the following is likely to occur:

- A useless backup may be generated. Where the filesystems in use do not support exclusive file locking, the database backup may continue, but the data being backed up will be inconsistent and not useful for recovery purposes.
- The database may be corrupted, requiring recovery. Where the filesystems in use perform exclusive file locking, the backup may have open handles on database files when the database is started. This can result in creating inconsistencies between files as the database processes those files upon startup. Typically, such inconsistencies can be only resolved through recovery.

Advantages of cold database backups

- Complete disaster recovery or total database recovery is very easy and thus does not normally require intervention from an application or database administrator.
- Results in minimum software investment.
- If a database does not support any other backup method without access to snapshot technology (either filesystem or array based), this may be the only way to achieve a backup.

Disadvantages of cold database backups

- Database is unavailable for the duration of the backup. This may not be acceptable, depending on business needs.
- For most databases, using cold backups does not allow for incremental recoveries or point-in-time recoveries of the database.
- If the startup and shutdown sequence for the database is handled incorrectly, it may result in useless database backups or database corruption.
- Databases frequently perform data caching to improve performance over time. If the database is shut down every night, the benefit of that caching is lost at the start of every backup.
- Guarantees maximum use of backup media, as incremental cold backups are not possible.

3.10.2 Hot Backup

A hot backup refers to keeping a database up and running while the backup is performed. It is the equivalent of an online backup for filesystems. When a backup product supports a particular database, it usually means that it has a module or plug-in that allows the database to be backed up while staying available to end users. When a backup module or plug-in is not used, hot backups are still possible, though may require additional scripting to integrate them into the backup environment safely.

The process of performing a hot backup will significantly differ depending on whether it can be done with a backup product module, or whether it must be done external to the backup product.

If a backup module performs the hot backup, the process will typically be as follows:

- Regular filesystem backups occur for the client as per normal.
- Backup server initiates a special database backup, using an alternate backup command on the database server.
- The command on the database server runs a hot backup, feeding data back to the backup server for inclusion with standard backups to tape or disk.

In some cases, the structure of the data being sent to the backup server will be all that the server will understand — the actual content will remain the proprietary format of the database product.

When hot backups are performed without a database module, there are two slightly different backup methods that may be used. The optimal method will be where the backup server initiates a "pre-backup process" that performs a hot database backup to a spare area of disk. At the conclusion of this pre-backup process, the actual filesystem backup is performed, during which time the backup software excludes from the backup the live database areas, and instead backs up the database copy that was just generated. The sub-optimal method, however, is where the hot database backup is scheduled to occur at a particular time, with the expectation that it will be completed before such time as the filesystem backup runs, or that if there is an overlap, the filesystem holding the database copy will not be accessed by the backup agent prior to the actual database backup completes. It is obvious, however, that this is a somewhat hazardous backup strategy, which has been known to lead to serious data loss when timings have not been correctly controlled.

Advantages of hot database backups with a backup module

- Backup is controlled and initiated centrally. Backup reports and status therefore remain centralized as well.
- Database server does not (necessarily) need its own hardware to back up itself.
- Recovery is typically straightforward, as it may be controlled via either the recovery utilities provided by the backup software, or the recovery utilities provided by the database vendor. This may allow such recoveries to be performed without an application or database administrator being available.

Disadvantages of hot database backups with a backup module

- To be enabled, database backup modules/plug-ins typically require additional licensing.
- More complicated than cold backups. (It should be noted, however, that while some may think that configuration of database backups is unnecessarily complex, by and large it is actually straightforward although it requires more steps and has less room for error due to the underlying complexity of the data.)

Advantages of hot database backups without a backup module

- May be the only method of achieving hot backups when there is no backup module available.
- For smaller databases, this may be cheaper (initially) than using a backup module or plug-in.
- Sometimes seen by DBAs as "simpler" than using a backup module. (It can be argued that this is rarely the case, however.)
- A copy of the database is typically present on the database server most of the time.

Disadvantages of hot database backups without a backup module

- Consumes at least twice as much space as a direct-to-backup-media strategy. There needs to be sufficient disk space available to hold a second copy of the database. (Alternatively, if compression is used during the database backup as the files are copied, this drastically increases the backup time and the performance impact of the backup on the database server, and may result in more-challenging recoveries.)
- Recovery typically requires a DBA to be present.
- If not scheduled correctly, this can result in backing up the filesystem before the hot backups are generated (or while they are still being generated), which may prevent recovery.
- Recovery can become a two-step process, or even longer if compression is used on the database backup files.
- Typically, encourages a "full backup daily" policy, which forces disk growth for the backup region that would not be required if a module/plug-in were being used.

- May arbitrarily extend the actual backup window, as two backups of the database must be performed — one to back up to disk, and one to back up the disk.
- Recovery typically requires the database to have been previously created, whereas with a module/plug-in based recovery, the database may be able to be created on the fly as part of the recovery process.

3.10.3 Export Backup

A database export is typically a series of plaintext commands that can be used to recreate the database content and permissions. For example, the following is a section of a database export from a PostgreSQL database:

```
CREATE TABLE anywebdb_saved_query (
  id integer DEFAULT nextval('anywebdb_saved_queries'::regclass) NOT NULL,
  name character varying(75) NOT NULL,
  "object" character varying(175) NOT NULL,
  username character varying(16) NOT NULL,
  private character(1) NOT NULL,
  query text NOT NULL,
  max_results integer,
  sort_field character varying(32),
  order_by character(1)
);
ALTER TABLE public.anywebdb_saved_query OWNER TO preston;
```

A trap with export backups is that unless explicitly stated by the database vendor, the database export may not actually be consistent. That is, activity during the export may result in an export file that cannot be used to restore the database. Therefore, before making use of this option, it is important to confirm that the database supports hot exports. If hot exports are not supported, cold backups or cold snapshots should be favored instead.

Advantages of database export backups
- If exports are supported while the database is being accessed, and there are no other hot backup methods available, this may present a better availability strategy than cold backups.
- This may allow a backup of a database on one operating system (e.g., Windows), with a restore on another platform (e.g., Linux).
- Depending on how the database has been designed and how compliant it is to SQL standards, it may even allow for a backup of a database from one database product and a restore to another database product. However, it should be noted that because many databases use proprietary extensions, this frequently means that exports are not as platform- and application-independent as one would like.

Disadvantages of database export backups
- An export may take up even more disk space than the original database, as an export contains more than just the content of the database, but also the commands to recreate the database structure. Compressing the export as it is generated may result in significant space savings, but at a cost of high CPU load during the backup.

- Typically, the export does not actually contain instructions to recreate the database itself, merely the internal structure. The complexity/time of this task needs to be factored when planning recovery times.
- The export has to be scheduled carefully in the same way as cold backups and hot backups with a module, to ensure that the resulting export file is properly backed up.
- An export of a database may take longer than a simple copy of the files associated with the database depending on the amount of data in the database.
- Some database vendors have additional requirements to achieve exports where BLOBs (binary large objects) are involved.
- The export may not result in the recreation of meta-data surrounding the database. For instance, user accounts and passwords may not be recreated as part of an import. This can result in the requirement to create these first, so that permissions are correctly applied during the import process.

3.10.4 Snapshot Backup

A snapshot backup is where the following process occurs:

- If a hot snapshot is to be performed, the database is either quiesced (paused), or put into hot backup mode. If a cold snapshot is to be performed, the database is shut down.
- Filesystems that the database reside on have snapshots generated.
- For hot snapshots, the database is resumed or brought out of hot backup mode; for cold snapshots, the database is restarted.
- The filesystem or volume snapshots that have been generated are mounted somewhere else — possibly even on another system — to be backed up.
- At the conclusion of the backup, the snapshots may be released immediately, or retained for a particular period of time to permit a faster recovery if required.

Note that for systems that do not allow a cold database backup, cold snapshots may still be acceptable — for instance, for a database requiring 23.5/7 access, a six-hour cold backup window would be unacceptable, but a brief outage measured in minutes in the middle of the night to allow the snapshot to be generated safely may be acceptable.

Advantages of snapshot database backups

- Interruption of database in preparation for backups can be quite small.
- Can be used to create "cold, full" backups without having an outage that lasts the length of the backup.
- May allow for a hot backup to be performed without a module or plug-in for the backup product, while simultaneously reducing the amount of disk space required for the hot backup.
- May allow for multiple backups to exist without needing to run a real or offline backup, allowing for more-stringent SLAs regarding maximum data loss to be met.

Disadvantages of snapshot database backups

- Typically, this cannot be achieved without complex filesystem, volume, or array management software.

- Depending on the snapshot technology used and the space made available for snapshots, a snapshot could result in a situation whereby the database can no longer be updated due to the snapshot region filling. This could have disastrous consequences and thus additional planning and monitoring is required to avoid this scenario.
- It is necessary to ensure that storage for snapshots is as fast as the storage holding the production copy of the database. If slower storage is chosen (usually done so as it is perceived as being much cheaper), the performance of the database while a snapshot is active may be unacceptable.

3.11 Backup Initiation Methods

There are two primary methods of backup initiation: server initiation or client initiation. Regardless of whether or not backup media have been centralized, we typically consider client-initiated backups to be a symptom of a decentralized backup policy, whereas server-initiated backups are representative of a centralized backup policy. The aim at all times should be to achieve server-initiated backups.

3.11.1 Server Initiated

Server-initiated backups refer to the backup server software on the "master" server starting the backups for one or more machines at a designated time. Almost all backup software contains backup scheduling capabilities that allow backups to be started at nominated times and dates. (Indeed, it can be easily argued that the lack of such scheduling capabilities should unconditionally disqualify software or solutions as being capable of enterprise protection.)

The advantages of server-initiated backups cannot be overstated. This gives the backup administrator control over the timings of backups, which directly affects the resources available to the backup server to provide those services. When a backup server initiates the backup process, it should have an accurate understanding of what resources will need to be allocated to allow the backup to complete. Furthermore, centralized timing and scheduling of backups are critical in reducing administrative overhead of the backup environment.

3.11.2 Client Initiated

Client-initiated backups refer to the individual machines running their own backup processes as required — either manually or via automated jobs scheduled to start at particular times from the client side.

Client-initiated backups should be frowned upon in an enterprise backup environment in most circumstances. One of the core goals of enterprise backup software is to provide a centralized method of control over the backup process, and having scheduling maintained at the client level significantly breaks that model. Under such a model, the backup administrator may not even be able to adjust the schedules and resources accordingly, as he or she may not have access to the individual clients that initiate backups.

One area where client-initiated backups may be an acceptable option is for the backup of machines that may only intermittently connect to the corporate network — for example, laptops. In this scenario, it may be conceivable that, once connected to the network, a user's laptop contacts the backup server and indicates that it is ready to commence a backup. Conversely, however, for any machine that is continuously connected to the network (e.g., a server in a data center), client-initiated backups should be an extreme exception, not a rule.

If client-initiated backups are to be performed, consider the following questions:

- Is the backup server processing other activities that might be interrupted by a client-initiated backup?
- Will the client-initiated backup have, or affect, recovery dependencies?
- For how long should a client-initiated backup be retained?
- Will the recovery from a client-initiated backup be different than the recovery from a server-initiated backup?

It is not unheard of to see companies install a backup product capable of centralized backup initiation, but retain a decentralized/client-initiated backup regime. More often than not, as the number of backups to be performed increases, this can cause backup failures due to the inability of the backup server to properly load-balance what are deemed to be "ad-hoc" backup requests. This can result in the following situations:

- Backups randomly fail as the server's concurrent-operation settings are exceeded and it rejects new backup attempts. If a backup server is initiating backups, it will typically have mechanisms to ensure that the automated backups do not exceed these values, but if backups are initiated from another location it may not be able to put new backup jobs properly on hold pending the allocation of new resources.
- The server suffers a performance degradation, or worse, a backup software failure from being "swamped."
- When there is a mix of server- and client-initiated backups, server-initiated backups may not run correctly.

Additionally, using client-initiated backups makes maintenance operations on the backup environment more problematic — e.g., disabling 60 backups from one host is trivial in comparison to disabling one backup each on 60 hosts.

With all this in mind, to keep backup operations simple and centralized, client-initiated backups should be avoided unless absolutely necessary.

3.11.3 Externally Scheduled

Technically, externally scheduled backups will either be backup server-initiated or client-initiated. However, the use of an enterprise-class job scheduling system for backup initiation warrants an independent discussion. (By enterprise class, we are referring to products such as Computer Associates' Unicenter AutoSys Workload Automation.)

Although there are distinct advantages to server-initiated backup management, it shouldn't be forgotten that there is more to an IT environment than just the backup and recovery system.

Backup product scheduling systems can be described as somewhat primitive. They allow for the scheduling of specific activities such as:

- When a backup job should be run, and at what level

- Whether a backup should be retried if it fails, and possibly how many times it is retried before abandoned
- Various maintenance and data migration activities; for instance, products that support backup to disk will typically support the configuration of policies to migrate data to offline storage as required

However, because total job scheduling is not the primary purpose of backup software, anything above and beyond this is a considerable bonus within even an enterprise backup product. In a complex environment, there may be significantly more advanced scheduling requirements that organizations would like to use, and in these cases, enterprise-scheduling systems may be required. These might include such functions as:

- Only allow a full backup of systems on the first (or last) consecutive Friday/Saturday/Sunday of a month
- Ensure that backups can only run for key systems after batch processing has completed, and a complex set of applications across multiple hosts have been quiesced first for snapshot generation
- Schedule backups between multiple backup products (e.g., a workgroup product for satellite offices, and an enterprise product for the data center)
- Schedule backups between multiple master backup servers that all share tape library resources
- Schedule backups across a multinational organization where processing in one country affects when and how backups are to be performed in another

Of course, there could be a variety of other reasons, some based on technical requirements, and others based on corporate policies. In some cases it may be possible to force the backup product to perform the scheduling required with various levels of success — for instance, the first example above can be met through periodic revisiting of manual setting of schedules at the server level, and the second could be met using server-initiated backups that run pre- and post-backup commands that perform maintenance operations on a variety of hosts before initiating other backups.

If choosing to schedule backup activity via an enterprise job-management system: (1) wherever possible, interface with the server-initiated backups, i.e., if the backup server software offers a mechanism to initiate what would otherwise be a scheduled backup, use that interface; and (2) it will be necessary to perform resource monitoring on and contention avoidance for the backup server.

Therefore, although it may be required to perform external scheduling of backups, it remains the responsibility of the backup administrators to ensure that this does not impede resource management or compromise backup and recovery performance.

3.12 Miscellaneous Enterprise Features

There is a collection of features that do not in themselves warrant entire categories, but can be pooled together to form what we would describe as enterprise features — i.e., facilities that should be found in some way in an enterprise backup and recovery product. In this section, we will give an overview of some of those features.

3.12.1 Pre- and Post-Processing

Pre- and post-processing refers to the ability of the backup agent to initiate commands on individual clients prior to the start of the backup, and following the completion of the backup, respectively.

Examples of where pre- and post-processing might be used include the following:

- Prior to backup, a database is put into hot backup mode, and following the backup, the database is brought out of hot backup mode.
- Prior to backup, a hot export is performed for a database.
- Prior to monthly backups, the database is shut down for a cold backup rather than its regular hot backup, and following the backup, the database is restarted.
- Following successful backup completion on Friday nights, a client might be rebooted to allow system updates to take effect.
- Prior to starting backups, a map might be built of a dense filesystem, and the configuration for the client automatically adjusted to support massively concurrent backups of the dense filesystem to improve performance.

The possibilities are (almost) limitless when a product supports pre- and post-processing. The following limitations will need to be considered when comparing products:

- Is there a set timeout period for the commands, or can the administrator define an arbitrary period?
- Is it necessary to establish a command execution environment prior to running the pre- and post-processing commands?
- Are pre- and post-processing commands done for each filesystem, or before the first and after the last filesystem is backed up, respectively?
- For applications with more than one host, is it possible to schedule pre- and post-processing across multiple clients using dependencies?
- Is security provided to prevent the execution of arbitrary commands?
- Does the backup agent run under a user account that will have the authority to execute the commands that must be run? If not, can the user account be changed?

3.12.2 Arbitrary Backup Command Execution

Arbitrary backup command execution means being able to replace the native backup mechanism with a custom backup tool for particular machines so as to be able to process data that the backup vendor did not anticipate (or did not feel sufficient commercial pressure to support). For instance, companies have been known to use arbitrary backup command execution to perform hot backups for databases for which there is no backup agent, or to simulate such a backup by detecting and reacting differently to database files.

Although it may be rare that companies would need to extend a backup product to this level, some backup products use arbitrary backup command execution as their mechanism for providing database and mail backup capabilities (i.e., this is the facility by which the modules or plug-ins are integrated with the backup product).

3.12.3 Cluster Recognition

For a cluster to be effective, the end users of the cluster should not need to know or care which node in the cluster is currently being accessed. They certainly shouldn't be in a situation where they need to reconfigure their access manually when a cluster node failover occurs.

At the other end of the service spectrum, backup administrators should also not need to keep track of cluster failover manually — the backup software itself should be able to achieve this, either automatically or as a result of an initial configuration providing it details of nodes in a cluster.

For instance, in any *n* node cluster providing *y* virtual machines, a typical configuration might be (1) *n* client instances for the physical cluster nodes, used to back up their private data; and (2) *y* client instances, one per virtual cluster machine (or service), used to back up the shared/presented data and applications (where a cluster presents databases or applications, the virtual cluster machines would be the ones that perform database/application backups).

The goal of cluster recognition is to avoid a situation whereby, to recover the data or application presented by a cluster node at any particular time, the administrator has to be able to work out which physical node in the cluster was acting as the primary node (assuming an active/passive cluster configuration). In active/active cluster configurations, the goal will be to ensure that multiple backups of the cluster presented data or applications are not performed — although it's always better to back up a little more than not enough, the line should be drawn at multiple simultaneous or redundant backups of the same data just because the backup product doesn't understand that two physical hosts are the same virtual machine.

It is important to note that not a single backup product supports every cluster product on the market, and thus it will be necessary to choose cluster — or backup — products accordingly.

3.12.4 Client Collections

At the most primitive, a "collection" of clients is a set of one or more clients whose backup starts at the same time. Typically this can be handled in two ways: (1) each client has a start-time/schedule associated with it and starts independently of other clients, and (2) the backup product provides a collection configuration resource that allows the logical grouping of similar clients to force a common start time (and possibly even a common backup schedule).

Various names exist for these collections, with three of the most common being "group," "policy," and "class." When a backup product allows such groups, the administrative overhead of the configuration becomes simplified. For instance, assume 50 Windows servers normally get backed up at 21:35. If it is decided that these machines should instead start their backups at the new time of 22:35, it is far more convenient to adjust a single group configuration to which all clients belong than to adjust the configuration for each of the 50 individual clients (even if that configuration is maintained centrally on the backup server).

Although it is possible to have centralized backup services without client collections, little is achieved by this configuration, and thus a minimum goal of a centralized backup system should still be client collections.

3.12.5 Backup Segregation

Backup segregation refers to specifying what data can be sent to which collection of backup media. Typically, such groupings of backup media are referred to as pools. Following are examples of backup segregation requirements:

- Offsite versus onsite media: Without segregation, a situation might occur where a copy of data that is to be sent offsite resides on a volume that was meant to be kept onsite.
- Data separation: If providing backup services to multiple companies, or involved in backups for an organization where data must legally be kept separate by division, such data should be kept separate not only on the production copy, but on all other copies, including backups.
- Backup retention periods: If performing daily backups with six-week retention periods, and monthly backups with ten-year retention periods, it is not practical to have both sets of backups written to the same media (some products offer "media migration" to get around this problem, but this simply increases the administrative workload of the backup server to the detriment of the real work requirements of the backup server).

Primitive backup products will provide "segregation" based on simple and unreliable mechanisms such as:

- Which backup media is currently in a stand-alone device?
- Which slot number backup media resides within a tape library?
- Which label has been assigned to media?

In order words, the segregation is done at the initiative (i.e., workload) of the backup administrator, operators, or both. As such segregation is manual, it is not reliable enough for an enterprise-level backup environment.

To qualify as an enterprise backup product, automatic data segregation should be available at least based on the following scenarios:

- Originating client collection
- Originating client
- Whether the backup is an original or a copy
- Intended retention period for the backup
- Backup level (e.g., fulls versus incrementals)
- Type of data (e.g., database backups may need to be written to different media)

By offering segregation based on these options, a backup product can provide automated data separation that is sufficient to meet the needs of most organizations.

3.12.6 Granular Backup Control

Granular backup control refers to the alteration of the backup process for a particular host based on one or more criteria being met. One form of this has already been touched upon in the context of data selection methods. Exclusive backup products work by automatically backing up everything on a host except for what has been excluded from the backup process — this in itself is a form of granular backup control. For instance, it may be necessary to configure granular backup control such that even though all filesystems are backed up on a particular host, any file with an ".mp3" extension is excluded.

There is, however, much more to granular backup control than just excluding multimedia files. Following are examples of other types of granular backup control:

- Forcing software-based client-side compression or encryption for particular files or types of files
- Preventing database files from being backed up as part of the filesystem backup when they are protected by a database module
- Forcing the inclusion of additional filesystems that are not picked up as part of the automated probe of filesystems (e.g., a network filesystem that the backup product would otherwise assume is backed up elsewhere)
- Suppression of error or warning messages about active files for system logs, etc., which don't need to be backed up quiesced
- Changing how files are selected for incremental backups — e.g., if a Windows host has an application running on it that uses the archive bit to set whether or not a file has been processed (an altogether-too-frequent case), this may interfere with the backup product; in these instances, it may be required to instruct the backup software to choose files based instead on the date file contents were modified
- Force an exclusive lock to be taken out on a file being backed up so that it can't be modified during the backup process

With fine-grained control of the backup process for individual hosts, the backup system can be modified to work with systems that the backup software designers had not necessarily anticipated during the design of their product, rather than having to shoe-horn systems into a backup product in such a way that it detracts from the usability of the environment.

3.12.7 Backup Schedule Overrides

All backup products will support scheduling of some sort — and we've already discussed the levels associated with scheduling. A common schedule, for instance, is "daily incrementals with full backups on Friday night."

To reduce administrative overhead, however, it is important that a backup product offer some mechanism to set overrides to the schedules that have been established. For instance, the schedule above works well if only daily backups are performed. However, if monthly backups are also required, it will be necessary to ensure that the full daily backup does not run at the same time as the full monthly backup. It is the ability to alter automatically the default assigned schedule that we refer to as "schedule overrides."

Without schedule overrides, backup administrators may find themselves either having to intervene manually, or establish their own schedule override scripts to disable backups on particular dates, or resort to manual scheduling. This detracts from the centralized control and, if not managed properly, can result in the non-execution of backup jobs that in fact should be running at a particular date and time.

3.12.8 Security

There are two aspects to backup security that are not necessarily complimentary: (1) to back up everything on a system, backup software needs reasonably complete access to that system; and (2) due to the above, if backup security is breached, the potential or data theft or destruction is severe. With this in mind, it's imperative that organizations maintain tight, secure control over the backup environment, and that the backup software supports this. At bare minimum, enterprise backup product should be able to:

- Restrict who can administer the backup server
- Restrict who can interact with devices
- Restrict who can recover data on a per-client basis
- Provide reports/logs/details on activities performed within the backup environment

A common security flaw introduced into many backup environments allows too many users (either deliberately or inadvertently) access to the backup administration role. Like all other aspects of IT, security via obfuscation is not sufficient, and the implications of a security breach on the backup server should be seen as extreme for any organization. After all, if the security for the backup server is breached, all data protected by the backup server is potentially compromised.

3.12.9 Duplication and Migration

This topic will be discussed in great detail in section 8.3, "Protecting the Backups," but we can summarize for now by saying that backup duplication is the method by which the IT environment (and by extension, the company) is protected from a failure of a single backup. Returning to our insurance analogy, it is akin to the insurance company having an underwriter. If a backup and recovery product doesn't offer backup duplication capabilities, it should not be considered enterprise ready.

Backup migration, on the other hand, refers to moving a backup from one physical piece of media to another. Following are examples of where backup migration is an essential feature of enterprise backup software:

- Moving backups that were generated to disk across to tape for longer-term storage
- Evacuating readable backups from failing media — e.g., if it is determined during routine tests that there are physical errors on a piece of media, it must be possible to transfer all readable backups from that piece of media to new, reliable media
- Transferring long-term and archival backups from a decommissioned media type to a new media type
- Media consolidation — in particular, a necessity if backup segregation based on retention time is not an option, this will be needed to migrate backups of differing retention times
- Legal requirements — if ordered to destroy particular data, it may be necessary to migrate data on the same media that must be kept to alternate volumes prior to destroying the original

3.12.10 Alerts

Running a GUI against a backup server and observing the current state is one thing, but not all organizations employ 24/7 staff, and even when they do, staff may not react fast enough to issues if there are activities to be performed.

With this in mind, it's important that a backup product have alternate methods of alerting users, operators, or administrators of events that require attention other than expecting them to be directly in front of a GUI when the event occurs.

Some within the industry get obsessed over whether a product offers a particular alert method — e.g., SNMP, paging, mobile phone SMS, etc. However, thinking outside the square, so long as a backup product offers custom alerts (i.e., arbitrary command execution in response to a particular event), any form of required alert can be accommodated with a little scripting or data massaging. Therefore, if the preferred alert mechanism for a company is not directly supported by a backup product, using custom alerts, it still can be integrated.

In section 10.2, "Reporting Options," some of the automated reports or alerts that should be available in a backup system will be covered in more detail. For the moment we can say that at bare minimum, execution of arbitrary commands in response to particular events as custom alerts is a required feature of enterprise backup products.

3.12.11 Command Line Interface

Although it may be said that a picture is worth a thousand words, a GUI is not worth a thousand command line options.

Graphical user interfaces fulfill a particular function — they simplify interaction with a computer program or operating system so as to make the system more accessible to users. This in itself is an admirable function. Certainly in backup products, GUIs often allow users to get a better view of the "big picture" of the configuration for a server, and do indeed make some administrative functions easier for many users. However, GUIs typically have their limits:

- Can't be easily automated
- Don't allow for much extensibility
- May be slower to display information across sub-LAN speed links
- Don't provide all the functionality of every single aspect of the backup system, or replicate every option of every function
- May not provide the same level of error/log messages as command line options
- May not provide the full functionality for retrieving all data required from the backup product

For instance, consider an environment where the backup system is continuing to scale, and new systems are being added at a rate of, say, ten per week over a period of one year. For the most part in this environment, it will be necessary to have a set configuration for each client, and therefore each new machine will be added in exactly the same way as the one before it. When working within a GUI, it is not immediately obvious as to how this may be automated. Even if a "screen capture" session is run, and mouse movements/keystrokes are replayed, it may not necessarily create a new client instance, but instead try to recreate the same client instance whose creation was recorded. Mileage will certainly vary on a per-operating-system basis.

Alternatively, using a text editor, it should be possible to write a short batch or shell script that calls the backup software's command line interface to create the configuration for a new client. The script could be invoked with an argument of the new client name, and the administrator could then allow the script to do the work. Although this may sound in itself like a small saving, it is this ability to automate perhaps more than anything else that makes command line access to a backup product useful.

Command line access to a backup product can also be instrumental in remote support, monitoring, backup, and recovery operations. Many backup administrators who do not use the command line for anything in the office may find themselves making use of the command line when dialed in from home or on the road, to review the status of the backups.

By their very presence, command line interfaces support ongoing extensibility of a product. This promotes integration and long-term maintenance of a product, and often allows a product that cannot natively perform a particular function to be extended with minimum scripting so as to simulate that function.

3.12.12 Backup Catalogues

A key differentiation between a good backup product and a backup product not worth the time it takes to say "worthless backup product" is whether there is an online catalogue system for the backups. The use (or non-use) of a backup catalogue has a fundamental impact on how a recovery is approached.

Without a backup catalogue, the system administrator must approach recoveries as follows:

- User wants to recover file(s).
- Determine when the files were lost.
- Retrieve media generated on or before that date.
- Read media and retrieve files.

This may sound like a reasonable scenario, but only for stone-age environments where data loss is acceptable and infinite time is available. This is truly the worst approach to recoveries; no backup product that uses this methodology as its principal recovery mechanism should be considered eligible in any environment. This approach forces the administrator to know what media was generated on what dates, and what the content (or likely content) of each piece of media is, based on its label or generation date.

Indeed, this method confuses the entirely disparate items of "media label" and "media contents." For example, what happens if an administrator recalls all the "Monday, Week 1" tapes to perform a recovery, only to find out (after much investigation) that a new operator, unfamiliar with the backup procedures, started loading Tuesday tapes at five past midnight on Tuesday morning during the Monday backup?

Data Security Starts with the Tape Label. Although security through obfuscation is not a desirable model, it remains the case that security starts with using barcodes on tapes — or, for that matter, any form of removable media. In addition to preventing casual theft or interception of removable media based on "interesting" appearing volume labels, it forces the use of the media database for identification of volume content.

Moving on to real backup products, when using a backup catalogue the backup administrator deals with recoveries as follows:

- User wants to recover files. When were the files lost?
- Using a filesystem browser tool either provided by the backup software or integrated into the system filesystem browser tool, view the filesystem as of the nominated date and time, and select the files required for recovery.
- If desired, request a list of the volume(s) required for the recovery.
- Initiate the recovery.
- Backup software advises of volumes to be used for recovery.

The use of a backup catalogue is critical to achieve reliable recoveries. At a bare minimum, a catalogue should:

- Track the media that is in use by the system
- Track the backups that are on each piece of media
- Prompt the administrator for the required media when recoveries are initiated

Preferably, a backup catalogue should also contain features such as the following:

- Sufficient indexing to allow fast-forwarding through media to the location of a backup, rather than needing to read through all the media
- Searching for files and directories that users would like recovered, but can't recall where they were originally
- Media usage information — how often a piece of media has been labeled/rewritten, how many times it was mounted, when it was originally added to the backup system, etc.
- Online, hot backup of catalogue data
- Automated and manual checking of consistency
- Recovery of catalogue data at a minimum granularity of per-client or per-volume
- Regeneration of catalogue data on a per-volume basis
- The option to retain backups for longer than per-file details for each backup is retained, in case per-file details are not required for particular backups

Previously, many backup products needed a mechanism to separate the time that a backup was kept, and the time that the backup could be recovered or browsed on an individual level. This restriction was primarily imposed by the high cost of disk. Previously a necessity, maintaining separate browse periods to the retention time of a backup should now be considered an exception, not a rule. (For example, last-backup "archives" might fall into this category.) Unfortunately, some companies still insist on keeping a very small file-browseable backup index in comparison to the life span of the backup, claiming a cost saving as a result of this.

See "Scenario for Maintaining Per-File Catalogues for the Lifetime of a Backup" for a brief demonstration of how much of a false economy such decisions usually are. This is not a convoluted example. Companies repeatedly make such frugal decisions in relation to backup systems, never understanding the flow-on cost to the rest of the business. When tapes, disks, and backups were small, the reduction in catalogue size through such decisions did have a tangible financial benefit, but these days it makes no economic sense.

Scenario for Maintaining Per-File Catalogues for the Lifetime of a Backup. "Lawsuits 'R' Us" is a company with approximately 30 lawyers and a small IT/admin staff supporting their activities. They have a centralized fileserver that receives nightly backups. End of month backups are retained for ten years, while nightly backups are retained for six weeks.

Due to space considerations, management require the backup system to be configured so that the most recent four weeks of the nightly backups retain per-file catalogues. For the last two weeks of the six-week retention time, backup indices are automatically purged. Only the per-file indices for the most recent monthly backup are retained.

The fileserver has approximately 800 GB of data on it, which is backed up to LTO Ultrium 1 tapes. This takes three tapes to back up, as some gains are made with compression of data.

Recoveries for backups in the first four weeks of their retention time are generally quite quick, as the backup software targets the required volumes for a recovery and does not load or use any extraneous backups.

Of the recovery requests received, 75 percent come from data lost within four weeks of backup; 20 percent come from data lost within weeks five and six; 5 percent come from data from monthly backups; and all requests are for single files or individual directories.

Ignoring the monthly recovery requests let's consider the two requests on average received per week for data aged between five and six weeks. Adding to the calculations, we'll include the following: IT staff are paid $35 per hour on average; legal staff are paid $100 per hour on average; and legal staff are charged out to customers at $400 per hour on average.

Ultrium 1 tapes take 1 hour and 54 minutes for a complete end-to-end read, which would be required for the purpose of rebuilding a catalogue. Therefore we can say that every week six tapes must have their indices rebuilt. This results in operational delays of between 11 and 12 hours, assuming tapes are changed very quickly during the process, or only one tape is used per operation.

Assuming 12 hours, we can add up the cost of not keeping catalogues for the last two weeks of the nightly backup retention: 12 hours of IT staff time at $35/hour = $420; 12 hours of lawyers' time at $100/hour = $1200; and 12 hours of client billable time at $400/hour = $4800.

This represents a total of $6420 per week due to the need to rebuild media catalogues. As IT staff are present to support legal staff, and salaries have to be paid regardless of what duties are undertaken, we can assume that the $1620 in wages is a fixed cost regardless of who is doing what. However, this still leaves $4800 per week in lost invoicing. Assuming that legal staff mind spending half an hour searching for files before issuing recoveries, this halves the lost invoicing to $2400.

Extending this over three years (the normal time-consideration for hardware purchases), this will cost "Lawsuits 'R' Us" $374,400 in lost invoicing.

Although per-file index space does take up tangible space, it is typically not ridiculously high. Even a reasonably large environment might need no more than an additional 200 GB of index storage space for the backup server for three years of monthly backups as well as six weeks of daily backups. When viewed in this light, such space savings are false economies in the extreme.

Although it may seem trite to say so, disk is cheap. Long-term system administrators may remember having to drag managers kicking and screaming into signing purchase orders for SCSI drives as small as 2 GB or even 500 MB. However, this is not really an issue now.

For an SATA-based backup server, having a mirrored 500 GB region for backup indices that cost significantly less than AU $1000. For a SCSI-based environment the cost may be more, but not so much so as to negate the comparative cost savings. Even in a SAN-based environment, adding sufficient space for this additional storage will be cheap by comparison to the alternative.

3.13 Media Handling Techniques

3.13.1 Spanning

Spanning refers to a single large backup encompassing more than one piece of backup media. This should be seen as a fundamental requirement of backup software, yet otherwise perfectly sensible companies still periodically choose to implement backup solutions that can't perform media spanning.

A "single backup" can refer to any nominated item being backed up, whether that is a filesystem, a database, a mail store, or even a single file.

Without media spanning, backups become more difficult to manage. For example, let's consider a filesystem slightly over 200 GB being backed up to DLT 7000 drives. These drives use DLT IV media, which have a native capacity of 35 GB when used with DLT 7000 drives. Without compression, a ~200 GB filesystem would require six tapes to back up.

With spanning and an automated media changer (e.g., a tape library or jukebox), the backup product would automatically load the next tape whenever a tape fills, thus continuing to write the backup onto the new tape.

Without tape spanning, the backup becomes tricky. Assuming we can't get any compression on the media, to back up the ~200 GB filesystem we have to break it down into a series of smaller, artificial units. (Indeed, many organizations that use non-spanning products choose to disable backup compression — hardware and software — to avoid any issues it may create with media calculations!)

For instance, looking at a single 204-GB root filesystem on UNIX, we may have the following first-level directory structure:

- /home — 150 GB
- /var — 40 GB

- /boot — 500 MB
- /opt — 9.5 GB
- /bin — 400 MB
- /sbin — 600 MB
- /lib — 2.4 GB
- /etc — 18 MB

At the first directory level, the directories "/boot," "/opt," "/sbin," "/lib," and "/etc" can fit onto a tape, with a used capacity of approximately 13.4 GB. As this leaves approximately 21.6 GB free on a 35-GB tape, we must look to see where else we can source data from.

Evaluating "/var," we may see a large imbalance in the directories contained therein; "/var/lib" has 20 GB, whereas "/var/cache" has 15 GB, and there are another ten subdirectories in "/var" that use the remaining 5 GB of space.

Because we've got another 21.6 GB of space remaining, we'll backup the "/var/lib" directory onto the same tape. At this point, because we want to be able to handle a modest amount of data growth, we'll leave the tape with a little spare room and move on to the next tape.

On our second backup tape, we'll back up the rest of "/var," which will put 20 GB on the tape, leaving us 15 GB. We must then approach "/home," which has a total of 150 GB, spread pseudo-randomly among 35 user accounts, with the smallest account directory consisting of just 38 kB of data, and the largest having 48 GB of data. As user accounts are not static, this distribution changes periodically, sometimes between backups, requiring an administrator to revisit constantly the allocation of directories to tapes.

This is a tiresome exercise, yet it is sometimes faced by administrators of backup systems that don't do tape spanning on a daily basis. Depending on the number of hosts involved in a backup system that doesn't do tape spanning, this may require a full-time backup administrator solely to check and adjust artificial backup set allocations on a daily basis.

For these reasons, backup products that fail to perform media spanning should be removed from any consideration in any backup environment.

3.13.2 Rapid Data Access

This goes hand in hand with both spanning and backup catalogues. If we revisit our 200 GB filesystem from the previous section (which we've thankfully decided to back up using a product that can span media), we need to evaluate what happens when we want to recover a single file from somewhere within the filesystem.

Rapid data access in this case refers to whether the backup product is able to identify (via the catalogues) only those pieces of media that really need to be used for a recovery, and, within those pieces of media, as small a portion of data that must be read so as to retrieve the requested files. In this example it may be that the backup spanned four tapes (with hardware compression). The file to be recovered may be on the third tape. Enterprise backup software at this point should only need to load the third tape and read from it rather than having to read through all the media searching for the file.

In addition to being able to choose only those tapes that literally contain the data we need to recover from, advanced backup systems will be able to quickly seek to the position on tape that contains the data we want. This is typically done by file and record markers — in this case, "file" refers to "portion of tape," not "file as was on the client." For instance, regardless of the size of the data being backed up, a backup product might record an end-of-file marker on tape after, say, every 2 GB of data has been written.

In addition to this, the product may associate record markers within each "chunk" of data on tape. These might be generated every, say, 10 MB. Within the backup system's catalogues, individual system/user files that are backed up would then be tagged with their starting tape "file" and "record."

If a user requests the recovery of a particular file, the backup product checks with its catalogue to determine the following:

- What tape does this file reside on?
- At what tape file marker does the backup of this file start?
- Within the selected tape file marker, what record number does the backup of the file start with?

Practically all tape drives support the following operations:

- Forward space file (FSF) — Seek forward the nominated number of end-of-file markers on the tape.
- Backward space file (BSF) — Seek backward the nominated number of end-of-file markers on the tape.
- Forward space record (FSR) — Seek forward the nominated number of records on a tape.
- Backward space record (BSR) — Seek backward the nominated number of records on a tape.

Once a tape has been loaded into a drive, an enterprise backup product will use its catalogue information to seek forward the number of end-of-file markers required, then seek forward the number of records required to minimize absolutely the amount of data that has to be read from tape to facilitate a recovery.

This style of catalogue interaction can significantly reduce the amount of time taken to perform recoveries.

What about Backups to Disk or Virtual Tape? Although our discussion has focused on tape, the same (or similar) details can be used for rapid access to backups that are stored on disk, or virtual tape (in the case of virtual tape libraries).

Because virtual tapes are accessed the same way as regular tapes, exactly the same operations will apply, though they might be proxied to alternate operations by the virtual tape library.

For backups that have been written to disk, similar information will be relevant. If all backups are written to a monolithic file, then information will still need to be retained on where within the file any individual backup is stored. If each discrete backup is written to its own file, then information will still need to be maintained to indicate where, within that file, various chunks of data reside for faster access.

Using our previous example, even reading from high-speed disk, reading 200 GB of data to recover a single file is neither efficient nor fast. Therefore, regardless of whether backups are being written to tape, virtual tape, or disk, such rapid access techniques will remain mandatory.

3.13.3 Multiplexing

Media multiplexing refers to writing multiple backups simultaneously to the same piece of media. This is covered in depth in chapter 6, "Performance Options, Analysis, and Tuning." To summarize, however, it is necessary for backup products to support multiplexing so that data from slower machines may be written to the same media, not allowing any one machine to slow down the backup (thereby extending the backup window) significantly.

3.13.4 Media Tracking

Most backup products will offer at least some primitive form of media tracking. This typically refers to annotations in the system that may be used to indicate the location of a particular volume. If available, the media tracking can be used to provide human-readable instructions on the location of the volume (e.g., V09113 is in the location "Fireproof Safe," whereas V09119 is in the location "Offsite Vault").

This may not always be suitable for the needs of a company. For instance, some companies still choose offsite media vault agencies that box media. In this case, a company does not necessarily issue a recall notice for a volume, but a box.

When this occurs, companies tend to fall back on spreadsheets or databases to track where their media is. For instance, they may know that Box 33 contains the tapes:

V09110	V09111	V09112
V09113	V09114	V09115
V09116	V09117	V09118
V09119	V09120	V09121
V09122	V09123	V09124
V09125	V09126	V09127
V09128	V09129	V09130
V09131	V09132	V09133

In such a scenario, if a recovery is performed which requires, say, V09117, a recall notice is not issued for that single tape, but (after looking up which box contains the tape) Box 33 instead.

Box-based media vaulting agencies should be avoided, as they violate a fundamental principle of media offsiting: media are sent offsite to provide protection against site failure. Therefore, arbitrarily recalling a potentially large number of backup media just to allow access to one piece is inappropriate and may represent a potential for loss of long-term data storage. More advanced media vaulting agencies not only allow reference to individual volumes, but also frequently are capable of providing software that can either hook into enterprise backup products or be used in conjunction with enterprise backup products to facilitate media recall and in-vault tracking.

Chapter 4

Backup

4.1 Introduction

This chapter will provide a clear understanding of the planning and choices that have to be made when determining what should be backed up (and how) within an environment.

When considering what to back up, always remember the rule that it is better to back up a little more than not enough. This doesn't mean to go overboard and deliberately back up items that are known not to be required (e.g., useless filesystem backups of open database files that require special backups instead) — such actions invariably artificially inflate the backup window and cause headaches. What the rule does mean is that companies should not be miserly with their backup media — if it's a 50/50 choice between whether something should or shouldn't be backed up, and there is no real pressing argument either way, the choice should be to perform the backup.

For technical personnel, this should assist in building a checklist for backup environments (regardless of whether they are in planning, newly commissioned, or existing/legacy systems). For management, this should help to explain some of the complexity that goes into considering a holistic approach to backups.

4.2 What to Back Up

Choosing what is to be backed up is not as simple as usually thought. This section will evaluate not only the items that may immediately spring to mind, but also those that may not immediately be apparent. Sometimes the decision on what to back up comes down to a risk-based decision. However, sometimes there is a little more thought involved — particularly in areas that an organization may not have previously considered.

Ultimately, there is only one rule when it comes to determining what should be backed up: everything that may be needed to effect recovery or be otherwise required due to legal or financial considerations. This may sound blasé, but it is the simple truth.

It is a dangerous reality that within many companies a disparity will be found between what should be backed up and what is backed up. Although the goal of a company should be to eliminate the gap, if that gap cannot be 100 percent eliminated, it is important that it be acknowledged and agreed to by all affected parts of the business.

4.2.1 Servers

Typically, the backup operations that occur for the servers owned by a company are a core component of enterprise backup systems. These are fundamental components of the IT backbone for any company, and are the most obvious systems requiring backup.

Questions to consider when deciding the backup regime for the servers (on a server-by-server basis) include, but are not necessarily limited to:

- What SLAs are required for this server?
- What is the role of this server? The role will have a direct impact on the backup options and requirements for it, and will directly feed into the remaining questions to be considered for servers. Sample server roles might include production, development, test, and quality assurance (QA).
- Are there any special backup handling requirements for applications on the server?
- Are there any special backup handling requirements for data on the server?
- What times can the server be backed up?
- What times are backups not allowed to occur?
- What types of backups should this server receive? At minimum, most organizations will need to evaluate the necessity of the following:
  - Daily: What rotation between fulls, differentials, and incrementals are required?
  - Monthly: When should the monthly backup occur? If the daily full backups would occur on the same date as monthly full backups, what should be done? Should both backups be run concurrently, should the daily full be skipped, or should the daily full be run on an alternate day?
  - Yearly: Are yearly backups required? (Typically "no" if monthly backups are kept indefinitely.)
- Does this server have any special features that will make backup activities problematic? For example:
  - Is it WAN rather than LAN connected?
  - Does it need to be backed up in a particular sequence (or at exactly the same time) in relation to another server, or servers, within the environment?
  - Does it have any applications that must be backed up in a special way?
  - Does it have an operating system that is not supported by the backup software? If so, what plan will ensure its backups are recoverable?
- Will the backup impact the usability of/access to the server?
- Will the backup impact the usability of/access to other servers or systems?
- If the backup fails on this host, should it be restarted or left until the next scheduled backup execution?
- Is there a cut-off point at which backups must not be running, even if it means aborting a currently running backup? (Systems should be designed to avoid such scenarios; designs requiring such arbitrary job halting typically require consideration of alternate backup methods.)

- Who "owns" the host to the point that they should be notified of changes to the backup system?
- Who is authorized to request changes to how the backups for the system are to be handled?
- Who should be notified of backup failures?
- What is the priority of backups for this system? (A scale should be used and acknowledged throughout the company, and each server should have a rank on that scale to indicate its importance.)

To have a well-formed backup plan for each server, all of these questions need to be answered. There may be additional questions appropriate to the individual operational requirements of a single organization, and each new server that is added to the backup system and made available for use should meet any site- or corporate-specific requirements for backups.

A common strategy within organizations is to back up production servers only, or production and active development servers only. Although this works much of the time, if established as a blanket rule it may result in either data loss or needless repetition of work. For example, consider a situation whereby a QA system is being used extensively to check proposed upgrades to a key database. If this is refreshed from a cold/offline backup of the production system each Sunday, and the QA system catastrophically fails on a Monday, then one of the following must happen in theory:

- QA must halt until the following Monday
- QA must halt until some time Tuesday, with system staff needed to:
  - Rebuild the QA system
  - Generate a cold backup of the production system (thereby causing a production outage)
  - Refresh the QA environment

Neither of these options may be particularly desirable, particularly when evaluated on a cost basis, or when evaluated against possibly tight deadlines. In comparison, a short retention backup scheme for the QA system for the duration of testing may allow easy restoration from such failures within minimum wasted time. Having a blanket rule regarding what can and can't be backed up can result in an unpleasant set of circumstances later, and in such situations, no one ever remembers a few dollars saved on backup media.

4.2.2 Storage Devices

Between 2002 and 2005 we saw the first strong signs of shifts in enterprise environments away from DAS, with combined NAS and SAN sales outstripping sales of direct attached storage. This growth in NAS and SAN storage has created additional backup requirements and procedures for organizations.

4.2.2.1 SAN

Because it effectively emulates direct attach storage, SAN storage is frequently backed up as part of the normal backup regime for hosts with SAN volumes attached. However, for each new SAN allocation that occurs, consider

- Will this be attached to a server that can host the backup of its data?
  - If not, how will the data be backed up?
  - If it is necessary to perform non-host attached backups of the data, does recovery depend on having the same type of array available as was used to back up? If recovery is dependent on the presence of the same type of array, is there sufficient documentation and processes to ensure that the array is kept for the longest retention time of backups to be performed? (That is, what would happen if in three years time a change is made to a new array manufacturer, and two years after that it is necessary to recover from an end-of-financial-year backup made using the old array?)
- Will SAN-based backup devices (e.g., fiber-attached tape, or shared virtual tape) be utilized to perform a "local" backup of hosts with SAN storage attached?
- Is there any configuration stored on the array that should be protected in the event of a catastrophic failure? (For example, LUN mappings, disk layouts, etc.) Although highly redundant disk arrays should do their utmost to protect this information, a fire in the enclosure or general vicinity may render such internal-only protection irrelevant — i.e., it is possible (though admittedly unlikely) to lose the configuration information of a SAN, but not the actual LUNs and volumes configured on the SAN.

4.2.2.2 NAS

There are two ways to back up NAS data — either by backing up the host that mounts filesystems from it (forcibly including the network mapped drives if necessary), or by performing an NDMP (Network Data Management Protocol) backup. Some of the aspects of NDMP backup have been introduced in section 3.9.2, "Serverless Backups," and are covered in section 6.2.1.2, "NDMP."

An illustration showing the process in an NDMP backup of NAS data is shown in Figure 4.1. To explain the diagram, the process is as follows:

1. The backup server, at the appropriate scheduled time, instructs the NAS host to commence an NDMP backup.
2. The NAS host commences reading its filesystem(s) and transferring its data to the backup device designated for use of the backup server.

The host(s) that mount the filesystem(s) being backed up by the NAS host are not aware of, nor do they participate in the backup. (They may however, experience some form of IO impact.)

If intending to back up NAS storage via an NDMP backup, consider the following questions:

- Does the backup product support NDMP backups?
- Does the backup product support the NAS being used?
- If this NAS host is supported, do both the NAS host and the backup server support a common version of NDMP?
- What forms of backup device connectivity does the NAS host support? (Can it only back up to locally connected tape? Can it back up to another NAS host with a tape library attached? Can it back up across the network to a regular host?)
- What types of recovery will be available? (For example, file level only? Block level only? A mix?)
- Will there be any limits placed on recovery? (Some NAS hosts, for example, may not support a recovery of more than 10,000 files at once without reverting to a block-level complete

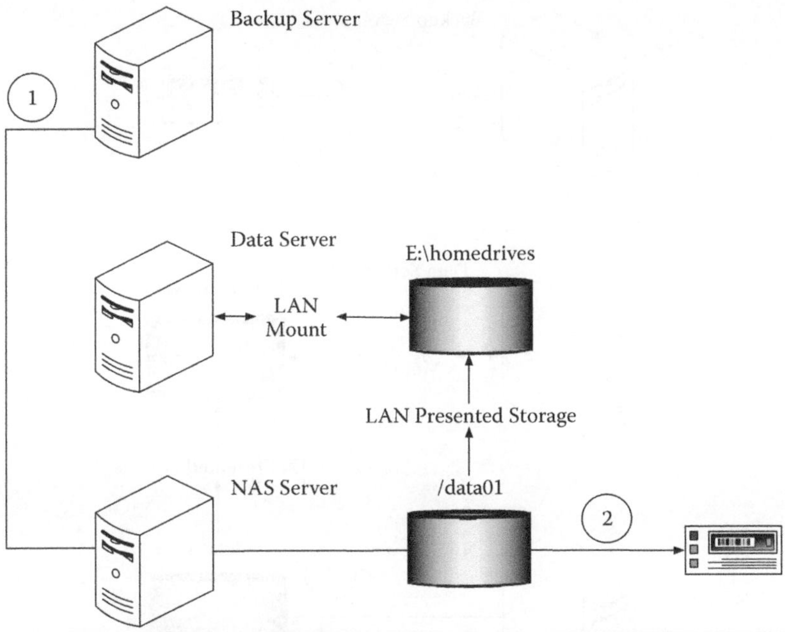

Figure 4.1 Overview of NDMP NAS backup

filesystem recovery, and therefore larger directories may need to be recovered in multiple operations.)

- Will this type of NAS host need to be retained for recoverability from long-term retention NDMP backups? (Few, if any, NAS hosts support NDMP recoveries from NAS devices belonging to other vendors, and it is unheard of for a regular host to be able to perform recoveries from NDMP backups generated by a NAS host.) If so, is there sufficient documentation and processes to ensure that the NAS is kept for the longest retention time of backups to be performed?

The alternative process for performing a regular host-mount backup of a NAS hosts' filesystems is shown in Figure 4.2. The process flow for a regular host-mount backup of a NAS filesystem is as follows:

1. Backup server instructs the host mounting the NAS filesystems attached to commence backup.
2. As part of the backup, the host reads data from the NAS mount, and transfers this data across to the backup server (or another nominated storage node/media server).
3. Backup server or other nominated host writes backup to the backup media.

This method (although simpler for implementation and licensing) results in a double-transfer of data. That is, to back up 1 GB of files from the NAS host, 2 GB have to be transferred across the network. The first gigabyte of network traffic comes from the mounting host reading data from the NAS system, whereas the second gigabyte comes from the mounting host then transferring that data across to the backup server or nominated storage node/media server. Even if a private network exists between the NAS system and the mounting host, there is still twice as much data transferred to achieve backup.

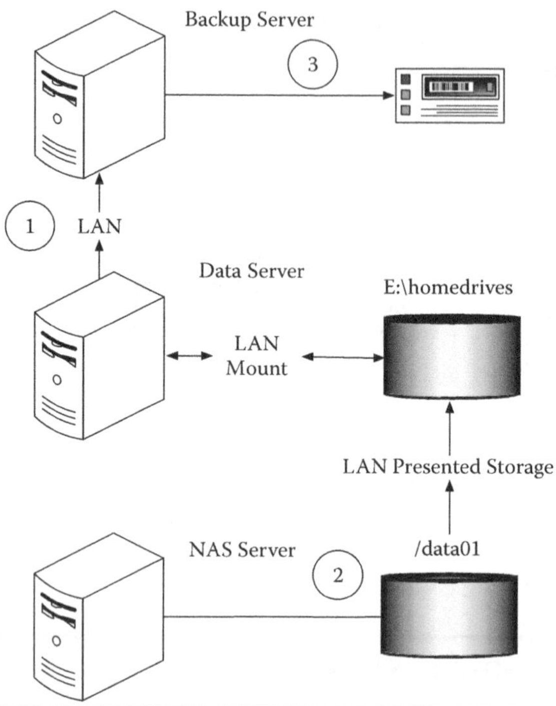

Figure 4.2 Overview of host-mount backup of NAS

If intending to back up NAS host storage via a regular host-mount, first consider the following questions:

- Will access control lists (ACLs) be backed up properly? (Typically, if a filesystem is shared to only one type of operating system, ACLs should be preserved. However, if the filesystem is shared to multiple operating system types, the NAS host must maintain "meta-ACLs" that are not necessarily stored on the filesystem presented, and therefore unlikely to be backed up as part of this strategy.)
- How will the configuration of the NAS host be protected? This covers such aspects as definitions of share points, permitted access to share points, allowed administrators, network configuration, operating system patch level, etc.
- What will be the network impact of the double-transfer involved in the backup? (In many organizations, network-based backups of NAS hosts may be fully approved until such time as the network administrators are asked to comment on or approve of the backup plan!)

This method can sometimes be seen as more acceptable if the host mounting the NAS volume is also a storage node or media server, but this is not always an option. Even if this is the case, it only solves the double-transfer problem, not the ACL or NAS configuration backup problem.

Although NAS hosts provide easy connectivity of storage without undue extension to existing infrastructure, they do introduce what can sometimes be significant administrative overhead to protect them.

4.2.3 Non-Traditional Infrastructure

Quite a bit of critical infrastructure within an average computer room is never backed up at all. Examples of such infrastructure include, but are certainly not limited to:

- Network switches
- Fiber-channel switches
- Hardware-based firewalls, virus scanners, document indexers, etc.
- PABX systems
- Fiber ↔ SCSI bridges

It is necessary to consider how the configuration of each of these types of devices will be preserved in such a way that it can be restored or recreated in the event of a failure. Although most systems use non-volatile RAM or other configuration protection for loss of power, they may still suffer data corruption in the event of a power-spike, or lose their configuration if the non-volatile RAM fails. Further, human error can play a part in these systems "failing."

For smaller environments, it may be that the most cost-efficient way of going about this protection is to record the configuration manually and be prepared to re-key it in the event of a failure. For larger environments, however, this may quickly become impractical, and more-efficient mechanisms may be required. One such mechanism that is not often considered is the ability of most enterprise backup systems to allow users to design custom backup scripts. When combined with the typical remote login and command-line access capabilities offered by most of the above devices, it is possible to automate configuration backup processes for these devices. This can be done along the following lines:

- Backup is triggered for a particular "normal" (and secured) host.
- For each special device on the network, the host runs a special "pre-backup" script that performs the following actions:
  - Sets up an output-capture session
  - Logs into the remote device
  - Runs the commands required to generate a text-based dump of the configuration
  - Exits the remote device
  - Saves the output captured to a text file on the server in "raw" format
  - Parses the output captured into human-readable format and saves this to an alternate file
  - If possible, parses the captured output into a format that may be used to "replay" the creation of the configuration once logged onto the device, and saves this to an alternate file
- Regular operating system backups occur after the details for each remote device have been captured.

This style of enhanced data center backup operation is not frequently considered, but can provide significantly better protection to a company's IT (and even telephony) infrastructure with relatively little effort.

4.2.4 Desktops and Laptops

Despite having typically been considered as too inconvenient, costly, and error-prone to back up, many companies are now being forced by government regulations to back up desktops and laptops to avoid the risk of company data being lost that is otherwise legally required.

If the decision is made not to back up desktops and laptops, consider the following questions:

- Does the environment allow users to store data on their local machine(s)?
  - If yes, can an automated replication procedure be developed or implemented to copy their data to a server that does get backed up?
  - If a replication procedure can't be developed, strongly consider changing corporate policy and disallowing users from storing data on their local machines, or else backups should be considered mandatory.
- If the environment does not allow users to store data locally:
  - Has this been tested?
  - Is there an SOE (Standard Operating Environment) image or rebuild tool to allow a rapid reconstruction of a desktop or laptop?
  - Are there SLAs to ensure that a user is quickly helped if experiencing network problems?

If backups of desktop PCs and laptops are to be performed, consider the following questions:

- Will the backup be automated — i.e., will it start without user intervention?
- Has the backup process been tested to ensure that it does not unduly impact user productivity? (More computer-savvy users may very well "hunt down" processes that appear to be slowing their machine and kill them off, which may at times be the backup process depending on the design of the overall system.)
- Following the above, has the backup system been configured to prevent the user from blocking backups?
- Will recoveries be user initiated?
- How will backups and recoveries of laptops be handled when they are not in the main office?
- If laptops are routinely disconnected from the network, how will backups be initiated when they are reconnected?
- If planning to back up desktop PCs overnight, has this policy been communicated successfully to users so they understand that they can't shut down their machines when they leave for the day?
- How will the backup system cope with a (potentially large) number of machines to be backed up that are not connected or not responding? (Desktop PC/laptop backups often see a failure rate is high as 50 percent due to laptops not being connected, desktop PCs having been shut down, etc., despite the most carefully worded corporate policies.)

Remember when planning backups of user desktops and laptops that strategies that rely on users to initiate the backup inevitably fail.

4.2.5 Hand-Held Devices

It used to be the case that if any particular person in an organization lost or damaged their PDA or mobile phone, it was likely to be completely insignificant to the organization, regardless of the significance to the owner. For many organizations, it may still be, but considering the growing amount of storage space available on hand-held devices, it is becoming more plausible that a situation can occur when business-critical information ends up being stored on only one of these devices. Therefore, these devices need to be considered when planning backups.

Unfortunately, backup products do not typically support the backup of hand-held devices (one could argue that this is a market waiting to be tapped), and so the onus of performing a backup falls (regrettably) to the user of the device, even though we have previously stated that relying on users to perform backups is fraught with danger.

With it not being readily possible to address the primary issue — the automation of the backups for these devices — it becomes necessary to address the secondary issue — storage of the backups when they are made. If nothing else, an organization should set a standard location for backups of these devices to be stored, with that location being backed up as part of the standard server or desktop backup process. (For example, it may be that instead of synchronizing their mobile phone or PDA device to local storage on their desktop or laptop, users profiles will be configured to store synchronization data to a network share.)

4.2.6 Removable Storage: Devices and Media

Until recently, for most organizations the term "removable media" referred to floppy disks or perhaps CD-ROMs. However, these days it usually refers to non-volatile RAM media capable of storing large amounts of data. Such media include CompactFlash cards, SmartMedia cards, SecureDigital cards, USB or USB-2 memory keys, etc. By late 2006, such devices commonly had storage in excess of a gigabyte, and continued to grow rapidly in size. Further, "removable devices" can include multi-gigabyte hard drives and portable music devices that potentially can store a large amount of corporate data.

For instance, consider a "mobile" user with a workstation in the office and a computer at home, but no laptop. To have access to the data both at work and at home, this user may store critical data on a portable hard drive and not on a fileserver. This may quite likely be done without any real knowledge of the system administrators of the environment. As these devices can run at a speed similar to that of hard drives in desktop PCs, some users may work exclusively from these devices to avoid copying files back and forth.

As removable devices/media with useful data capacity are only now just becoming reality, there have been few mechanisms developed to ensure that a loss of someone's portable music player or hard drive doesn't result in the loss of corporate data. Thus the focus is usually on corporate policies. With this in mind (and when also factoring in security policies), some companies forbid the connection of portable storage devices to the network, and do not permit the purchase of desktops/laptops with CD/DVD burner units. Some companies physically ensure this by damaging or otherwise blocking all user-accessible ports on computers to prevent the connection of new equipment.

If users will be allowed to connect portable storage devices to their machines, consider the following questions:

- Do the users understand the importance of not leaving master copies of corporate data on their devices?
- Does the operating system allow system and backup administrators to be alerted of the connection? This can be useful to keep track of who is connecting what, both for security considerations and to be able periodically to confirm with users that they are not using the device(s) to hold master copies of data.
- Should backups of the storage be provisioned if PCs and laptops are also being backed up? For instance, one solution may be that if users have their portable storage devices connected during the backup, the system will automatically backup the portable storage device as well. (Because so many portable storage devices are also portable music players, it is usually necessary to obtain legal advice on whether it is permissible to back up another person's music prior to doing so.)

Chapter 5

Documentation and Training

5.1 Introduction

At the conclusion of this chapter we should have established an understanding of the level of documentation that should be received with, and maintained for, a backup environment. This covers both the configuration and the operational aspects of the solution.

For enterprise-level backup products, it should not be automatically expected that all staff who interact with the backup system will be capable of configuring and maintaining the system without some form of training. Enterprise-level backup software often has a reasonable level of complexity and many more options than are immediately apparent just from reviewing the vendor documentation.

Therefore, while documentation is quite important for a backup system, training is an equally important requirement for stable and reliable operations.

5.2 Documentation

It almost goes without saying that a critical requirement of any backup system is adequate documentation. This covers both the operational aspects of the system (how to change tapes, how to initiate ad-hoc backups, etc.) and also a configuration overview that can be used to provide new staff with an understanding of the backup process.

In the case of a backup system, "adequate documentation" means the documentation is

- Comprehensive
- Complete
- Each segment targeted at the appropriate usage level
- Readily extensible

An overview of the documentation that should always be available for a backup system is detailed in this chapter.

5.2.1 System Configuration

This should be a living document that provides a comprehensive, ongoing overview of the configuration of the backup environment. The goal of the system configuration document is to serve as reference material for the backup/system administrators, and to be able to bring new staff up to speed on the way in which the backup system works. This should contain at least the following:

- Operating system and application configuration details of the backup server, including items such as:
  - Network configuration — host resolution method, details of any hard-coded host entries required, etc.
  - Performance characteristics — does the system become heavily loaded during backups?
  - Process listing — what would a "typical" list of backup-related processes resemble?
  - List of installed packages or applications
- Explanation of any design decisions that may not be readily apparent (e.g., "this system is running version X of the operating system because..." or "despite the corporate standard, disks need to be partitioned in this fashion to facilitate..."). This avoids someone "fixing" a design which, although not the normal for the operating system or the company, is actually required for the backup product
- Licenses installed in the backup environment
- Contact details for support providers along with information on the SLAs in place with those providers. Where there is no "single point" for support, a breakdown listing the vendors responsible for supporting each aspect of the system should be provided
- Physical (hardware) layout covering all forms of media used
- Ongoing capacity planning and reporting
- An overview of each backup schedule in use, and deviations from the norm (e.g., "full backups occur on Saturdays except for server Y, which has a full backup performed on Sunday due to batch processing requirements")
- Any abnormal steps involved in the configuration of the backup product that would not be immediately obvious
- Media management policies with respect to the movement of media once extracted (physically) from the backup system
- If the system was designed and commissioned by a third party, references to any purchase orders, tender documents, statements of work, design briefs, etc., so that everyone involved can understand immediately whether an aspect of the configuration is "original" or "new"
- Reference to any corporate policies that must be followed in relation to the use of the backup system
- References to acceptance test documentation that was produced during the commissioning of the backup environment
- References to other documentation that can be used when working with the backup environment

5.2.2 System Map

A system map can best be described as a network diagram/map showing systems connectivity as well as system and application dependencies. In this case when we refer to dependencies, we are referring not to backup-level dependencies, but operational dependencies, which can have a significant impact on the recoverability of systems in an environment. It should form a core component of the IT environment documentation for all organizations, but in actuality mostly exists in the minds of IT staff, and then only in segments — i.e., different areas in IT will have different views of the system map.

If a network diagram is too complex (i.e., too large) to include a system map, it may be necessary to produce the system map as a table that accompanies the network diagram. A basic network diagram without backup services might resemble Figure 5.1, which shows the various components of the IT network as a whole. However, it doesn't show us (1) how the components relate or (2) what mappings they have to corporate functions. Thus, the standard network diagram is only ever at most half the full picture. For example, there's nothing in Figure 5.1 to indicate that, say, the intranet server hosts a Web-based call-management system that interfaces with the database server, using the authentication server to ensure that only those users who are allowed to access the system can retrieve data.

Without this sort of information, there is no clear mechanism to determine the criticality of systems or even a recovery order in the event of a catastrophic data center failure. A common consequence of this is that even IT staff may not fully appreciate which hosts require recovery first. For example, in an environment that fully relies on centralized host resolution (i.e., DNS), a network diagram does not show that the DNS server may need to be recovered first simply to allow other systems to contact each other and be recoverable in turn. Perhaps even more importantly, the diagram does not show such requirements and dependencies to management, key, and end users who would want to know why in a disaster the IT staff appear to be busy recovering their own servers rather than recovering the "real" systems such as e-mail, file, and print servers.

By having a system map, not only can these system and application dependencies be recorded visually, but they can be referred to during disaster recovery activities and planning exercises to ensure that systems are evaluated in the correct order. A system map might extend the network diagram as shown in Figure 5.2.

There is no standard or "best practices" approach to drawing a system map, and different organizations will utilize methods that are most appropriate to them. In the Figure 5.2, we have mapped the following dependencies:

- Each core piece of infrastructure is numbered.
- In addition to the equipment shown in the network diagram, we have also introduced business functions. It is imperative that the functions of the business (i.e., activities and products) be included in the system map. This ensures that we identify not only the individual systems, but the "net products," which the business sells and relies on.
- Each system is labeled with its function and also its dependencies. For example, the figure shows that the file/authentication server (1) depends on the DNS server (5).

System maps are very straightforward when servers perform only one function. However, when multiple functions are performed, they may need to show generic systems and also the core applications on multi-function systems if the dependencies differ between those applications. This means that the system map may become unwieldy pictorially, and as such it might be necessary to construct a system map as a table that accompanies the network diagram. The table-based approach to the previous system map might resemble Table 5.1.

Regardless of which mechanism is used to build a system map, the goal is to ensure that system, application, and business function dependencies can be seen quickly. With this in place, the

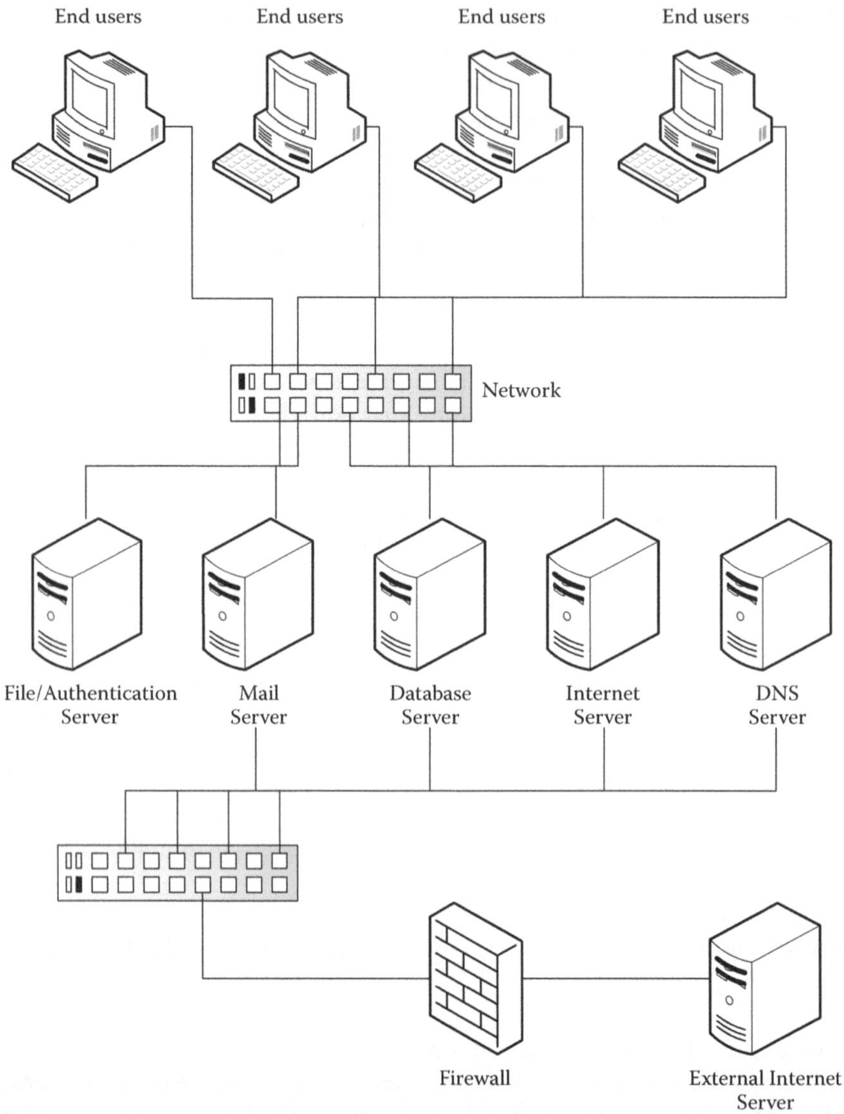

Figure 5.1 Basic network diagram

level of "importance" can be assigned to a system not just by the perceived user importance, but by the number of systems that depend on it. This in turn may reveal the importance (from a recovery perspective) of systems not previously seen as high priority. For instance, many companies make the mistake of assuming that DNS servers are non-critical. When evaluated in light of a system map, this quickly changes.

Based on Table 5.1, we could say that (1) the higher the number of dependencies, the earlier a system requires recovery, and (2) the smaller the number of dependencies, the more visible a system is to the company or end users.

Some organizations feel that system maps are only required for extreme circumstances, such as if all system administrators were unavailable. It is believed in these situations that risk mitigation (e.g., having company policies prohibiting all system administration staff from traveling

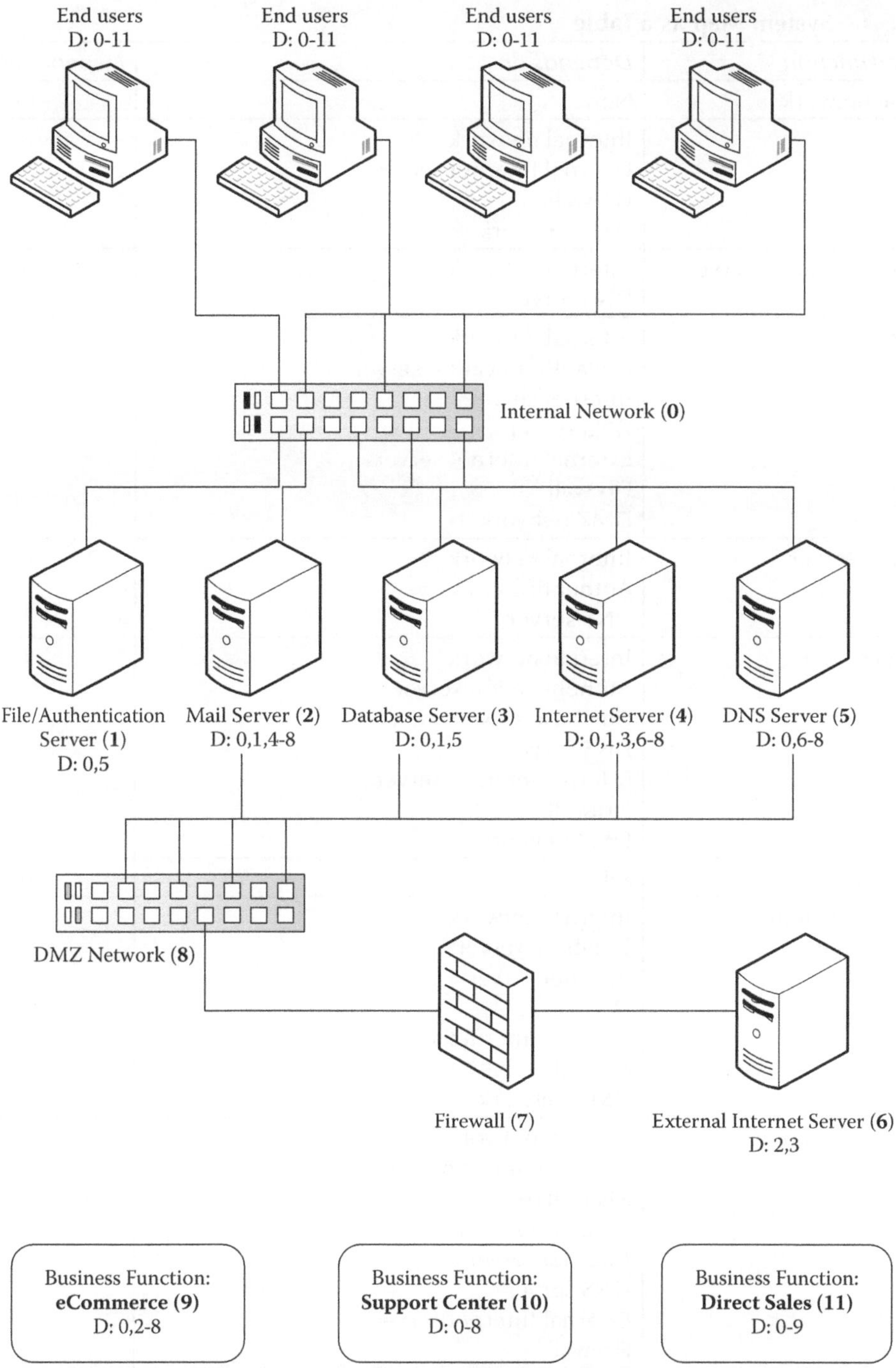

Figure 5.2 Network diagram extended to act as a system map

Table 5.1 System Map as a Table

System/Function	*Depends on*	*Dependencies (#)*
Internal network	None	10
DNS	Internal network External Internet server Firewall DMZ network	8
File/authentication server	Internal network DNS server	5
Mail server	Internal network File/authentication server Internet server DNS server External Internet server Firewall DMZ network	4
Database server	Internal network Authentication server DNS server	6
Internet server	Internal network Authentication server Database server DNS server External Internet server Firewall DMZ network	1
End users	All	0
Business function: eCommerce	Internal network Database server Internet server DNS server External Internet server Firewall DMZ network	1
Business function: Support center	Internal network File/authentication server Mail server Database server Internet server DNS server External Internet server Firewall DMZ network	0

Table 5.1 System Map as a Table (Continued)

System/Function	*Depends on*	*Dependencies (#)*
Business function: Direct sales	Internal network File/authentication server Mail server Database server Internet server DNS server External Internet server Firewall DMZ network eCommerce	0

together, etc.) resolves this problem. However, system maps do not address just this particular need. Instead, they serve a far more important business need — they help to ensure that IT activities and systems are correctly aligned to business functions, activities, and products. Without a system map, many businesses end up in situations where the IT environment does not properly address business needs.

5.2.3 *Administrative Operations*

This documentation must cover "regular" activities on the backup system, and should be targeted at the skill level of backup and system administrators, rather than aiming to be readily accessible to all possible users of the system. This would include at least the following information and procedures:

- How to configure new backup clients
  - Operating system/filesystem backups
  - All existing database and special application backups
- If an operating system, database, or application has special handling requirements, those details must be clearly stated; for instance, this might cover such items as, say, "ActiveDirectory databases must be exported prior to backup" or "licenses for X must be maintained separately as the backup account doesn't have authority to access those files"
- How to configure new devices
- How to adjust the configuration of existing clients
- How to decommission backup clients
- How to adjust overall server and backup policy configuration items, such as
  - Multiplexing settings
  - Who can administer the server
  - The frequency of backups, etc.
- Reference to any corporate policies that must be followed in relation to the use of the backup system
- Reference to other documentation to be used when working with the backup environment

5.2.4 Media Handling

This documentation doesn't always need to be separate from regular backup administration documentation. However, if it is separate, it can be more easily provided to backup operations staff without providing a flood of information they may not need to use. This documentation should be written for operator-level readers, and should cover the following:

- How to add tapes to the tape libraries or stand-alone drives
- How to remove tapes from the tape libraries or stand-alone drives
- Handling of any special backup media (e.g., magneto-optical (MO) devices, disk backup units, etc.)
- Physical media handling requirements (e.g., minimum/maximum storage temperatures, sorting/stacking procedures, etc.)
- Authorities for access of media
- Contacts for offsite media vaulting
- Reference to any corporate policies that must be followed in relation to the use of the backup system
- References to other documentation to be used when working with the backup environment

5.2.5 Backup and Recovery Operations

Depending on who performs the various types of recoveries, there may need to be multiple versions of this documentation produced. For instance, if backup and system administrators perform all operations, then there will only need to be one document, covering all of those items listed below. In situations where different staff groups are expected to perform the various activities of the environment, each staff group may need its own documentation, specifically targeting those staff. For instance, help desk staff may only receive documentation for file/directory recoveries, database administrators may only receive documentation for file and database backup/recovery operations, and so on.

The complete set of documentation for backup and recovery operations should cover at minimum:

- Recoveries
  - How to recover individual files
  - How to recover entire directories or filesystems
  - How to recover each type of database (or application with special handling requirements) in the backup environment
  - How to recover backups without the use of file indices if the backup software (and situation) supports it
  - How to recover from backup duplicates or media duplicates if supported by the backup software in use
  - How to re-index backups for file-browse recovery or in the event of backup software database corruption
  - How to recover the backup system, its configuration, and associated databases
  - Each type of recovery should be documented for each type of operating system in use, even if it is not technically required; this facilitates the use of the documentation by

multiple administration groups, and also prevents such issues as "I can't find the documentation to recover my operating system — it only gives examples for operating system X"
  - Any caveats with the recovery process (e.g., "database X must be shut down to allow recovery to take place," or "recoveries cannot be started within an hour of the backups commencing without management approval," etc.)
  - References to any SLAs that will be used to guide the recovery process
  - If parts of the environment are outsourced, documentation on the roles and responsibilities of both company-internal staff and staff from the outsourcer must be included
- Backups
  - How automated backups run
  - How to initiate a pre-configured backup manually
  - How to initiate a manual/ad-hoc backup on a per-operating-system basis, using both the GUI and the command line if possible
  - Details on how to initiate a manual/ad-hoc backup for each application or database with special backup requirements
  - Any caveats associated with running any of the above backups (e.g., "when running ad-hoc backups make sure the retention time is set, or else the backup system will set a retention time of one year")
- Reference to any corporate policies that must be followed in relation to the use of the backup system
- References to any other documentation that can be used when working with the backup environment

5.2.6 Disaster Recovery Operations

Unless a company has a very good reason, this documentation should be written with the intention that it will only be used by system and backup administrators, as these people have the best experience and training for dealing with the unexpected.

For each type of operating system that is being protected, the disaster recovery operations guide should include the following:

- Expectations of whom shall perform the recovery (for instance, if the recovery can only be performed by a system administrator rather than, say, an operator, it should be clearly stated)
- Pre-recovery instructions for any preparatory work required (e.g., installing an SOE (Standard Operating Environment), notifying management, recalling media, etc.)
- Where to source any documentation or configuration information associated with the recovery operation, e.g.:
  - Electronic and hard copies of the latest system configuration details, such as, say, volume layout details, hardware configuration information, copies of critical files or licenses, etc.
  - Vendor, third-party, and internal documentation for key applications on the system as appropriate for the environment
  - Vendor, third-party, and internal documentation for the operating system

- Locations for any media required for the recovery (regular tapes, OS CDs/DVDs, install media, boot tapes, electronic copies of media or system images, etc.)
- Detailed documentation of the recovery process for each type of operating system and "core application" combination; e.g., there might be one recovery procedure for Solaris using Sun's Disk Suite system, and another for Solaris using Veritas Storage Foundation Suite, etc.)
- Reference to any corporate policies that must be followed in relation to the use of the backup system
- References to any SLA documents that will guide the recovery process
- Reference to the system map
- References to the regular recovery documentation
- If parts of the environment are outsourced, documentation on the roles and responsibilities of both company-internal staff and staff from the outsourcer must be included
- References to other documentation that can be used when working with the backup environment

5.2.7 Troubleshooting

For the most part, troubleshooting documentation should be written so that it is readily accessible for all users of the backup environment. This should be a living document that contains the following:

- References for diagnosing common faults
- For the support contract with a vendor or third-party support provider, the document should cover all the initial diagnostic steps required/expected by that external party prior to logging a case
- Whenever a new fault is discovered that can be rectified by local staff with the appropriate information available to them, this should be added to the document
- Reference to any corporate policies that must be followed in relation to the use of the backup system
- Reference to other sources of troubleshooting information, knowledgebase articles, online help forums, and so on, where useful information may be found, either for the backup system directly or for any operating system, system hardware, network infrastructure, storage device, application or database connected to or protected by the backup environment
- References to other documentation that can be used when working with the backup environment

5.2.8 Acceptance Test Procedures

A company's acceptance test documentation should contain details of every test conducted on the backup environment prior to commissioning. Many companies perform acceptance testing, but don't retain the documentation produced with the rest of the backup system, which represents a considerable loss of knowledge of the capabilities of the backup environment, particularly when staff move on.

The acceptance test procedures should be the first point of reference in allowing administrators to answer the question "can we do this?"

Obviously the acceptance test procedures need to have covered the appropriate components of the implementation. At bare minimum, during implementation, acceptance test results should be noted for:

- Each operating system type
- Each major database and application type that requires its own backup or recovery procedures
- General backup/recovery testing
- Operational testing of key hardware such as tape libraries, virtual tape libraries, disk backup units, etc.
- Witnessed signatures
  - If the company installed the system itself, then the staff who conducted the testing should be noted, as well as the manager responsible for assigning them the testing.
  - If a vendor (integration or product) facilitated the installation, each test should be signed both by an appropriate staff member and a vendor representative.

5.2.9 Test Register

In addition to formal acceptance test procedures and associated documentation, a test register should be maintained. This will be used to record the results of periodic backup and recovery testing performed within the environment. This should be available to all administrators (backup, system, and application/database), as well as management.

A record of each test conducted should include the following details:

- Nature of the test
- System the test was conducted for
- When the test was run, when the test was previously run, and when the test is next expected to be repeated
- Results of the test
- If the test was unsuccessful, the following should be noted:
  - Errors or failures that occurred
  - How the failure has been escalated
  - Results of the escalation, once the issue is resolved
  - Details of any documentation changes that need to be made as a result of the failure
- If the test was successful, the following should be noted:
  - Any anomalous output that occurred during the test
  - Details of any documentation changes that need to be made

Note that this list is equally applicable to the formal acceptance testing conducted. (Appendix C shows a sample acceptance test form, and a sample acceptance test register can be found on the Web site.)

5.2.10 Vendor-Supplied Documentation

If vendors (either the original manufacturer or any third-party integrator) have supplied any documentation outside of that discussed above, the documentation should also be kept together with all the documentation of the backup system.

5.2.11 Release Notes

Although we normally think of release notes as being a part of vendor-supplied documentation, they are important enough to warrant individual consideration.

Release notes typically provide the following information:

- New features in a backup system
- Known limitations
- Updates that did not make it into the main documentation
- Changes to how the system works
- Details of bug fixes

Obviously, every time a backup vendor releases a new version of product, it is not feasible (or even appropriate) to read the entirety of the documentation again. However, administrators must make sure they read at least the release notes before planning any upgrades. In particular, backup products over time may change the available functionality or licensing required for particular functions. It is much less traumatic to read the release notes and act accordingly prior to performing an upgrade than it is to discover after the fact that additional licenses are required or a particular type of operation can no longer be performed. Additionally, the release notes should help administrators plan both the upgrade and any backout/contingency options that may need to be followed if an upgrade fails.

5.3 Training

5.3.1 The Case for Training

Depending on who will interact with the backup system (and in what way), a variety of training options are available to choose from, though some of those options may not immediately be obvious. For instance, when evaluating formal training courses, do not stop only at the courses offered by the original backup software vendor(s). Although these courses can be very valuable, it can often be said that they teach the "marketing" or "up-sell" approach to operating a particular backup product, and may not offer a holistic approach covering all aspects of backup. Third-party vendors, such as systems integrators and professional consultancy agencies who offer their own training courses on the product, may offer an alternate training path that provides staff a broader coverage than that offered by the vendor training course. In many cases, systems integrators will develop more experience (particularly in the local environment) with a product than those at the backup software company who write or deliver the training courses.

Always remember that staff must have human backups as well. Having only one person trained in a backup system is a foolish concentration of knowledge that should be strongly discouraged, no matter how small the environment. At least two, preferably three people should have sufficient skills in the backup system to be able to administer it. This allows one person to be on leave, one person to be sick, and the system to continue to be maintained.

One or fewer than one person trained in the backup product is not appropriate. Unfortunately for small to mid-sized organizations in particular, it is far too common to have only somewhere between zero and one fully trained staff members. This might be caused by:

- The only skilled person leaving without training anyone else
- Staff being too busy to participate in the installation and configuration when being conducted by a third party
- Staff participating in the installation and configuration, but with frequent disruptions
- Staff not able to attend any training

Companies tend to experience the most problems with enterprise backup software when they don't allow staff to develop skills in the software properly, or refuse to accept that daily administration of backups is part of the IT role. There is always a direct correlation between the level of customer staff involvement in the installation, configuring, testing, and training and the quality of the experience they have in using the backup product. That is, staff who are untrained tend to have the most issues. When staff are untrained, or only minimally trained, the ultimate goal of the backup system — that being a corporate insurance policy — is put significantly at risk.

5.3.2 Backup Administrators

If there are dedicated backup administration personnel, they should definitely receive training on the backup system, which should cover the following:

- Standard administration activities
- Backup and recovery operations for all operating systems and applications involved in the backup system
- Troubleshooting activities — how to diagnose and rectify standard faults that may occur in the environment
- Operational activities such as tape/media movement
- In short, everything that all other staff would be trained on (as documented in the following sections) in relation to the backup system should be taught to the backup administrators, as they will become the key point of reference for an organization once the system is commissioned; they will also become the key people responsible for training new staff members when courses or resources are not readily available

This training may not necessarily come only from formal training courses. For instance, if a third party is involved in the installation of the backup environment, it will typically have allocated consultants to work on each of the above activities as part of the commissioning. These consultants are likely to represent a valuable knowledge base that should be mined by staff during the installation phase. That is, staff should be involved in a knowledge transfer as part of the implementation of any new system.

5.3.3 System Administrators

If there is no dedicated team of backup administrators, or there is only one backup administrator, then clearly the system administrators will need the same level of training as the backup administrators described above. However, if there is a differentiation between system and backup administrators, the system administrators may be able to receive less training. In this case, they should be taught at minimum:

- How to initiate ad-hoc backups
- How to perform recoveries
- How to monitor recoveries
- Security and procedural aspects of recoveries
- An overview of the architecture of the backup system
- How to troubleshoot backup and recovery operations for their systems
- Where to find the documentation for the backup system

Of course, in a well-rounded environment it would be appropriate for one or more system administrators to be able to take over the role of a backup administrator if necessary, but it may be that only one team member from each system administration group is targeted for complete backup system training. (Preferably though, for larger organizations, there should be at least two per team.)

Further to the training outlined above, system administrators should also be involved in any acceptance test activities for a backup system that affects their systems. This involvement can constitute valuable hands-on training with the system as implemented at a company. Doing so may provide a better learning experience than formal classroom training following standard course material that may have few similarities to the installed configuration. (This is particularly so if the configuration used in standard training has little relationship to the installed configuration.)

5.3.4 Application and Database Administrators

It should be noted from the outset that very few backup courses concentrate significantly on how to back up and recover particular applications or databases; such courses either require special design, or are offered as adjuncts to the main courses, and only for the most prevalent applications or databases.

Typical backup courses cover the following:

- Theory of backup
- Nomenclature and layout of the backup package
- Installation and configuration of the backup package
- General usage of the backup package

Spending a useful amount of time on each of the applications or databases that can be protected by the backup software in a "core" training course will usually be impractical, if not impossible. For this reason, application and database administrators do not frequently find much use in attending formal software training courses for enterprise production products. Instead, with application/database administrators, training should:

- Provide one-on-one or specialised group instruction that teaches the fundamentals of the backup product in use, as it applies to them
- Teach how to initiate backup and recovery operations for their applications or databases
- Instruct in the security and procedural aspects of recoveries
- Involve the administrators in the acceptance test procedures for their applications or databases to ensure they feel comfortable with the product, and how it works
- Cover how to troubleshoot backup and recovery failures that would apply to their roles
- Inform where they can locate the documentation for the backup system

5.3.5 Operations Staff

Depending on the environment, operations staff may be responsible for many aspects of the day-to-day running of the backup system, or alternatively they may be engaged simply to function as protein-based autoloaders.

Operations staff engaged solely for tape-changing operations will simply need to be taught the following:

- How to add and remove media to and from the backup system
- How to locate media for the backup system
- How to allocate new media to the backup system
- How to monitor the backup system
- How to react to media requests from the backup system for recoveries, duplication, and backup

Operations staff who are expected to carry the daily operations load of the backup environment (i.e., where there is some overlap between the function of a backup administrator and the operations staff) will also need training in:

- Media and monitoring functions as above
- Adding (and potentially removing) hosts to/from the backup environment
- Installing backup agent (client) software on hosts
- Performing ad-hoc backups and recoveries for all the systems they are involved with
- Security and procedural aspects of recoveries
- Troubleshooting operational aspects of the backup system, as well as general backup/recovery issues; this is particularly the case in environments where the operations staff continue to monitor and work with the backup system after system and backup administrators have left the office
- Where to find the documentation for the backup system

This training should typically be a combination of informal, hands-on training, and formal course training. In particular, operations staff who are responsible for overnight monitoring of the backup system will need to understand the system sufficiently well as to be able to assist administrators with the environment.

A common mistake made by many companies is to provide operators with insufficient (or no) documentation, instead relying on on-the-job knowledge transfers. This has a direct impact on the frequency at which operators need to escalate issues to backup and/or system administrators. With access to documentation as well as on-the-job training, operators frequently become very knowledgeable in the backup systems they help to maintain, and can prevent minor issues from requiring escalation or becoming more serious problems.

5.3.6 Help Desk Staff

For some organizations, the terms "help desk" and "operations center" are synonymous. However, when there are different groups, it typically comes down to help desk staff being user-facing, and operations staff being server-facing. That is, help desk staff will directly interact with users and their systems, and operations staff will involve themselves primarily in day-to-day running and maintenance of servers.

Help desk staff who deal with end users rather than servers therefore will need to be trained in:

- How to perform recoveries
- How to monitor the backup system (so as to observe a recovery in progress, or determine for instance why a recovery hasn't started)
- Basic troubleshooting for recovery operations
- Security and procedural aspects of recoveries
- Where to find the documentation for the backup system

This training will be done typically through informal, hands-on mentoring by other staff members (such as the backup administrators, or help desk team leaders who have attended training), but may also involve custom training (usually developed internally to the company itself) targeted specifically at the activities likely to be performed by the help desk staff. However, they should have access to documentation (as per the operators) so as to reduce the frequency with which they need to escalate problems to the backup and system administrators, or even operators.

5.3.7 End Users

Even when end users don't perform recoveries themselves, they still require some training, albeit typically procedural training. Users who don't perform their own recoveries will need to know the following:

- How to request recoveries
- What can't be recovered (e.g., individual message recovery unless a user is in management, etc.)
- How far back (and with what levels of accuracy) files can be recovered; by accuracy, we refer to the frequency of backups over time (e.g., daily backups may be retrievable in an organization for one month, whereas monthly backups may be retrievable for ten years, but only allow recovery of files and data present on, say, the last Saturday of every month)

It is equally important that users understand how they can interact with data. That is, procedures should be in place regarding data deletion, file/directory renaming, etc. If these are not present, users might assume whatever backups are in place are a blank check to do whatever they want. (For instance, a mistake sometimes made by end users is to assume that with backups in place, they can free up space by deleting any file they choose, then request it later when required again — i.e., using the backup system as archival storage.)

When designing procedures for end users to request a recovery, remember two facts: (1) end users will be at least as vague in their recovery request as they are permitted to be, and (2) end users cannot be expected to understand fully the complete layout of all systems they attach to.

These are essentially contradictory facts, and there is a fine line to be walked between them. For instance, "please recover 'letter to the editor.doc' on my H: drive" could be a perfectly sounding request from an end user, and depending on the known layout of the data, it may also be a sufficiently precise request. However, if H: is a mapping to a corporate fileserver and the user could have stored the file in any one of a thousand or more directories, it is sufficiently fuzzy as to cause significant hair-tearing by IT staff.

One way to alleviate this problem is to teach users how to request recoveries properly. For instance, a form that they need to fill in may require them to specify fully the path to the file, and may also include a disclaimer that if the full path can't be provided, the recovery may take longer while staff find the file in the backup environment. A sample recovery request form that users might be required to fill out can be found in appendix B of this book. Users should also understand that finding files that have been deleted when the original directory they resided in is unknown is typically not an easy task.

Every recovery facilitator from help desk staff through to backup administrators will have their own horror stories of imprecise recovery requests. Users understandably dislike losing their work, and without a procedure to guide them through, the recovery request may become vague due to the stress and irritation involved. In this situation, they can make requests such as "I lost a file. I think it was called 'letter.' I saved it in the usual place that Word prompts me to save it. I'm not sure when it disappeared — I'm sure I worked on it last week. Please get it back!" (Many staff of course will have received requests that say no more than "I lost my file, please get it back!")

As discussed in section 3.12.12, "Backup Catalogues," a critical feature of enterprise class backup software is searchable backup indices. Depending on the product, the search functionality may be advanced (e.g., "list all files with the word 'letter' in it backed up in the last week from these systems…") or it may be very simple (e.g., limited to searching an individual filesystem or machine at a time).

The implication of this is clear — users who simply request recoveries need to understand the recovery time will be directly dependent both on how recently the backup was performed and the preciseness of their recovery request.

Moving on to users who are permitted to run their own recoveries, they will need to be taught the following:

- How to initiate the recovery (providing them a "cheat sheet" with, say, one to two pages at most, explaining what to do in typical circumstances is appropriate)
- How to monitor the recovery
- How to check server activity
- How to report errors to staff for diagnosis
- How to escalate recovery requests if they are urgent, or not working

Without this information, users may find the recovery system confusing, and may actually impede the activities of backup and system administrators by registering faults regarding the system that are in actual fact merely caused by an insufficient understanding of the product.

5.3.8 Management

Certainly at the high-management level, there makes little sense in a CEO or even a CIO being completely conversant with the ins and outs of the backup product implemented at a site. At that level, as we stated at the start of the book, management should be able to expect that the backup system is working unless otherwise notified. However, senior management should have access to a simple high-level overview of the backup environment.

However, turning our attention to less-senior management — team leaders and operations management — it is important that this management tier has some overview of the backup system. Management are typically able to fulfill two important functions in the backup and recovery environment: (1) presenting budgetary requests to more-senior management, and (2) acting as liaison between senior management and technical staff for reporting, analysis, audits, and testing.

While management can attempt these functions without any knowledge of the backup system, it does somewhat reduce their effectiveness. Without a basic understanding of the system, reporting feedback at best will be rote recitation of technical feedback, or worse, confused and garbled statements that will hinder, not help.

At a bare minimum, management should have an understanding of the basic enterprise backup features including, but not limited to:

- Backup topology
- Scheduling and levels
- Data availability (offline, online, and snapshots)
- How exclusive backup schemes are required to get insurance out of a backup product
- How server impact can be mitigated
- Options available for database and special application backups
- How backup performance and recovery performance are intimately related
- How SLAs need to be balanced against real-world system features or budgetary increases
- How duplication of backup is not an "optional extra," but a required feature to ensure that backups do not become a single point of failure

Additionally, for an individual environment, management need to know the following:

- How the backup and recovery system has been designed (overall layout, design principles, etc.)
- Backup retention times for each frequency backup being performed (e.g., daily backups kept for one month, monthlies kept forever, etc.)
- Who the valid backup administrators and operators of the environment are
- How to access reports that are required for their feedback to upper management (even if this is "the report will be e-mailed to management weekly")

Chapter 6

Performance Options, Analysis, and Tuning

6.1 Introduction

In this chapter, we will cover the various factors that need to be considered when investigating backup performance, regardless of which backup product is used. This will cover areas such as:

- The various types of performance enhancement techniques used by backup products
- Determining where bottlenecks may exist
- Choosing appropriate backup hardware for the requirements of the business
- Balancing the need for backup performance with backup efficiency
- Balancing the need for backup performance with recovery performance

The last point is actually one of the most important factors to be considered in a backup environment. When companies plan new backup environments, usually one of the first requirements discussed is a need to achieve backups within an *x* hour backup window. Although the window size is sometimes chosen for real processing or operational reasons, it is sometimes chosen arbitrarily.

In actual fact, the more important question is always "What is the recovery window?" We will see in this chapter that some of the common techniques used to improve backup performance can, if misused, compromise recovery performance.

Two different factors need to be considered when considering backup performance: (1) backup bandwidth, which refers to the maximum amount of data that can be backed up in a given time; and (2) backup efficiency, which refers to how well the backup product makes use of available resources.

Although it would be desirable to have a 100-percent overlap between these two types of performance, we will show how backup bandwidth can sometimes only be achieved to the detriment of backup efficiency, and vice versa.

When tuning the backup performance (either for efficiency or bandwidth), it is important at all times to remain cognizant of the impact that performance tuning may have on recovery requirements.

6.2 Performance Techniques

Backup products can employ a variety of features to provide backup performance, and to analyze and tune backup performance, it is necessary to have an overview of those features and the issues that can come into play with their use.

6.2.1 Backup Bandwidth

6.2.1.1 Multiplexing

As a simple definition, multiplexing refers to combining several items into a single consolidated item, which in turn can be split back out into its original component forms. Typically, we multiplex to reduce processing requirements, or improve communications efficiency or performance. This can be represented as shown in Figure 6.1. Obviously, to have a multiplexing system, there must also be a demultiplexing system, which works in the reverse, as shown in Figure 6.2. That is, a single consolidated stream is converted back into its constituent parts.

Depending on the backup product, multiplexing can be referred to in a variety of different ways including, but not limited to "multiple streams," "parallelism," and "concurrent backups." Some backup products have a high capability in this area, and others (typically workgroup or plain operating system tools) will have little or no multiplexing capability. Those that have little or no multiplexing capabilities may be fine for small-office or home-office environments, but offer little benefit to data center/enterprise backup environments.

There are typically three types of multiplexing that can be used within an environment:

1. Server multiplexing — the ability of the backup server to accept multiple incoming streams of data
2. Client multiplexing — the ability of a client to send multiple streams of data during backup, or receive multiple streams of data during recovery
3. Device multiplexing — the ability of a device to read or write multiple streams of data

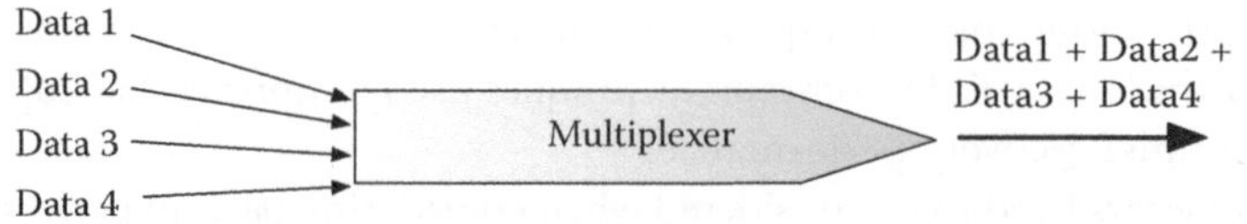

Figure 6.1 Multiplexing

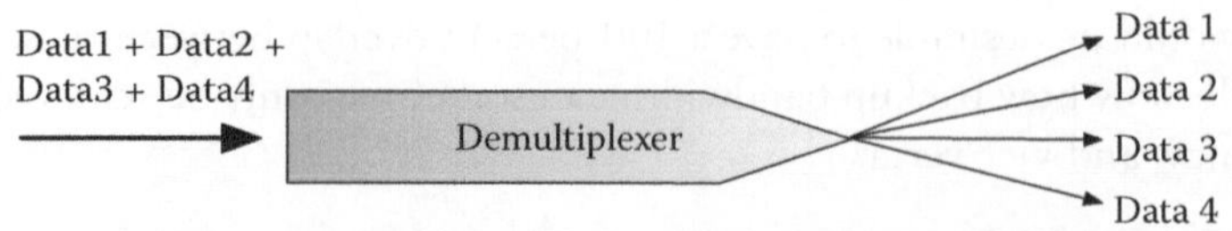

Figure 6.2 Demultiplexing

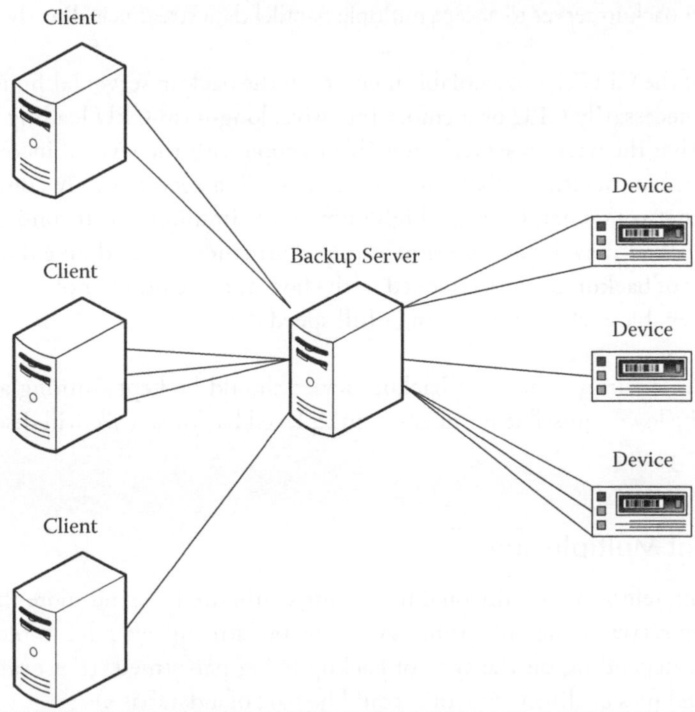

Figure 6.3 Multiplexing in a backup environment

Various products may offer additional areas where multiplexing can be configured, but these three are the core areas most likely to be seen within a backup product.

An example showing these three types of multiplexing is shown in Figure 6.3.

6.2.1.1.1 Server Multiplexing

In the most primitive form, server multiplexing is the extent to which the backup server supports receiving or sending multiple streams of data, and is an absolute prerequisite to a product being classed as enterprise, or even workgroup ready. For example, if there are three clients of a backup server, and the backup server has three tape drives, simple server-based multiplexing means that the server should be able to back up all three clients simultaneously.

A backup product obviously requires server-based multiplexing before it can offer any other form of multiplexing.

The configuration of server multiplexing makes a profound impact on the performance of the entire backup environment. If set too low, not enough data will be sent to the backup media, increasing the length of the backup. If the backup exceeds the backup window, there is obviously an increased risk of data loss — after all, backup windows should be chosen as the best time to ensure data protection occurs.

If, on the other hand, server multiplexing is set too high, the backup server can be "swamped" with excessive amounts of data transfer and be unable to service each backup stream efficiently. This can lead to slower backups (at best), or backups that are very slow to recover from (worse), or backups that fail due to server resources being exhausted (worst of all).

The ability of a backup server to accept multiple parallel data streams is directly affected by:

- The speed of the CPU(s) and available memory in the backup server (although backup activities are not necessarily CPU or memory intensive, long-term CPU loading or memory use is a sure sign that the backup server is not able to cope with the level of incoming data)
- The network bandwidth available to the server — if a server is only connected to a small bandwidth network, then having a high number of simultaneous incoming data streams to the backup server may act as a detriment to performance rather than enhancing it
- The number of backup devices attached to the host and the number of simultaneous streams required to enable each device to run at full speed

In an optimum environment, each backup device should be kept running at its highest possible speed with the lowest possible number of multiplexed backups. (We will discuss multiplexing at the device layer soon.)

6.2.1.1.2 Client Multiplexing

Client multiplexing refers to an individual host being configured to send more than one stream of data to the backup server at the same time. Typically, by "stream" we refer to filesystems, but this could be different depending on the type of backup being performed. (For example, it may be a collection of named files or directories, or it could be part of a database.)

Client multiplexing is used so that a single host can send more data to the backup server so that its backups complete sooner. The capability of a client to send multiple streams will be highly dependent on the following factors:

- Other processing activities occurring (and most complete) on the client at the same time
- CPU/memory capabilities of the client
- Underlying disk subsystem or filesystem performance
- Whether the client is performing any software encryption or software compression of the data prior to sending it to the backup server
- Whether another software agent is scanning the data the client sends to the backup server
- Network link between the client and the server

To a lesser degree, it is also dependent on the speed of the target backup device, but we will cover that more when we cover device multiplexing. In newer environments, another factor that will come into play is whether the client has been virtualized, and if so, whether any sibling clients (i.e., virtual machines on the same virtual machine server) are also being backed up.

The performance of the underlying disk subsystem or the filesystem is a key factor in client performance that often takes people by surprise when evaluating multiplexing options for individual clients. When systems are being used for random file access, many design or layout issues (either at the operating system or system implementation level) may not be readily apparent — but during large sustained sequential reads of the filesystems, previously unnoticed issues may be highlighted.

Hosts in a backup environment could have any of a very large number of types of disk structures, so we'll consider just a few common scenarios from which a large number of multiplexing settings can be extrapolated. For these examples, we will assume that the backup product performs multiplexing where each filesystem on a machine is assigned a single stream — the most-common form of multiplexing.

There are no magic rules to follow when trying to determine an optimum client multiplexing value. Instead, there may be multiple tweaks performed before an optimum setting is achieved. However, if looking for a quick rule to follow when planning the multiplexing setting for a client, there's only one that can be readily suggested, even though it may appear to be the opposite of our topic: for client multiplexing, always start with a value of 1 and work up.

Obviously, some machines will need higher multiplexing values than 1; however, a common mistake in many backup environments is to configure all clients with unnecessarily high multiplexing settings — when configured this way, the net result may actually be a performance detriment rather than an enhancement.

Scenario 1: Simple Disk—Consider first a standard x86 low-end server that might have a single hard drive divided into two partitions — one for the operating system, and one for the applications and data. Under Windows, this might be drives "C:" and "D:"; under Linux, it might be "/" and "/home."

It is important to note that few (if any) backup products actually look at the underlying disk structure when evaluating what to back up. With this in mind, most backup products, if configured for client multiplexing of two or more, would simultaneously backup both filesystems. With such a configuration, however, the disk will be forced into a situation where it receives an ongoing stream of read requests from two physically separate areas on its platters. For example, the disk could be logically represented as shown in Figure 6.4. The consequences of two-way multiplexing on a disk with two filesystems like this should be obvious. The disk drive must service both sets of requests, which means the heads will be continuously seeking across a large amount of the surface of the platters. Although disks are designed for random access, this constant long-seek across the platters is certainly sub-optimal. Indeed, the backup scenario we're describing is actually a worst-case access method.

Typically, we describe this style of configuration as a "disk head exercise routine." Clearly a multiplexing setting of 1 should be used in this scenario. This allows a clean read of each filesystem one after the other without undue work on the part of the disk drive. It is not uncommon, however, to see clients with this type of disk configuration to have two-way multiplexing enabled.

When considering multiple disks in a system, it is still important to consider the partition layout, rather than simply assuming that multiple disks automatically allows for higher multiplexing settings. For example, consider the layout shown in Figure 6.5, where we can see that the C: and D: filesystems reside on the same physical disk, with the E: filesystem being on a disk by itself. In this case, invoking a two-way multiplexed backup of the client may still fail to deliver optimum performance. If, for instance, the backup agent processes filesystems according to alphabetical order, then the C: and D: filesystems would again be processed simultaneously, with the backup for the E: filesystem initiated only after the backup for one of the C: or D: filesystems completed.

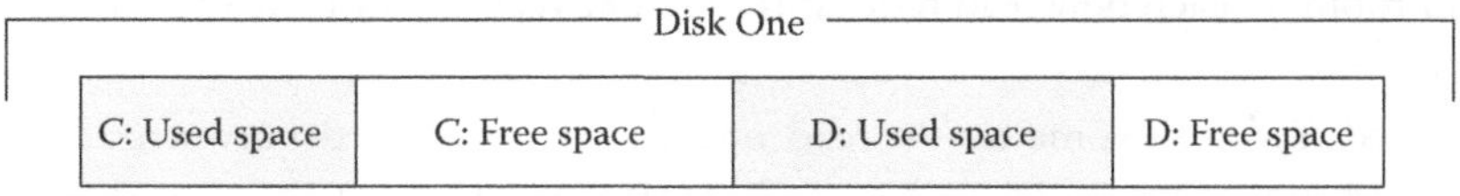

Figure 6.4 Simple disk with two filesystems

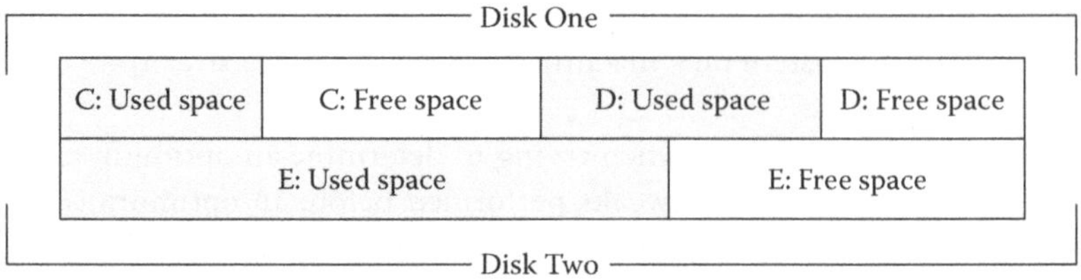

Figure 6.5 Sample three-filesystem, two-disk layout

An alternative may simply be to "tell" the backup software to back up drive C, drive E, and then drive D, in that order. However, by doing so, we slip into an inclusive rather than an exclusive model, which can then result in data loss (i.e., what happens if someone adds an "F:" filesystem?). However, even if an inclusive mode is used, and an explicit list of filesystems is provided, sub-optimal backup performance can still occur — e.g., if the "E:" filesystem is backed up simultaneously with the "C:" filesystem, but has few files to back up, the backup software may still end up backing up "C:" and "D:" simultaneously.

As long as the rest of the backup environment will handle it, the following guidelines for simple disk configurations can be assumed: (1) for n disks providing n filesystems, with a 1:1 mapping between disks and filesystems, multiplexing should never be set higher than n; (2) for n disks providing $n + x$ filesystems, multiplexing should be set to 1 unless absolute guarantees can be made that the backup software will not attempt to back up two filesystems on the same disk.

Scenario 2: RAID—A mistaken assumption is that as soon as a system has RAID storage, then a higher multiplexing value is the most appropriate setting. This is not always the case, and there will still be dependencies on the hardware in use, regardless of the RAID type deployed. We will first examine RAID presented by either a software level or a "cheap" controller level (as opposed to a SAN, which will be covered in its own scenario). Note that RAID-0 (striping, or concatenation) will not be considered because it offers no form of redundancy.

Scenario 2.1: RAID-1 (Mirroring)—The multiplexing setting used with RAID-1 disks will be strongly dependent on the following factors: (1) other processing that is occurring during the backup that will require disk activity, and (2) the read optimization techniques offered by the RAID system.

There are three typical read techniques available for RAID-1:

1. Dedicated-read — this is almost like an "active/passive" RAID where only one disk is ever used to read from, unless it fails
2. Round-robin — each new read request rotates between the mirrors that are available for the RAID
3. Optimized-read, or geometric — read operations are divided between areas of the disks (e.g., one disk may be used for all reads from the "first half" of the filesystem, and the other disk may be used for all reads from the "second half" of the filesystem)

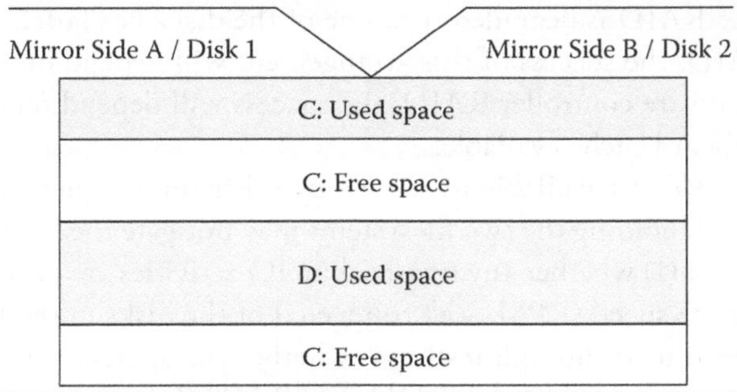

Figure 6.6 Two-way mirror with two filesystems

Consider, for instance, a two-way mirror hosting two filesystems. This might be represented logically as shown in Figure 6.6. For a dedicated-read RAID-1 system, multiplexing should not be used — i.e., for read performance the RAID system will only function as well as a simple-disk environment.

For round-robin and optimized-read RAID-1 systems, start at first with no multiplexing for the backup to ascertain a base performance figure, then increase to two-way multiplexing to determine which method provides the best performance. The amount of non-backup IO processing that occurs during the backup will often govern this setting.

Scenario 2.2: RAID-3/RAID-5 (Striped with Parity)—Consider a small RAID-5 or RAID-3 system consisting of the minimum three disks (common for DAS inside a host). Assuming this provides, say, "/" and "/home" for a UNIX system, this might result in a layout such as shown in Figure 6.7. This style of configuration is quite common, and it also common to see backup configurations where a two-way multiplex backup is performed. However, during large-scale sequential read operations (i.e., backups) the improved read performance of RAID-5 does not guarantee high-speed multiplexed backup, particularly when there are only a few disks in the

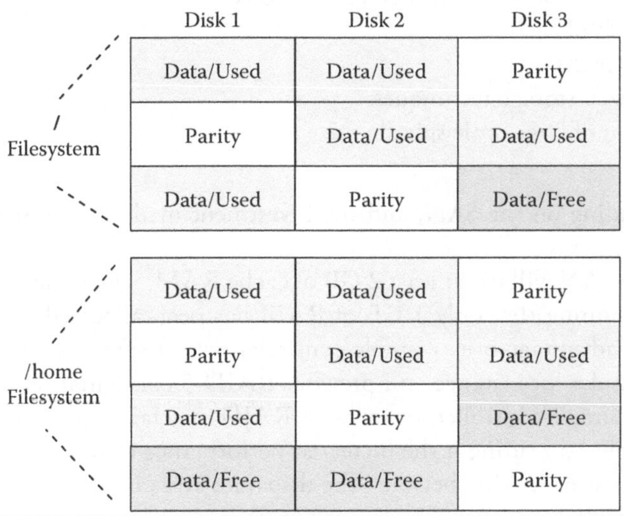

Figure 6.7 Simple RAID-5 unit providing two filesystems

RAID grouping. If the RAID is degraded (i.e., one of the disks has failed), this is even more the case. For software RAID, the success of this arrangement will depend on the host processor and memory. For local hardware controller RAID, the success will depend on the quality of the unit and the amount of onboard cache available.

Despite having three disks available to service two disparate sequential reads, the seek time between the areas on disk holding the two filesystems may mitigate the striping performance. Two key factors influence this: (1) whether any non-backup IO activities are occurring at the same time as the backup, and (2) the speed (RPM, seek time, etc.) of the disks in the RAID.

What must be determined through testing is whether the aggregate performance from backing up all the filesystems provided by the RAID-5 or RAID-3 device simultaneously exceeds the performance of backing up each filesystem one after the other. For example, if two filesystems provided by the same RAID-5 or RAID-3 volume can be multiplexed at 8 MB/s each (a combined throughput of 16 MB/s), this may seem like an acceptable result; however, if each individual filesystem can be backed up one at a time at a speed of around 18–20 MB/s, the multiplexing choice should be clear.

Like RAID-1, the decision to multiplex or not should not be an automatic one. Rather, when a system is being commissioned, tests should be run first to gain a benchmark of performance of reading one filesystem at a time, then multiplexing settings should be increased to determine an optimum setting. At most, in a RAID-3/5 environment, multiplexing should never exceed one less than the number of disks in the RAID group, and should only be increased if this target of tests continues to demonstrate increased backup performance.

Scenario 3: SAN Storage—Although SAN devices typically provide the same type of RAID levels discussed previously, they offer additional advantages over software or simple-controller RAID. These advantages extend well beyond "simple" improvements such as higher-speed disks, and even in the event of a SAN having the same speed disks as a JBOD or DAS RAID, it will typically provide better performance. This can be attributed to:

- Off-host processing of RAID-related calculations
- Significant levels of caching
- Dynamic data paths
- Highly optimized storage techniques
- Easy facilitation of large-scale spindle use

Note that depending on the SAN, and the investment made in the SAN, these variables of course will fluctuate.

A typical quality SAN will use at least 2 GB of cache RAM, which may be split between reads and writes. Even assuming that only 1 GB of RAM has been allocated for reads, this gives the SAN a considerable advantage over a simple controller or software RAID for reads, particularly during backup. Consider for instance, our previous RAID-5 configuration — three disks providing two filesystems. Simple controllers or software RAID may fail to perform well in this configuration during multiplexed reading if the increased performance of reading from multiple disks is outweighed by the cost of seeking between the disparate areas on disks that hold the data to be retrieved. SANs typically eliminate this through their read cache. When a read request for x KB is requested by the SAN, it will read $x + y$ KB, where y is the number that brings the read up to a logical buffer size — i.e., it anticipates that the next read may be from a similar area. Although operating systems and onboard RAID controllers also perform this caching, it is not as efficient or guaranteed as SAN caching. For OS caching, it competes with regular memory usage, and so is highly dependent on the memory requirements of the applications running on hosts at the same time as the backup. Operating systems invariably abandon filesystem cache to reclaim memory for applications to avoid swapping. However, as SAN cache-RAM is used only for caching purposes, the performance boost during backup operations is tangible. For onboard RAID controllers and local cards, the amount of cache RAM is usually significantly less than the SAN cache — e.g., 16 –64 MB is a fairly typical cache size (shared between read/write).

Furthermore, SANs give storage administrators the option of spreading the load for critical performance volumes across a significantly larger number of disks. If a fileserver using direct attached storage were providing a 300-GB file-share to all the users in a department, the options might be to use 2 × 300 GB SCSI drives in a mirror, or 5 × 73 GB SCSI drives in a RAID-5 arrangement, etc., depending on the number of drive bays available for storage. With a SAN, however, a much-higher number of disks could be allocated to the volume if performance is critical. A 300-GB file-share might instead consist of 10 × 30 GB mirrors striped together. That is, 20 disks each providing a 30-GB slice, with slices mirrored, creating 10 × 30 GB mirrors. These 10 × 30 GB mirrors might then be striped, forming a 300-GB volume. During backups, such a volume will not be hampered by the IO performance of the array subsystem. (The remaining capacity on disks can either be left unallocated for future expansion, or allocated to other systems with complimentary access requirements.)

When using SAN storage, a key area of consideration, however, is the performance needs of other hosts that also use the SAN during the backup. Although clients that make use of direct attached storage may be tested in relative isolation to determine optimum local read performance, this is not the case with SAN attached clients. Therefore when evaluating optimum client multiplexing settings of a client that makes use of SAN storage, it is necessary for backup and storage administrators to work together to evaluate the IO load and options available (e.g., if ten machines use the same SAN and are all backed up at the same time, multiplexing levels of all ten machines will need to be evaluated against the performance capabilities of the SAN).

6.2.1.1.3 Network

One standard concern in configuring client performance is ensuring that the network link between the client and its backup server is not underutilized. However, equally important is the need to avoid swamping the network. For example, consider a 100-megabit connection between the backup server and a client, where the client can sustain a throughput of 9.5 MB/s or faster reading from a single filesystem. In this scenario it makes little sense in the client being set to provide a higher degree of multiplexing. If, on the other hand, gigabit Ethernet is in use and the client can support three simultaneous reads at 9.5 MB/s, then choosing to perform three-way multiplexing may be appropriate.

A common mistake seen with multiplexing in sub-gigabit network environments is that "multiplexing won't hurt" when it is not needed. To evaluate that decision, consider a 100-megabit network where a single filesystem read/transfer can fill the network to capacity. It is quite regular in these instances to see the multiplexing value on a client tuned up to a higher number than necessary. In fact, this can result in a slower backup due to less data being sent. Taking a "best-case scenario" (and for ease of rounding), let's assume that the client can transmit data to the backup server at 10 MB/s.

What must be understood is that when a client transmits 10 MB/s of data, it's not 10 MB/s of user data that is transmitted. (By "user data," we refer to the actual intended data.) TCP/IP communication introduces a data overhead, as data is broken up into packets and sent across the network. These packets need to be clearly identified to ensure that they:

- Arrive at their destination
- Are reassembled in the correct sequence at the destination
- May be retransmitted in case of error

Therefore, for every x bytes of user data sent, $x + y$ bytes are actually sent where y is the metadata added to control and direct the packets properly. As such, we can say more accurately that during any one second, we transmit not x bytes of user data, but $x - y$ bytes of user data. This is no different than, say, posting a box to someone with a present inside — the weight and size of the item being sent is a combination of the contents of the box (what actually needs to be sent) and the box itself.

If we take two filesystems that can be each streamed at 10 MB/s over a network that can only handle 10 MB/s, and try to send them to the backup server simultaneously, then we don't send as much data as if we were sending each filesystem one after the other. Assuming that each filesystem stream gets equal share of the network being sent simultaneously, this would mean each stream would get 5 MB/s.

However, in any one second we don't backup x bytes across the network, but $x - y$ bytes, where y is our overhead. If we send two streams, we get $2x - 2y$. This isn't an improvement though; x dropped from ten to five, meaning that $2x$ is still the original ten, but we've now doubled y, the overhead. Returning to our box analogy, imagine a standard size door. One quite large box could fit through by itself, or several smaller-sized boxes could fit through. However, each box takes up measurable space, decreasing the amount of content passed through the door at any one time when multiple smaller boxes are used.

This goes to highlight that in backups, sometimes "less is more" — i.e., by reducing the amount of activity at any moment the overall backup bandwidth can actually be increased.

6.2.1.1.4 Device/Media Multiplexing

Device multiplexing concerns itself with how many simultaneous backup streams a given backup device will perform. This can also be referred to as media multiplexing, as it is ultimately the media in the device that receives the multiplexed streams — the device is simply the transfer mechanism.*

For people moving out of operating-system-specific backup tools or workgroup tools, a common question is "if the backup product mixes the data on the tape, how do I know I'll get it back intact?" There are two answers for this: (1) backup vendors have extensively developed and tested the multiplexing functionality at the device level, and (2) backup software manufacturers would have been sued out of business long ago if there were common problems in data retrieval due to

* Although media multiplexing can occur when the backup device is disk, we will restrict ourselves to tape at this point.

Table 6.1 Various Tape Streaming Speeds

Drive Type	*Speed (MB/s) Native*	*Speed (MB/s) Compressed*
LTO Ultrium 1	15	30
LTO Ultrium 2	35	70
LTO Ultrium 3	80	160
Quantum DLT 8000	6	12
Quantum SDLT 220	11	22
Quantum SDLT 320	16	32
Quantum SDLT 600	32	64
StorageTek 9840A	10	40

their multiplexing algorithms. The second answer may sound trite, but perhaps it helps to highlight why there is a difference between simple backup tools and enterprise backup tools.

The goal of media multiplexing is to ensure that a tape keeps on streaming. By streaming, we refer to the tape reading or writing at full native speed (or better) that has been quoted by the vendor. For example, some common streaming speeds are given in Table 6.1. Based on this table, we can say that, to keep an LTO Ultrium 1 tape streaming at full native speed, we must be able to keep 15 MB/s of data running to the drive at all times.

The consequences of failing to keep a tape drive streaming is not immediately obvious until one considers the physical activities involved in writing to tape. When a tape drive writes, it has to advance the tape to do so. Streaming therefore refers not only to the writing of the data at a particular megabyte per second, but also to moving the tape at a consistent and optimum speed. Thus, a write of 15 MB/s is almost the "human readable" implications of the true tape speed — the number of centimeters per second at which the tape is advanced.

It is also worth noting that tapes are not designed for true random access. Unlike disk, their seek times are measured in human-observable time — i.e., seconds or minutes rather than milliseconds. If data cannot be kept streaming to the tape, then the drive may have to seek back, or come to a halt, which will result in slowdowns, or outright pauses in the backup.

While modern tape drives typically employ a buffer to avoid stopping every time there is a pause in data, there is a fixed size to these buffers, and when a tape drive can no longer keep a tape running at its full streaming speed, it typically starts shoe-shining. This refers to having to stop the tape, wind back, wait for the next piece of data to arrive, and start again. If this happens frequently, it has a similar effect on the heads of the tape as one might experience having a manual shoe-shining operation done —hence, the term.

The net result is that if a tape drive is considered to stream at, say, x MB/s, and only $x - y$ MB/s is supplied, then typically less than $x - y$ MB/s is written; indeed, we might say that $x - y - z$ MB/s is written, where z is the lag introduced by overheads associated with stop/start (seek) operations. (In practical terms, this might mean that if, say, only 8 MB/s is capable of being sent to an Ultrium 1 tape drive, it may only write 7 MB/s. This doesn't mean that data is lost, it simply means that the shoe-shining of the tape becomes the bottleneck over and above whatever other factors have resulted in slower throughput.)

Some modern tape drives take the approach of performing "speed-stepping" — that is, either at a firmware or a configuration level, they can be scaled down to a lower streaming speed to avoid shoe-shining (e.g., they might be able to run at 50 percent, 75 percent or 100 percent of their rated

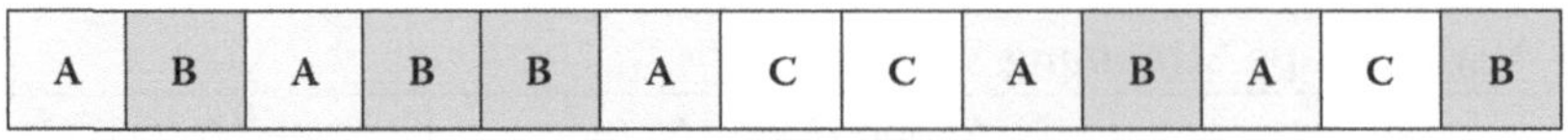

Figure 6.8 Logical representation of part of a multiplexed tape

speed.) Although this can be an improvement, it should be seen as a workaround, not the actual solution. That is, even if the tape drive is able to step down to a lower streaming speed, there is still a performance problem in the environment that needs to be addressed.

The ultimate goal of media multiplexing is to keep enough streams of data running to the tape drive so that it will not shoe-shine. Consider again LTO Ultrium 1. With a native speed of 15 MB/s, a single client connected to a 100-megabit network will never be able to keep the tape drive streaming — the network is simply not capable of it. However, if the backup server were directly connected to a gigabit backbone, and 100-megabit switches the clients were plugged into were uplinked to that backbone, it would be possible instead to use two clients from different 100-megabit switches to keep the tape drive streaming.

A segment of a multiplexed tape (at the logical level) might look like Figure 6.8.* Consider the figure where:

A: Host = belle, Filesystem = /Users/preston
B: Host = ajax, Filesystem = /home
C: Host = shrike, Filesystem = C:\

In this case, it is conceivable that three clients had to be used to perform three-way multiplexing to the device to keep the tape streaming. We can infer that while both belle and ajax were able to stream data relatively efficiently, shrike for some reason was not able to — it may have been doing more-intensive overnight processing, or it may simply have been connected over a slower network interface.

It is this style of performance issue that device/media multiplexing is designed to provide a workaround for — keeping media streaming. The net result is that, with device and media multiplexing, there is significantly less risk that the speed of a backup will be limited to the speed of the slowest client.

Device-level multiplexing can be absolutely necessary to achieve high-speed backups, depending on the environment and available equipment, but it can have a deleterious effect on the most important component of backup — the recovery.

Consider again the example of our multiplexed tape. Depending on what size each chunk of data is on the tape, individual file recovery may be relatively unaffected by the multiplexing. However, let's examine what would be required to read, say, the entire client belle /Users/preston filesystem from the tape. This would result in:

- Read first chunk of A
- Depending on chunk size, seek forward or read through and ignore the first chunk of B
- Read second chunk of A
- Depending on chunk size, seek forward or read through and ignore the next two chunks of B

* This is not designed to be analogous to any particular backup product, as each product that implements multiplexing has its own way of going about it.

- Read third chunk of A
- Depending on chunk size, seek forward or read through and ignore the first chunk of C
- Read fourth chunk of A

and so on.

Depending on the fragmentation level that has occurred on tape due to multiplexing, large-scale recoveries can in fact take significantly longer than a simple end-to-end read of the tape. As such, it is important to consider and test the effects of media multiplexing on recovery performance.

If looking for a rule of thumb for media multiplexing for backup performance, aim to have the sum of all media multiplexing values to be equal to the server multiplexing setting. If backups must be recovered as fast as possible, the aim instead should be to avoid media multiplexing, enabling single contiguous reading of media.

This is one of our first prime examples of the contradictory nature of designing for backup performance versus recovery performance.

When multiplexing to disk backup devices or VTL, the multiplexing values usually do not affect even large recoveries, because disk seek operations are orders of magnitude faster than tape seek operations, and disks are designed for this type of random access.

6.2.1.2 NDMP

Network Data Management Protocol was developed/introduced to facilitate the backup of network appliances (typically NAS hosts) without a conventional operating system on them — i.e., that do not support the installation of a traditional backup agent. Depending on the NDMP capabilities of a backup product, however, it may also refer to Never Does Much Protection. Because NDMP has been an evolving protocol, the level of protection and interaction offered by NDMP is directly affected by the version available to the NDMP device and the backup software deployed. Using NDMP also requires considerable cooperation between the storage team responsible for the appliance and the backup team, due to the risk of upgrades to either product altering or even breaking NDMP functionality.

NAS hosts are fantastic for organizations that want or need to absolutely minimize the amount of management involved in shared storage, as typically configuring all of the following activities are quite simple:

- Adding a new share
- Allowing multiple hosts to concurrently read/write a share
- Allowing multiple operating system types to concurrently read/write a share

Typically, all this occurs without any outage required, even if the host has not previously accessed the NAS appliance. In comparison, adding a new host to a SAN will require zoning changes, an outage to add fiber Host Bus Adapters (HBAs), driver installation, and SAN-level configuration to grant access to logical unit numbers (LUNs) — as well as possibly another host reboot to allow the newly presented LUNs to be visible (depending on the operating system).

However, returning to the NAS, as a wise man once said, there's no such thing as a free lunch. The day-to-day management simplicity offered by NAS comes at a price. The cost of NDMP is felt in the field of backup and recovery; therefore when considering NDMP from a recovery perspective, there is some justification in suggesting it can create headaches that outweigh some or many of the perceived benefits.

Although NDMP devices are typically capable of backing up their own data to directly attached (or SAN-attached) tape drives without any further intervention, the goal of NDMP is to be able to integrate into enterprise-class backup products. Thus, a typical NDMP backup should consist of:

- Backup server determines that NDMP-capable host *X* needs to perform a backup.
- Backup server loads a tape into a particular drive that *X* can access.
- Backup server instructs host *X* to write a backup to the tape in the given drive.
- Host *X* writes an NDMP backup to the available tape.

The differences between regular backups and NDMP backups are quite significant:

- The enterprise-class backup software typically does not "understand" the NDMP data.
- NDMP backups can't be recovered to regular hosts (i.e., they need to be recovered back to another NDMP host).
- NDMP backups typically can't be recovered by another type of NDMP host — e.g., a NetApp Filer can't recover an EMC NAS NDMP backup, and vice versa.
- Depending on the version, NDMP may not support multiplexing, resulting in a "one filesystem at a time to one device at a time" backup scenario, which may actually stretch the backup window.

Additionally, depending on the "age" of the NDMP implementation (in the NAS device or the backup software), other limitations may occur, particularly with respect to the placement of backup devices in the environment. Common restrictions depending on the version of NDMP have included the following:

- Tape devices had to be locally attached to the NDMP host.
- Tape devices could be attached to another NDMP host, but only of the same type.
- Tape devices had to be statically mapped — i.e., they could not be dynamically shared between NDMP and non-NDMP hosts.
- Once NDMP backups have been written to a tape, the tape could not be used for regular backups, and vice versa; this could create somewhat artificial sizing requirements in a tape library.
- NDMP backup indices may not be properly maintained by the backup product, resulting in the need to manage dependencies manually, etc.
- NDMP hosts may have artificial limitations placed on a restore — e.g., "if more than 10,000 files need to be restored, the entire filesystem must be restored or the restore must be run multiple times selecting at most 10,000 files per restore operation."

It cannot be overemphasized that the key limitation introduced by NDMP is the need to retain the NDMP device (or a compatible one) for the duration of the backups performed. Because NDMP vendors typically do not support each other, using NDMP for long-term backups does effectively represent a form of vendor lock-in. Even if this is deemed acceptable, it must be kept in mind.

6.2.2 Backup Efficiency

Although it would be pleasant to assume that there will always be sufficient bandwidth for a backup, there are situations where bandwidth is at a premium. This typically occurs in any of the following situations:

- Satellite offices with servers or critical data — these environments may have a moderate bandwidth connection to the head office, but bandwidth is measured in kilobytes per second or small amounts of megabytes per second, rather than LAN or even half-LAN speeds.
- Dial-up situations for consultants, sales people, and executives on the road — in a worst-case scenario this may literally be modem connectivity and bandwidth, though of late a reasonable DSL connection can often be assumed; again, however, the available bandwidth will be considerably less than would be required for a traditional backup.
- Slower-speed NICs may be present in older servers whose business functions cannot be migrated to a newer type of host. For instance, it is not unheard of to still find a 10-megabit machine whose functions cannot be transferred to a faster machine.

In each of these cases, one or more of the following may be available as a potential backup performance option.

6.2.2.1 Client-Side Compression

All enterprise tape drives support hardware compression, which typically occurs without prompting from the administrator. For this reason in most cases client-side compression is seen as unnecessary — particularly in light of the fact that attempting to compress a previously compressed file will (1) slow down the backup, and (2) potentially result in a larger amount of data backed up than the resulting file from the first compression.*

However, client-side compression may still be needed occasionally. With client-side compression, the backup agent on the client compresses the data before it is sent to the backup server or the nominated storage node/media server. Although this can reduce the amount of data the client actually sends over the network, it does have several downsides, with the most notable detriments being

- Backup has a much-higher CPU and memory impact on the client.
- Software-compressed data is more susceptible to media read failures; that is, decompressing a file may require access to the entire file. If hardware compression is used and a portion of the tape is damaged, the tape drive may be able to supply the data "around" the damaged portion, allowing partial file reconstruction. However, software compression may require the entire file for any form of decompression to occur.
- The data sent to the backup server may come in at a slower rate due to compression. This can result in or exacerbate shoe-shining.

* This can easily be demonstrated. Create a compressed archive of several files using maximum compression. Then, make a compressed archive of the compressed archive, again using maximum compression. The second archive is likely to be larger (even slightly) than the first archive.

6.2.2.2 Bandwidth Limiting

Bandwidth limiting refers to setting a maximum transfer speed per second (or percentage of available link speed used per second) for the purposes of the backup. With the exception of those products specifically designed to back up hosts over poor speed connections (e.g., temporary dial-up lines, etc.), few products support this feature.

If it is required to offer backup services for remote clients such as on-the-road laptops, it will be necessary to consider products that allow for bandwidth limiting. This avoids the inevitable user backlash in the event of them connecting in a hotel of an evening and being unable to use their link to the office for the first hour while files are transferred at full connection speed.

Depending on the requirements, if the product itself doesn't support bandwidth limiting, it may be that routers or switches can be configured to limit usage based on the TCP/IP ports the communications occur over.

6.2.2.3 File Consolidation

Often a feature more to be found in workgroup and laptop backup products as opposed to enterprise backup products, file consolidation refers to the backup product "understanding" that replicated files only need to be backed up once. In organizations or situations where backup efficiency (most notable tape capacity utilization or overall bandwidth reduction) is considered to be of more importance than backup performance, file consolidation becomes a valuable tool. Although there would be considerable benefit for many companies if this feature were present in enterprise-class backup software, it has been mostly ignored as a software option by most enterprise backup vendors to date. Only recently (circa 2006 onwards) has there been major investment by enterprise backup software in this arena.

Consider an example environment consisting of 50 laptops, each with SuSE Linux Professional installed on them. A typical operating system install including office applications, Web browsers, etc., might take between 2 GB and 6 GB depending on the package solution.

Assuming an average, we might have a situation with 50 laptops each having approximately 4 GB of space occupied by the same operating system binaries, the same application binaries, etc. Using a conventional backup system, a full backup of these 50 laptops will occupy 200 GB. This to some represents considerable wastage. It may be for instance that 95 percent of the files in that 4 GB of space per laptop are common to one another, leaving only 5 percent of the non-user data files on each laptop being unique.

Using file consolidation, the backup could be reduced from 200 GB to:

$$1 \times (4\text{ GB} \times 95\%) + 50 \times (4\text{ GB} \times 5\%)$$

Instead of a 200-GB backup, at this point we have 13.8 GB backed up, which represents a space saving of almost 15:1. This for instance gives us considerably more scope for a longer retention time due to the more efficient use of media. (Indeed, many companies would revisit decisions not to backup laptops or desktops if file consolidation were available in their deployed software.)

As a further example, consider a scenario where a proposal document is shared among multiple staff; although some staff may make edits to the document, others may simply store a copy of the document for review later. In this case with file level consolidation, only those copies of the document that are altered (along with one original copy) need to be backed up.

In Figure 6.9, the copies stored by Tim and Jill are modified, whereas the original copy and the copy stored by Gary are both the same; as such, the only backup that needs to be performed for Gary's document is a reference to it existing; the actual data used to restore this if necessary will be the data saved for the original file.

This space saving does not come without an impact. It is entirely possible after all to have two systems which:

- Have two or more files with the same name, but completely different content and size
- Have two files with the same name and the same size, but different content
- Have two files with the same content, but different names

Therefore the only way file-consolidation backups can safely and efficiently occur is via checksum calculations. A checksum is where a "unique" (or sufficiently unique) number or string is generated based on a computation on the data content of the file. (The filename is irrelevant.) If two files have the same checksum, then they are considered to have the same content. If the checksums are different, the files are considered to be different. (An example of such a checksum is the md5 algorithm.)

As such, file consolidation requires potentially two reads per file — the first read to calculate the checksum, and the second read to send the file to the backup server/device in the event of it not having a matching checksum. The backup process becomes

- Read the file, calculating checksum.
- Confirm whether the calculated checksum exists in the checksum database (typically held on the backup server).
- If the checksum already exists, note reference to the checksum for recovery purposes, back up metadata and move on to the next file.
- If the checksum does not exist, add it to the database, and back the file up before moving on to the next file.

Note that even if a file is determined not to require backup in itself, there are likely to be attributes for the file still requiring backup; this would include the owner user, the last open date, the location of the file on the filesystem, etc. (Obviously the file just can't be sent to the backup server as part of the first read of the checksum calculation, as the goal is to reduce the overall bandwidth used.)

In a predominantly small-file environment, the double-read of a file may not represent a significant cost. Although the CPU computation time for the checksum remains a factor, given that most modern operating systems perform caching in spare memory of recently read files, it can often be assumed that the second read will come from cache rather than needing a second physical read from disk. However, in environments where the files are larger, or where clients are simultaneously performing significant processing activities during the backup, the file cache may be insignificant for the task, requiring a second physical read.

Between checksum calculations and double-reads of files, file-consolidation techniques can have a tangible impact on the performance of the backup in all but the smallest of environments. As such, these backups are usually deployed in organizations or situations that match one of the following: (1) small organizations where tape or other removable media usage must be minimized for cost considerations, and (2) situations where actual network bandwidth available for the backup is at an absolute premium — for example, laptop backups over dial-up connections, and

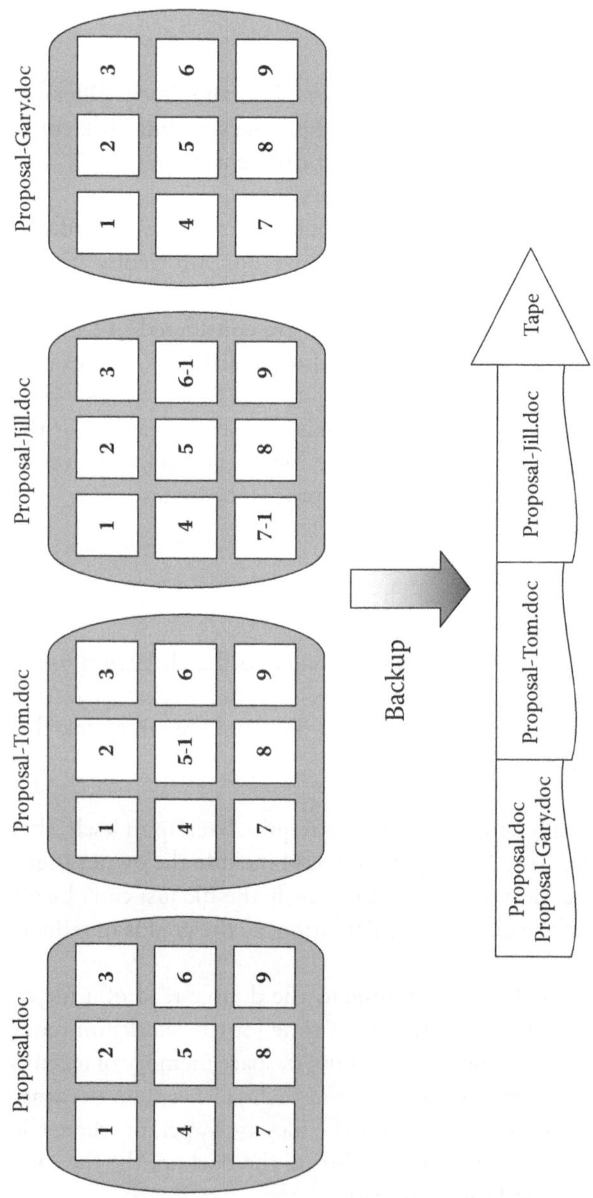

Figure 6.9 File-consolidation backups

in certain remote or satellite office situations. Thus, the overall aim is to reduce the amount of data transferred across the network or going to backup media across all hosts. For many smaller companies, the cost in time will be acceptable when evaluated against the backup efficiency. For larger companies, however, where backup windows are smaller and performance is a higher requirement, this cost in time may eliminate file consolidation from being an option. (It should be noted that this does not excuse enterprise backup software vendors who have been lax in incorporating such feature sets into their products that could be enabled as an additional option.)

6.2.2.4 Block-Level Backup

Although not supported by all software and systems, several enterprise-class backup products do offer support for block-level backups. These backups offer both increased backup performance and increased backup efficiency, but that can come at a cost of recovery performance, as we will see shortly.

To understand a block-level backup, it is first necessary to revisit the relationship between filesystems and blocks.

Almost all filesystems are formatted with a particular block size, which refers to the "default" storage unit for the filesystem. For example, a larger filesystem might be formatted with an 8-KB block size. This means that chunks of space are allocated in multiples of 8 KB by the system. (Some filesystems circumvent blocking by making use of extents, but this is outside the scope of this book. However, even if extents are used, comparable problems as per block-based filesystems will still exist at backup.)

Using block-based filesystems, files will occupy one or more blocks. Using our 8-KB block size above, a 3-KB file for instance will still take up an entire 8-KB block, and a 31-KB file will take up 4 blocks. A 2-GB file would take up 262,144 blocks in an 8-KB blocking scheme.

In a conventional file-based backup, the backup agent will walk through the filesystem, stepping into each directory, reading the required files and progressing on to the next directory until the filesystem has been completely processed.

Conversely, a block-level backup merely reads the individual blocks on the disk in order and transfers them to the backup media. Because it is necessary to be able to conduct file-level restores, block-level backups will have two components: (1) the backup of the blocks containing the data, and (2) the metadata providing a link between the blocks and the files.

We can represent the first component of a block-level backup as shown in Figure 6.10. Although we have a series of files on the host filesystem, for the purpose of the backup all that will be written is a sequential series of blocks, effectively eliminating any filesystem performance factors from the transfer to media. That is, rather than the tape containing "File1 … File2 … File3 … File4 … File5," the tape instead contains "Block 1 … Block 2 … Block 3 … through to … Block 24."

This can result in a very efficient backup, both for fulls and incrementals. In comparison to full filesystem backups, this avoids the need to walk the filesystem tree, which can eliminate a significant portion of the backup overhead. (This is covered in more detail in section 6.3.2, "Client Performance Analysis.") Note that incremental backups might be achieved either by scanning through and looking for changed blocks or, if a kernel-level agent is installed, by maintaining a bitmap of blocks that have changed since the last backup. In either case, the backup is still much faster without filesystem constraints.

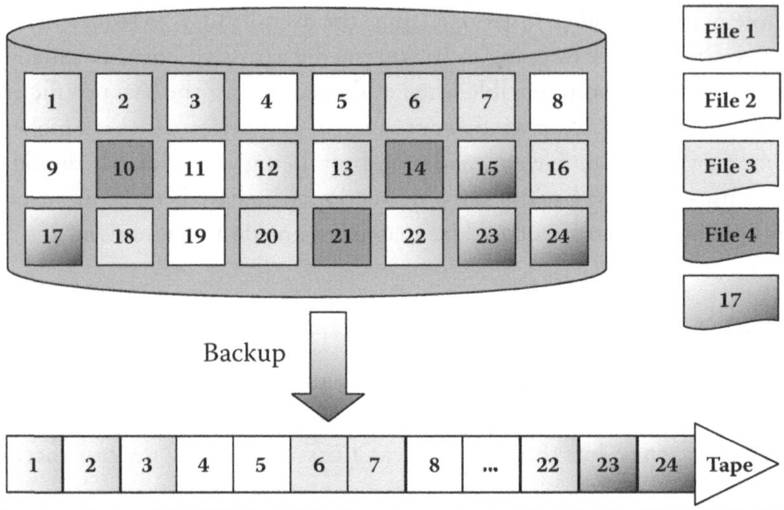

Figure 6.10 Block-level backup

Block-level backups work best for recovery when an entire filesystem must be recovered to a disk of equal or greater size than the original. In this case, a complete block-level restore of a filesystem should only take as long as it took to generate the backup in the first place.

Unfortunately, the cost of block-level backups is the file-based recovery performance, and the recovery cost increases significantly depending on the fragmentation and size of the original file. As the backups are performed at a block level, the only way to accomplish file level recoveries is to use a cache (see Figure 6.11).

When a file level recovery is performed, all the blocks that comprised the file are first recovered into the cache. Next, they are reassembled into the cache as a real file, before being copied across to the intended recovery location. Remembering that we must read the blocks back from the backup media to reconstruct the file, the time taken to recover the file is directly related to the size of the file (as it is for a regular filesystem backup) and the fragmentation level of the file. That is, if all the blocks that the file is stored in are not contiguous, the file recovery will take longer. Consider for instance our previous example of a 2-GB file consisting of 8-KB blocks. To recover this file from a

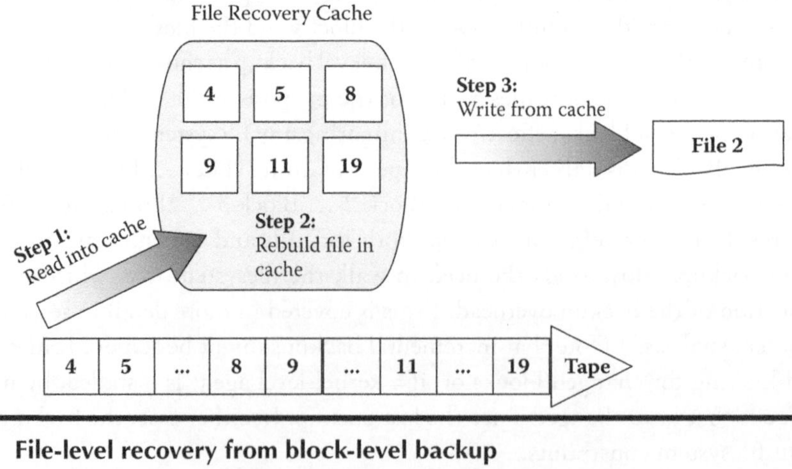

Figure 6.11 File-level recovery from block-level backup

block-level backup, 262,144 blocks will need to be retrieved into the cache before the file can even be reassembled in its correct order. As the fragmentation level of the file increases, the amount of data that must either be read or scanned past to recover all its constituent blocks will increase. If the file in this case belonged to a 200-GB filesystem, and due to fragmentation the file was spread over a range of 20 percent of the filesystem, this would necessitate reading or scanning through 40 GB of data just to recover a 2-GB file.

It is somewhat ironic that while block-level backups were designed to solve dense filesystem backup issues and thus allow high-speed backup of fileservers, they can result in tediously slow recoveries for even relatively small amounts of data!

Examples can get worse when we consider multiple file recoveries or very large file recoveries. Caches must use tangible disk space, and that space is going to be at a premium. If the block-level backup system provides, say, 10 GB of cache for file-level recovery, it means that every time more than 10 GB of files are to be recovered, there may be multiple media scans. If it is necessary for instance in this scenario to recover 15 GB in files, at least two passes will need to be made over the requisite media. The first pass might retrieve up to 10 GB of block-level data. Following the cache reaching or nearing capacity, the block-level agent would need to reconstruct the files that it has recovered the blocks for. The reconstructed blocks would then be discarded from cache, and the remaining blocks would be read in before another file reconstruction occurs. Although this is certainly better than the worst-case scenario — a tape scan per file (possible if storing very large files, and every file which is to be restored is as large or larger than the cache) — it can still result in multiple passes over the backup media to recover a relatively small amount of data. As such, the decision to implement block-level backups must be weighed up against the styles of recovery that will be required in an environment.

When considered for backup performance, block-level backups are primarily used to eliminate issues created by dense or ultra-dense filesystems that traditional backups cannot resolve.

Moving on to backup efficiency, block-level backups assist in reducing the size of incremental backups for files on a client. Bandwidth efficient block-level backups leverage not only savings through the backup of dense filesystems, but depending on the integration with products, can also result in considerably smaller backups when dealing with large files that have minor changes. For instance, consider Microsoft Outlook .pst files. These are local mailbox stores for a user in an Exchange environment. These files may grow to several gigabytes in size for many users, and a traditional filesystem incremental backup would need to back up the entire file, even if only a single message has been received, or worse, marked as read.

When implemented for efficiency, block-level backups are typically designed to work on regular files and specific database formats. Laptop backup products for instance typically support Outlook and Notes database files, but don't provide guarantees for other database files that may reside on a machine.

In these cases, bandwidth-efficient block-level backups would only transfer the individual blocks within the files that have changed — thereby making it entirely feasible for instance to perform incremental backups of a machine via a dial-up link.

6.2.2.5 Data Deduplication

Some backup systems that offer data consolidation perform that consolidation not at the file level, but at the block level. This may be either fixed block-size deduplication, or variable block-size deduplication. (Unlike our previous discussion on block-level backups, the blocks referred to in data deduplication are typically not as small as individual disk blocks due to practicality considerations.)

As previously discussed with file deduplication, there can be considerable amounts of duplicated files throughout a corporate network. However, this duplication does not just apply to individual files, but can be extended to apply to blocks within files.

For example, consider the following work process:

- Lynne writes a proposal outlining a new market the company could enter into, and e-mails it to the 20 colleagues in her team for peer review.
- Some of her team members make modifications to the document and e-mail it back to Lynne so that she can integrate the changes she wants.
- Having completed the proposal, Lynne forwards it to her boss, Laura, for review.
- Laura updates the document, making changes, then forwards it on to her immediate boss, Peter.
- Peter reviews the document, making changes, then forwards it to the rest of the management team for review.
- The other 30 managers in the organization review the document, suggest changes, which Peter passes back to Lynne via Laura.
- Lynne produces the final document, which is then forwarded to the board of directors for consideration.

This style of collaborative review, editing, and updating of documents within an organization is quite common, and leads to significant data duplication.

In the example above, there may be 60 or more copies of the document stored throughout the organization. Although some copies may end up having no changes, others will end up being slightly different. Based on traditional file consolidation through checksum analysis, each file with even a single letter changed will be different, and therefore must be backed up separately.

However, when considered at a block level, each file may have significant amounts of data duplication. If on average just one paragraph is changed in each file, this may result in less than 1 KB of variance between each file and its predecessor or sibling document.

Using our example diagram from file-level consolidation (Figure 6.9), we might instead see a backup process such as shown in Figure 6.12. In this case, most of the contents of each file are the same, and only require one backup; by contrast, Figure 6.9 shows that only three blocks of data on top of the original nine need further backup. When considered at a larger filesystem level, or even across an entire network, data deduplication does have the ability to reduce significantly the amount of data to be sent from the client to the backup server.

When discussing file-consolidation backups, it was explained that the consolidation occurs at the cost of needing to perform a checksum of each file for accurate data comparison. For data deduplication backups, the cost is an even higher one — a checksum must be made of each block within each file to determine whether it is a duplicate or a new piece of data that needs to be added to the backup. This checksum consolidation/deduplication is very processor intensive, and as such, data deduplication backup environments typically will not demonstrate high megabyte per second throughput, either at backup or recovery — in such environments, efficiency is king.

As may be imagined, although data deduplication systems can result in phenomenal space savings, it can result in a significantly slower backup if a traditional schedule is used (e.g., full weekly, incrementals daily). As a result of this, data deduplication backups usually offer the option of "full once, incrementals forever," and in this case such a schedule style is appropriate. As blocks age

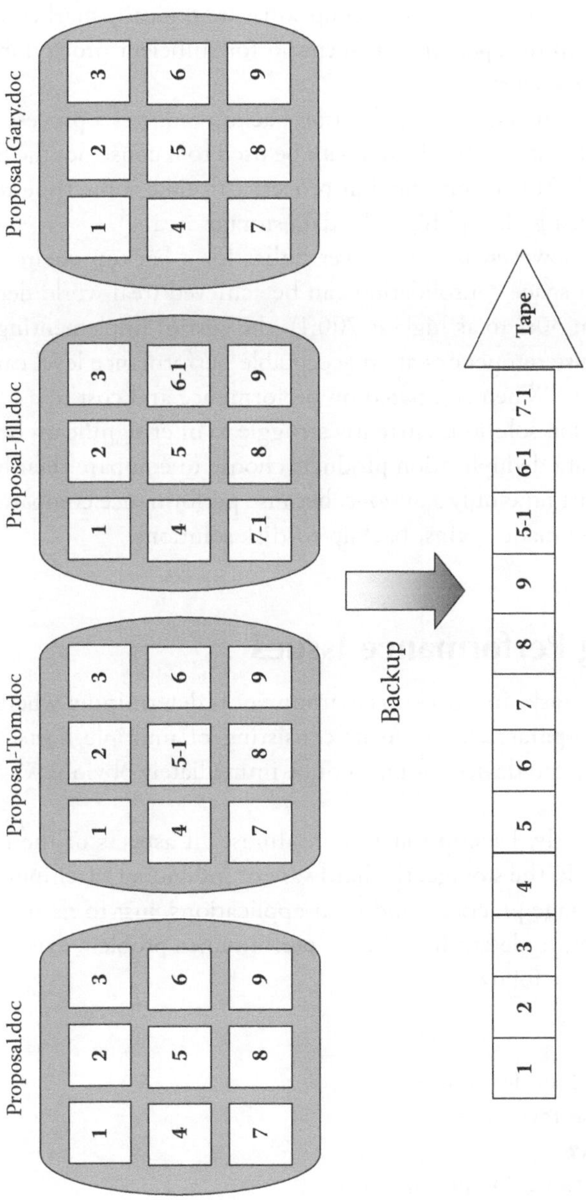

Figure 6.12 Data deduplication backup occurring at a block level

and are no longer required for the recovery of any file being protected, they can be automatically removed from the backup cache. Although the first full backup may take a considerable period of time (possibly several days depending on the system, or even more than a week), all subsequent backups will typically be fast, as only files that have altered on disk will need their blocks evaluated for protection.

Vendors who offer data deduplication backup software typically market it as a means of completely eliminating backup to tape. (In this scenario for sufficient protection it is necessary that backups be replicated between sites.)

Reconstructing files from a data deduplication backup requires a process similar to that done in block-level backups; that is, the blocks that can be used to reconstruct the files must be collated into a cache for retrieval. This reconstruction process can take some time to complete, because each individual block must be found from the data storage area.

Data deduplication, however, is not a silver bullet for a backup environment. Even in sites where very high levels of space consolidation can be achieved (real-world deployments have seen savings of anything from 30:1 to as high as 700:1), the cost of implementing data deduplication in such a way that the system operates at an acceptable performance level can easily rival that of a traditional tape solution. When compared on performance and cost to a tape-and-disk backup solution, data deduplication solutions currently struggle to offer significant benefits. Indeed, most organizations that sell data deduplication products choose to compare their backup and recovery performance solely against tape-only solutions, because performance comparisons become significantly less favorable when made against backup-to-disk solutions.

6.3 Diagnosing Performance Issues

One of the less-enjoyable tasks in a backup environment is determining where performance problems are rooted. In a disparate environment consisting of multiple hosts, switches, filesystem types, operating systems, and devices, it may not be immediately obvious why performance issues are occurring.

As mentioned previously, backup touches on almost all aspects of the infrastructure for an organization. The network, the storage, the hardware of individual machines, their operating systems, filesystems, file storage practices, and their applications, just to name a few, all impact the backup system. Therefore, to determine where a performance problem exists, it may be necessary to examine any or all of the following:

- Network
- Client hardware/OS performance
- Client filesystem performance
- Device performance
- Backup server hardware/OS performance

6.3.1 Network Performance Analysis

Unless a problem is clearly identifiable as originating elsewhere, network analysis is always a good, first starting point to diagnose performance problems. The sheer number of times that backup performance issues come back to network issues is staggering, even in larger, more-controlled environments.

Network analysis is frequently skipped during performance diagnosis, usually for one of the following four reasons:

1. It is forgotten.
2. It is assumed that the network and its settings are not subject to change.
3. It is assumed that someone else is keeping an eye on the network.
4. It is assumed that network issues will also manifest outside of backups, and therefore don't need to be checked.

6.3.1.1 Ping Test

This is a simple test that is assumed to have relevance only in checking connectivity issues. This simply has a series of pings performed between the backup server and client (and vice versa) to ensure that no packets are being dropped.

In anything other than a WAN-connected or firewalled network, it should be possible to perform hundreds of pings between two hosts without dropping any packets. Assuming LAN-connected clients without firewalls, etc., it should be possible to have a client ping a server at least 100 times (and vice versa) without any packets dropped. If any packets are dropped, it may be indicative of flaky hardware or configuration problems at the network layer that will, under heavy load, either fail completely or result in poor performance. The occasional dropped packet may have negligible impact on random/intermittent access, but can have a substantial impact on large, sustained transfers.

6.3.1.2 Speed and Duplexing

If a ping test exits without fault, the speed and duplex settings of the client, server, storage node/media server used, and intermediary switches should be checked. Make sure that all of the following questions can be answered in the affirmative:

- Is the client NIC hard-set to the full speed of the network?
- Is the client network switch port hard-set to the full speed of the network?
- Is the backup server NIC hard-set to the full speed of the network?
- If a storage node/media server is in use, is its NIC hard-set to the full speed of the network?
- Is autonegotiate turned off at all locations (primarily Ethernet and fast Ethernet locations)?
- Is full-duplex turned on at all locations?

Note that in each case the question starts with is, not has. When diagnosing performance problems, never assume these settings are unchanged — particularly if multiple people have access to the environment. This of course doesn't mean that someone is maliciously going to change the configuration, but for some operating systems it is relatively easy to change a setting accidentally while reviewing the configuration.

A common misconfiguration in environments (particularly those that have grown from unmanaged to managed switches) is the proliferation of autonegotiate. Autonegotiate for Ethernet

(10 megabit) and fast Ethernet (100 megabit) is really designed for desktop connectivity so as to reduce administrative headaches. It has no place in a backup environment. For Ethernet and fast Ethernet, autonegotiate can reduce the rated transfer speed between hosts by up to half of the rated speed.

6.3.1.3 File Transfer Test

Often directly related to speed and duplex settings, the file transfer test is used to confirm that data can be sent directly between the client and its server at a speed that is as close to the full rated network speed as possible.

To conduct this test properly, assemble large files that can be transferred between the client and the server. Optimally, the area of disk that is to be read-from on the source, and written-to on the destination, should both be relatively unfragmented.

If there is a choice of protocol, use FTP to perform the transfer before using another protocol such as SMB or NFS. FTP is an efficient file transfer protocol that introduces little data overhead. Both SMB and NFS introduce additional overhead that can skew the results. If these protocols must be used, restrict tests to very large files to mitigate the overhead as much as possible. Note that tools that employ compression or encryption (such as secure copy — scp) should definitely not be used for this style of test.

The minimum file size for these transfer tests should be a size that exceeds the amount of RAM on either the source or the destination host. If this is not possible, then the minimum useful file sizes are 1–2 GB; anything smaller than this and the file size is of no benefit to the testing.

In a 100-megabit environment, FTP should transfer at approximately 9.5–9.9 MB/s, allowing for overheads from the TCP/IP protocol. So long as the network is not the bottleneck, a 2-GB file should take, at 9.5 MB/s throughput, 215 seconds, or 3.6 minutes to transfer from one machine to another. (Revisiting autonegotiate, it would not be uncommon to see an FTP test of the same file, with autonegotiate turned on, peak at a performance of around 6–6.5 MB/s.)

6.3.1.4 Name Resolution Response Times

Often not considered, the speed at which the backup server and clients can resolve hosts in the environment can have a significant impact on the performance of the backup environment. At the point where a backup server attempts to resolve a client hostname, it may execute a blocking call to the OS, ceasing further activity on a multiplexing stream until the name is resolved. If name servers in an environment are misconfigured, and periodically suffer timeouts, or need to bounce resolution requests from one server to another, this can result in unexpectedly poor backup activities, timeouts, or even failures.

A good test mechanism is to maintain a batch or shell script on the backup server that contains a name resolution command for each active client in the configuration, performing at minimum:

- Forward resolution on the simple hostname
- Forward resolution on the fully qualified domain name
- Reverse lookup on the client's IP address

When run, the script should execute with no pauses or delays, seamlessly cycling through all the tests for the configured hosts. If delays occur, there are likely to be issues when it comes time to perform backups. (Additionally, no contradictory results should be returned.)

6.3.2 *Client Performance Analysis*

6.3.2.1 *Hardware*

To confirm whether client hardware is limiting backup performance, the following must be checked

- Are the multiplexing settings for the client set in such a way that they conflict with the layout of filesystems on disks, thereby causing thrashing during the backup process?
- If a client is backing up to locally attached tape (direct or SAN), confirm that media block sizes are configured in such a way as to get the best throughput, remembering to balance against compatibility requirements from other systems. (For example, in a SAN environment with dynamically shared tape drives, all hosts typically need to write to tape with the same block size settings, or be configured such that hosts with different block size settings do not attempt to access media written with a higher block size.)
- Monitor CPU, RAM, and network performance during backup operations. This should not be a one-off activity, but maintained for at least as long as the shortest backup cycle. That is, if performing a full backup once per week, with daily incrementals, then monitoring should be maintained for at least a week — preferably longer in case there were individual discrepancies. The key factor to watch for is whether any ebbs or other issues in backup performance correlate with spikes in CPU/RAM utilization or other activities occurring on the host. Also, the network throughput experienced during backup should be checked against the throughput going to the backup media — particularly if no other operations are occurring for the client.

6.3.2.2 *Filesystem*

Filesystem performance analysis is usually the next logical step to perform after file transfer tests have been completed satisfactorily. When file transfer tests were previously discussed, it was from the viewpoint of transferring small numbers of very large files. Those transfers are specifically designed to ensure that the network connectivity between the client and the backup server is sufficient for backup purposes, but usually serve little practical use when evaluating filesystem performance. The filesystem layout and content can be critical bottlenecks in the backup process, and must be evaluated separately to large file transfers.

> **Large File Transfers Are Only One Half of Throughput Tests.** A customer once ran preparatory testing of file transfers between a backup server connected to a gigabit backbone and several 100-megabit clients. It was reported that each client could transfer data between hosts at the full rated network speed, with the backup server able to receive all transfers simultaneously without noticeable performance impact.

When the backup software was installed and performance tests started, however, no individual client could backup faster than 5 MB/s, and some clients experienced data transfer speeds as low as 2 MB/s.

Testing showed that while the FTP tests passed with flying colors, each machine had a large number of files and (where it could be tested), a reasonably high fragmentation level on the filesystems, i.e., the FTP tests had verified the "raw" transfer speed, but did not factor in the filesystem.

One of the more interesting problems that has plagued operating system vendors for some time is dense filesystem performance. The point at which a filesystem is considered to be dense is somewhat fuzzy, but typically it is indicative of a very large number of small files, potentially spread across a very broad or very deep filesystem. Following are examples of what might constitute a dense filesystem:

- A 400-GB filesystem with 20,000,000 files
- A 1-GB filesystem with 500,000 files
- A filesystem with, say, 500,000 files stored in very few directories.

Regardless of the above examples, the best way of defining a dense filesystem is that it is one where the cost (in time) of walking the filesystem significantly slows the process of doing a sequential read of the files encountered. This cost is often not considered when diagnosing backup performance issues.

An in-depth analysis of the cause of dense filesystems and poor performance is well beyond the scope of this book, but the following summary should be sufficient for our purposes.

Almost all filesystems are referenced by the operating system via some form of tree data structure. For example, in the simplest form, a very small part of a filesystem might be represented using a tree structure as shown in Figure 6.13. Let's consider based on this model what is referred to by a "filesystem walk," starting at the "/home" directory:

- Backup system enters "/home". Directory listing shows two subdirectories.
- Walk subdirectories.
  - First subdirectory, "preston":
  - Walk subdirectories:
    - First subdirectory, "Technical":
    - Walk subdirectory:
      - Backup file "quantum_encryption.pdf"
      - Backup file "ultrium_4_proposal.pdf"
    - Last file — exit subdirectory.
    - Next subdirectory, "Science"
  - and so on.
  - Second subdirectory, "bob":

and so on.

As can be seen from the above (a very incomplete example), we have a lot of filesystem walking going on that takes real time to complete. Although the time taken to walk the filesystem to reach

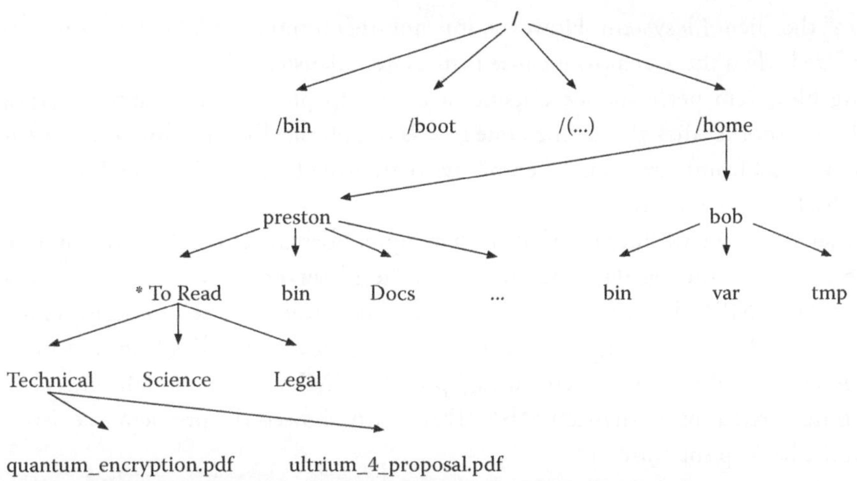

Figure 6.13 Part of a filesystem as represented by a tree data structure

a single file is barely noticeable, backup software works in a completely different way, and thus is affected considerably by filesystem walk times.

> **Watch a Backup at Least Once in Verbose or Debug Mode if the Product Supports It.** If a backup product supports extremely verbose modes or debug modes that show what it is doing on a per-file/directory level, it may be beneficial to perform a backup at least once (even a moderately small/ad-hoc backup) to observe how the backup process works. Obviously, the results will vary depending on what product is used, but it can be tremendously useful to help understand what is involved in the backup product walking a filesystem.
>
> Note that regular backups shouldn't be performed this way — just like quantum physics, where the more closely something is observed, the more the results are skewed, generating significant amounts of debug information for backups will slow the backups down.

Most data structures lend themselves to good performance for one of random or sequential access, but not always both. In this case, making them very suitable for directory structures, trees are optimized for fast, random access along any particular branch. In particular, with a tree, the cost of reaching any leaf (endpoint — file) is on average a small fraction of the total number of nodes in the tree.

However, a sequential walk of the filesystem can have a high cost due to the need to back out of the traversed paths. This is particularly the case if the tree walk is being handled via recursion. As can be expected, a backup can result in a costly tree walk. However, in dense filesystems with small numbers of changes, the cost can be very high, as the time taken to transmit data to the backup server may be considerably less than the time taken to walk the tree.

By comparison, linked lists can have a much higher cost for "random" because accessing any node in the list may result in the traversal of every node in the list. However, linked lists don't suffer from a high walk cost to walk the entire list when evaluating sequential access performance.

There is no doubt whatsoever that different backup products will have varying performance capabilities depending on (1) how well they've been written, and (2) what level they are able to "hook into" the client filesystem. However, it is not uncommon to see performance issues cited as backup-related when the actual root cause is filesystem density.

Testing filesystem performance outside of a backup product is a relatively straightforward activity. Using another disk device (i.e., one that is not physically providing the same filesystem(s) that are to be read from), create an uncompressed archive of a typical subsection of the filesystem for which backups are required.

In one such test, a customer felt that the backup performance of a departmental fileserver was very poor given that during daytime operations the fileserver showed an average read speed of approximately 25 MB/s. During overnight backups, however, the backup performance peaked at a maximum of 5 MB/s. Testing the creation of uncompressed zip files from the fileserver to the backup server resulted in a sustained throughput of 5.5 MB/s, even though individual large files could be transferred at more than 20 MB/s. This clearly showed the problem as existing at a lower level than the backup software.

6.3.2.3 Software

This topic can almost always be reduced to the following statement: configure virus scanners to leave the backup software alone.

There are some software activities that can be considered mutually exclusive to a backup operation. In particular for organizations with Windows environments, this is most noticeable with corporate fileservers and virus scanners.

The default configuration of a virus scanner is to:

- Scan each file as it is accessed to ensure that it is virus free
- Scan incoming data to ensure that it is virus free
- Scan outgoing data to vet it for viruses

Given the high potential for viruses on such systems, this is typically a required activity for user-related access. It should not, however, be required for backup-related access.

For random access by end users, the impact of performing virus-scanning operations is usually barely noticeable. Consider that on a large fileserver with a large number of users, virus scanning will only affect those files being currently accessed, which may be a tiny percentage of the total number of files on the filesystem. However, a backup server will need to read a large number of files on the host (for full backups, this will likely be all files). The small impact caused by the virus scanner during production hours operations becomes a considerable overhead for mass file access.

Almost all virus scanners can be configured to exclude particular processes from scanning on a host. In this case the processes (i.e., executables) associated with the backup software should typically be exempt from virus-scanning activities. In some cases, this has been known to improve the backup performance by a factor of three or more.

Moving beyond virus scanning, if other software running on a machine makes intensive demands during backup, it is usually necessary to look at reducing simultaneous load on the host (through rescheduling backups, implementing serverless backups, etc.), or increasing host performance capacity.

6.3.3 Device Performance Analysis

The ability to perform device performance analysis will vary somewhat based on the operating system in use. Although most backup products come with performance analysis tools, depending on the nature of the issue being encountered it may be necessary to test performance both within and outside of the backup product — at the operating system layer — to determine where an issue lays.

There are several factors that must be considered when evaluating device performance:

- Raw read/write speed — just how many megabytes per second does the backup device offer?
- Load and unload speed (if applicable) — depending on the environment, this may make an impact on the ability of the system to meet the performance requirements.
- Seek speed — as per load and unload speed, this may make an impact on the system to meet performance requirements.
- Optimum block size — is there a recommended IO block size for use on this device?

It is of course important to ensure that the backup devices in use represent a good performance fit for the environment requirements, particularly in hierarchical storage management or mass-recovery environments. In Table 6.1, we examined the streaming performance in megabytes per second for many standard tape backup devices.

Although tape read/write performance is almost always examined, the speeds for load, unload, and tape seek are not always considered or as frequently published. Compare, for instance, Super DLT 220 and STK 9840A series tapes.

On a casual inspection, given that SDLT 220 has a streaming speed of 11 MB/s and the STK 9840A has a streaming speed of 10 MB/s, it might be assumed that the SDLT 220 should "win" in any performance analysis between the two units. However, this depends on the requirements. The average load time on an SDLT 220 tape is around 35 seconds — that is, after a tape has been physically placed in a tape drive (presumably by a robot arm), it takes approximately 35 seconds for the tape to become ready for use by the host. By comparison, the load speed for the STK 9840A series tapes is just four seconds.

For an environment that does few recoveries, the SDLT 220 is the more-likely winner in a performance comparison between the two for any data backup amount past a few gigabytes. However, consider an environment with a large number of recoveries, where the recoveries are usually no more than a gigabyte.

With the faster load time, the STK 9840A tape has 31 seconds of usable time before the SDLT 220 is ready for the first tape positioning command. As races go, this is a bit like the hare and the tortoise. Assuming we start reading from the front of the tape in both cases, at 10 MB/s native read speed, this equates to 310 MB read from the STK 9840A before the SDLT 220 even starts its read.

The "read" times for 1 GB of data, when including the load time, becomes (1) 4 seconds load + 102.4 seconds read for STK 9840A, and (2) 35 seconds load + 93 seconds read for the SDLT 220.

Assuming we're using the same robot mechanism in each place, we can eliminate as equal the time taken by the robot arm to pick a tape and put it in the appropriate drive. This leaves us with a restore time of 106.4 seconds for 1 GB of data from a STK 9840A, or 128 seconds for 1 GB of data from a SDLT 220; this is a restore time difference of 21.6 seconds.

If we factor in unload times, assuming that the drives will be left unoccupied after the restore, the difference increases further. Just another four seconds will be added to the time the STK 9840A is in the tape drive, whereas another 35 seconds will need to be added to the time the SDLT 220 tape is in a drive.

If an environment has few restores (say, a few a week, or even one a day), there would be little reason based on restore performance to pick a lower capacity, lower speed tape.

However, consider an environment with a higher number of restores — say, 20 a day. Alternatively, consider a hierarchical storage management (HSM) environment where there might be hundreds of restores a day. At 20 × 1 GB restores per day, approximately 7.2 minutes of operational time would be lost to SDLT 220's slower load speeds. At 300 × 1 GB restores per day, this represents 108 minutes — or almost two hours — of operational time lost with the implementation of SDLT 220.

Clearly, the first aspect of any device performance analysis is to determine whether the drive is even suitable for its current use. Although 300 restores a day may be more akin to HSM operations, larger sites do make heavy use of recoveries in daily operations.

In backup products that use fixed block sizes for tape operations, picking an optimum block size setting can make a significant impact on the performance of the backups; the usual aim is to have as high a tape block size as possible. By comparison, disks tend to use smaller block sizes to optimize capacity usage of the filesystem — having a smaller block size in filesystems helps to reduce wastage, particularly when high numbers of small files are created. The overhead of reading a large number of blocks is usually not a problem due to the random access capability of disk drives, except in circumstances of high levels of fragmentation.

For tape devices, a small block size can cause serious impacts when it comes to having a high-performance system. Therefore many environments find it necessary to increase the default block size for tape IO activity to achieve higher performance read and write operations. The default block size will actually depend on all of the following:

- Media type
- Vendor of the tape drive
- Operating system type
- Fiber or SCSI host bus adapter type, vendor, and driver

Usually this means that the default block size for tape drives is at the lower end of the spectrum — even on high-performance drives, it is often configured around the 32-KB or 64-KB mark.

Experimenting with higher block sizes for media can result in significant performance increases, but can do so at the risk of compatibility. If, for instance, a SAN shared-tape library is in use, and one operating system has a limit of 64-KB block sizes for tape, then having other operating systems write tapes with 256-KB block sizes may create media errors later.

Altering Tape Block Size Can Affect Recovery

A company deployed a dynamic tape-drive-sharing configuration, which at the time necessitated the installation of a fiber-SCSI bridge for their tape library, and fiber HBAs in their backup server and storage nodes. After approximately 12 months of operation, the redistribution of data in their environment eliminated the need for dynamic drive sharing, so the fiber-SCSI bridge was removed, and a simple library-sharing arrangement was used instead between the backup server and a single storage node. (The server had dedicated access to some of the tape drives, and the remainder were dedicated to the storage node.) This allowed the return to SCSI HBAs. When the first restore was required from data backed up during the period where a fiber-SCSI bridge was used, it was determined that the tapes could not be read in the SCSI environment. The reason was that a block size of 128 KB had been used within the fiber environment, but when the plain SCSI environment was re-established, the only SCSI adapters that could be used had a maximum block size of 64 KB. Although the tape drives themselves had not changed during the entire period, the interfaces created a scenario where data was recoverable only by reverting to a prior hardware configuration.

For the most part, block size settings will be based on a standard binary progression — 32 KB, 64 KB, 128 KB, 256 KB, etc., although some media formats have been known to use more-obscure block-size settings; some vendor variants of DLT 7000, for instance, used a default block size of 96 KB.

Many organizations will achieve sufficient backup and recovery performance using the default IO block size for devices in use, with one notable exception. Regardless of whether the default block size is suitable or not, in a tape-sharing arrangement, where media created on one host might be mounted for use on another host, it will typically be necessary to set the tape IO block size forcibly across all nodes to the same size. This avoids situations where varying block sizes cause media incompatibility issues.

When experimenting with default block size settings, it is important to:

- Know exactly where the block size settings must be made; this will vary depending on the operating system, HBA, and backup product.
- Know whether a reboot or service restart is required after changing the settings.
- Try each block size setting on a brand new, previously unused tape.
- Start with the default block setting and work up, rather than starting at a very high setting.
- If multiple operating systems or multiple host bus adapter controller cards are in use, ensure that data written in one drive is readable in all other drives.
- Test writes in the following sequence:
  - Large, mostly uncompressed data from the host attached to the tape drive. This measures whether the block size change makes a direct impact on sustained write speed to the drive.
  - A large number of small files from the host attached to the tape drive. This determines whether the higher block size works when random IO occurs on the read source. Very large block sizes may work when backing up very large files, but may result in poorer performance if files considerably smaller than the tape block size are the norm, or if shoe-shining is a common factor.
  - Large, mostly uncompressable data from a client of the host attached to the tape drive (i.e., a network transfer). This shows whether the network offers sufficient performance to work with the new block size being used.
  - A large number of small files from a client of the host attached to the tape drive. This checks whether the small file access considerations, as described above, when coupled with a network transfer, work with or against the larger block size.

- Test a read of each of the above types of writes to determine whether the higher block size setting may have an impact on read performance. (If the effect is a negative one — i.e., reads are slower — it may be necessary to work with a smaller block size depending on SLAs in place.)
- Test a read of data written using the previous "default" block size to confirm it is still recoverable. If it is not, confirm there is a valid and non-interruptive recovery mechanism for data. (For example, changing the block size settings back to the prior default when historical recoveries are required may seem like an acceptable solution, but is usually not suitable in practice depending on how busy the backup server is and whether a sufficient number of drives can be made available.)
- If multiple hosts will have write access to the tape, test an append operation from each host to (1) ensure that media is compatible across all hosts with the selected block size and (2) no host demonstrates reduced performance from the increased block size.

To summarize, when evaluating device performance consider the following:

- Are devices appropriate for their use?
- Can each successive component of the environment (interface cards, attached servers, network, end clients, etc.) provide sufficient transfer speed to allow the device to run at full streaming speed?
- Can all devices attached to the system stream concurrently? If not, can settings be established to force as many devices as possible to stream at full speed?
- Does changing the block size setting result in faster write performance? Does it have a positive (or at worst, a neutral) impact on read performance? Are the changed block size settings compatible for all hosts and devices that might access such written tapes?

6.3.4 Backup Server Performance Analysis*

Except in large environments or when using very fast tape devices, CPU capabilities and memory capacity requirements of a backup server should normally be reasonable. The areas that typically affect a backup server and therefore need to be investigated as a result of diagnosing performance issues are

- Backplane speed of the server
- Incoming and outgoing network bandwidth
- Configuration of access to the backup devices

The first mechanism for conforming backup server performance capabilities is to ask whether the server can pass through at minimum the sum of the vendor-rated transfer speed of all the backup devices attached to it simultaneously. Obviously, if an environment has 2 × LTO-3 tape drives attached to it (each with a rated throughput of 80 MB/s native), but only has a single 100-megabit interface, the tape drives cannot be run optimally.

* While this section refers to backup server analysis, it can be equally applied to any machine in a multi-tiered backup environment that would have read/write access to backup devices — i.e., storage nodes or media servers.

Thus the simplest starting point to this analysis is to perform a calculation based on the number of devices in the environment and their combined throughput — both for compressed and non-compressed speeds.

Using our 2 × LTO-3 tape drive example, this means that the backup server must be capable of a sustained throughput of 160 MB/s to keep the tape drives streaming at native speed, but realistically with tape drive compression in use, must actually be able to sustain throughput of 320 MB/s. This information can be used to ensure the system is configured for sufficient performance. For example, in a fiber-channel connected environment we could draw the following conclusions:

- Using 1-gigabit HBAs or switches, 2 HBAs must be used to stream the drives at their native speed of 80 MB/s.
- To run the tape drives with compression — 160 MB/s — each drive will need to be connected via its own dedicated 2-gigabit HBA to a suitable switch, or be connected via a single 4-gigabit HBA/switch.
- It will not be suitable to have disk devices on the same HBAs as the tape drives.

Assuming the server is able to sustain the 320 MB/s output performance to the tape drives being used, the next step is to confirm the network can receive (or sustain) 320 MB/s of incoming data to keep the tape drives running at full speed.

If in a LAN-based environment, this would imply that the backup server will need 4 × 10 gigabit network connections, trunked, or alternatively, 1 × 10 gigabit NIC. Assuming gigabit rather than 10-gigabit network is in use, this would require potentially six occupied expansion slots just for the backup functionality. (Some dual interface cards may be applicable, but these have to be judged against shared access to the same backplane location.)

Although this is a somewhat simplistic example, it is important to understand that the key performance analysis that can be done on the backup server is to determine (based on examples of simple calculations above) that the server has sufficient data throughput capabilities to handle the transfer of data volumes required for streaming performance in the backup or recovery.

Ensuring that there is sufficient performance to achieve media streaming solves a large number of performance factors that might otherwise be investigated individually.

A factor sometimes forgotten is other processing that may be required of the backup server during backups. One of the unfortunate factors of backups being seen as a "secondary" activity in IT is that the backup server can be installed on a host that has other processing requirements — e.g., database, file, and print or Web services.

For smaller organizations where it is not possible to have dedicated servers due to cost constraints, this may have to be accepted as a necessary evil. However, in larger organizations, or organizations where there is a large amount of data to back up, there is no excuse for backup services being piggy-backed onto servers that already have other functions. In this regard, the only performance advice that can be offered is to accept backups as primary functions requiring dedicated servers in all but the smallest of environments.

Once a backup server can stream and is a dedicated host, the main area of outstanding performance issue that can occur relates to the handling of databases associated with the backup — i.e., the indices that hold details of the files that have been backed up for the various clients, and the information regarding the backup media used. If the file indices must be updated in parallel with the backups, they can become a critical bottleneck in the backup process. A server needing to back up 16 or 32 concurrent streams, for instance, will potentially be hampered by needing to update indices for all these streams to a single pair of mirrored disks concurrently.

A common mistake made by companies wishing to "save" on their backup server costs is to deploy a machine with slower hard drives in a software-mirror. Although the machine itself may have the throughput capacity to transfer data from the network to the backup devices in a timely fashion, it may not have sufficient local IO throughput capabilities to maintain index information concurrently to the backup.

Any machine that stores metadata regarding the backup, and most particularly file indices, should have high-speed storage made available for this region. One simple rule of thumb is to ensure that the index regions on backup servers use disks that are at least as fast as any production host they protect. As the number of streams to be backed up concurrently increase, the layout of those backup database/index regions must also adapt — a mirrored pair of disks may be fast enough for a small number of streams, but if this becomes a bottleneck, this region may need to be expanded to a stripe of several mirrors, or a parity-RAID arrangement.

6.4 Improving Backup Performance

Backup performance may be improved in an almost unlimited number of ways, with the right combination to use ultimately based on the results of the analysis of the various performance bottlenecks in an environment. In this section we will consider a variety of techniques that might be used to improve backup performance.

6.4.1 Multi-Tiered Backup Environments

In simple backup products there are only two types of hosts within an environment — the client and the server. This is sufficient for smaller environments as it resolves the primary consideration — the need to centralize control and only have one "master" server. For larger environments, though, this model starts to fail, as it can enforce artificial restrictions on the backup based on the requirement to stream all data across the network, or deal with all aspects of all backups from a single machine.

To be truly enterprise class, a backup product must support a three-tier model. This model introduces an intermediary host that exists at a layer between the server and the client. There is no standard name for this type of host, but two common terms used are "storage node" and "media server."

The goal of this type of host is to remove some of the load from the backup server by writing, at minimum, its own data to local media (or SAN-accessible media), and possibly by also writing the data from other hosts to its media. This is represented in Figure 6.14, in which three clients backup and retrieve their data directly from the backup server itself. To share the backup load and reduce the hardware requirements for any one host, the other three clients backup and retrieve their data directly from a storage node. This could also be used to reduce the amount of incoming data bandwidth required for any one host.

As shown in the diagram, there are actually two types of communication occurring within the environment — a data stream, and a metadata/control stream. Although the data stream obviously contains the data being backed up, the metadata/control stream is used to coordinate backup and recovery activities, as well as to transmit information about the backup (e.g., the file index information).

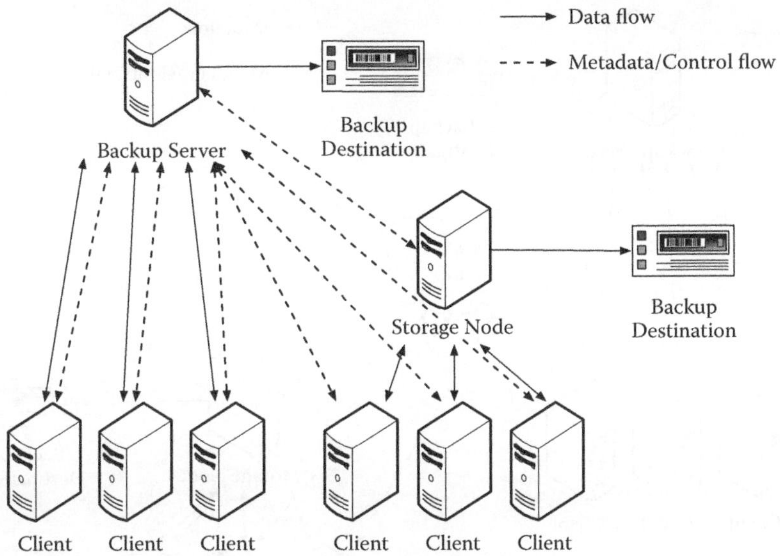

Figure 6.14 LAN-based three-tier backup architecture

So long as there is a segregation between control data and real data in a backup environment, the option exists to configure a fully centralized backup environment across a WAN. Obviously, backing up significant amounts of data over WAN links (e.g., T1, xDSL or ISDN) is not feasible. For workgroup backup products that do not support (or do not properly support) multi-tier backup environments, this means that a separate backup server must be located at each WAN-located site.

Enterprise-class backup products will, however, cope with a single centralized backup server coordinating the protection of multiple WAN-connected sites. In this sense the remote clients send their actual data to a storage node in their local environment. This can be represented as shown in Figure 6.15. The three-tier backup environment approach allows for incremental growth of a backup solution, and a broadening of the backup load, which in turn can make a significant impact on the level of hardware expenditure required. For instance, trading in a tape library with a maximum of six tape drives to buy a twelve-drive tape library may be significantly more costly than simply buying a second six-drive tape library. In particular for products that license library usage by the number of slots than the number of drives, a combined purchase of a newer, larger library may result in significant budgetary requirements.

Consider moving to a multi-tier backup environment in situations such as the following:

- It is necessary to perform centralized multi-campus backups in the same general area
- It is necessary to perform WAN-based backups without sending all the data across a slow communications link
- Where key hosts have a significant amount of data that is impractical to stream across the network
- Where the backup server is of itself unable to provide sufficient processing for the backup, but can, with load removed, coordinate a larger backup system

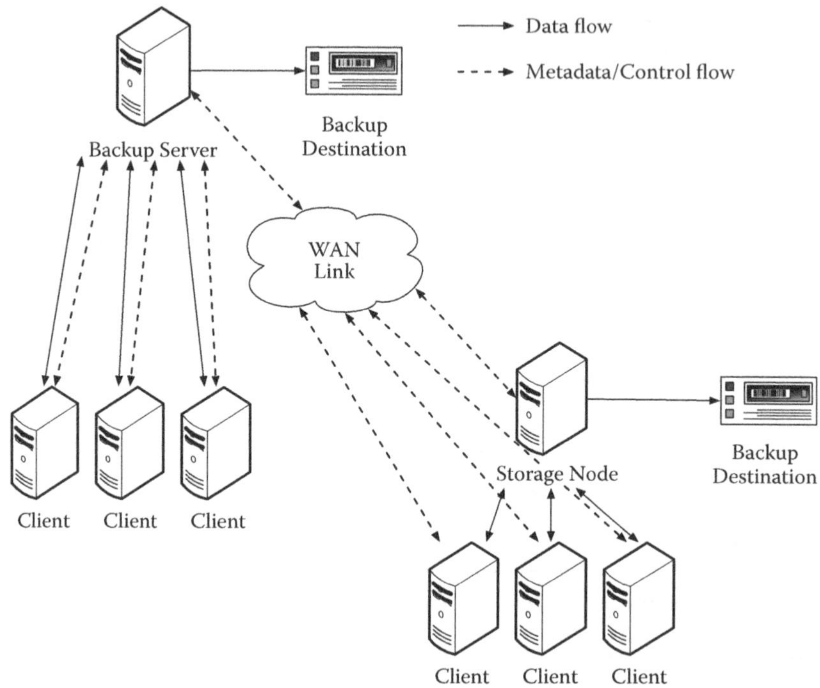

Figure 6.15 Three-tier backup architecture in a WAN environment

6.4.1.1 *Incrementals Forever, Revisited*

When examining the various backup levels found in enterprise backup software, we briefly covered systems that offered "indefinite incrementals" — i.e., after an initial full backup, only incremental backups are run, with backup media consolidation performed to reduce the number of physical volumes that backups reside on over time.

Some backup products advocate that by using the system of infinite incrementals, they do not need to provide a three-tier backup environment. This is a somewhat flawed argument, particularly when we consider the option of a centralized backup environment operating over a WAN.

Although (in theory) a two-tier architecture could be used to backup a WAN-based backup environment, taking advantage of infinite incrementals to reduce the amount of data streaming across the WAN, it fails to address the reason for backup — to recover when necessary. Or rather, such products continue to hedge bets on never needing to recover too much data at any one time. It also fails to account for more-complex backup scenarios — for example, how comfortable would DBAs be recovering from 1 × full + 365 × incremental backups of either Oracle, SAP/R3, or Microsoft SQL databases?

Don't ever be misled — a fundamental requirement for a package to be a true enterprise-class backup product is the support of a three-tier backup structure.

6.4.2 *Upgrade Hardware*

Sometimes the only way to improve backup performance is to upgrade hardware. This may be literally a case of replacing hardware with faster and more-powerful equipment, or it may be extending the capabilities of the environment by expanding the amount of hardware. (An example of the first might be to buy faster tape drives, the second might be to buy additional tape drives.)

Hardware upgrades should typically be considered in situations where it is apparent that the bottleneck is one or more of the following:

- The backup devices stream, but cannot backup all the required data in the given window
- The backup devices would be able to stream with newer hardware at the backup server, client, or network infrastructure level
- The established SLAs require one or both of the following:
  - A faster recovery time than can be achieved through a direct read from the backup devices
  - Less data loss than can be offered by the frequency at which the backups are performed (e.g., recovery to within an hour of data loss, but backups can only be run once per day)

Although purchasing additional hardware or upgrading infrastructure can in some cases be the most-costly option in a backup environment, if it is necessary there are usually few options to avoid it.

6.4.3 Tape Robots

For businesses that are growing beyond stand-alone tape drives, the decision to switch from staff changing tapes to robot autochangers is often a difficult one due to the price. However, using tape libraries, autochangers, etc., to service tape change requests can make a substantial impact on how much can be achieved during the backup window.

Example: The Cost of Not Accepting the Need for Autochangers

One company had the policy that because operators were employed overnight to collate print-outs, etc., they could perform tape changing. This company also chose to use a distributed backup environment (i.e., one server = one tape drive), which resulted in a large number of tape changes for each evening's backup processes.

With over 30 servers, even incremental backups required a lot of operator attention. To exacerbate the problem, operators were located six floors away from the computer room. Finally, to add insult to injury, DDS-3 tape drives were purchased as they were the cheapest drives available from the vendor of choice, but only DDS-2 tapes were allowed to be purchased, as DDS-3 tapes were considered too costly. Full backups would mostly exceed a DDS-3 tape capacity, let alone DDS-2 tape capacity.

It was almost as if this backup system was designed from the simple principle of "make it as worst-case as possible."

In this environment, the backup window (supposedly eight hours) would be exceeded every night, and always be blamed on the operators. However, the operators had to collate a very large number of print-outs every night for analysts while also performing other system maintenance functions.

Due to the separation of the computer room and the operations area, when it came time for a tape to be changed the operators would typically wait for up to half an hour for other tapes to need changing also, so as to save time. (On average, systems required two to three tape changes per backup.)

The most depressing aspect of this entire scenario was that this was in 2000, not 1990 or 1980.

Moving away from this worst-case scenario to a more-reasonable scenario (hopefully) whereby operators are physically located near the servers they perform activities on, and larger capacity tape drives are in use, we can still see room for improvement with some simple calculations.

Operators — even the best of operators — are not able to react instantly to tape change requests. Whereas a robot changing mechanism within a tape library would normally service a mount or unmount request immediately, a human operator must:

- Notice the alert
- Have free time to act
- Physically access the next piece of media
- Physically access the host requiring media
- Eject the previous piece of media
- Place the new piece of media and notify the host it is available
- Place the previous piece of media in its appropriate holding location

Not including the time taken to load/unload media, which will be the same regardless of whether a mechanical or a protein-based autoloader is used, there may be a significant difference between the speed of the operations. Even a slow tape library should react within ten to twenty seconds, whereas the reaction time for an operator would be in the order of several minutes, if not more.

Such a time lag affects the overall backup window capacity. This capacity is the megabytes per second speed of the backup media in use multipled by the number of seconds available in the standard backup window. For instance, 2 × LTO Ultrium 1 drives, with a streaming speed of 30 MB/s each (compressed) over an eight-hour backup window sees an overall backup window capacity of 1,687.5 GB.

LTO-1 drives, when writing at full speed without interruptions take around one hour and 50 minutes to fill, which we'll round to two hours. Over an eight-hour backup window, assuming the tape drives have been pre-loaded, each drive will require three tape changes.

We can assume that a tape library robot might take 15 seconds to perform the following tasks:

- Take a piece of media ejected from a drive and put it in a nominated library slot
- Pick the next piece of requested media from its nominated slot
- Place the media in the nominated tape drive to initiate a load operation

A 15-second delay at 30 MB/s represents 450-MB data gap during the backup window. If, on the other hand, an operator takes ten minutes to notice the need for media, pause what they're currently doing, and then change the tape, we have a data gap of 17.6 GB.

With two tape drives each requiring three media changes, the tape library induced data gap will be 2.6 GB over eight hours, and the human operator induced data gap will be 105.5 GB. The data gap difference — approximately 103 GB — would be sufficient to back up a small fileserver, several smaller clients, or a small database server. Taking a simplistic approach over the course of a year, this data gap will be 949 GB for a tape library, or 37.6 TB for a human operator.

Does a tape library really cost more than missing out on backing up more than 35 TB? This type of argument can be quite helpful in understanding that tape libraries can quickly pay for themselves due to the efficiencies they introduce just at the backup level. (The efficiencies introduced to recoveries are in some cases even more significant.)

Even simple autochangers can play a role for smaller businesses. Such businesses tend to, say, kick off a backup before leaving in the evening and require that the first person on-site change the tape the next business day if necessary to complete the backup. This results in a lengthy delay, can result in data loss, and may unnecessarily impact system performance while the backup continues to run the next day. As such, an organization that cannot afford a fully fledged jukebox or library should at least consider a carousel or autochanger to accommodate the longest consecutive number of public holidays in the year.

6.4.4 Faster Backup Devices

Following from hardware upgrades, faster backup devices can, depending on the performance bottleneck, make for a substantial increase in performance. The simple caveat with deploying faster backup devices (or at least faster tape-based backup devices) is to ensure the rest of the hardware and systems in the backup environment can keep the drives streaming without an unacceptable recovery impact.

Consider deploying or upgrading to faster tape drives when it is apparent that the primary performance bottleneck is the speed of the current backup media, and it can be verified that the environment will allow the proposed media to stream. However, do not consider deploying or upgrading to faster backup devices when it is apparent that other components of the environment cannot provide data fast enough to keep drives streaming.

6.4.5 Backup to Disk

There are two approaches to disk-based backup devices — disk backup volumes, or virtual tape libraries.

6.4.5.1 Disk Backup Units

For a long time, support from backup vendors of disk backup was quite poor, even laughable. For instance, some vendors treated disk backup as if it were tape — allowing one read operation or multiple concurrent write operations, but not both simultaneously.

As backup systems increased in complexity, many of the backup vendors realized that a number of issues (particularly relating to performance) in backup environments could be addressed through the use of disk backup devices. With this in mind, there has been considerable effort put into disk backup systems for enterprise backup software, making it much more useful for organizations.

Disk backup systems offer the following key performance benefits that cannot be underestimated:

- They do not shoe-shine, meaning that slow data transfer speed from any one client does not impact the write speed of the device.

- They support multiplexing without resulting in a tangible impact on recovery speed.
- Parallel recoveries can be accommodated, even if it means performing multiple disparate recoveries from the same piece of media (the number of parallel recoveries allowed will be product dependent).
- There is no load time associated with disk backup volumes, meaning that recoveries can start instantly.
- Recoveries and backups can occur simultaneously.
- Tapes generated from disk-based backups (either through duplication or transfer of backup images) are typically written in a demultiplexed fashion, meaning that even the tapes are faster to recover from.

As backup-to-disk systems continue to grow in popularity, some industry analysts have confidently asserted that backup-to-disk will finally see the death of tape. This is unlikely to be the case, even when using inexpensive disks. (One example of why this is not likely to occur is simple — how would recoveries be accomplished if a malicious worm strikes the backup server and corrupts five years worth of online backups?)

Backup-to-disk should therefore be seen as an intermediary step, or an adjunct to tape backup — particularly for longer-term retention backups.

Unlike many other performance-enhancement techniques that improve backup or recovery performance, but not necessarily both, disk backup can and often does result in both improved backup times and improved recovery times.

Disk backup units should therefore be considered when:

- Data cannot be streamed fast enough from LAN-based clients to keep the tape drives streaming, but a direct data transfer from storage attached to a server with tape drive(s) can stream the tape drive(s)
- Slow recovery times caused by high multiplexing values on tape are unacceptable
- Recoveries from recent backups must start "instantly" without the need for loading, positioning, etc.
- More than one recovery per device/volume is required concurrently

6.4.5.2 Virtual Tape Libraries

A virtual tape library (VTL) is a disk array masquerading as a tape library to the backup server. It may literally be an array with a "black box" attached to it to provide that masquerading, it may run additional software on the backup server to perform the masquerading, or it might be achieved through an entirely dedicated server attached to the array.

This may result in a situation where, for instance, 3 TB of formatted, RAID-protected space is seen by the backup server as an 85-slot DLT-7000 tape library with an administrator-nominated number of tape drives in it.

VTLs typically offer the following performance-based improvements to a backup environment:

- Shoe-shining is not an issue, which means that backups can be written to virtual tape with higher levels of multiplexing
- There are no volume load/unload times, assuming that a virtual tape drive is free

- Can be deployed into products that do not support regular backup to disk
- They usually support the configuration of an arbitrary number of virtual tape drives — a SAN-connected VTL, for instance, may be shared among a large number of storage nodes/media servers, allowing for massively distributed backups, which would be too costly using conventional backup-to-disk or physical tape drives

Non-performance-based advantages of VTLs in comparison to disk-based backup include (1) media not "mounted" in a drive is treated as offline, and therefore not as prone to accidental or malicious deletion; and (2) if replacing a real tape library, there may be no need to alter licenses. However, they do have some disadvantages that must also be factored in:

- Media can't be "removed" for true offsite storage without using a physical tape library or drives (note that the same applies to traditional disk backup).
- Hardware compression capabilities are typically a "costed extra," and therefore they may not necessarily deliver all the functionality of a real tape library — in some instances, users of VTLs have found that the cost of adding hardware compression functionality is more expensive than simply doubling the amount of disk space in the array.
- They do virtualize some of the bad aspects of conventional tape, such as limiting parallel recoveries when data must be retrieved from the same virtual tape.

VTLs do provide several performance gains over conventional tape libraries, but still suffer from similar disadvantages as conventional disk backup (notably the inability to offsite media), and so will rarely be a complete replacement for tape.

The choice of deploying either backup-to-disk or VTLs will be very much dependent on individual site requirements.

6.4.6 *Dynamic Device Allocation*

Dynamically allocated (or shared) devices are most likely to be found in a SAN, though they can introduce debugging and maintenance overheads that some organizations may find distasteful. A dynamically allocated device environment extends our previously discussed multi-tier backup environment to allow shared backup device infrastructure between the server and storage nodes/media servers. This avoids the need to have backup devices (normally tape drives) permanently allocated to any individual host.

In an environment using dynamic device allocation, a limited number of backup devices are owned by a backup server or a media server, and shared out to other hosts for LAN-free backup and restore as required. A sample dynamic device sharing configuration is shown in Figure 6.16, which consists of three SAN-connected hosts — cerberus, hydra, and omnibus, as well as a three-tape drive library (that happens to be connected via a SCSI to a fiber-channel bridge). Although all three hosts physically can see the tape drives in the library, for the purposes of this example we will say that the backup server omnibus "owns" the drives. This means that access to the drives is authorized (within the backup program) only by the owner of the tape drives, regardless of whether they can be physically accessed.

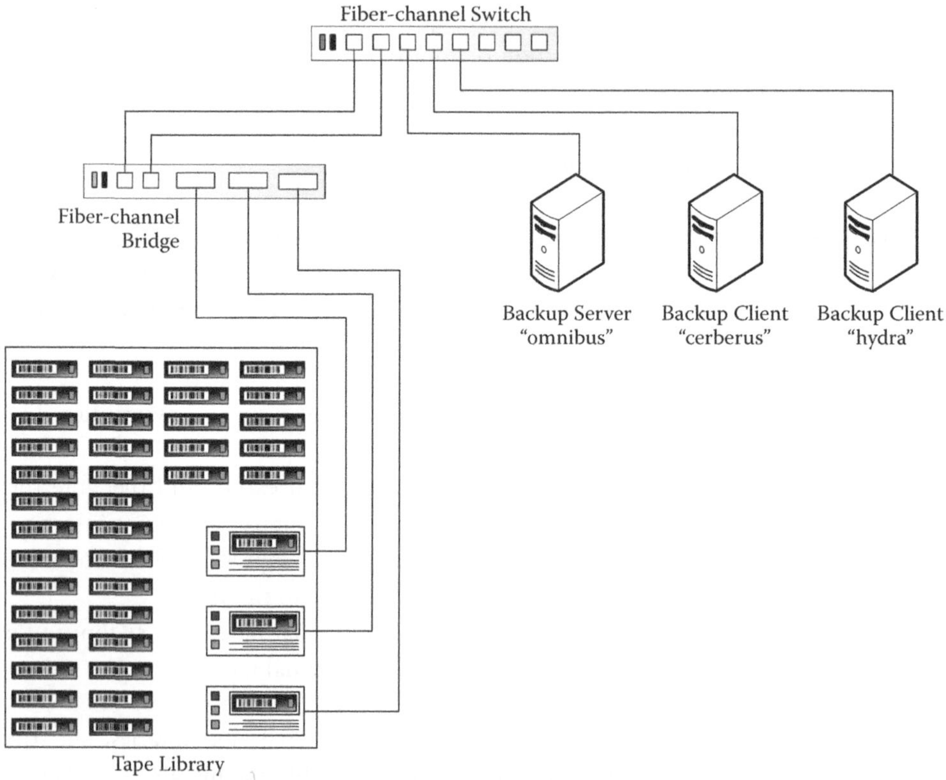

Figure 6.16 Sample dynamic device-sharing configuration

If a backup for the client cerberus is to be run, the process typically runs as follows:

1. Omnibus initiates a tape load, placing a tape in one of the three drives it shares with cerberus.
2. Omnibus instructs cerberus to commence a local backup, writing the backup to the nominated shared tape drive (omnibus will know both its own mappings to the tape drives and the mappings of all other hosts that share access to the drives).
3. Cerberus performs a local backup, notifying omnibus if additional media is needed, and notifying omnibus when it has completed the backup.
4. In the event of additional media being required, omnibus will instruct cerberus to stop using the currently allocated tape, dismount it, and return to step 1.
5. When the backup completes, omnibus instructs cerberus to stop using the currently allocated tape, dismounts it, and then flags the drive as being free for the next host that requires access (or itself).

(This process is logically similar for recovery operations, and is not limited to only one tape drive per host.)

Improvements offered by dynamic device sharing include

- Ability to perform local backup and restore operations on a series of hosts rather than over the network

- Ability to service more local backup and restore operations than could be accommodated on a one host = one drive arrangement
- By reducing the amount of data streamed over the network, the impact of the backup or recovery on the overall environment is reduced

Challenges introduced by dynamically shared devices include

- Different operating systems may use different block sizes, and without rigorous control it is possible to end up with a system whereby a tape labeled or formatted on a particular system can be physically loaded into another system, but not mountable, thus causing errors.
- Ensuring that SCSI resets are masked between systems. Typically when a host reboots, it sends a SCSI reset to all attached devices. (Remember that fiber-attached devices are typically treated as SCSI.) If such a reboot occurs on a host that is zoned in to access the tape drive, and it impacts the tape drive while another host is using the drive, it can result in major backup errors — for instance, it can cause the tape drive to rewind mid-operation, or even result in the accessing host completely losing its connection to the drive.
- Drive contention must be carefully balanced — i.e., while one host is using a particular tape drive, no other host can make use of the drive.
- For hosts with direct attached storage only, dynamic drive sharing can introduce greater cost due to the need to add one or more fiber HBAs to access the SAN for tape.
- Expanding somewhat on the previous comment, many vendors recommend that HBAs allocated for disk-based SAN should not also be used for tape-based access, and vice versa. Thus if two HBAs are used for redundant data path access to disk, at least one more HBA will need to be added for single-path access to tape. (It should be noted that few backup products support redundant paths to tape drives with automatic failover between those paths.)
- For some backup products, once a host has finished with a tape in a drive, it will need to be rewound and unmounted before the drive may be reallocated to another host — ostensibly to protect against SCSI resets — even if the same tape is to be used in the same drive for another host.*
- Problems can be more difficult to debug due to the increased number of hosts that can access individual backup devices — instead of a single path between a host and a backup device, each backup device can be visible to multiple hosts, increasing the number of factors to consider when debugging issues.

Dynamic device sharing should be considered for deployment when:

- The network is not fast enough to support the throughput requirements for keeping tape drives streaming.
- "Key" hosts are SAN attached and have a significant amount of data on them.
- The backup devices are SAN attached, or can be otherwise shared.
- HBAs and switches can be configured to mask SCSI resets and other deleterious commands from hosts not currently accessing backup devices.

Note that combining VTLs with virtual device allocation can create a very flexible backup and recovery environment.

---

* The fact that some products don't need to do this demonstrates that it is a rather flimsy excuse for those that do.

6.4.7 Serverless Backup

So far the performance options discussed have focused on ensuring the data owner host is able to push the backup devices fast enough (and that no intervening layer poses an impediment). However, sometimes the only way to improve the backup performance is to remove the host that owns the data from the configuration.

There are two primary ways in which the owner-host can be bypassed — NDMP and snapshots.

6.4.7.1 NDMP

As discussed previously, NDMP is a backup strategy to be deployed in situations where the data provider does not have a traditional operating system and it is necessary to avoid a double network-transfer backup. NDMP backups should be used in the following types of scenarios:

- The data provider (as opposed to the data owner) host supports it.
- The data is provisioned to multiple operating system types that cannot preserve or access each others' access control lists (ACLs).
- Both the backup software and the data provider support sufficiently new-enough versions of the NDMP protocol to support the required flexibility in location and use of backup devices.
- The network is not fast enough to support the sustained, complete transfer of all data on the data provider.

6.4.7.2 Snapshots

When used to facilitate serverless backups, filesystem, or LUN snapshots result in the snapshot generated mounted on a host other than the data owner. For optimized backups, this other host will either be the backup server or a storage node/media server, so that the data can then be written directly to the backup media without needing to be streamed across to the network.

This style of backup becomes eligible for consideration when:

- A SAN is in place, but the backup devices cannot be placed on the SAN, or dynamic device sharing is not an option.
- The LAN is insufficient for the backup process.
- The backup server (or storage node/media server) that is SAN-connected can successfully mount the filesystems requiring backup.
- The data owner cannot have its performance impeded by the backup operation.

This is in some senses the reverse of dynamic device-sharing backups. Instead of sharing the backup devices, a copy or snapshot of the original source data is shared to another host.

A key restriction of this mechanism is that the mounting host needs to be of the same operating system type of the data owner. This can sometimes introduce the need for storage nodes that might not otherwise be required — one storage node per operating system for which snapshots are generated. Of late, some advanced filesystems offered by vendors have started supporting cross-platform mounting, but this does not necessarily fully preserve metadata such as ACLs, etc.

6.4.8 Multiplex Larger Filesystems

Previously, we discussed the impact of dense filesystems on the backup process. At the filesystem level, there is often not a lot that can be done to improve the backup process, but depending on the underlying disk structure there may be improvements that can be made via multiplexing.

Consider, for instance, a SAN-based system. For general performance reasons it is reasonably common to see a large filesystem provided as a stripe of several LUNs presented from an array. For instance, the array might provide 5 × 100 GB RAID-5 LUNs, each comprising five disks. Either the operating system or the array will then stripe these LUNs into a single 500-GB volume. At this point there are a large number of disks available to service read requests.

In almost all dense filesystem cases, the walk-cost of the filesystem is not a CPU or memory-intensive one, but rather it originates from the performance of the data structure referencing the filesystem. Furthermore, filesystems are designed to support multiple concurrent operations, particularly when the underlying disk structure supports it, such as in the above example.

In this case sufficient backup gains may be achieved by performing multiplexing at the filesystem level. Consider, for instance, a university fileserver providing home accounts for thousands or tens of thousands of students. This is very likely to lead to a dense filesystem that would be too slow to back up as a single stream.

Such a filesystem could be broken down into a series of concurrent streams in one of two ways, depending on how it is laid out: (1) if the system administrator has chosen a flat structure, each home directory could represent a single backup stream; and (2) if the system administrator has created a hash structure where a series of accounts are stored in subdirectories of the parent directory (e.g., /home/a-c/alex, /home/a-c/brian, /home/a-c/charlie, /home/d-j/darren, etc.), the middle directory layers could each represent a single backup stream.

It should be noted that we are not suggesting every potential stream is backed up simultaneously, but rather, multiple subdirectories are processed concurrently. If the filesystem is broken into many smaller streams, and each stream represents a considerably smaller portion of the filesystem directory structure to walk, faster performance can be achieved than backing up a single monolithic stream.

For example, a "/home" filesystem may have a series of directory entries such as:

```
/home/aaron
/home/alex
/home/alfred
...etc...
/home/beatrice
/home/betty
/home/bill
/home/billy
/home/bob
...etc...
/home/zara
```

Although a single stream backing up all of /home may represent a dense filesystem backup and suffer walk-speed constraints, backing up, say, eight home directories at a time as individual streams would result in considerably faster performance (so long as the underlying disk structure could support that many concurrent reads).

If implementing individual filesystem multiplexing, such a backup stream breakup must be automatically performed as part of the backup process, rather than being hard-coded (which has considerable potential for data loss if new subdirectories are added).

Although such a solution may produce better backup performance, it is important to keep in mind: (1) if backups are written directly to tape rather than to a disk backup unit, the multiplexing value may significantly impact large restores or backup duplication; and (2) with more incoming streams, there will be a higher process load on the backup server itself, and this will (a) impact the performance of the backup server, and (b) decrease the number of other streams that can be serviced simultaneously.

Multiplexing on single filesystems should be considered where:

- The vast majority of the data present in the environment reside on the larger filesystems.
- The backup product does not provide a block-level agent, or the denseness/fragmentation of the filesystem significantly impedes recovery from block-level backup.
- Either the backup product natively supports multiplexing, or it is possible to automate the building of the multiplexed streams in such a way that the backup remains exclusive rather than inclusive.
- The filesystem is laid out in such a way that streams do not become imbalanced (e.g., running eight streams of departmental data storage areas makes little sense if seven departments use less than 10 GB each but the eighth department uses ten times that much, and has ten times the number of files than the other departments).

6.4.9 Filesystem Change Journals

This technique is quite specific to particular operating systems and filesystems, and as such only has limited applicability. It is also appropriate to only particular backup types and levels — that is, regular file backups using a non-full level. In particular, for full backups of dense filesystems this technique will offer no performance improvement because change journals are irrelevant during full backups.

For smaller or less-dense filesystems that suffer the fate of having a very small incremental backup change, the performance cost for the backup is usually experienced in finding the files that have changed since the last backup. In this case we can say that the filesystems experience sparse changes.

In such cases, filesystems or operating systems that use change journals can be instrumental to improving backup performance, so long as the backup system can leverage those techniques. The goal of a change journal is to maintain a history of files that have changed since a particular point in time. Considering this in respect to backups, the activity sequence would be

Day 1: Backup product does a full backup, ignoring change journal
Day 1–2: Change journal maintains a list of files changed
Day 2: Backup product queries change journal for a listing of files that have changed since the previous day's backup
Day 2: Backup product performs a backup of the files the change journal has reported as having changed, stepping through the list of files rather than searching for them on the filesystem
Day 2–3: Change journal maintains a list of files changed

Day 3: Backup product performs a backup of the files the change journal has reported as having changed, stepping through the list of files rather than searching for them on the filesystem and so on.

To understand why this is a useful technique it is necessary to understand how incremental backups are done without using a change journal. In these situations the backup server has to walk the filesystem, comparing the file creation/modification date to the known date/time of the last backup. Although this comparison is not necessarily a lengthy process, when coupled with walking the filesystem, the backup can be significantly slowed, particularly if only a very small percentage of files have changed.

For very sparse filesystems, incremental backups can actually result in timeouts, depending on the backup product. Although it seems a logical necessity that a backup agent traversing a filesystem should periodically send a "heartbeat" signal to the backup server to state it is still active, even if it hasn't sent any data for a while, not all backup products perform this function, thus relying on backup data to remind the backup server the agent is still running and has not hung. Using change journals not only speeds up the backup, but by implication, avoids situations where the lack of a heartbeat signal might result in the incorrect termination of a sparse backup.

As we've seen already, a change journal is not a magic bullet — for instance, it can't help during a full backup. There is another cost to the change journal, however, and that is its size: this will grow in direct proportion to the number of files that change between instances where the journal is periodically reset. If filesystems have sparse changes, this is not an issue; however, if there are large numbers of changes, this can either impede the performance of the data owner, or result in the journal being dumped, necessitating a reversion to regular filesystem-walk backups.

Therefore, even on operating systems or filesystems that can make use of a change journal, it is necessary to evaluate carefully where the performance impact occurs before the use of change journaling is enabled.

Change journals should be used for backup when:

- Full backups succeed, but incremental backups experience performance problems or timeouts.
- The number of files that change on the host between incremental backups are quite small.
- Filesystems remain mounted between backups (e.g., change journals typically can't assist for remote-mounted snapshots, etc.).
- The operating system uses a change journal.
- The backup product can access the change journal.

6.4.10 Archive Policies

Archive policies (whether manual or automated) can play a valuable part in the improvement of backup performance, and over time as filesystems continue to grow in size, the importance of archiving will grow.

Consider a simple filesystem with, say, 500 GB of used storage. This filesystem might contain corporate documents and downloads of important software used by staff during consulting activities.

If a full backup is done each week to say, LTO Ultrium 1, then this will take approximately nine hours at uncompressed speed. This may in fact be too long a window for the backup, but at the same time, purchasing faster backup devices or eliminating other bottlenecks from the infrastructure may not be feasible. That is, there are situations where there is literally too much data to be backed up.

If the required backup window is six hours, it could well be that the real requirement is that the user data must be backed up in six hours. If say, 50 percent of the content of the filesystem is software images, then these images may be able to be archived to alternate media, or another server, thus reducing the overall amount of data to be backed up. In this scenario, the primary fileserver storage would be used just for user data, and the other data might be moved to another server that receives less-frequent full backups. This can have an added benefit of increasing media efficiency, because less data would be backed up weekly.

Archive Is Not HSM

Note that archive policies are not synonymous with hierarchical storage management (HSM) systems. HSM sees infrequently accessed data moved to slower devices, with an access stub left behind that has the same name as the original file. When a program or user attempts to open that stub, the original file is retrieved and provided to the requesting process. Although filesystems employing HSM can result in considerably smaller amounts of data to be backed up, as more files are moved to slower storage, more stubs (tiny files) are created — thus, HSM filesystems can become very dense filesystems, which as we've already discussed, are a bane to backup performance.

6.4.11 Anti-Virus Software

Computer viruses have been around for almost as long as computers themselves. *The Jargon File* (or *The New Hacker's Dictionary*) provides several examples of viruses stretching back as far as the 1970s (with a personal favorite being the story of the Robyn Hood/Friar Tuck virus designed for the Xerox CP-V system). This probably goes to prove the cliché "wherever there's a will, there's a way," and thus virus scanners are likely to remain an integral part of core operating system services until such time as system security becomes sufficiently advanced that there are no "gaps" left for virus writers to exploit.

Anti-virus software can have a profound impact on the performance of the backup software, most notably in Windows environments where the virus definition databases are now very large. While not wishing to appear to be picking on Windows, it must be said that the plethora of viruses available for that platform creates backup performance considerations (and problems) that are almost, but not quite unique to it.

Particularly in Windows, a typical server installation usually involves installation of an anti-virus agent that scans

- All files periodically
- Any file being transferred to local storage
- Any files being read from local storage
- Any data transmitted across a network interface

All of these functions are completely incompatible with backup performance. That is, anti-virus software should always be configured as follows for hosts that are backed up: (1) do not perform a comprehensive scan at times when there will be known backup activity, and (2) ignore activity generated by the backup software.

Most anti-virus software allows the specification of applications or executables whose activity (read, write, and network transfer) will not be scanned, and a significant impact will be experienced on the host without this enabled for backup software. If the anti-virus software does not support this facility, it may be necessary to suffer the performance impact or change anti-virus software, because the alternative of disabling the anti-virus software during the backup may be somewhat unpalatable. (Surprisingly, some anti-virus vendors actually recommend this as a solution, which seems to be an invalidation of the purpose of their product — protection.)*

6.4.12 Slower Backup Devices

Although not an option that is considered in many environments, it can be argued that in some situations the best possible way to remedy a backup performance issue is to revert to slower backup devices.

Consider, for instance, a corporate backup environment where there are remote offices that must be backed up to the corporate data center. With an available backup bandwidth of say, 1 MB/s between each remote office and the data center, even "old" enterprise class tape drives such as DLT 7000 will experience significant shoe-shining unless a large number of streams are multiplexed. Obviously with a small link between the data center and the remote site this would imply using multiplexing across a large number of remote sites, or combining remote site backups with local backups.

Of course, this amount of multiplexing will impact recovery performance and possibly other backup maintenance/protection activities. Additionally, once the incoming data speed drops below a certain threshold, the risk of errors during the backup has a tendency to increase. For instance, an LTO-1 tape drive that streams at 15 MB/s at best will suffer significant performance problems with a 1 MB/s throughput. At worst, running at less than 1 MB/s for long periods of time may result in errors — tape wastage or even backup timeouts.

In this case, deployment of slower backup media may achieve the requirements (for the least cost). For instance, a DDS-3 tape drive works with a streaming speed of between 1 and 2 MB/s, meaning that the device will cope significantly better with a reduced bandwidth than an enterprise drive would.

However, using slower, older devices creates new challenge. It is not in the best interest of vendors to continue to sell older styles of backup devices, so to use slower devices, it may be necessary to pay exorbitant hardware maintenance fees, or maintain a pool of second-hand equipment.

The deployment of slower backup devices can introduce more administrative overheads than the problem they initially solve, and therefore should not be considered unless other options such as backup to disk have been considered and discounted.

* A more subtle impact can occur when the anti-virus software runs with a different set of permissions than the account running the backup software agent. For instance, this can produce unpredictable results during recoveries, resulting in "permission denied" errors that are caused by the client, not the backup server.

Chapter 7

Recovery

7.1 Introduction

Keeping our insurance analogy, a recovery is when a company needs to make a claim against its policy. Something has gone wrong (or at least this is the scenario most of the time), and data must be retrieved from backup.

Just like a regular insurance policy, an IT insurance policy comes with an excess fee when making claims. The amount of excess faced with an IT insurance policy is based largely on the initial investment. If a company has not invested properly — if it only takes the cheap options — recovery will cost more: more time, more money, and a higher risk of data loss.

Although recovery operations themselves are product-centric, some common procedures and practices for recoveries exist regardless of the product or technology in use. These items fall into the following categories:

- Backup system design — how recovery requirements should be a primary consideration when designing a backup system
- Recovery best practices — procedures and guidelines to follow during recovery processes
- Disaster recovery considerations — although notionally a disaster recovery is simply a special type of recovery, there are often more aspects of disaster recovery than are considered during the implementation of a backup system
- How service level agreements (SLAs) influence the recovery process and system architecture
- How to plan and perform recovery testing

In this chapter, we will examine each key category in detail to gain a greater understanding of the recovery process, and how to minimize excess when making an IT insurance claim.

(It is worthwhile noting that, in a perfect world where everyone understands everything there is to understand about backup, a book about backup and recovery should actually cover recovery first, because it is the more important topic.)

7.2 Designing Backup for Recovery

Our goal in this section is to discuss how a backup system needs to be designed to facilitate recoveries. As mentioned in our introduction, the purpose of a backup is to provide a mechanism to recover, and therefore it follows that the backup system must be designed to allow those recoveries to take place with as little effort or cost as possible.

7.2.1 Recovery Performance

In the earlier topic regarding backup performance, we briefly discussed the idea that performance considerations for recoveries must be considered when planning a backup environment, and we'll now examine this principle in more detail.

For many organizations, backup environments are scoped on a backup window, regardless of whether that backup window is real or imaginary. Remember, though, our original definition of backup — a copy of any data that can be used to restore the data as/when required to its original form.

This creates what should be a self-evident rule — the recoverability requirements of the system must play a more significant role in the planning of the backup environment than the backup requirements.

> **Example:** Consider a simple case where an organization implements a new backup system, and configures all backups with four-way multiplexing across each of the three tape drives to ensure that backups complete within a six-hour management-stated backup window. Two large fileservers consume almost the entire backup window, starting first and finishing last, therefore taking up one unit of multiplexing on a tape drive each for the entire duration of the backup.
>
> Following the installation of this configuration, simple random file recovery tests are performed and succeed. Backup duplication is trialed and found to take too long, but because the previous backup system could not duplicate anyway, this is not seen as a loss of functionality, so the system is declared ready and put into production use.
>
> Five months after installation, one of the key fileservers suffers a catastrophic failure at 9 a.m. on the last business day of the month when a destructive virus causes wide-scale data corruption and deletion. The most recent backups are called for, and the recovery commences.
>
> At this point the impact of multiplexed backups come into play. Although the backup of the system completes just within the six-hour window, a complete filesystem read from the tapes generated for the host takes approximately twelve hours to complete. On the final tape, a failure occurs in the tape drive, damaging the tape and resulting in the loss of several directories. These directories need to be restored from the older backups. As a result, (1) the system has been unavailable for the entire last day of the month, resulting in loss of invoicing revenue for the company; and (2) some records of invoicing were lost due to the tape failure, and during the following month revenue has to be recalculated following complaints from customers due to double-billing.

Clearly, this is not a desirable scenario for a company to find itself in. Although it is not necessarily easy to redesign a backup system after it has been put in place (particularly when it results in a request for additional budget), the recovery requirements must be clearly understood and catered for in the backup environment. At bare minimum, management must understand the risks the company is exposed to in relation to data protection.

As seen in chapter 6, "Performance Options, Analysis, and Tuning," a multitude of ways exist in which performance can be improved given the type of challenge to the backup environment. Even when a reliable mechanism to achieve appropriate backup performance has been found, it may be that the performance comes at the cost of rendering the recovery untenable.

Backup to Recover. When implementing an upgrade to a new backup system, a company wanted to resolve performance problems in backing up its two main filesystems, which were both around 400 GB in size.

Backups for these filesystems had reached the point where they crawled through at speeds not exceeding 2 MB/s to DLT-7000. Unfortunately, LTO Ultrium 2 (the chosen tape format to replace) was not going to perform any better given the filesystem was dense.

As various backup products now support block-level agents on hosts, the block-level agent for the backup software deployed was trialed on the Windows 2000 fileserver. The backup window immediately dropped from approximately fifteen hours to four. (Due to the need to allocate only one tape drive for block-level backups and the agent's inability to multiplex at the time, this meant that the backup window in fact dropped from fifteen hours for two filesystems to eight hours.) This was still seen as a considerably better backup improvement.

Complete filesystem recoveries also went through at full tape speed, resulting in a 400-GB recovery performed in three to four hours.

As the filesystems were rigorously protected by virus scanning, volume mirroring and array replication, the customer had never needed to perform a complete filesystem restore. Therefore the key recovery test was actually an individual directory recovery. The directory initially chosen for recovery testing was approximately 40 GB, and that recovery took approximately eight hours.

Investigations showed that the filesystems were both in the order of 50 percent fragmented, with the directory chosen exhibiting the worst symptoms, with most files suffering serious fragmentation problems. This highlighted the performance problems that can arise from file-level recovery from block-level backups.

As individual file/directory recoveries were seen to be more important, the business decision was made instead to optimize the filesystem backup via generating multiple simultaneous backups from each filesystem, which provided somewhat better performance. This, of course, resulted in a situation whereby a complete disaster recovery of the filesystem would take considerably longer to complete due to the multiplexing involved, but this was seen as acceptable, given the reduced need for such a recovery in comparison to the day-to-day file and directory recoveries required.

In this case, after trying to design the system for backup performance, the company elected instead to optimize recovery performance.

A more-significant problem can occur in WAN-based backup environments. For some companies, WAN-based backups are designed to centralize the location of backups, with an understanding that the "trickling" of a backup across the WAN is an acceptable occurrence. However, is the same "trickling" acceptable to a recovery? Unsurprisingly, the answer is frequently no. In this case, the recoverability of a remote system may depend on such options as:

- Recovery of the remote machine's hard drive to an identical machine in the backup server's computer room, then shipping the hard drive out to the remote site
- Shipping a tape and a stand-alone tape drive out to the remote host for recovery
- Recovery to a spare machine in the computer room local to the backup server, and then sending the entire replacement server out to the remote site
- Contingency plans to allow users to work with remote fileservers while a trickle-back recovery occurs

It should be noted that when such "trickle" remote backup systems are deployed, it is frequently done to eliminate the need for dedicated IT staff at the satellite offices. The lack of dedicated staff at the remote offices in turn can impact how the recovery can be performed.

All of these examples and situations should serve to highlight one very important rule — designing a system to meet a backup window is one thing, but ensuring that it can be used to recover systems within the required window may require some compromises to the backup speed, and very careful consideration in advance of just how recoveries will be performed.

7.2.2 Facilitation of Recovery

When designing a backup system, it is necessary to consider various key questions that deal with how recoveries will be facilitated.

7.2.2.1 How Frequently Are Recoveries Requested?

See Table 7.1.

7.2.2.2 Backup Recency Versus Recovery Frequency

Typically, a backup environment design should aim to meet an 80-percent immediate start rule for recoveries — that is, 80 percent of recoveries should be done without a human physically needing to change or load media. To achieve this, it is necessary to understand the frequency of the recovery requests compared to how recently the backup requested for recovery was performed.

For example, a company might find that its recovery requests are balanced against the backup recency as follows:

- 40 percent of recovery requests are for data backed up within the last seven days
- 20 percent of recovery requests are for data backed up within the last seven to fourteen days
- 30 percent of recovery requests are for data backed up within the last two to six weeks
- The remaining 10 percent of recovery requests come from monthly and yearly backups (i.e., are more akin to retrieval from archive)

Table 7.1 How the Frequency of Recovery Requests Impact Backup System Design

Frequency	*Implications*
Frequent recovery requests	If recoveries are performed frequently, the goal of the backup system should be to ensure that the hardware and configuration is such that recoveries can start with minimum intervention and delay. In a tape-only environment, this will require • Sufficient slots in the tape libraries to ensure that a copy of all backups covering the most-common recovery time span can be held in the libraries for a fast restore start • A sufficient number of tape drives that there will always be a drive available to perform a recovery from (or at least one tape drive set aside as read-only) • An environment featuring backup-to-disk, and tape that also has frequent recoveries, should be designed such that the backups most likely to be required for recovery reside on disk backup units rather than tape, wherever possible When recoveries are performed frequently, procedures for the recovery will need to be documented, but there should also be sufficient "in-memory" understanding from the users involved in the recovery as to what steps will be involved.
Infrequent recovery requests	If recoveries are only infrequently performed, then design considerations may be somewhat different. For instance, potentially spending tens of thousands of dollars on a dedicated recovery tape drive used maybe once a month may be unpalatable to a business with limited financial resources, i.e., taking a risk-versus-cost decision, the business may elect to wear the risk so as to avoid a higher capital cost. Therefore, when recoveries are few and far between, the key design consideration will become the procedures and documentation that describe the recovery process. This will be because users and administrators will be less experienced with recoveries, and will need more guidance and prompting than those in environments with frequent recoveries. (Recovery procedures should always be detailed and readily understandable by any administrator of the system they are referring to, but it becomes especially the case when the recoveries are performed only infrequently.)

With this in mind, it's clear that the backup system for this environment should be designed in such a way that no less than the first 14 days worth of backups are readily recoverable at minimum notice. (It would be preferable for the first six weeks to be recoverable with minimum notice as well.)

In a purely tape-based environment, this implies a tape library that is large enough to hold one copy of all the tapes generated for this critical-recovery period. For many companies, this turns out to be their "smallest" backup retention period — e.g., if daily incrementals (with weekly fulls) are kept for five weeks, this would mean having a tape library capable of holding five weeks worth of backup tapes.

In a combined disk-and-tape backup solution, backups should be migrated from disk to tape only when the age of the backup has entered the "less frequently recovered" period.

Obviously, many companies will have different recovery frequency-to-age ratios (though the 80 percent rule is a good starting point if no data or trends are available on the subject), but the end result should be the same: ensure the highest frequency recoveries are served fastest.

7.2.3 Who May Want to Perform Recoveries?

This is often a controversial topic within an organization, and the answer is rarely the same in two companies, even in the same line of business. Therefore, here are a few answers to this question that are commonly heard, some of which overlap, and some of which are contradictory:

- Only system administrators should perform recoveries.
- Only backup administrators should perform recoveries.
- Application administrators should perform the recoveries for their own application.
- Help desk staff and operators should be able to perform user-file recoveries.
- Help desk staff and operators should be able to perform all recoveries, including complete system recoveries.
- Help desk staff should not have access to the backup system.
- End users should be able to recover their own files.
- End users should not be able to recover their own files.

Based on this common subset of answers received to this question, it is obvious that there are no industry-standard responses.

When it comes to designing the system with recovery in mind, always remember the following: the further removed someone is from actually running the backup server, the less they'll understand about backup and recovery. This can be presented as shown in Figure 7.1.

If there is a difference between the backup administrator and the system administrator, the backup administrator should usually understand more of the backup environment than the system administrator does. In turn, a system administrator will typically understand more of the backup environment than an application administrator does, and so on.

The point of this "onion skin" approach is to highlight that the further away users are from administering or interacting with a backup system, the less they'll understand about it. We introduced the idea of the amount of information a user might receive about the backup system in the training section (see chapter 5). As it is not practical to train all people who might interact with

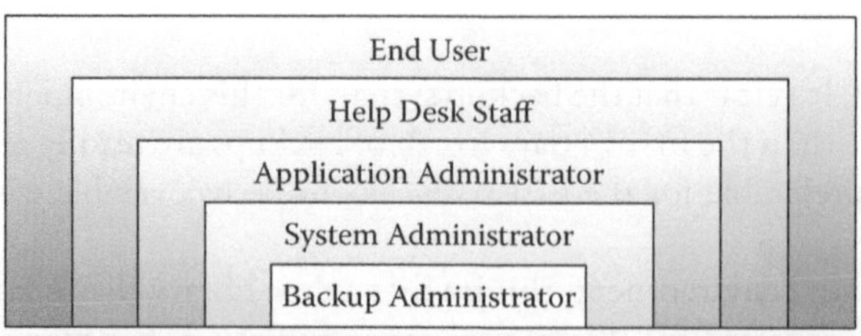

Figure 7.1 Role relationship with backup systems

the backup system to the same level, it stands to reason that the way in which these people interact with the backup system will be different.

Therefore, for each "tier" away from the backup environment a user is, it is necessary to provide a progressively simpler mechanism for the user to interact with it, and the more necessary it is to deal with contingencies automatically on behalf of the user, perhaps without the user even being aware this is occurring. Examples of impacts this makes include, but are not limited to:

- Ensuring that recoveries don't need to wait for media to be retrieved from off site (for end users, this sort of "unexplained wait" may result in multiple cancellations and restarts of the restore process before logging a fault with the administrator of the system).
- Ensuring that each role has appropriate documentation for the type(s) of recoveries they may be reasonably expected to perform. This is directly related to actually deciding the extent to which the different roles can perform recoveries. For instance, many system administration teams are happy with the notion of providing recovery capabilities to operators and help desk staff for file and directory recoveries, but will not hand over responsibility for application and system recoveries. The level of documentation provided will primarily be based on the types of recoveries expected.
- Backup software should be configured in such a way that the permissions of the user performing a recovery are reflected in what is recovered. For instance, does the backup product disallow the recovery of employee payroll data (which legally can be accessed only by human resources staff) by a help desk operator? (Additionally, watch out for anti-virus software running as a different user account than the actual user performing the recovery. When not properly configured, this can block the recovery due to not having sufficient permissions to scan the data being retrieved.)
- Does the backup software provide some form of auditing to let administrators know that (1) a particular user is trying to recover files or (2) a particular user has recovered a particular set of data?
- Does the backup software provide a simple monitoring mechanism that doesn't compromise system security, and is straightforward enough that users can see their recovery request in progress, and what might be impacting its ability to complete?

7.3 Recovery Procedures and Recommendations

Various backup products will support a variety of recovery techniques, and the general principles of these techniques have been discussed in section 3.8, "Recovery Strategies."

The purpose of this topic is to move beyond the simple aspects of what can and can't be done, and try to address the more challenging issues — what should or should not be done.

7.3.1 Read the Documentation before Starting a Recovery

Always read the vendor-supplied documentation regarding recoveries carefully, and before it is time to perform a recovery, not just when it is time to perform a recovery. The reason for this is quite simple — by being familiar and comfortable with the recovery procedure before it is used, an administrator can concentrate on the recovery, not the documentation. Also, if for some reason the documentation mentions what must be done as part of the backup for a successful recovery, discovering this information only when it's time to attempt the recovery is unpleasant, to say the least.

The documentation — or some distillation of it — needs to be available to anyone who may need to perform recoveries, with any annotations regarding environment specific changes or features. (As a backup consultant, it is very common to encounter situations where staff more intimately involved in the deployment of a backup product have not provided any documentation to operations staff, expecting them to manage the day-to-day functions of the backup server based on demonstrated activities only.)

It also needs to be recognized that there is some difference between documentation on how to perform a recovery and documentation on how to recover in a specific environment. For example, documentation on how to perform a recovery will cover such things as:

- Launching the recovery program
- Browsing for files to recover and selecting those files for recovery
- Identifying the media required for the recovery
- Starting and monitoring the recovery process

However, documentation on how to perform a recovery within a specific environment should cover somewhat more than this, encompassing all of the above steps as well as:

- Which processes or authorities need to be gone through to allow a recovery
- What system activities need to be quiesced (if any) on either the client or the backup server to facilitate the recovery
- Organization standards or practices for where files and data should be recovered to, under various circumstances (e.g., recovery of user files, user mail boxes, applications, and databases)
- Where backup media are to be sourced from, if not available in a media changer, and who should be contacted to authorize the release or return of that media
- The procedures or processes to follow at the end of a recovery — differentiating between what needs to be done at the conclusion of a successful recovery from an unsuccessful recovery
- How to remove and return media that were not in an automated media changer following the recovery

Of course, depending on the size and complexity of an organization, there may be changes to the above lists. However, some compilation of procedures will be required — not necessarily to document the actual recovery itself, but all the corporate procedures regarding the recovery.

7.3.2 Choosing the Correct Recovery Location

It goes without saying that if not handled correctly, a recovery could conceivably result in a loss of even more data than that being recovered. One of the worst ways that this can happen is to recover data to the wrong location. If a backup system supports directed recoveries, this can aggravate the problem further, and if the backup system supports cross-platform directed recoveries, the implications of a poor recovery location selection become even worse.

Therefore, it is very important to confirm the recovery location before initiating the recovery, and to understand any limitations that may exist on where file(s) or data can be recovered to.

Examples of recovery locations include

- The original host and original location of the data
- The original host but another location for the data
- An alternate host with the same location
- An alternate host with a different location

Each option has different advantages and disadvantages. For instance, being able to perform a recovery to the original host and location is obviously critical when performing disaster recoveries, but can also be important for recovering critical files or system data that has been accidentally deleted, as well as recovering partially deleted directory trees.

Recovering to the original host but a different location is typically a useful function for backup administrators, operators, or help desk staff. This is particularly the case if they perform the recoveries for end users who are unsure as to exactly which file(s) they want recovered. In this case, it is not unusual for an entire directory tree to be recovered to an alternate location, with the end user asked to winnow through the recovered tree to locate the required file(s) before deleting the recovered tree.

When recovering to an alternate host, recovering to an alternate directory path is often useful — but sometimes this won't be required. For instance, if an environment features a production system and a development system configured exactly the same way, the development system could easily be refreshed periodically with a copy of the production data via a recovery to the same location on a different host.

When end users make recovery requests and can cite the exact files or exact location of files to be recovered, many help desk and operations staff will recover these back to their local machine and simply e-mail the files back to the end user.

One recommendation when performing recoveries is that, before clicking the button or typing the command that finally starts the recovery, always ask the following questions:

- Have the correct file(s) been selected?
- Was the correct host logged into, prior to running the recovery command?
- Has the correct recovery location been selected?
- Is the recovery going to run to the correct destination host?

This typically amounts to 30 seconds or less of checking, but being in the habit of performing these checks can prevent some of the worst types of recovery mistakes that can be made.

By having reviewed documentation relating to recoveries prior to performing them, any limitations to redirecting recovery locations should be clearly understood — and the implications of attempting to redirect recoveries when they can't be done. (For instance, special types of data may be treated like "database" data rather than file data during a recovery such as, say, the Windows registry hives, and therefore instead of being recovered as files, they may be recovered as an import into the registry. Such a type of recovery may not be relocatable, and it is these types of limitations that should be known in advance.)

7.3.3 Provide an Estimate of How Long the Recovery Will Take

There are two types of recoveries — those that can be performed while talking to the user who is currently requesting the recovery (e.g., "you want this file back? Hmmm, how's the weather?" [running recovery in background]), and those where the recovery will take time to prepare or to run, therefore it will be necessary to inform the person(s) who requested the recovery once it is complete.

When in a situation where a recovery can't be performed as soon as it is requested, it is important to provide an estimate of how long the recovery will take to run. For instance, if a user requests the recovery of a single file (particularly if it is a verbal request to a backup administrator or operator), the user may expect the file will be back and available momentarily, and may not start any new work. If, however, the backup operator or administrator believes the recovery will take an hour to complete because a tape will most likely need to be recalled, the user should be told, so that he or she can schedule other activities rather than waiting for the file.

In some instances this estimate might be quite accurate, but in others it will be somewhat like the question "how long is a piece of string?" In the cases where the recovery time really can't be predicted, at least some form of *guestimate* should be provided ("I'm not sure — maybe four hours?") so that the user is aware of some initial time frame and that the time frame is not a hard certainty.

By being provided with an estimated recovery completion time, users can schedule their work around when the system or data will be available again. Like the personnel performing the recovery, it's entirely likely they'll have a multitude of other tasks they could be doing while longer recoveries are running.

7.3.4 Give Updates during Recoveries

Following from the need to provide recovery estimates, it is also important that updates are periodically provided on how the recovery is progressing, even if those updates are "still recovering, no problems." This allows everyone to understand where recoveries stand. Consider the scenario of a four-hour recovery where a tape fails during the recovery process. For instance:

Time	*Action*
09:30	Recovery requested.
09:45	Recovery initiated. Estimate of four hours to recover provided to users.
10:15	Update to users – recovery is progressing, no errors.
10:45	Update to users – recovery is progressing, no errors.
11:15	Update to users – recovery is progressing, no errors.
11:45	Update to users – recovery is progressing, no errors.
11:55	Tape fails.
12:15	Update provided to users – issue with recovery, tapes holding backup duplicates will be recalled from off site. New estimate for recovery time is 5 p.m.

Now, consider the situation when updates are not given:

Time	*Action*
09:30	Recovery requested.
09:45	Recovery initiated. Estimate of four hours to recover provided to users.
11:55	Tape fails.
13:00	User requests update and is told that issues have occurred, and the recovery will take longer with tapes to be recalled from off site.

In the first example, users have seen that progress has been made throughout the recovery and have been informed when issues have arisen. Even though a failure has occurred, and they may be facing a longer-than-four-hour wait to get access to their files or systems again, at least they've been aware of the progress that was made.

In the second example, however, users have requested a recovery and, after not hearing of any progress for almost three hours, have found out that a tape has failed. Psychologically, this makes the reaction to the change in a recovery situation quite different.

The personnel performing the recoveries are not the only ones under pressure. The owners and users of the system are probably even more interested in the success of the recovery than those performing the recovery, and the best way to avoid staff being asked every few minutes how the recovery is progressing by a different person is to provide regular updates to everyone.

For instance, if people still have e-mail access, they should be informed that updates will be provided at regular intervals — and then those updates must be provided. If people don't have e-mail, regular phone updates should be provided to a particular person, and they can then inform others of the progress. This is the best way to avoid "shrapnel" recoveries whereby a particular person flies to pieces at the thought of data loss and incessantly pesters the people performing the recovery. By providing regular updates (and on time) personnel have little need to interrupt the recovery process asking for an update on it.

7.3.5 Write-Protect Offline Media before Using

A silly but not unheard of mistake when loading media into a tape drive or library for recovery is that instead of issuing a command to load and inventory the volumes, the command to load and label the volumes is issued. This of course doesn't happen to all people, but some people have felt that "oh no!" moment.

Nevertheless, this style of problem goes to highlight that off-site media in particular are most vulnerable to data destruction when reloaded into a media unit — that's the nature of off-site media: we remove media from site and from active/on-line storage to prevent mishaps. (As a side note, this is why disk backup units should not be considered for long-term/indefinite storage of long-term (monthly or yearly) backups, as such backups should typically remain "offline" for safety.)

Although most backup products feature a "soft read-only" setting for media, nothing guarantees read-only more than actually physically turning on the write-protect tab on media (short of not using the media at all). Therefore if needing to use offline media, always physically write-protect them before returning the media to online usage for the recovery.*

This type of strategy ensures that offline media remain "as protected as possible," and protects not only from the type of mistake mentioned above, but from a variety of other potential media-overwrite situations that could make a critical recovery a critical disaster.

An alternate policy used by some companies, which is perhaps even more focused on data protection, is that rather than write-protecting offline media before they are used for a recovery, all media have write-protection enabled as they are removed from online storage. This happens regardless of when the media would be re-used and where they are destined to go. The write-protect tab is only turned off for the media when reloaded into online units with a formal notification that the media are to be re-used. At any other time when the volume is requested, the media go back into the online storage with the write-protect tab left on.

Although this can potentially result in situations whereby tapes might be occasionally loaded for re-use with the write-protect tab on, it more closely follows the rule of taking as many steps as necessary to protect backups, and therefore should be considered a useful option for organizations.

7.3.6 Don't Assume a Recovery Can Be Done if It Hasn't Been Tested

A mistake made particularly when implementing new backup software, or new features of existing backup software, is to assume that particular recoveries can be done without actually testing those scenarios. This can lead to serious issues if the system goes into production untested.

This is not to say that the recovery of every single file must be tested, but as more of a reminder that if a new backup system is to be installed, it has to be tested. For instance, if installing backups for a new database for the first time, recoveries should be tested rather than assumed that they'll work.

Not only should tests be performed, but the results should be permanently/officially noted to serve as a reference point in future. Where possible, it should be extrapolated what might happen over time — e.g., are there planned upgrades or changes that could alter the success of a recovery despite previous tests?

> **Systems Grow, Test Results Change.** This was highlighted in particular once when a customer was testing a block-level agent for Windows to back up a dense filesystem. They were implementing with LTO-1 tapes, with a native 100-GB capacity. One of the features of the block-level agent software was to be able to do a disaster recovery of the entire filesystem as a block-level retrieve without reference to any indices, which was a significantly faster method of disaster recovery.
>
> These tests worked, and over multiple tests we found that the tapes filled at approximately 130 GB written.
>
> Towards the end of the testing, the customer mentioned a plan to upgrade the filesystem from 100 GB to 300 GB. It was of course important then to test how the recovery would work over multiple tapes. This could be simulated by running two backups in a row and recovering from the second backup, which naturally spanned two tapes.

* This implies, of course, that once the media is no longer required for the recovery, it should be removed and its write-protect status cleared before being returned to its previous location.

This test showed that the product was incapable of doing this fast style of recovery when backups spanned multiple tapes, and therefore was incapable of surviving system growth.

Of course, it isn't possible to test for every possible contingency or every possibility of future growth. However, as much as possible should be tested prior to system implementation, and only recovery strategies based on what has been tested should be advertised to the business.

7.3.7 Recall All Required Media at the Start of the Recovery

This not only harks back to using backup catalogues that can list which volumes will be needed for recovery, but also serves as a reminder that a recovery should be planned rather than run in an ad-hoc fashion. By planning the recovery, and knowing what volumes are needed to recover from, it is possible to anticipate the needs of the backup product and thus avoid unnecessary delays waiting for media to be returned.

Don't start the recovery and then ask for volumes to be recalled — ask for the volumes to be recalled and plan to start the recovery once they are available. Even if the recovery is started beforehand (for instance, some media may already be on site and can therefore be recovered from first), ensure everyone understands that the successful completion of the recovery is contingent on retrieving tapes from off site.

Additionally, if media are recalled, remember to ask how long it will take for the media to arrive, and then confirm arrival at the appropriate time. If the media have not arrived, escalate immediately rather than just restating that the media are required.

7.3.8 Acclimatize Off-Site Recovery Media Whenever Possible

Reading the fine print on most backup media, there will be reference to optimum humidity and temperature conditions for the use of that media. If moving media around (e.g., arranging them to be brought back on site from the tape storage vendor), give the media time to adjust to the temperature and humidity of the computer room before loading in a tape drive whenever possible. (For instance, companies operating in the tropics in far north Australia typically encounter humidity problems on tapes, if the tapes are unprotected, simply when moving them from one building to another in the same campus, a walk of perhaps 100 meters.)

Obviously, giving acclimatization time is not possible in all situations (particularly if it is a critical recovery), but it remains a recommended step. A logical extrapolation from this is that the chosen off-site vendor should (1) store media in an environment with an optimal temperature and humidity, and (2) transport media in bags or boxes that protect them from significant environment/atmosphere differences.

It's worth remembering that because there should be at least two copies of each backup, with one being off site and one being on site, that it is only on rare occasions that there should be a need to refer to off-site media, typically only if the on-site media fails. On-site media that is offline should be stored in an environment as similar to the computer room as possible, if not in the room itself. That way any offline, on-site media can be used near to immediately in a drive without fear of insufficient acclimatization times.

7.3.9 Run Recoveries from Sessions That Can Be Disconnected From/Reconnected To

It is the nature of recoveries to take a variable amount of time to complete. It may be a quick recovery, or it may be a recovery that takes literally days to complete depending on the volume of data and other activities.

It is frustrating enough having a recovery fail due to faulty media or hardware, but it is a particularly frustrating and time-wasting experience to have a recovery fail simply because the connection was lost to the server or host that the recovery was running from. It's also quite likely to happen if a recovery is initiated from a dial-up or remote connection.

Alternatively, it is rather unpleasant to be forced to stay back in the office for an unknown period of time to track a recovery simply because:

- The recovery was started from a laptop.
- The laptop can't be taken home without aborting the recovery.
- The recovery can't be monitored from home without the laptop.
- The recovery can't be aborted and restarted without causing problems or delays.

To avoid these scenarios, long recoveries should be run from sessions that can be disconnected and reconnected from another location, with the recovery still running while disconnected.

Under UNIX systems, this typically can be accomplished from running a command-line recovery under a "screen" session, or if the recovery program works via the GUI only, it should be initiated from a VNC desktop that can be disconnected from and reconnected to later. For Windows systems, consider directing recoveries from a remote desktop session or via VNC, which will again allow a disconnect and later reconnect.

7.3.10 Know the Post-Recovery Configuration Changes

Depending on the type of recovery being performed, it may be necessary to make post-recovery configuration changes — particularly if an application or database is recovered from one system onto another system.

For instance, a common method of refreshing the development, test, or QA database for a corporate environment is periodically to recover the production database into the other database(s). This ensures that people working with the development/test/QA databases are working with a reasonably up-to-date copy of the current production data, and will therefore be working with the most appropriate sample data available.

Following the completion of the recovery in these instances, the configuration file(s) associated with the restored database or application must be updated so that, once started, it doesn't "impersonate" the production system, thereby causing real production problems. Although this is often referenced as a step in recovery instructions, the consequences of not following the procedure is not always clearly elaborated.

7.3.11 Check Everything before It Is Done

This comes down to being absolutely certain that actions that are about to be taken are correct. That is, taking the time to confirm

- The correct host has been logged into.
- The correct recovery location has been chosen, or it has been confirmed that the recovery is definitely to go to the original location.
- The correct files have been selected for recovery.
- There is sufficient capacity on the filesystem(s) to support the recovery.
- Users are not accessing the system if this is not recommended/allowed during the recovery.

These may seem like trivial, unnecessary checks, but it's precisely those reasons that we need to perform the checks — making assumptions when working in a situation where there has already been data loss may result in more data loss or downtime than the company is prepared for.

> **Example: The Sort of Recovery No One Wants to Perform.** When still a relatively new system administrator, I found it quite frustrating watching a more-experienced system administrator work on a recovery — before pressing "return" to run a command, he would always double-check what he had typed to be confident that it was correct. This seemed like a complete waste of time.
>
> That of course was before I rushed through a recovery too quickly, and recovered /dev from a Linux host into /dev on a Solaris host, all because I failed to double-check what I was running. (Or to be more precise, *where* I was running the command.) Given that the Solaris host was the backup server, this significantly exacerbated the recovery activity.

These types of checks take almost no time but can save considerable angst. There's obviously a line that must be drawn between careful checking and procrastination or needless checking, but there is more to running a recovery than just clicking some buttons or running some commands — quality assurance plays a factor.

If concerned about how long these checks take, remember that spending an extra one or two minutes performing final checks before initiating a recovery is a trivial amount of time in comparison to making a mistake and having to restart the entire process or run extra recoveries not planned for initially.

7.3.12 Remember Quantum Physics

Monitoring can be useful, but excessive monitoring results in skewed results. Therefore the level of monitoring should be carefully chosen when performing recoveries.

Recoveries are no different from any other activity — the more they are monitored, the slower they run, or the less accurate the monitoring will be. For example, if recovering a few hundred files there may be little impact in seeing a file-by-file listing of what has been recovered. However, if recovering a million files, the display of each file may become a limiting factor in the ability to obtain accurate updates of where the recovery is up to. This can be particularly the case when performing recoveries on, say, a dial-up connection or a UNIX system console.

> **A Watched Recovery Never Completes.** When running a disaster recovery once on a Solaris backup server via a 9600 baud console, the recovery appeared to take six hours to complete. But when the recovery finally "finished" and the server could be accessed again, it was observed that the tape devices had been idle for two hours — i.e., it had

taken four hours to conduct the recovery, and an additional two hours to finish displaying all the files that had been recovered.

Recoveries often need to be monitored, but can frequently be monitored through better mechanisms than simply which file the recovery is up to — particularly with larger recoveries. Less-intrusive ways to monitor include periodically checking the amount of used space on the recovery target, or monitoring the amount of megabytes or gigabytes reported recovered through a backup administration application.

7.3.13 Be Patient

Almost everyone would have been told when growing up that "patience is a virtue," usually in response to wanting something faster, sooner, or better. As computers and data transfer speeds increase in speed, patience is sometimes forgotten. This comes down to a "brute force" approach to solving problems — if it isn't fast enough, don't optimize, just throw more memory/CPU/spindles at the problem and hope that it goes away. One area where this rarely works, and where it is important to remember the virtues of patience, is when it comes time to perform a recovery.

Sometimes particular steps or activities take a while to happen, and regardless of how much of an emergency exists, it is not always possible to speed up the process at all. For instance, if a tape library has difficulty unloading a tape, it may take a while for it to drag itself out of the error. Think carefully about whether it is faster in failure situations to wait for the error to be corrected/dealt with, or to intervene. In a situation whereby a tape unload fails, the intervention may be to stop the backup software, manually remove the tape, let the library re-initialize, start the backup software, have it re-establish library state and then attempt the activity again. If performing a recovery, this may require the operation to be aborted, and therefore taking a little longer than desirable for the system to free itself from the failure may save considerably more time.

In particular, focusing on tape libraries for a moment, administrators and operators should always "meet" their tape libraries before they go into production, or before a major recovery is performed. Rather than shaking the robotic hand inside the library, what this refers to is actually sitting near the library, in line of sight, and observing how long each of the following activities takes:

- Tape load commands
- Tape unload commands
- Tape deposit and withdraw commands
- Tape load commands that necessitate an unload of media first

Not All Libraries Are Created Equal. When doing an install for a customer who was using a tape library I'd not dealt with before, only by watching the library could I understand why it was taking so long from the time that a tape was put in its CAP to the time that the backup software registered the tape. The CAP was too high to accommodate the barcode scanner on the library robotic arm, so the robot had to move the tape to another slot, scan the barcode, and then return the scanned tape to the CAP. Only at that point did the backup software register that a tape was present.

For the most part, tape libraries end up in rooms that are not necessarily the same location that administrators and operators work from. This therefore results in a physical disconnect whereby users of the system aren't necessarily always aware of what is going on within them. If administrators and operators know how long activities take, it enables considerably more patience during a recovery — and it allows users to know more confidently that the time for patience is over.

7.3.14 Document the Current Status of the Recovery

Many backup and system administrators have faced a 24- or 36-hour recovery experience. (Since Murphy's law seems to prevail in IT as much as anywhere else, this is usually prefaced by having gone into the office having not had much sleep the night before.)

Frequently people stay involved from start to finish in such lengthy recoveries due to either being the only people available to do the work or, having started the recovery, feel uncomfortable with passing on the recovery to someone else. Obviously, if an administrator is the only person available to do the work, this is not an easy limitation to overcome, but it is something that the company must understand and plan for — a single person with knowledge of a particular system represents just as significant a single point of failure as, say, not RAID-protecting the filesystems on that system.

While it's difficult to do something about being the only person available to do the work, it should be possible to hand over the restore to someone else as long as the status of the restore is maintained. If there is a published list of steps (i.e., documented restore procedure), this may be as simple as keeping track of the step number that is currently being executed. If there is no published list of steps, then some record should be kept of where the recovery is up to. (On UNIX systems, a common way of achieving this is to "script" the entire session, i.e., capture all input and output during the recovery.) It is also just as important, if not more important, to keep a running record of what errors or issues have occurred, so that when the recovery is passed on to someone else, they are aware of the current state of play in the system.

This ensures that if the person who starts the recovery has to abandon it for some reason (e.g., a family issue, prior plans, or occupational health and safety requirements that force staff to return home), the recovery process can be passed on to someone else so they can continue it.

7.3.15 Note Errors, and What Led to Them

A critical activity in recoveries — or even to be performed after recoveries — is to keep track of any error that occurs, and a synopsis of the events that lead to the error.

If it is a non-critical error and doesn't affect the recovery, it can be raised with the support vendor afterwards. If it is a critical error, it will be necessary to have all the information required by the support vendor in the first pass to diagnose the problem.

Although this applies to all situations (i.e., regardless of whether errors are being researched or being escalated), it is quite critical that the error messages received during recovery are noted — and without wishing to sound curmudgeonly, these errors should be noted exactly, including any particular spacing, punctuation, or grammar/spelling mistakes. For instance, there might be a significant difference between `failed' and 'failed' in an error message. Sometimes screenshots can help in this, as they irrefutably show what has occurred.

It is important as well to note not only the error message itself, but the circumstances that led to it. Did an error only occur after the restore was started without the first tape in a tape drive? Did an error only occur after the tape library's SAN port experienced a temporary glitch and an LIP occurred during the middle of a restore? Obviously for some errors, it will not be possible to note exactly what led to the error. However, even if it is simply noted what was being done on the system at the time, a good head start will be provided to someone who will investigate the problem. In the same vein as noting what led to the errors, this should include the capturing of system state — grab application and system log files to review what else was going on within the system at the same time.

7.3.16 Don't Assume the Recovery Is an Exam

Certification exams often work in the following two ways: (1) student is "locked" into a room without any notes, manuals, etc.; and (2) no communications in or out of the room are allowed during the exam time. This is hardly a "real world" situation — or at least it shouldn't be. Although the purpose behind a certification exam is understood, it's also worthwhile noting that such exams fail to deal with knowledge acquisition and aggregation — the ability to pull in information from a variety of sources and construct solutions from those sources.

During a recovery situation, always remember to leverage any information or access to support that exists, whenever it is needed. Obstinacy does not guarantee results in most cases, nor does getting flustered to the point of not evaluating other options.

It is not uncommon to observe people struggling with recoveries for an extended period of time without checking documentation or calling support. What starts off as a small problem when there is plenty of time to spare in the recovery window can end up becoming a critical problem when the recovery window has almost expired. Therefore, why exacerbate the problem by treating it like an exam?

It's easy to become so focused that other options are forgotten, but it's important to avoid doing so. A side point to this is never to forget the usefulness of a Web search engine. For instance, support staff in many organizations have solved a tangible percentage of support cases logged by customers simply by typing the error message reported into Google or another publicly accessible forum. The lesson to be learned is that not all sources of information are official sources. The vendors may have a lot of information available in their knowledge bases, but this may be sanitized, or it may not cover a particularly obscure subject. When this happens it doesn't mean that no one else in the world has encountered the error. It could be that the error message will appear in some other vendor's support database — for instance, companies like Sun and Microsoft (just to name two) maintain large knowledge bases that often overlap knowledge from other areas, or third party products where their staff have been involved in the diagnosis of a particular failure.

It also could be the case that the error being encountered is indeed the first instance of that error seen anywhere in the world. Maybe no one else in the world has tried to back up a Plan 9 server to an LTO Ultrium 3 drive attached to a Novell NetWare backup server using an AIX storage node, in which case, it's not just the error message that matters, it's the state of the environment that matters. Both items are needed for successful problem diagnosis and repair.

7.3.17 If Media/Tape Errors Occur, Retry Elsewhere

This is a perfect example of why backups must be protected by duplication. If an error occurs, it is not always immediately obvious where the error occurred. If a tape error is reported, for instance, the error may have occurred with the tape media or a tape drive — or if it has occurred with tape media, it may have actually caused a problem in the tape drive as a result. (Some administrators advocate that once an error is received in a drive, even if it is shown to be a media-only error, then a cleaning cartridge should be run through the drive before any other tape is used to ensure that the drive does not then malfunction with the next tape.)

Quite simply, the second (and potentially only other) copy of the data needed for recovery should not be risked in the same tape drive as has just encountered a failure unless absolutely necessary. If for some reason it is necessary to retry in the same tape drive, at least try a cleaning cartridge and another data cartridge first to ensure that the drive either wasn't the cause of the problem or wasn't affected by the problem.

Where possible, however, retry the recovery using a different tape drive, and preferably a different tape holding a duplicate of the data to be recovered.

7.3.18 Ensure the Recovery Is Performed by Those Trained to Do It

There may be a wide variety of people available to perform the differing types of recoveries that the system may be used for. For instance, simple file/directory recoveries may be able to be performed by anyone from an end user to application/system/backup administrators. However, as recoveries increase in complexity, the level of training required for someone to be able confidently and successfully to perform the recovery may increase — database recoveries may very much need the involvement of an application administrator, and complete system recoveries may need the involvement of a dedicated system administrator for that particular operating system.

Recoveries should be performed only by those people who are trained (and thus qualified, whether officially or unofficially) so as to ensure the operation is completed correctly. This is not by any means a reflection on those people who have not been trained to do the recovery — they may very well be capable of performing the recovery with suitable training — but it makes sense to have the most knowledgeable people performing a recovery. Such people are thus able to handle abnormalities and deviations from the expected process with minimum fuss, and adapt the process to ensure the recovery completes. For instance, consider a complete operating system recovery. It may be possible for an operator or help desk staff member who has no real system-administration experience to complete a recovery by following a careful set of instructions as long as all systems are built to the same exacting circumstances. However, they may be unable to cope as well as a system administrator would to an unexpected error. This may result in them attempting to continue with the recovery or needlessly restarting the recovery, assuming that they have performed a previous step incorrectly. (This, of course, may have nothing to do with the fact that, say, for instance, the fiber-channel cable has also failed and therefore SAN access becomes an issue, with IO errors reported when they try to format a disk.)

If the recovery should be performed only by a system administrator, don't try to get an operator or a help desk agent to perform the recovery. (If operators and help desk staff have to learn how to perform such recoveries, that's what test environments are for.)

(A corollary to this is to ensure that staff are trained. Backup consultants frequently find managers who are reluctant to train their staff in the administration and operation of the backup product they've just purchased, which is quite frankly a disturbing prospect.)

7.3.19 Read and Follow the Instructions if They've Never Been Used Before

We've said before that it is important that the documentation should be read before the recovery is started. Unfortunately, this may not always be an option, particularly if the person who normally performs the recovery is unavailable.

In such cases that staff performing the recovery are not normally tasked with such activities, the documentation for the recovery must be read in its entirety, and the steps followed very carefully. Even for staff who normally perform the recoveries, using the instructions as a quick "refresher" or introduction for the recovery prior to starting is a helpful way of focusing on the activities to be performed.

If the documentation includes particular steps and there are questions as to the value of those steps, be very careful about deciding not to follow them. Although there's always the chance that they actually aren't required, keep in mind that it's far better to follow procedures and have the recovery take a little longer than may be necessary than it is to skip a step, only to have to restart the recovery process because it was later determined to be required. If it turns out the steps were not required for the recovery being performed, the documentation should be updated (or a reference-able addendum written) to state that the steps were successfully skipped.

7.3.20 Write a Post-Recovery Report

This may not apply of course to every single recovery that is performed — for instance, system and application administrators will periodically perform recoveries of system/application files that are not necessarily visible to users, and are restored primarily for referential purposes — such restores normally occur without users or even management being particularly aware that they are occurring.

However, for any "official" recovery, it is important to provide some report upon completion of the recovery. For simple recoveries, this may be as minor as an e-mail to the user(s) that requested the restore, or completion of the recovery request forms. For more-complex recoveries, or recoveries where issues were encountered, a more-formal report of activities completed may be appropriate to finalize the restore.

If issues occurred during the restore that could be avoided by a change of corporate procedures, backup practices, or additional budget, a formal recovery report is the absolute best place to make mention of those issues — and what might be done to resolve them so that they do not occur again. Indeed, if the recovery was required due to failures in systems that could in the future be avoided, it is pertinent to mention these so that organizations can undertake improvements to their processes or systems. (Although it may sound blunt, few things get to the point more than a post-recovery report written after a 24-hour outage by the person that worked on the recovery the entire time.)

7.3.21 Update Incorrect Instructions

Although we have briefly touched on the subject of updating instructions, it warrants a mention of its own that procedures and documentation should remain relevant at all times in a backup/recovery system so as to avoid unfortunate failures.

There's a general rule that most system administrators seem to follow: an administrator can make the same mistake exactly once. It's when the same mistake is made multiple times that there starts to be a problem. Thus, if performing a recovery and discovering that the documentation for the recovery is incorrect, it should immediately be updated while the recovery is still well remembered to ensure that the same problems do not occur again later. (This is somewhat different than noting steps that can be skipped, instead referring more to steps or sequences that are blatantly wrong.)

If simply noting that some steps are redundant, considerable caution should be felt about removing those steps from the documentation. They may very well be there to cover a scenario that didn't occur in the specific recovery performed in this instance. Instead, aim at providing an alternate documentation procedure rather than removing all evidence of the steps that didn't need to be followed during the most-recent recovery. This avoids situations where, over successive recoveries, the same content is removed and then re-inserted because there are either alternate ways of going about the same recovery or there are actually slightly different recoveries that can be performed using similar but not completely identical procedures.

Failing to update incorrect documentation almost guarantees that at some point in the future someone will follow incorrect documentation and suffer the same recovery failures again. A cavalier attitude towards documentation for systems and backup/recovery environments should be avoided.

7.3.22 Preserve the Number of Copies of Backups

If copies of backups (cloned or duplicates) are generated, then there should be the same number of functioning copies at the conclusion of the recovery process as there were at the start of the recovery. This means that if a particular copy or duplicate failed during the recovery (necessitating a recovery from an alternative copy), then a necessary step at the end of the recovery process is to recreate the copy that failed (and any other backup copies that existed on the media if the entire piece of media failed) so that the original number of copies have been preserved.

Therefore the recovery process could be said to be along the lines of:

- Recover from local media
- If local media successfully recover, no need to continue
- If local media fail:
  - Recall off-site media
  - Recover from off-site media
  - Regenerate a copy of the on-site media using the off-site media
- Send the off-site media back off site

Failing to do this could result in a second recovery attempt from the same backups becoming a complete disaster in the event of another media failure.

This also ensures that any legal obligations regarding the number of copies continues to be met.

7.3.23 Send Off-Site Media Back Off Site

Although we try to avoid it, periodically some recoveries will need to be performed using media that does not normally reside on the primary site. In these cases, media will need to be recalled from an off-site location to the required site so that it can be read from.

A common mistake is that such media are not returned to their off-site location at the conclusion of the recovery (or a suitable grace period thereafter). This goes directly against the reason behind off-site media. We send media off site to ensure that the backups they contain are protected from the types of failures that can affect on-site media. By leaving such media on site after they are no longer required, we lose that added degree of protection that they were generated for in the first place.

Leaving off-site media on site may open a company up to a new set of problems later, and therefore once certain that the recovery is complete, media should be sent back to the off-site location. Once this is done, don't forget to update any media tracking records — it may be that this is handled automatically when the media are originally sent off site. However, it may need to be done manually when media are returned to the off-site location.

An additional factor, other than the practical protection provided by off-site media, could very well be legal requirements. If an organization is legally required to create backup duplicates and send them off site, it creates a legal obligation to ensure that once a recovery is complete, the off-site copy is sent back off site so that the organization does not potentially fail in an audit or inspection. For instance, if the only off-site copy is on site the day that it is being used for a recovery, an auditor is most likely to find this acceptable. However, if it is still on site a month after the recovery, auditors may report it as a violation of corporate or legal policies.

If a company is legally required to keep off-site copies of backup media, there may also be legal requirements to the use of that media. For instance, it may be that it is not permitted to retrieve these copies, and it is necessary instead to have a tape drive at the off-site location to use for recovery.

7.3.24 Remind Vendors of SLAs

Support and maintenance contracts — regardless of whether they are for hardware or for software — cost businesses real money. It's the price of insuring the backup system (and IT systems in general) against failure. If someone breaks into a person's home and steals equipment, the victim will tend to force the insurance company to act in a timely manner and honor the policy that was taken. It's a logical response to the situation, and one that is entirely appropriate.

However, recoveries have been observed to take significantly longer because vendors could not meet their SLAs for the supply of replacement hardware. Staff must understand that the failure of a vendor to meet an SLA needs to be escalated to senior management for discussion with the vendor's senior management. For example, is it really the concern of staff performing the recovery if a vendor has agreed to a four-hour parts-and-labor SLA, but has to fly in equipment from another city? The short (and only) answer to this is "no." If the IT department has promised/agreed-to SLAs with the rest of the business on the basis of the SLAs provided by vendors, then staff should be prepared to enforce those SLAs with the vendors.

Obviously when escalating SLA issues, it is worthwhile remembering that the people in the front-line support at the vendor may not actually have any say in how quickly issues can be addressed, and this is why it is necessary to have an escalation process provided by the vendors as part of support and maintenance contracts. In short, be very reluctant to agree to a vendor not meeting their SLA requirements — while the vendor may be gracious about being "let off the hook," management may not be so pleased or grateful.

7.3.25 Cars Have Bandwidth, Too

There is a timeless statement, often attributed to Andrew Tanenbaum, which is typically quoted as "never underestimate the bandwidth of a station wagon full of tapes hurtling down the highway." This has become particularly relevant in recovery situations — and even more so in remote recovery situations.

This does not specifically mean of course to consider only vehicles as a means of transferring data between sites, but more that non-immediate data transfer methods should be considered in a data recovery environment where appropriate.

If recovering a significant amount of data at a remote site with poor throughput, it may be faster and more efficient to attend the site with the required media and equipment for reading that media. Of course, this actually should be planned long in advance of the recovery, but it may become an option in an emergency.

Examples of where this style of recovery scenario might be appropriate include

- Low-bandwidth links to remote offices do not need to mean a significant outage in the event of a system failure. If spare equipment is kept in the main production site (or a suitably equipped satellite office with sufficient bandwidth), the systems from the low-bandwidth sites could be reconstructed on the spare equipment, and the equipment is then shipped out as a whole to replace the failed systems, thus avoiding any significant bandwidth transfer. A 24-hour turnaround to build and courier remote equipment might be significantly faster than sending a large amount of data over a slow link, or acceptable in comparison to the cost of maintaining a high-speed link between the sites just for disaster recovery.
- Rather than trying to run backups over a slow link, or paying for a more expensive link, it may be cheaper to run backup systems remotely, with tapes generated remotely sent to the production site for protection, only to be returned for re-use or recovery.

7.4 Disaster Recovery

Obviously, everything stated in the previous topic on regular recoveries is applicable for disaster recoveries, in addition to the specific items below.

7.4.1 Maintenance Backups

7.4.1.1 Perform a Backup before Maintenance

Before performing system maintenance tasks (for example, application or system upgrades, installation of patches, etc.), a backup should be performed so that in the event of maintenance failures the system can be backed out to a point just prior to the maintenance attempt. If it is necessary to fall back to the next most-recent backup, this may result in the loss of more data than the business finds acceptable.

For example, consider the following scenario:

1. Backup occurs on Tuesday evening at 9 p.m., finishing by 11 p.m.
2. System is used as per usual on Wednesday.
3. At close of business Wednesday, the logical volume management software is upgraded. Unfortunately, a step on the release notes was not followed and the filesystem became corrupted.
4. The filesystem is reformatted and the data is recovered.
5. On Thursday, users have to recreate all data generated on Wednesday.

Although this may seem a somewhat extreme example, even seemingly innocuous changes can result in such data loss. Murphy's law plagues IT environments as much as it does other areas, and therefore a deliberate decision not to take the extra hour to perform an incremental backup before the upgrade can be a very costly one.

Some companies will state at this point that they simply do not have the time to keep systems down for the length of time required to back up and then patch. If this is the case, it is worth considering that this implies a more highly available solution is required — one that will not only allow for backups and patching, but will also address general availability requirements. For example, if a system can be shut down for half an hour for patching, but not two hours for backups plus patching, it could very well be the case that in reality a cluster is required, at which point in most cases the cluster nodes can be individually patched without affecting service availability. (Alternatively, options like array snapshots may be required so that the entire operating system change can be easily "rolled back.")

7.4.1.2 Perform a Full Backup Following Maintenance

As per the above, this can be explained best with an example:

1. Full backup occurs on Friday.
2. Incremental backups run Saturday through Tuesday.
3. System or application is patched on Wednesday.
4. Incremental backup performed on Wednesday night.
5. System fails on Thursday morning and requires recovery.
6. Recovery encounters problem due to need to recover any full backups and incremental backups spanning different versions of a product.

Although there may occasionally be exceptions, a policy should be followed such that after the completion of system or application maintenance activities, a full backup is run. This gives a new starting point for recoveries, which reduces any issues caused by different data, system, or application versions between full and incremental backups.

7.4.1.3 If Time Permits, Backup after Recovery

Consider performing a full backup immediately following a disaster recovery. This may present some initial impacts to users who are starting to access the system again (assuming it was not possible to leave users locked out of the system until the recovery was complete), but provides a fresh "snapshot" of the new version of the host. In the event of a second failure, this may considerably reduce recovery time and complexity.

This is particularly relevant if the nature of the failure was an operating system or application flaw that resulted in the need to apply a patch to properly recover the system and resume operations. This may not be a necessary step, particularly when it was only necessary to recover from a full backup, but can be useful for mixed-level recoveries.

If a full backup cannot be performed immediately following verification of successful recovery, an alternative strategy is to schedule a full backup overnight, rather than performing incremental or differential recoveries.

7.4.2 Avoid Upgrades

Disaster recovery is not the time or place to perform additional upgrades or changes to a system. This may seem somewhat contradictory given the final statement in the above topic, but generally a patch being required for a recovery is the exception, not the rule.

The purpose of disaster recovery should be solely to return the system to a usable state. Introducing changes or upgrades to an already-critical situation will almost invariably make the situation worse.

Consider the following scenarios:

- System fails, and disaster recovery is performed. At conclusion of the recovery, because patches have not been able to be applied for a while, the latest patches are applied. One of the patches, however, is incompatible with the system and shortly after handing the system back to the users, it starts behaving erratically.
- Database suffers significant corruption. Before recovery the administrator decides to install the database server 8.1.3.4 even though 8.1.3.2 had previously been installed. However, the DBA had been trying to get a window to perform the upgrade so this seems like a good enough time. Recovery fails because the API used for hot backups has a slight change. As a result after several failed recovery attempts, 8.1.3.2 is re-installed and the recovery finally succeeds.
- System fails, so user installs operating system version *X*+1 even though the previously installed version was version *X*, mainly because the install media for version *X* could not be found. (This has been observed even in "extreme" conditions, such as trying to perform a disaster recovery of a Windows NT machine to a Windows 2000 machine.)

None of these activities (or any other similar activities) are appropriate in a disaster recovery scenario. In such a scenario the only permitted activity should be the recovery of the system, with any other suggested activities to be deferred to a later maintenance window.

7.4.3 Read the Documentation before the Backups Are Performed

Disaster recovery should never be done while reading the recovery documentation for the first time. Many backup vendors, for instance, include "disaster recovery guides" and these sometimes outline not only how to perform a disaster recovery, but also provide details and procedures to ensure that systems are backed up properly in the first place.

Examples of information commonly found in vendor disaster recovery documentation are

- Operating system databases that require export prior to backup
- Operating system and application licenses that cannot be backed up
- System configuration information that needs to be restored to another location
- How open files must be handled during the backup process

All of this information should be known and understood by all the administrators of the system before the recovery is ever attempted.

7.4.4 Disaster Recoveries Must Be Run by Administrators

Although standard recoveries can often be handed over to help desk staff or even end users, disaster recovery operations should for the most part be considered essential functions of the appropriate administrators of the systems and applications that have failed.

A system administrator (whether it be through formal qualifications or field experience) will have an in-depth understanding of operating systems that regular help desk staff may very well not have. This might include such things as:

- How filesystems are laid out
- What activities are required to "re-join" a computer to the rest of the network
- What other system-level activities need to be performed on a host following its recovery

Most importantly, the system administrator should understand what to do if things go wrong. If a help desk staff member has difficulty recovering an individual file or directory, this is not typically a major problem, as many will know what to do to work around common backup software error messages or operating system errors. However, a failure during an operating system recovery may very well be handled quickly by a system administrator (e.g., "that's not important, we can deal with that later") whereas a help desk staff member may feel obliged to restart the entire procedure and only after it has failed a second time contact a system administrator.

7.4.5 Test and Test and Test Again

As much as regular recoveries, disaster recoveries should be tested long before they are actually required, with appropriate changes made to the backup environment to compensate.

> **Confirm, Don't Assume Everything Is in Place.** A (relatively small) company once outsourced its Solaris systems management to a small firm that handled all aspects of the installation, configuration, and maintenance process. This included configuring the backup environment.
>
> When the company I worked for at the time took over the management of the system, the first activity was to conduct an audit of the environment. It was discovered that the backup software was a custom-written backup tool from the IT consulting company that ran cpio for each filesystem, backing it up to locally attached tape. To protect proprietary routines (presumably), the original outsourcing team, from what

we could tell, had written the backup routine as a C program and then installed the compiled software.

The customer was very impressed with this tool because, despite the summed size of all the filesystems exceeding double the capacity of the tape drive attached to the system, they were still not needing to change tapes during the backup process.

This set alarm bells ringing in our team, and not having access to the source code we watched the backup via list-running processes to confirm how the backup ran. Unfortunately, it showed that the compiled software used the rewind version of the device for each filesystem it backed up. That is, the sequence for backup became

```
Backup /
Rewind tape
Backup /opt
Rewind tape
Backup /usr
Rewind tape
Backup /var
Rewind tape
Backup /data
Rewind tape
```

Having assured ourselves that we'd caught a disaster in the making, we convinced the customer of the problem and the customer agreed to change the backup environment and purchase additional tapes. We then assumed that all was well.

Months later when the system failed, we asked the customer to place the Solaris boot CD into the CD-ROM for the host so we could start an install process, to which the customer responded, "We never got any CDs with our system."

The importance of recovery testing will be discussed in greater depth later in section 7.6, "Testing," and its importance prior to disaster recovery operations cannot be underestimated. In general follow the rule that whenever significant system changes are made, new disaster recovery tests should be performed.

7.4.6 Use the Same Hardware

Depending on the type of hosts in use, it may be possible to get away with a relaxation of this rule to "use similar hardware," but there will always be limitations. Operating system disaster recoveries will typically replace/overwrite almost everything on the system with a previous instance of the system. This will include whatever installed drivers have been put on the system.

Common mistakes that have been made in disaster recovery situations include

- Recovering from a SCSI-based system to an IDE-based system (or vice versa)
- Recovering from one CPU architecture to another
- Having a different physical layout of IO cards in the machine being recovered to than the machine being recovered from (this is most typically seen in Intel-based systems where device paths are typically allocated/defined based on the physical slots that cards are plugged into)

- Leaving network interfaces that were previously configured "unconfigured" prior to disaster recovery
- Attempting to recover between significantly different architecture from the same vendor — e.g., recovering a Sun E6000 to a Sun Netra T1
- Although not specifically related to hardware, recovering a production machine to another host to avoid having downtime on the production host and leaving the other host connected to the same network, resulting in an outage when two hosts come up with the same names and IP addresses
- Recovering a system to compatible but inadequate hardware — e.g., a production system had 2 GB of RAM, but the system recovered to only has 1 GB of RAM

In these cases when a disaster recovery fails it is not unusual to find "blame" attributed to the backup software. However, at all times remember that the backup software sits at a layer above the operating system, which in turn sits at a layer above the hardware. Backup software is responsible for protecting not only everything that sits above it, but also the operating system. However, as stated before, backup software requires suitably working hardware and operating systems — not only for the purpose of backup, but also for the purpose of recoveries.

7.4.7 Know Dependencies (and How to Work around Them)

More so than regular recoveries, disaster recoveries become subject to architectural dependencies in a computing environment. For example, consider what might happen if, say, the only DNS server for a computing environment fails. Obviously, it becomes critical to get the system recovered, as systems will have interconnectivity problems without a DNS server. However, the backup server may also rely on the DNS server to be able to resolve clients properly so that unknown hosts do not recover data. Thus, to be able to recover the DNS server it may be required for the DNS server to exist, so that the backup server can perform a DNS query on the client before it allows the data to be recovered. Dependency loops should be avoided!

> **Name Resolution: The Forgotten Dependency.** Name resolution systems are frequently forgotten in system dependencies. A customer once ran disaster recovery testing of their backup server in an isolated network with no DNS servers available. The customer noted the backup server processes on the newly recovered machine took well over an hour to start. When run in debug mode, it became apparent that the backup software was trying to resolve each registered client on startup, and taking almost five minutes per client to time out the name resolution.

Ensure wherever possible that all the dependencies in a computing environment are properly plotted, with sufficient planning in place to allow there to be a "work around" so that the environment can be bootstrapped if required. This means that even if the backup system normally depends on other systems (such as DNS or directory servers) during day-to-day operations, it should be configured such that in an emergency it doesn't need those services. For example, one solution to avoid DNS dependencies is to register the backup server as a secondary DNS server.

7.4.8 Keep Accurate System Documentation

This can be reduced to two key factors: (1) deployment of backup systems should not be seen as an excuse to avoid documenting key system components (e.g., licensing, application configurations, etc.); and (2) there reaches a point on a system that a backup system does not probe any further. An example for this is that backup systems are typically not "array" or "volume" aware — they are incapable, for instance, of rebinding LUNs on a SAN, or re-creating RAID-5 volumes before conducting the restore of the volume.

Maintaining accurate system documentation should be considered an essential part of the roles of system and application administrators, regardless of how effective the backup software actually is. This documentation should be maintained in hard-copy format and soft-copy format, with the aim being that the soft copies should be available to administrators when they are performing disaster recovery operations, and the hard copy can be obtained and referred to in the event of a site disaster. (This necessarily implies that hard and soft copies of this information should be stored off site.)

Examples of appropriate system documentation policies include, but are not limited to:

- An automated process should periodically run that generates a comprehensive dump of configuration information in both human- and computer-usable format. This information will have been verified as being all the information required during destructive disaster recovery testing. For most environments, a monthly generation of this information should be sufficient.
- Administrators should be able to force the running of the above configuration report at will in the event of performing anything but the most mundane of system changes or updates. This ensures that the "hard copy" of the configuration can be regenerated at any time that significant changes are made, so that there is no risk of a failure occurring after the alteration but before the next monthly run of the report.
- Hard and soft copies should be stored in locations immediately available to system administrators in the event of ordinary failures.
- Any passwords required to access this recovery information should also be stored securely in an appropriate corporate location for use by an external system administrator in the event of a major failure. Techniques for this include things as mundane as passwords written down and stored in a key-locked box, which is then stored in the company's fireproof safe, with the keys stored with suitably senior managers. In more-secure environments, using offline-accessible encryption with multi-key protection may be appropriate.*
- Hard copies of this information should be stored at an off-site location. In the event of a multiple-site company, storage at another company site may be acceptable.
- Soft copies of this information should be stored at an off-site location. Although this can be another site in a multi-site company, that site should not be vulnerable to the same failures, or to corporatewide failures (e.g., fast-moving destructive worms). Otherwise, many vendors are happy to oblige customers by holding secure copies of this information, and many companies can be found that are willing to do a shared-protection arrangement.

* This should not only cover **current** passwords, but any password used over the retention-span.

7.4.9 Do You Know Where Your Licenses Are at 1 A.M.?

Although hinted at in the above point, this deserves special mention. There is more to a disaster recovery than just restoring data. Indeed, if handled correctly, the data restoration component should be the most-straightforward and least-interactive part of the entire process.

The best-laid disaster recovery plans can come unstuck for the simplest of reasons. What if the backup software won't install (or activate required functionality) without the licenses? Sure, the licenses should be able to be restored, but to do that, the backup software will be required, which needs the licenses. Always ensure that disaster recovery documentation includes complete details of all licenses used by the systems, so that these may be manually re-keyed if required.

7.4.10 Disaster Recovery Exercises

Disaster recovery exercises form a valid component of activities that a business should be periodically performing to check the health of their backup environment. Many larger organizations will periodically perform disaster recovery exercises. This is where a disaster is declared, and IT staff, management, and regular staff must provide details of what would be done to restore the functionality of the business. However, such exercises should not be limited to large companies; all organizations need to confirm they are able to survive a disaster.

Unfortunately, these exercises are rarely audited by an external party, which should by all rights be a logical component of the activity. A common complaint from companies is that they perform disaster recovery exercises only to discover later that the results of the exercise were less than accurate — for example, a system is deemed to be recoverable within four hours, but months later when it really does crash it takes sixteen hours to recover it.

Although involving external auditors in the disaster recovery simulation does not guarantee accuracy, it does significantly increase it by providing an independent third-party assessment of the steps that will be performed during the recovery. This kind of third-party assessment may even be legally required, depending on the industry and country.*

At a bare minimum, the following "scenarios" should be considered required aspects of disaster recovery exercises:

- In the event of a total site loss, will data be preserved?
- How will a recovery be performed in the event of the key system administrator for a system being unavailable?
- How will recovery be affected by the loss of the tape or backup media originally chosen for recovery?
- What would be the impact of a secondary failure? For example, what would happen if a system failed, and then during the recovery process the tape library used for the recovery also malfunctioned?
- As an addendum to the previous point, when planning disaster recovery exercises it is necessary to evaluate SLAs with all vendors for equipment associated with the exercise. Do teams involved in the exercise take these SLAs into consideration?
- How would an inability to access e-mail or corporate/workgroup fileservers affect the ability to perform a critical restore?

---

* For maximum accuracy and independence, the audit should be performed by an organization that will not be awarded any sales from recommendations relating to the recovery.

- Although not wishing to dwell on extremely unpleasant circumstances, has the system been configured and documented sufficiently such that in the event of the loss of the system administration team, a trained administrator who previously has not worked in the environment will be able to restore it?
- How fast can the company react to a destructive worm/virus?
- Is disaster recovery dependent on vendor-supplied hardware?
- How would the recovery be achieved in the event of a loss of directory or authentication servers in addition to the critical system? Examples of directory or authentication servers include, but are not limited to:
  - Novell eDirectory
  - Microsoft ActiveDirectory
  - Kerberos servers
  - NIS / NIS+
  - DNS servers
  - LDAP servers
- How would the recovery be performed if the only system administrator available was remote and could only connect to the network via a dial-up connection?
- How would the recovery be performed in the event of a loss of physical site access? (For example, systems other than the failed system are still running, but the site itself is cordoned off?)
- If planning for a truly massive disaster, would the loss of essential services (for example, any combination of power, public transport, communications, etc.) either prevent the recovery or render the recovery unimportant?

Of course, it is possible to plan disaster recovery contingencies seemingly forever, and still not cover every possible disaster scenario. However, in a risk-versus-cost environment, most enterprises will need to plan for at least the previously stated contingencies.

7.4.11 Off-Site Storage

Off-site storage of backups and related system documentation is essential for any organization where site and complete data loss would result in significant business interruption (which would cover almost all businesses).

Items that should be stored off site include, but may be extended to cover company-specific requirements:

- Copies of backups
- System disaster recovery documentation
- Backup server recovery documentation and data
- Copies of passwords that may be required in the event of a loss of, or an unavailability of the system, database, or application administration staff

Where possible, these should be stored in a secure location that is sufficiently distant from the production computing environment and is not prone to the same risks as the production computing environment. For example, the generally accepted minimum distance between a production area and off-site storage is 10 kilometers. Depending on the types of disasters that need to be considered for an organization, planning off-site storage that is not vulnerable to the same failures as the original site may be difficult. For instance, a company could plan for a cyclone by storing the above items in a secure underground bunker. However, storing off-site media in a high-rise building when the most-significant threat to a computer room is an earthquake is not entirely appropriate.

For particularly sensitive companies that may be targets of hostile physical action, it will also be imperative that off-site storage is private and hidden. As moving a large number of tapes in the event of the "hidden" storage being made public or otherwise known, this may introduce the need for media double-handling — i.e., tapes sent to a publicly known site first and then picked up by the off-site storage company, or tapes sent to the off-site storage company rather than their retrieving them. Somewhat akin to regular computer security, security by obfuscation is no guarantee of security, and thus companies should not expect their off-site storage location to remain hidden forever. With this being the case, other means of securing the off-site data will also be required, and an organization relying solely on hidden off-site storage will need to plan to move the storage should it be discovered.

If concerned about the notion of storing passwords off site, remember that we are at all times referring to secure off-site locations — after all, if the physical backups themselves are not stored in a secure site, there is little point in securing passwords.

7.4.12 Keep the Disaster Recovery Site Current

If there is a disaster recovery site, it's important that steps are maintained to ensure that the equipment in it is up to date and able to take over production operations (or a known percentage of production operations). This means ensuring that:

- There are sufficient hosts in the disaster recovery site.
- Each host has sufficient CPU and RAM.
- Each host has sufficient disk space.
- If licenses have to be registered to a particular host ID, MAC, or IP address, ensure that those licenses are registered to the production machines as well as the disaster recovery machines (if permitted), or a mechanism of transferring the licenses that can be done at any time of the day or night within a few minutes is available. For example, some software companies (backup software included) may offer for free, or a small fee, permanently authorized "disaster recovery" licenses under an affidavit that they will not be used concurrently with the production licenses.

A common strategy for many "budget sensitive" companies is to follow the policy that once a server is "retired" from production and a new server purchased, the retired server is relocated to the disaster recovery site for use as the disaster recovery server for the machine which has been purchased to replace it. In some instances, it may be that this is actually possible. However, for the most part, consider that servers are typically replaced for one or more of the following reasons:

- Server has run out of resources for the application.
- Server has become sufficiently old enough that its hardware is not reliable.
- Server has become sufficiently old enough that it is no longer maintained by the vendor, or if it is maintained, it is done so at a cost-prohibitive price.

To determine whether a disaster recovery site is up to date, see that the equipment and systems at the site have been vetted to ensure that an agreed percentage of the normal production load can be achieved, and that equipment is under maintenance. If not, there are some issues to be addressed so that a disaster does not become unmanageable.

7.4.13 Hot or Cold Disaster Recovery Site?

Obviously, a key consideration when preparing to implement a disaster recovery site is whether the site will run "hot" or "cold. " A hot disaster recovery site sees some of the day-to-day production equipment hosted at that site as well as the primary site — i.e., both sites perform part of the day-to-day processing for the corporate environment, and both have the capability of taking over the full processing load of the environment in the event of a failure. Although this sees a more-active return on investment, it needs careful planning with periodic testing to ensure that no dependencies creep in between the two sites that would see all the planning made moot. It also requires LAN-level (or better) links between the two sites, which may prove to be costly depending on the location of the two sites.

A cold disaster recovery site can in some cases be cheaper to maintain due to the reduced link requirement between the two sites, but is often quite difficult to gain management approval as it essentially requires the purchase of equipment that will for the most part go unused — to the point that years on from the purchase, the equipment may be decommissioned and replaced having never been used by anyone other than application and system administrators. Typically, testing a cold site is more involved than testing a hot site, as there is more equipment to bring up at any one time. However, one key advantage a cold site has over a hot site is that it can be configured to be completely isolated from the production system's network. If agreed-to by the business, cold disaster recovery sites can also be invaluable for in-hours disaster recovery testing.

One of the key criticisms of hot disaster recovery environments is that they don't offer protection for all the same failures that cold disaster recovery sites offer. In particular, while both sites adequately protect against hardware failure or site loss (in fact the hot site may offer faster restoration of system availability), by making the disaster recovery site a hot site it remains vulnerable to the same viruses, worms, Trojans, and network outages that can impact the production site — in essence it is no longer as secure as its cold counterpart.

Both hot and cold disaster recovery sites can lead to additional costs for an organization, particularly as the level of equipment and services scale up — for instance, if an organization moves to SAN-based storage and uses a disaster recovery site, then it can be practically guaranteed that the organization will need to purchase a SAN for both the primary site and the disaster recovery site. This may also necessitate purchasing a sufficiently fast-enough link that array replication can occur to keep sites up to date depending on the type of disaster recovery site being implemented, which in turn will drive up costs considerably.

7.5 Service Level Agreements

SLAs must be considered when planning a backup system — most typically when it comes to determining what sort of recovery options can be made available, but also in determining what type of backups will be performed. When planning a backup system start with the SLAs and work back to a system that meets those agreements, rather than planning a backup system and hoping that it will meet the SLAs.

SLAs typically come in two forms, and the type of SLA will considerably impact the kind of infrastructure required to meet it: (1) Recovery Point Objective (RPO), those that govern the amount of data that can be lost in the event of a failure; and (2) Recovery Time Objective (RTO), those that govern the maximum length of time it can take to resolve a failure.

The establishment of SLAs must be a two-way agreement between those who want the SLAs and those who must meet the SLAs. This may result in changes to business practices where necessary. For example, some companies prepare SLAs, but then decide they can drop some requirements when it becomes apparent that considerable expenditure will be required to meet service levels stated as "required" which were in fact really only "desired."

SLAs will differ considerably depending on the type of system or business they have been created for. Examples of systems that will have different SLAs might include

- Core bank finance system
- Air traffic control system
- Power facility control system
- Library database server
- Corporate or departmental fileservers
- Development server
- Test server
- End user desktop system
- Personal digital assistant
- Mobile phone

In each case, the SLA will be different both in terms of how long it takes to perform a recovery, and also how much data can be lost. For instance, customers of a bank will not accept the loss of a transaction that deposits their pay, nor will airline passengers accept that their booking (fully paid for) was lost due to a computer failure. "Your bookings weren't covered in the SLA" is not something that a group of irate passengers at an airline check-in desk will accept as a reason when they're told they can't board because their previously purchased seats had been reallocated.

It may be completely acceptable, however, for a fileserver to lose a full day's worth of information, particularly if a company receives most of its information via e-mail and the e-mail server is separate from the fileserver. For an end user desktop system, it may be perfectly acceptable to lose up to a week's data, depending on the requirements of the organization and the importance of the user. Alternatively, even if the user is an important user, if system policies prohibit data storage on local PCs it may be acceptable for all data on a PC to be lost.

7.5.1 Recovery Time Objective SLAs

Recovery time SLAs typically refer either to how long a recovery will take, or how long it will take before starting a recovery. Wherever possible, such SLAs (particularly generic, environmentwide ones) should aim to state the duration between the time that the recovery request is made and the time the recovery commences. When setting SLAs for recovery time there are three important factors to consider

1. Is there a maximum elapsed period after which time the recovery has to commence?
2. Is there a maximum elapsed period after which time the recovery needs to be completed?
3. Does the SLA refer to recovery operations or merely backup operations?

Although it seems logical and entirely required, the final point is often missed when establishing SLAs — particularly when outsourcing agreements are being discussed.

> **Example.** At a pub, a manager of an outsourcing company bragged of having just completed a successful agreement where the word "recovery" was never mentioned at any time throughout the entire contract. Although there were rigorous requirements in the outsourcing contract for backups (and strong penalties for non-conformance), the company whose IT department was outsourced failed to notice that they had placed no conditions on whether data or systems could actually be recovered.

Ignoring the somewhat dubious moral values of such an outsourcing agreement, it remains to be seen that without recovery criteria, the usefulness of backup SLAs are considerably diminished.

When recovery-performance SLAs are written, the following considerations must be followed

- Can the personnel targeted for involvement in the recovery commence the recovery in the given time frame? (For example, if the recovery must be initiated on site within an hour and one of the support technicians lives an hour and a half away, does this impact delivery?)
- Has the backup system been designed (via performance targets) to meet recovery times?
- Can systems and backup media stream fast enough to physically accommodate the amount of data transfer required to achieve the recovery?
- For disaster recovery sites where there are systems to be recovered to, can those systems meet the SLAs? (Or are there differing SLAs for whether the recovery occurs at the production site or the disaster recovery site?)
- Have SLAs and the backup systems been designed to ensure that SLAs can continue to be met even with data and systems growth?
- Additionally, when establishing SLAs, all parties must understand what requirements the SLA will create from vendors and other third parties who may be necessary in meeting the SLA. For instance, if a signed SLA states that recovery will complete within eight hours of failing, but there are no 24/7 support contracts with hardware vendors, or the support contracts are for next day parts and labor, a failure at 3 a.m. may very well result in a breach of SLA requirements.

All of these factors must be clearly understood when agreeing to SLAs for recovery targets.

Depending on the business requirements, very different SLAs will be established, but in general it is better to set SLAs that refer to the amount of time it takes to commence a recovery than the amount of time a recovery has to take. If, however, it is required to set SLAs for the amount of time a recovery has to take, the SLAs should be set on a per-host basis so as to ensure that key systems have appropriate SLAs while IT staff aren't distracted servicing difficult SLAs for non-critical servers. In these cases the SLAs will need to be revisited periodically to ensure that they can still be met given ongoing data growth — for instance, an SLA set for a maximum four hour recovery time in January 2006 may have little relationship with the real world in December 2008 with a yearly doubling of growth but no expansion to the backup system during that time.

7.5.2 Recovery Point Objective SLAs

SLAs for data loss essentially determine the frequency at which backups or other data protection operations must occur. These SLAs typically occur in environments with "high-9s" availability. For instance, banks and ticketing agencies will typically require availability targets of 99.99 percent uptime or higher, which creates entirely new operational requirements.

When SLAs restrict the amount of permissible data loss, it is quite possible that the backup system alone will not be able to be used to meet those targets. For instance, if an SLA requires no more than two hours of data to be lost in an outage, but backups take six hours to complete, then it is obvious that backups alone cannot meet this SLA.

The styles of protection that may need to be added to an environment with minimum data loss requirements may include

- Snapshots
- Asynchronous replication between sites
- Synchronous replication between sites
- Multi-site WAN clustering

For example, if an SLA requires a maximum data loss period of two hours, it would be possible to achieve this using snapshots, with a series of snapshots taken once every two hours throughout the day, and perhaps only one or two snapshots ever backed up each day. Operationally, this might result in the following scenario:

Time	*Activity*
08:00	Snapshot taken.
10:00	Snapshot taken.
11:15	Database becomes corrupt.
11:30	Filesystem rolled back to 10:00 snapshot.
11:35	Database restarted using 10:00 snapshot.
12:00	Snapshot taken.

With this in mind, when planning systems to meet data loss ensure that SLAs focus on more than just the backup software.

7.5.3 Planning SLAs

Planning SLAs is something that must be done jointly between the business and the IT department (or the IT outsourcer). Every business will have different needs when evaluating SLAs, but there are a core set of questions and practices that should be considered when establishing them.

7.5.3.1 Map IT Systems

Before SLAs can be determined for systems, it is necessary to know what systems exist. This should be done as part of a comprehensive system map that allows the "big picture" to be seen for the organization. If there is no system map, then SLAs cannot be accurately established, and therefore this should be treated as a preliminary exercise to the establishment of SLAs. Remember that a system map is much more than a network diagram, so although a network diagram is a good starting point, it does not in itself provide sufficient details for SLA development.

7.5.3.2 Establish SLAs on a Per-System Basis

The first sign of a poorly thought-out SLA is where it's based on sweeping statements — "at no point shall more than four hours of data be lost" or "systems shall be recovered within two hours." This type of SLA indicates little understanding of the disparate systems that form the IT environment for an organization and, to be quite frank, stupidly assumes that all systems are equal. Regardless of the area of industry a business operates in, it will have a variety of IT systems that are of different criticality — and sometimes the most important systems are ones that may not even be considered by non-IT staff when evaluating criticality.

After having mapped the systems in use, the next step is to determine the SLAs for each system.

For example, in Table 7.2 we have extended the previously developed system map table to also function as our SLA reference point. Note that there is an apparent inconsistency in the table, but only in extreme circumstances. The server "hydra," which had a maximum time down of one hour, depends on "oxford" and "collins," which have maximum time down definitions of two and four hours, respectively. This inconsistency can be borne when considering that (for DNS) "hydra" should be able to make use of whichever server is currently operational, and a risk is being taken that both servers will not be down at the same time.

7.5.3.3 Confirm SLAs Are Realistic

Although this is intrinsically a part of the previous step, it warrants explicitly mentioning as a separate step so as to highlight the need for negotiation on SLAs. Additionally, the exercise of confirming that SLAs are realistic is best achieved by determining what is required for each system to meet the established SLAs. For example, it might be entirely appropriate to the business that the server "delphi" can only lose two hours of data at any given point in time, but just because it

Table 7.2 Sample SLA Map

System	*Function*	*Depends On*	*Data Loss*	*Time Down*
oxford	Primary DNS server	N/A	1 day	2 hours
collins	Secondary DNS server	oxford	1 day	4 hours
hydra	Terminal server, authentication server	oxford/collins	1 day	1 hour
delphi	Database server	oxford/collins, hydra	2 hours	1 day
fortknox	Backup server	oxford/collins	1 day	4 hours
redback	Web server	oxford/collins, hydra, delphi	1 day	4 hours
mars	Mail server	oxford/collins, hydra	1 day	2 hours
dagda	Spare server	N/A	N/A	N/A

Table 7.3 Sample SLA Requirements

System	*Data Loss*	*Requires*	*Time Down*	*Requires*
oxford	1 day	Nightly backup	2 hours	On-site media, on-site spare parts
collins	1 day	Nightly backup	4 hours	On-site media, on-site spare parts or 4-hour repair SLA with vendor
hydra	1 day	Nightly backup	1 day	Same-day repair SLA with vendor
delphi	2 hours	2-hourly snapshots, nightly backup	1 day	Same-day repair SLA with vendor
fortknox	1 day	Nightly backup	4 hours	On-site media, on-site spare parts or 4-hour repair SLA with vendor
redback	1 day	Nightly backup	4 hours	On-site media, on-site spare parts or 4-hour repair SLA with vendor
mars	1 day	Nightly backup	2 hours	On-site media, on-site spare parts
dagda	N/A	Ad-hoc backup	N/A	N/A

is appropriate doesn't mean it will happen if the infrastructure doesn't support it. If it is the case that the existing infrastructure doesn't support it, the business will either need to fund additional infrastructure or re-evaluate the SLAs.

One way to confirm that SLAs are realistic is to note what will need to be done to meet those SLAs for each system. This might be shown as in Table 7.3.

If an organization does not operate 24/7, then it will most likely need two such tables — one for business-hours SLAs and one for out-of-hours SLAs, as these may be different in these circumstances. (For example, many companies that are not operational 24/7 will have recovery SLAs such as "two hours during business hours" and "either by start of business hours or two hours after recovery start if recovery is started outside of business hours" for the same system.)

The requirements for meeting SLAs that we have established in the two tables are reasonably accurate when considering only equipment and backup components. However, there's another resource involved in recoveries that is frequently not considered — the human resource.

Every recovery SLA makes an impact on the ability of system and application administrators to perform other duties. For example, an SLA states that systems must be recovered within four hours, and if only two system administrators are available, then sending them both on leave or even on a one-day training course together clearly is not an acceptable policy. Thus, to establish recovery SLAs, it is necessary not only to consider the technical aspects of the recovery, but also the personnel side. This should result in policies that govern how many staff in the technical areas have to be available during on-site and off-site hours.

Finally, when establishing SLAs, data growth must either be factored into place, or allowances must be made for periodic revisiting of the SLAs if data growth is too unpredictable. (A general rule of thumb applicable to most non-media/design businesses is approximately 50 percent data growth per annum.) If it is clear that in six months there will be twice as much data to protect, then the SLA must meet not only the current amount of data, but the expected system capacity as well. If this is not factored, the SLA will most likely not be worth the paper it is written on soon after adoption. Where growth predictions are factored into SLAs, those SLAs should have "use by" dates that indicate when they must be revisited.

7.5.3.4 Upgrade IT Environment or Revisit SLAs

Once preferred SLAs have been established for systems, the next step is to evaluate the "Requires" column (Table 7.3) for both the data loss SLA and the recovery time SLA, to determine

- What (if any) new infrastructure (software, hardware, etc.) will be required to meet the SLAs?
- Will additional staff be required to meet the SLAs?
- Will additional staff training be required to meet the SLAs?
- Will staff absence policies need to be adjusted to suit the SLAs?
- What business practice changes will need to occur to meet the SLAs?

The only way to make an informed decision on the implementation of SLAs is to determine a minimum of one-year cost to meeting the SLAs in new infrastructure and staff, and then evaluate whether this represents a higher or lower cost to the business than not meeting the SLAs. This is often where poorly thought-out SLAs come unstuck.

Consider, for instance, our database server "delphi." To achieve a two-hour or less data loss, we have to implement some form of snapshots. More properly, we may not have to implement snapshots — really what we have to implement is a two-hourly data recovery policy. This may be achieved not only via snapshots, but also through such additional options as hot exports (if the database supports it) or even frequent backups as long as the database is quite small. Assuming, however, that the database does not support hot exports and is too big to backup frequently, we are faced with the need to snapshot the database. However, it may be that the machine that "delphi" is running uses DAS, and that there has not been a SAN or other consolidated storage system implemented. It may also be using standard filesystems without any special volume management.

Thus we factor the cost of meeting the SLA as including the purchase of a SAN (or other consolidated storage system) and the purchase of more-complex volume management and filesystem technology that allows periodic snapshots to occur — most likely still with the purchase of additional storage space to hold snapshots.

This type of evaluation must be performed for each system that requires infrastructure or personnel that are currently not provided by the organization. Once the costs are available, the organization can determine whether these costs are worth meeting the SLA or whether the SLA needs to be "revised down" to something more achievable given budgetary constraints.

7.5.3.5 Failure Costs

Although a potentially unpleasant subject, no SLA is useful without a failure cost — i.e., the consequences of not meeting the SLA. When providing support or maintenance contracts for customers, this is often first broached by the customers rather than the company offering the support contract.

When discussing company-internal SLAs, the process is somewhat more difficult and, for the most part, unique to each company. There should be a clearly defined set of consequences in relation to the failure to meet SLAs, and both the IT department and the rest of the organization should agree to the consequences. These consequences should also have "escape clauses." For instance, if the IT department cannot meet SLAs because the budget has been cut, and the department has been unable to buy sufficient media to meet data retention requirements, then this is hardly the fault of the IT department — as long as the business has been informed of the consequences of making such a decision.

7.5.3.6 Formally Agree To, and Publish SLAs

Once the SLAs and the infrastructure, personnel, and policies to back them up have been established, they must be formally agreed to. This should be done between the business and the IT department, in writing, as it ensures that everyone is aware that there has been buy-in on both sides and an agreement has been made in consultation.

Having been formally agreed to, the SLAs need to be published in a corporate accessible location. Additionally, they must to be provided to:

- Key staff and management in each affected department
- All staff that would be involved in the recovery process
- Auditors and external consultants as required
- New employees in key departments as part of their "starter-pack"

An SLA does no good covered in a film of dust, sitting on the bookshelf of a single manager or even a group of managers. It must be published and shared so that everyone involved in the delivery of the SLA is aware of the requirements.

7.5.3.7 Enact Policies to Protect SLAs

When we were discussing "Risk Versus Cost" (section 1.4), we used the example of a corporate lawyer whose network fileserver connection was lost to highlight what can happen if risk-based backup policy decisions are not reinforced with staff and operational policies. This was essentially an example of an SLA that was not followed up with the appropriate policy.

Staff members should be aware that the establishment of SLAs logically requires particular activities to occur, or specific priorities to be assigned to issues.

Revisiting our "delphi" example where a SAN has been purchased to allow for two-hourly snapshots, we have an SLA but we don't have the operational policies yet. These policies need to be in force by the time the system is deployed (or the SLA is agreed to). For example, with "delphi" we might have the following policies:

- IT staff shall be aware that the snapshot has completed (and its results — successful or unsuccessful) within five minutes of the snapshot time.
- No more than three snapshots in a fortnight shall fail.
- If a snapshot fails it shall be re-run within 30 minutes.
- If two snapshots fail in succession, a severity-1 call shall be logged with the appropriate vendor(s).

Note the use of the word "shall" in this example. An alternate word is "must," but it is important to avoid potentially ambiguous words such as "should" or "may." For instance, "if two snapshots fail in succession, a severity-1 call should be logged with the appropriate vendor(s)" does not necessarily imply a hard directive. (It could be argued, for instance, that this implies staff can choose not to log a call with the appropriate vendor(s) if they believe the next snapshot will work, or they run the snapshot a third time and it does work.)

7.5.3.8 Verify SLAs

Periodic tests should be performed to ensure that SLAs can still be met. This might be performed as part of a disaster recovery exercise, or as individual tests where possible. It should be done by comparing completed recoveries with the established SLA times to confirm that the SLA was met. This may not happen for every recovery (particularly in an environment that requires a large number of such operations), but it should happen sufficiently regularly that trends can be determined.

As part of the verification process the business should be prepared to revisit the SLA should a trend develop that shows the SLA can no longer be met (e.g., unexpected data growth or changes in business work hours/system availability requirements). This would logically necessitate a return to the start of the planning process.

7.6 Testing

Backups should be tested periodically to ensure that they are recoverable. This refers to more than simply a physical read of the media to ensure that the system can process all the data on it. Just as important is the need to recover files and applications (and in some cases, operating systems) to confirm that the recovered information is indeed a legitimate backup.

A common mistake is to assume that a physical read of the media proves that a backup is recoverable. In actual fact, it only proves (at best) half of the recoverability requirement. Scenarios where this would not lead to a successful recovery in itself are

- Backup of the files for a live Oracle database without a hot backup agent
- Backup of Microsoft SQL on a Windows host via an open file agent that is not database aware
- Backup of a snapshot that was taken without the system quiesced
- Backup of an export file started before the export file had been completely written

When performing recovery testing, it is therefore vital to understand the difference between media verification and data verification. Media verification, often the simplest of the activities to perform, simply refers to making a read pass over the backup media once the backup is complete to ensure that there were no physical errors and possibly to compare backup checksums. Some products can automatically perform media verification as part of the backup process. If available, this functionality should be used even if data verification activities are also performed.

Simple physical error checking and comparison of backup checksums as stated previously, however, don't deliver full verification. If backup protection is employed — i.e., media or backup set duplication — then one type of media verification test is performed daily. (The duplication will fail if the media being read from is faulty.) However, even if duplication is being performed, it is still necessary to consider strongly performing media testing on the duplicates to ensure that they, too, are readable.

The resources available directly affect the level of testing that can be performed. However, as testing is an important facet of a well-running backup environment, companies should develop budgetary plans to perform the level of testing suitable for the environment and systems in place.

By way of introduction, here are some common mistakes people tend to make when performing tests:

- Same files or filesystems are recovered every time
- Data only recovered from one client
- Full backups only recovered from (it is, after all, more convenient and provides for faster testing than, say, recovering from a full backup and five incrementals; however, in a backup schedule with weekly fulls and daily incrementals, this only tests one seventh of the possible recovery scenarios at best)
- Test recoveries only run on a particular day (a derivation of the "full backups only recovered from" mistake above)
- Destructive testing without a suitable copy in the event of failure

These tests don't factor in the randomness of failure nor the need to protect against a failed test.

> **How Not to Test.** A customer once described how a manager in a previous job had a particular policy for keeping IT staff on their toes with respect to recovery. Periodically on a Friday evening after the backup completed, he would log on and delete an entire filesystem. System administrators were then instructed to repair the filesystem by start-of-business on Monday morning.
>
> While the manager's dedication to testing might be applauded, it was dangerous and flawed for several reasons. Failures in this method include (1) only testing backups from one time, (2) only testing full backups, (3) destructive data testing, and (4) a test method guaranteed to antagonize IT staff.

What is the scope of these failures? Let's examine them one at a time:

- Only ever testing backups from one time — it could very well be that, say, all of Friday's backups are successful, but some of Saturday's fail due to reboots of servers scheduled to take place at the same time.
- Full and non-full backups can have very different environmental interactions that can lead to failures for entirely different reasons. It could be, for instance, that the full backups always work, but incremental backups mid-week start failing due to dense filesystem issues.
- Although this may sound nonsensical, destructive backup testing should only be done after a reliable backup or copy of the data being tested against, and this should not be the backup that is being tested. Furthermore, in a live environment performing destructive testing on systems that were not quiesced during backup may induce data loss. For the purposes of system disaster, such small amounts of data loss may be acceptable, but would rarely be deemed appropriate for backup validation purposes only.
- Although it should not need to be said, forcing IT staff to perform what they would invariably see as meaningless activities that disrupt their social lives for no valid reason may (as it did in this case) guarantee a high staff turnover and thus a loss of long-term knowledge of the systems.

Two rules must be followed when performing recovery testing: (1) test randomly, and (2) do not allow testing to jeopardize the data that the testing is for.

For testing, it is important to understand the difference between type and unit testing. This typically comes out during initial system installation or disaster recovery testing. If there are 20 servers, performing disaster recovery testing on all of them (unit testing) may be an exhaustive and overzealous activity. Once confidence in the backup product is established, it should be possible to use type testing. This might result instead in a reduction to disaster recovery testing of three machines — one Windows host, one Linux host, and one Solaris host, if these are the operating system types in use.

When performing testing, a log should be maintained indicating

- Name of the person conducting the test.
- Signature of the person conducting the test.
- What tests were performed.
- When the tests were performed.
- What media were used for the tests.
- Success/failure results with additional details for:
  - Follow-up activities if a failure occurred.
  - Any anomalies in the output during the testing that requires investigation, either internally or with the vendor, with the subsequent results of the investigations noted.
  - Any alterations that need to occur to documentation as a result of the test (e.g., "Steps 3 and 4 in the disaster recovery guide need to be reversed for Windows 2003 servers"). An important but oft-forgotten caveat to notes such as this is to put them before the referenced steps in the documentation. Otherwise, the notes may be read only after the steps have been executed in the "wrong" order, particularly if the note is pushed over to a separate page as a result of formatting changes. Although we've stated before that documentation should be read completely prior to starting a recovery, it doesn't automatically follow that everyone does this. Although it is not possible to prepare for every eventuality (otherwise every step would be preceded by "make sure the previous step has been completed"), this is one variant that can be relatively easily prepared for.
- Reference to any SLA that covered the system(s) being tested.
- Success/failure results in meeting the SLA with additional details for:
  - If the SLA could not be met, a description of how this has been escalated, with the subsequent results of the escalation recorded as well.
  - Any observations on the SLA's validity (e.g., "only just scraped in — given the data growth on this system, SLA needs to be revisited"), with escalations to management (and their results) noted appropriately.

Tests are in themselves reasonably useless to anyone other than the person conducting the test if they are not formally recorded, so keeping an accurate test log that is accessible to appropriate users and managers ensures that everyone is kept in the loop on the ongoing status of the IT environment.

A sample test form included in appendix C can be used as a template for organizations wishing to adopt testing, but unsure how to structure the tests.

Chapter 8

Protecting the Backup Environment

8.1 Introduction

In the same way that it is necessary to ensure that no production servers have any single points of failure, it also highly important to ensure that the backup system doesn't represent a single point of failure to the business due to insufficient self-protection.

At the end of this chapter the requirements for protection of a backup server and the backups that it generates should be clearly understood.

8.2 Why Protect the Backup Server?

Unprotected backups are like having a one-way mirror — i.e., not all that reliable. Therefore, those backups should be duplicated in some fashion so that in the event of a failure, there is still a good chance of recovery.

Without wishing to appear to be superstitious, when evaluating backup redundancy it seems that Murphy's law holds as true or perhaps even truer in computer rooms as it does in other environments. For example, there is little more gut wrenching for system administrators than being asked to perform a complete recovery of a critical system where the eyes of the company are on them for the duration of the recovery. However, one thing that is more gut wrenching is watching the only tape that can be used for that recovery mangled and physically destroyed by a tape drive that encountered a catastrophic hardware failure.

Companies rarely hesitate to deploy strong protection and fault tolerance for mission-critical servers. What is less frequently considered is a simple corollary — the backup system is part of that protection, and thus is in itself mission critical. However, for organizations this is the "least important" machine to have backups of, yet such an attitude can result in an unmitigated disaster.

Various mistakes seen with backup servers include

- Using a desktop PC as the backup server for a large-scale backup environment — even performance considerations aside, this introduces considerably more scope for failure as desktop PCs rarely have the same level of hardware availability or fault tolerance as do servers
- Having a "next day" warranty arrangement with the hardware vendor for the backup server, or even worse, not having any warranty arrangement with the hardware vendor for the backup server
- Not using any form of redundancy on the backup server's disks — i.e., simple disk attach rather than RAID storage
- Not backing up the backup server
- Only performing infrequent backups of the backup server
- Backing up everything on the backup server other than the configuration and databases for the backup environment

These examples really only deal with mistakes concerning hardware redundancy or false economies on backup media. There are myriad other ways in which a backup server can be unprotected.

Backup servers frequently see the worst types of security controls, typically on the grounds that it makes the machine easier to administer, or backups easier to configure. If either system administrator access is obtained for a backup server or a backup server is too lax in whom it allows to alter its backup configuration, a nefarious individual can gain access to any data stored on any servers that the backup server protects, regardless of what type of security exists on those individual machines.

For example, the backup software EMC NetWorker allows people to administer the server from clients remotely, as long as those people attached to particular clients have been configured as valid administrators. This in itself is a good design consideration as it makes administration far more easy than having to do it all from only one location. Unfortunately, this creates a tendency among administrators at some sites to set the allowed administrator list to include the string "*@*," so they don't have to adjust the administrator list more than once. This opens administration of the server to all usernames connected via any host. When queried about this, companies often state that they trust everything attached to their network and that NetWorker is only installed on machines that are backed up, so therefore it is reasonably safe. Such trust is frequently misplaced.

Most Networks Are Too Insecure for Lax Security Policies on the Backup Server. With the exception of military-grade networks, I have only seen one site where a customer's stating they have a "secure network" actually had a modicum of truth. Five minutes after a system administrator connected my laptop to the network at a financial organization, the switch port attached to the network outlet that my laptop was plugged into went dead. After tracing the problem back to the switch port, the system administrator approached the network administration team and they re-enabled the switch port — they had been alerted that an unknown machine had attached to the network and they'd immediately shut down the switch port. In general, however, at almost every new site I have visited as a backup consultant, I could have easily made use of the established "non-existent" backup security to retrieve any sensitive corporate data that I wanted to.

Keep in mind that for most backup packages, any person who can be counted as an administrator of the backup server will be able to adjust the configuration of the server to allow him or her to recover data from any server protected by the backup environment. This could result in any, all, or more than the following:

- Data theft (recovering files from a fileserver onto a machine or device that can be removed from the site)
- System hijacking (backing up password files from an attacking machine and then recovering them onto a machine in the network, thereby granting access to an unauthorized user and simultaneously denying access to regular users — potentially including the system administrators without a physically attended reboot)
- Data destruction (overwriting data on a machine with a recovery from previous copies of that data)
- System corruption and outage

The backup server can either act as the keystone or the weakest link in the chain in an environment, depending on how it is configured — particularly in regards to the security for every machine in the environment. As such it deserves special, not lax consideration when it comes to security matters.

It is only recently that backup software vendors have started to come to grips with separating administrative functionality with access to data, and even still this is in its infancy. Unless a backup environment uses a hardware encryption layer with comprehensive key management, backups are typically no safer than the administrator password.

8.3 Protecting the Backups

8.3.1 Via Backup Software

Various backup products have their own names for this feature. Some, for instance, call it duplication, whereas others refer to it as cloning. The purpose of this feature is to generate a duplicate set of backups that can be used for recovery purposes in the event of the first set of backups failing.

Cloning backups is a key requirement to achieving disaster recovery capabilities — so much so that it can be argued that without cloning, an organization will not have a sufficient disaster recovery policy.

Typically, there are two methods of cloning in backup environments: post-backup cloning and inline cloning.

8.3.1.1 Post-Backup Cloning

Post-backup cloning is where the backups are not duplicated until either a pre-configured time or after each backup group has completed. Usually this occurs in one of two different ways — media duplication or backup duplication. Support for backup versus media duplication will be dependent on the design of individual backup packages.

8.3.1.1.1 Media Duplication

With media duplication, a simple media-to-media copy is performed, duplicating the media (usually tapes) generated during the backup process. This process can be considerably faster than backup duplication, but usually results in a requirement that the media being written to is of the same type as the media being read from. Even a slight variation in media length (e.g., a 195-m tape being duplicated to a 194.95-m tape of the same type) can result in duplication failure, or media wastage. Using the same tape length example, it may be that instead of failing the duplication, a second tape will be loaded to complete the last 5 cm of duplication for the source tape. Once the source tape has been completely duplicated, both tapes might then be unloaded, with a new tape used for the duplication of the next source tape, leaving the previous "end of duplicate" tape almost completely empty. Furthermore, media duplication may create an "all or nothing" environment. If the SLAs require duplication of only key systems, media duplication would require separate pools of tapes to avoid duplicating non-critical backups, whereas backup duplication would instead allow the copying of just those critical backups. Thus, although this method may initially appear to be attractive in comparison to backup duplication (described next), it can create issues that reduce its effectiveness.

8.3.1.1.2 Backup Duplication

With backup duplication, the process is somewhat different, particularly once multiplexing at the media level is involved. With this duplication method, one or more passes are made over the original media, generating copies of individual backups that were performed. Backup duplication may either make one pass of the media, in which case the copied backups remain multiplexed, or they may make multiple passes, in which case the copied backups are demultiplexed — typically one pass per unit of multiplexing on the media.

We can demonstrate demultiplexing duplication by revisiting the simple representation of a multiplexed tape in Figure 6.8. Assuming demultiplexed backup duplication were to occur, the process would run as shown in Figure 8.1. In the first pass, we would read all of the "A" backup, appending it to the media targeted to receive the duplication. Following the successful read of all the "A" backup, we continue onto the "B" backup, as shown in Figure 8.2. During the second pass, all of the "B" backup is duplicated to a contiguous region of destination media. Finally, the "C" backup is duplicated as well, as shown in Figure 8.3. At the conclusion of the duplication for the "C" backup (assuming this was all that was on our original backup), we have two very different physical copies of the backups that were on our source media.

There are several advantages (and one notable disadvantage) of demultiplexing duplication:

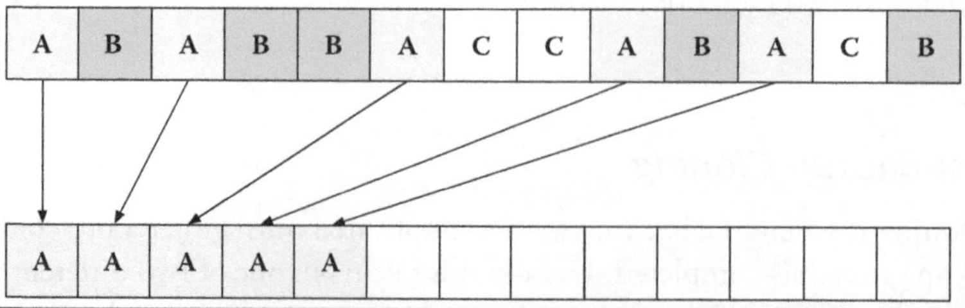

Figure 8.1 Demultiplexed backup duplication, pass 1 of 3

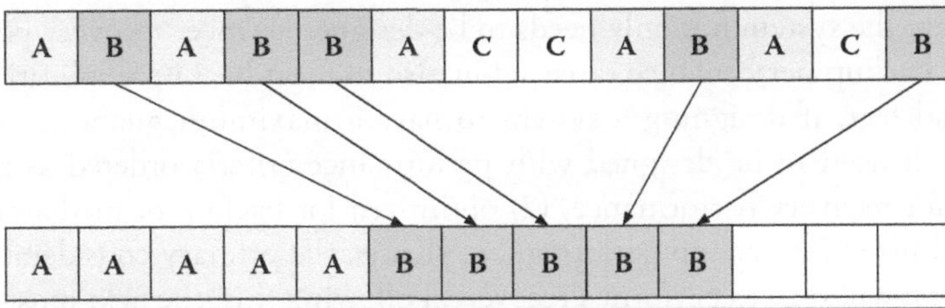

Figure 8.2 Demultiplexed backup duplication, pass 2 of 3

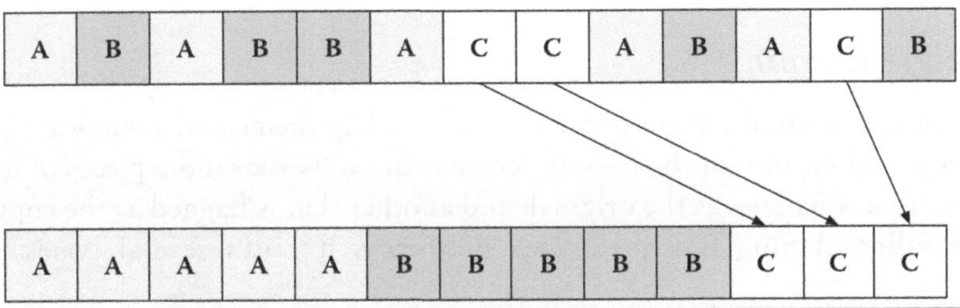

Figure 8.3 Demultiplexed backup duplication, pass 3 of 3

- Entire backup set recovery can be considerably faster from the demultiplexed copy than the original media.
- The duplication process does not require physically identical media. This means it is possible to duplicate from, say, disk to tape, or LTO-1 to 9840B, and so on. Although this may not seem immediately useful, consider duplicating backup images stored on disk to tape for off-site storage.
- This method can be used for targeted duplication without additional backup separation — for instance, it may be that only certain machines need to have their backups duplicated. With full media duplication the only way to achieve this would be to ensure that backups run to different sets of tapes.
- With multiple passes made over the source media, there is considerable media verification occurring as a result of the duplication process.
- On the downside, with multiple passes made over the original media, this method is directly affected by the level of multiplexing used during backups and may take considerably longer than the original backup time if the backups have been poorly tuned.

If the backup software in use or to be used offers multiple duplication methods, carefully weigh these factors before deciding which method is to be used for backup protection within the environment.

Revisiting Performance Considerations. In section 7.2.1, "Recovery Performance," we discussed that a backup system needs to be designed with the recovery performance kept in mind — i.e., if it only takes four hours to back up the system, but as a result it takes sixteen hours to recover it, there may have been a better way of going about the entire backup process. We can further extend that performance requirement now to include post-backup cloning — if the backup software performs post-backup cloning, it is clear that the system not only needs to be designed to meet recovery performance targets and backup performance targets, but also to meet backup duplication targets.

In actual fact, if designing a system to have a maximum guarantee of recoverability, it will need to be designed with performance criteria ordered as follows: (1) optimized for recovery performance, (2) optimized for backup or media duplication, and (3) optimized for backup performance. That is, the primary consideration should be how long it will take to perform a recovery. Following this, the next most-important consideration should be how long it will take to perform backup duplication. Finally, the system will need to be designed for backup performance.

8.3.1.2 Inline Cloning

Inline cloning refers to simultaneous generation of a backup image and a duplicate backup image. Typically, this would mean that the backup server writes to two or more pieces of media simultaneously — one that is flagged as the original, and another that is flagged as the copy.

Although inline cloning is a great idea in theory, it raises several issues that must be considered

- Inline clones will be no faster to recover from than the originals.
- There may be restrictions on mixed media — does the system allow mixed media types, and run the backup at the speed of the slowest tape, or does it require all duplicates to be written to the same media type?
- The same issues regarding differing media lengths as discussed for media duplication may apply here as well.
- Media verification does not automatically occur as part of the inline cloning process because there is no "source" and "destination" concept between the multiple copies of media — therefore, alternate media verification techniques will be required.
- Determining what constitutes a backup failure due to media in the case of inline cloning is somewhat interesting. If the end requirement is two copies of a backup, has the backup succeeded or failed if one piece of media fails? If the backup is re-run in this case, is the first generated copy "wasted media," is it re-used, or can it be referenced for recovery?

8.3.2 Storage of Duplicates

One copy of the backups should always be stored on site, and another copy stored off site. (If further copies are made, they will no doubt be stored according to the requirements of the individual business, but one copy on site and one copy off site should be the minimum goal.)

Where possible, on-site copies should be stored in an electronically accessible way. That is, when considering tape, on-site copies should be kept wherever possible in a tape library. (Obviously this is not possible in all cases, but for frequently accessed media, this should be one consideration in choosing the appropriate sized library.) When on-site copies cannot be stored in a media-changer unit, they should be stored in a suitably protected location — e.g., a fireproof safe or at minimum a locked room. This should feature the same environmental conditions (temperature, humidity, etc.) as surrounds the hardware used to access/read the media.

Off-site copies should be stored in a physically secure location (see section 8.3.3.4, "Physical Protection," for more details), which is not susceptible to the same types of site failures that the primary site is susceptible to — obviously within reasonable risks that can be afforded by the company.

Picking which copy remains on site and which copy gets sent off site can be an interesting choice, and the following factors should be considered:

- If performing inline cloning, then it physically shouldn't matter which copy goes off site and which copy is stored on site. Therefore the appropriate copy should be sent off-site depending on the way in which the backup product chooses copies to use for recoveries, and how frequently those recoveries are performed.
- If performing post-backup cloning, there are two schools of thought:
  - If the duplication demultiplexes the backups, some organizations favor sending the copy off site, so that in a disaster recovery situation they will then be recovering from the "fastest" possible copy of the backup.
  - Regardless of whether the duplication demultiplexes the backups, some organizations favor sending the original off site because in a disaster recovery situation they will be recovering from a copy of the backup that has previously been successfully read from.

There is no definite rule as to which copy of a backup should be stored on site and which copy should be stored off site — it will be dependent on the features of the backup software being used, and corporate policies.

8.3.3 Hardware-Level Protection

There are a few different types of hardware-based protection that can be deployed in a backup environment, ranging from internal hardware of the backup server to tape library and disk array options for the backups.

8.3.3.1 Hot-Pluggable Tape Libraries

In an enterprise or any other highly available environment, the backup server should not constitute a single point of failure, and a way to assist with this is to ensure that the tape library (or libraries) in use employ hot-pluggable components. Obviously when there is a single component (e.g., the robot arm), the options for hot-pluggable components shrinks somewhat, but it should be possible to replace a tape drive without having to shut down or reboot the backup server. (Obviously the backup software will also need to have some support for this — for instance, although the backup software should not need to be aware that a tape drive has been replaced, it will typically be necessary to instruct the backup software to "disable" the tape drive before it is replaced so that it doesn't try to use the drive during the physical replacement process. If it can't be disabled temporarily, then the risk is run of introducing errors into the backup environment if the drive is replaced while the backup software is trying to access it.)

Many enterprise tape libraries have supported hot-pluggable tape drives for some time now in the SCSI area, but sometimes support for hot-plugging fiber drives is lacking, or worse, available but not enabled by default.

A challenge with replacing fiber tape drives of course is that each fiber device needs to have a unique worldwide name (WWN), and therefore in a normal scenario replacing a tape drive would necessitate rezoning a SAN. Depending on the environment, this may lead to an interruption by way of a reboot, or worse, a need to reboot and to reconfigure the tape library within the backup software.

To address this problem, it is possible in some tape libraries to enable a feature that could be generically referred to as worldwide name masquerading. In this scenario, each "slot" in the library that a tape drive can plug into has its own unique WWN. It is this WWN that is zoned for access with the rest of the SAN. When a fiber drive is installed in the slot, the library internally handles the mapping from the "public" slot-WWN to the private drive-WWN, thus avoiding any reconfiguration or reboot requirement as a result of the drive being replaced. If this is available, it should be used.

8.3.3.2 RAIT

Some companies offer what could be loosely described as "RAIT" — a redundant array of independent tapes. This is where a series of two or more tape drives are used to write backups simultaneously (somewhat like an inline backup duplication) so that the system can recover from the loss of a single tape not via cloning but via standard RAID techniques.

Typically, this is offered in the form of either RAIT-1 or RAIT-5, and these options are analogous to their disk-based RAID numbers, coming with much the same pros and cons as their RAID equivalents. Some vendors, such as StorageTek, also provide enterprise-class RAIT via mirrored tape drives in large ACSLS-controlled silos, but at this price point the protection is beyond the budgets of many businesses.

In practice, RAIT suffers from media-management overhead:

- RAIT-5 offers increased tape backup capacity than RAIT-1, but the striping factor across multiple drives makes for significantly increased requirements for tape changing.
- RAIT-1 requires double the tape capacity for the same capacity backups as regular tape-based backups, and still suffers from the need for more tape changing in much the same way as RAIT-5.
- The same tape length issues that apply to inline and media duplication apply to RAIT devices as well, and therefore even more media may be used than anticipated depending on variable media length.

Typically, only companies with very large data centers deploy RAIT (typically as part of silo functionality) due to the increased media utilization.

*8.3.3.3 RAID for Disk Backup**

If implementing a disk backup solution, always ensure that the disks being backed up to are RAID protected to avoid loss of backups due to the failure of any one disk.

When planning disk backup solutions remember that the mean time between failure (MTBF) cumulatively decreases as more disk drives are added to a system. Although individual drive MTBF is quite high, the cumulative MTBF can be alarmingly low if there is a significant number of drives. Remember that disk is cheap — particularly compared to losing a large amount of backup.

---

* This applies equally to virtual tape libraries as conventional disk backup.

For example, consider the use of 320-GB drives for disk backup. If these are arranged as 5 × 320 GB drives in an unprotected stripe, there will be an unformatted filesystem capacity of 1600 GB. With RAID-5, this will drop to 1280 GB — i.e., a loss of 320 GB of unformatted capacity of the unit in return for protection against disk failure. With five disk backup units provided out of these two configuration types, there will either be 8000 GB of unformatted space (unprotected) or 6400 GB of unformatted space (protected).

This may sound like a large difference, and may tempt some to "save money" instead and run with unprotected disk. What this decision doesn't do is evaluate the cost of lost backups, however. What is the cost to a business if 1600 GB of backups are lost due to a disk failure in an unprotected stripe-set? On the other hand, by accepting 1600 GB less storage, the problem of a loss of backups is very unlikely to occur just due to a disk failure. If questioning why the configuration of five disks per RAID-5 set has been chosen, it is quite deliberate. Various benchmarks show that five- and nine-disk configurations give the best (average) RAID-5 performance, and in turn multiple backup vendors have advocated that five-disk RAID-5 configurations provide the best performance for backup to disk. Therefore, although using all 25 disks in a single RAID-5 set would provide 7680 GB of unformatted capacity versus the 6400 GB capacity discussed above, it is also likely to provide extremely poor performance.

Some hardware vendors of late have taken to publishing statistics showing best performance for disk backup using RAID-3 systems. Such claims should be reviewed and tested carefully on a per-environment basis, as the results achieved tend to depend on the local environment.

8.3.3.4 Physical Protection

It is imperative that backup media are stored in a location that does not compromise the physical integrity of the media. Similarly, the same considerations need to apply when the media is transported from one location to another.

This is particularly important in environments that suffer from considerable humidity, extreme heat/cold, or large temperature variations. Indeed, many tape vendors provide recommendations, for instance, that if tapes are moved from one environment to another they are given time to acclimatize before they are accessed.

Areas of physical protection that should be considered include

- Are off-site backup media stored in a location that is safe in comparison to the faults that may potentially take out the production sites?
- Are backup media transported in environmentally sealed containers or packs?
- Are the volumes stored at an off-site location that is suitably physically protected and secure?
- If some of the backup media are stored on site but not online (i.e., inside a medium changer) for part of its useful life, is that on-site location protected? (For example, are tapes stored in a fireproof safe, or just on a shelf somewhere in the environment?)
- Do people have to sign (or otherwise leave identification details) to access backup media or are they readily accessible?
- How are media that either (1) are considered too old to be used, or (2) have experienced a failure securely and reliably disposed of? A challenge here, of course, is that the absolutely most reliable and simple way of disposing of media would be to destroy it physically via something such as a fire, but this will create environmental considerations that are either

unacceptable or even illegal. (For instance, paying a temp worker to de-spool tapes physically into buckets of water before disposal may be cheaper than using secure destruction companies, depending on the level of destruction required.)

Backup media should be stored in a secure room with constant temperature and humidity appropriate for a computer room, and be transported in such a way as to ensure that there is a minimum alteration to the tape's temperature or environmental humidity.

8.3.3.5 Physical Security

This topic cannot be completed without reference to physical security. Backup media holds the same data and secure information as the systems that have been backed up, i.e., although not as immediately easy to access as the "real" system, backup media is typically far easier to steal than a server. With access to the same backup software, backup media can easily be used to misappropriate data from the originating server.

Unfortunately, this is frequently forgotten after the media have been removed from the device that wrote it. It is not uncommon, for instance, in an average computer room to find a plethora of backup tapes laying around with a diverse range of labels on them, some of them clearly indicating the content of the media. Although security through obfuscation is never a stand-alone security model, we restate the recommendation that tapes should always (and only) have barcodes (or other plain numerical sequences) on them to prevent someone from easily determining the importance of the data on a volume simply by the label written on it.

To someone with less than honorable intentions, having access to unguarded backup media is like a child being left in a candy store. What this means is that the security precautions that are applied to the systems which are backed up should also be provided for the media that holds the backup. If a swipe card is need to access the server physically, then it should also be needed to access the backup tapes. If a swipe card and a physical ID check is needed, then that procedure should be replicated for the access of the backup media.

Some products advocate the use of encryption of sensitive data prior to backup. However, this should be avoided in favor of hardware encryption as it introduces additional performance overheads in the backup and can increase the risk of a recovery-failure situation. On-the-fly encryption should be seen as a last resort if physical security cannot be achieved, not as a first step towards securing backup media. In particular, the use of on-the-fly encryption creates two requirements:

1. Hosts in the backup environment must have sufficient processor and memory capacity to handle the additional load of encrypting data before transmission, and decrypting data before receipt.
2. Backup cloning becomes mandatory. In the event of a backup containing a physical tape fault, depending on the product or the money that is willing to be spent there can usually still be some data recovery around the tape fault. With encrypted data, however, the chance of either recovering data or being able to send the tape away for third-party recovery decreases considerably. Thus it should be considered that encryption of backups necessitates the use of backup duplication.

Hardware-based backup encryption can be almost as fast as raw speed. Specialist data encryption companies sell "encryption routers" that reside in either a fiber-channel or a SCSI layer between servers and storage, ensuring that all data passing between is encrypted, and that correct keys are required to decrypt data. These solutions offer secure, reliable, and high-speed encryption mechanisms.

8.4 Protecting the Backup Server

Thankfully, when asked whether the backup server needs to be backed up, most people now answer "yes" without hesitation. This was not always the case, and occasionally some organizations may still be found where it is deemed that the backup server is not really a production machine, and therefore does not require regular backups.

However, the recognition that the backup server needs to be backed up doesn't necessarily result in a flow-on effect of ensuring the backup server is adequately protected in the same way as the machines that it protects. In this section we will discuss the various aspects to protecting the backup server.

8.4.1 Backup Server Components

Most backup servers will have the following components:

- Configuration data
- Volume (media) data
- File catalogue data
- Backup and system logs

Each of these components must be properly backed up to ensure that the backup server is able to be recovered properly.

Some backup products do not automatically protect this information, but instead rely on the users of the product to turn the backups on, or worse, periodically require users to force a run of the special backups manually to ensure that the backup server is recoverable. (This is quite the mark of a poor backup product.)

If the environment makes use of a SAN, it is strongly recommended to store this data on a SAN-connected volume. In this case, in the event of a failure of the backup server itself, it is possible to transfer ownership of those filesystems to another host to get backup/recovery operations running quickly. (Or alternatively, this protects from a catastrophic failure in the backup server that takes out the internal disks as well. This doesn't have to be just a fire event. A customer literally experienced a server "crash" when inserting a CD into a backup server. The service technician called out the previous day had forgotten to screw in the bolts holding the computer into the rack, and it fell the entire height of the rack, destroying not only its own disks, but also the disks of the server it fell onto.) Obviously this means that the backup server is dependent on the SAN remaining operational — for most organizations this is taken as a given, and where it is not, SAN replication is usually configured, in which case protection will exist from SAN failure as well.

Regardless of where these configuration files and databases are stored, it is important to ensure on a daily basis that backups of these items are performed so that in the event of a loss of the backup server, the system can be recovered, and operations kept running.

Many may wonder why backup and system log files warrant mentioning in the above list of "special" items on the backup server. Unfortunately, backups are not always simple to recover from. Sometimes the key pieces of media needed as part of a recovery may exhibit strange errors during access, or a file that was to be recovered didn't seem to come back during the recovery process.

There is considerable difference between being able to state that a failure has occurred and being able to report why the failure occurred. Obviously this is not always guaranteed and thus being able to retrieve logs from the time that the backup was generated can be vital in determining why the failure occurred. For instance, did the logs show that the file that could not be recovered was open at the time and therefore couldn't be successfully backed up? Did the logs show the tape that was to be recovered from filling at half its normal size? Did the system logs show SCSI reset errors during the time of the backup? Obviously in all of these cases it is preferable to be aware of these problems when they happen, not during the recovery. However, it should be possible to fall back on recoveries of these log files later for reporting in the event of either a recovery failure, or the need to make a report to an auditor. It may also be that it is not remembered that a failure occurred six months following the fact (or even six days) if it was a seemingly minor failure.

In addition to performing regular backups of the backup server, it is important to ensure that its backups have the same retention as the servers that it protects. A common strategy for companies trying to save money on media, for instance, is to reduce the backup retention period for "less important" servers, which almost invariably includes the backup server itself. In some cases, backup servers have had a retention period of as little as a week, on the understanding that "it doesn't contain any historical data." However, when we consider the backup databases (file/media databases, etc.) and logs, we can see plainly that this isn't the case. Additionally, changes to the configuration over time may be critical to the recoverability of a particular host from a long-term backup. Remember our axiom that it is always better to back up a little too much than not enough. This applies to the backup server as much as any other key production system in an environment.

8.4.2 Ensuring Availability

The backup server is a key server for the entire environment it protects, and therefore it should be considered as mandatory that (at minimum) low-level fault tolerance options such as RAID-protected storage and basic hardware redundancy are to be used for it. Typically an enterprise backup server should:

- Use RAID to ensure that no single disk failure can prevent backups or recoveries from running.
- Have redundant power supplies and fans.
- Have a same-day service level agreement with the vendor. Sometimes a backup server is relegated to "next day parts and labor," but think carefully about this: can a company really afford to wait 24 hours for a critical system recovery? (Alternatively, if same-day service for the backup server cannot be achieved, it may be necessary to consider keeping hardware spares available so that faulty parts can be swapped out while waiting for the vendor to arrive.)*

* In comparison to other servers in a larger organization, it may become apparent that the backup server needs considerably better service level agreements with the hardware and software vendors — for instance, if one system is down, it may introduce considerable impact to the business, but what is the potential impact to the business if no host in the corporation can be backed up while waiting for a replacement hard drive to arrive overnight?

In large-scale backup environments (and particularly in the backup services arena) it may even be appropriate to consider deploying backup software on highly available hardware, which allows for hardware maintenance to take place during system operations. However, this level of protection is unlikely to be required for most organizations.

A more-regular alternative to highly available hardware is clustering. However, clustering is a somewhat trickier concept with backup servers than it is with regular servers — typically due to the need to be able to attach a backup server to a media unit (i.e., tape library or other robotic media changer). As such, the level of support offered by backup vendors for clustering of their backup server software can be variable. Also, what may be desired may not be physically possible, as we'll discuss later.

In a SCSI robot-connected environment it would be quite easy to configure a cluster to do at least the following:

- Shut down a failing backup server
- Bring up backup services on a failover cluster machine (particularly when the server disk is on a SAN or other shared disk)
- Start up the new server as the old backup server

However, even at this point someone has to unplug the tape library from the failed server and plug it into the new server — i.e., a modicum of clustering can be achieved but human intervention is still required in the failover process. For this reason many organizations (even those with highly available production servers) choose to implement a fully manual failover system between the backup server and its failover server.

In full SAN-connected environments, fully automated failover becomes possible as long as every machine in the cluster can be simultaneously zoned in to see the tape library, but can be configured not to access it as a controller unless directed.

Sometimes when presented with these options, companies may choose to attach the tape library to another host (e.g., "storage node" or "media server"), or use a special library server such as StorageTek ACSLS or EMC AlphaStor to "present" the library to the running backup server as a virtualized unit. In both cases, these approaches merely move where the single point of failure is within the environment; they do not solve the problem. As such, if intending to "solve" the problem via this mechanism, it is necessary to understand that it simply relocates the problem rather than actually solving it.

Even where it is physically possible to dual-attach a backup server and a failover server to the same machine, there may still be more human intervention required during a failover than during a failover in a normal cluster. Again, this is primarily due to the physical components involved — most notably the tape library or media changer. If such lights-out transitions are required on such systems, it is imperative to ensure that a robot has a remotely accessible control system that allows it to be rebooted or reset. If the backup server fails during a backup process and failover is required, there is likely to be a need to have operator intervention on the tape library before it can be used by the failover host — for instance, it may require a reset due to hung communications with the failed server. Alternatively, it may need media manually unmounted/cleared from drives before the failover host can take over access.

Additionally, the choice of whether or not to cluster the backup server will be considerably dependent upon whether the backup software supports active/active cluster arrangements or active/passive cluster arrangements. This doesn't necessarily refer to both servers in the cluster acting as a backup server, but instead refers more to the idea of the "inactive" backup server acting as a media server or storage node — i.e., does the clustering support in the backup product allow for the failover node to be used to assist overall backup performance when it is not required for contingency activities, or does it have to remain totally inactive until such time as a failover occurs? (Even if the backup product does not natively support an active/active cluster configuration it may pay to consult with system integrators that work with the product, as they may have solutions that fill the gap.)

8.4.3 Historical Considerations

As mentioned in the introduction of the book, backups represent a stronger "forward thinking" requirement than any other IT system. Many organizations go through a three-year hardware refresh policy, and backup systems will also fall into this category.

Example. Consider a simple scenario of being required to retain backups for ten years due to legal or taxation record requirements. We might have a timeline such as the following:

1995	Backup software X purchased, DLT-4000 tape drives used.
1999	Backup software X retained, upgraded to DLT-7000 tape drives.
2002	Backup software Y purchased, upgraded to LTO-1 tape drives.
2005	Backup software Y retained, upgraded to LTO-3 tape drives.

This scenario is a common-enough example of backup systems evolution within an organization, but the implications on recovery are not always considered. Let's therefore add more to the scenario for 2005:

January	Tax department decides to do a random audit and requests files from monthly backups going back to 1995. Files for 2002–2004 retrievable immediately.
February	IT department no longer has a DLT-7000 tape drive. Management purchases DLT-7000 tape drive, most likely second-hand.
March	DLT-7000 tape drive attached to backup server. IT department determines old backup software required. Previously used version of software is no longer compatible with available operating system versions.
April	Old vendor requests payment of thousands of dollars in back maintenance on software to allow the installation of the latest version.

This type of scenario is not pleasant. Clearly what has occurred in such a situation is a lack of forward planning. Backups are often thought of as a "recover from yesterday's failure" system, even when monthly or yearly activities are being performed and are known to be required from the outset of the backup system implementation.

Even when no upgrades are planned, some historical considerations must come into play, and this is mainly due to media storage capabilities. Despite the fact that many tape manufacturers state that their media have a long shelf-life, this does not mean that an organization should assume that seven or ten years after being used, a cartridge will be guaranteed fault-free. Thus, tapes should be pulled out of long-term storage periodically, at worst, and their data integrity evaluated with a view to recreating the backups in the event of errors. More appropriately, over a long-term retention there should be definite time periods (well within the quoted shelf-life reliability of the vendors) after which backups on older tapes are recreated.

With these two factors in mind, two options are available to a company regarding long-term retention of backups — migration and maintenance.

8.4.3.1 Migration

Migration refers to moving backups from one piece of media to another, and most typically should be considered for regeneration of backups onto fresh media, or transitioning to new media types.

In some circumstances with lower-class backup products, migration requires the physical restore of the backups to original (or similar) hosts, followed by a new backup being generated from the restored data. This should be avoided wherever possible as:

- Unless done carefully, a "restore, then backup" may result in a slightly different set of data than the original data — particularly with regards to access control lists, etc.
- Courts and taxation officials may not recognize new backups of old data as the "real" old data (scenario: "why should the court accept that this is really June 1998 data when the files on tape were generated in October 2004?").
- Hardware and operating systems may have diverged sufficiently to increase the complexity of the operation.
- Regardless of whether the original hardware/operating systems are available, the process is an incredibly tedious one.

Moving on from the "restore, then backup again" scenario we can examine two more-realistic migration techniques.

A migration sees the backup product "copy" the content of the original tapes to the new tapes, thus extending the life cycle of the backup or refreshing the media type involved. In a worst-case scenario, this will be a registered copy of the original backup, with the original backup kept for referential purposes, but no longer used for recovery. A copy method of migration however induces a downside, that being the necessity to maintain backup system database records for the (essentially) defunct original.

Other backup software will offer a true migration, however, whereby after the copy is made the records for the original backup are removed, with the newly created copy registered as the "new original." This allows older media to be phased completely out of the system.

8.4.3.2 Maintenance

Maintenance refers to keeping previously used hardware or software available and operational in "read-only," thus even after a transfer to new backup media has been performed, or installation of new backup software is complete, the old hardware or software will be kept running for restores.

For example, maintenance would be used to allow a company that moves from backup software *X* to *Y* to continue to restore from backups generated using backup software *X*, even after backup software *Y* has been in use for several years.

Factors that must be considered for maintenance-style operations are

- Even with maintenance operations in place, migrations for long-term storage of backup media may still be required.
- Choosing to keep systems in maintenance mode requires all associated hardware to be maintained as well.
- Backup companies frequently offer a commercial incentive to swap out their competitors' products with their own. If such a deal has been struck, then legally it may not be permissible to retain licenses for older backup software.
- As operating systems age, their reliability tends to decrease in comparison to newer operating systems. Maintenance refers not just to maintaining the backup server software itself, but everything else it depended on (hardware and operating system) before it was decommissioned. (Virtualization can assist on this front.)
- Maintenance should literally be interpreted as keeping existing hardware and software running, with periodic tests conducted to confirm successful operations.

The last point cannot be overemphasized. The following scenarios are quite common with an upgrade from one tape technology (*X*) to another (*Y*) incompatible tape technology:

- No model *X* tape drives retained
- One tape drive for model *X* retained, but not connected to server or powered up
- One tape drive for model *X* retained, but backup server cannot be physically connected to it
- One tape drive for model *X* retained and connected to server/powered up but never tested
- As per the last example, but with the added "bonus" of vendor maintenance no longer being paid for the tape drive

If any of these strategies appear familiar, serious consideration should be given to data migration instead as a means of long-term recoverability. (A simple rule: if equipment is not maintained in a "ready for use" state, it is not being correctly maintained.)

Ultimately, like so many IT factors, choosing to keep a system in maintenance mode will appear to be the cheaper or easier option to start with, but as time goes by and support/service contracts continue to increase in price with the age of the systems being maintained, this may rise in cost eventually to eclipse the initial cost of backup migration considerably.

This option is typically more appropriate when a switch is made in the backup software used rather than when tape hardware is changed. When hardware is changed, the backup software should natively support migrating backups from one type of media to another — it is, however, somewhat difficult to believe that the major backup vendors will ever support reading each others' backups due to the risk this creates of losing an account.

8.4.4 Archives

Although archives and backups are technically separate activities with differing requirements, it stands to reason that in a large number of organizations a backup server is also responsible for storing archival backups.*

The migration and maintenance of archival backups will have the same requirements and considerations as other backups, but these will typically have an even longer life span than regular long-term backups. For instance, government departments that perform archival backups may be required to retain those archives for at least 30 years, or possibly even longer.

With this in mind, if the backup system is also used for archives, recoverability from archival backups must be ensured, particularly over extended periods of time.

When considering the implications of long-term retrieval from archival backups, always remember the following point: there is not a single specific format for electronic off-line storage that is exactly the same now as it was 30 years ago in computing. Obviously generic types of electronic storage (tape, disk) have been around for this length of time, but new systems are not being produced, for instance, that will work with tapes generated 30 years ago.

Therefore, archival, even more so than long-term backup, is not just about writing the data down somewhere and throwing it away. This is particularly so when, over extended periods of time, vendors, manufacturers, and standards associations may sometimes "revise down" the expected life span of a product. For instance, when first introduced, compact disks were meant to last "forever," so to speak, yet now it is generally accepted that the average life span of a compact disc is around ten years.

For this reason, archival is not simply a one-off activity, and at bare minimum it is required to:

- Keep track of all archives performed. For each piece of media an archive is written to, ensure that details are kept of the batch number the media came from, for two reasons:
  - If a vendor issues a recall notice against a particular batch number, then it is possible to recall, test, and evacuate all archives performed on media using that batch number.
  - If during testing a particular piece of media is found to be defective, all archive media written to using the same batch number can be recalled and tested.
- Perform multiple copies, preferably to multiple media types for each archive performed.
- If at all possible, maintain "meta" indices to the archives performed in addition to the databases maintained by the backup server. These indices should track:
  - Volume label/barcode that the archive is stored on.
  - Host the archive was generated from (the client).
  - Backup software used to generate the archive.

* It is very important that, if a backup system is used for archives, it is used properly for archives, with the knowledge of the backup administrator. A classic example that happens in some companies is that users deliberately delete data on systems that have minimal free space with the intention to restore that data later when required. This is a highly dangerous way of going about using a backup system, and if it occurs it should be seen as a significant warning of the urgent need to expand storage systems for users and applications. (A worse derivation of this once observed was that although IT staff were allowed to set disk quotas, they were forbidden by legislation to impose e-mail quotas. Users therefore zipped and e-mailed the entire contents of their home directories to themselves every time the home directories became full, before deleting the contents of the directory, thereby allowing themselves to stay under their disk quota.)

    - If the backup software generates a "unique ID" associated with each backup, note the unique ID.
    - The file(s) stored in the archive.
    - The permanent, archival location(s) of copies of the backup software that can be used to perform the recovery of the archive.*
- Test the recoverability from archives on a regular basis (e.g., yearly), with evacuation of archives to be performed in the event of a failure.
- Have a migration plan in place from the start of the archival service to relocate archives from media after the archive has exceeded a certain age. Obviously any newly generated archival media will need to be inserted properly into the archival testing and maintenance regime.
- Have an archival migration plan in place in case the backup software used to generate the archives is exchanged or replaced with incompatible software. As this may not be an instantaneous changeover depending on the number of archives generated, there will need to be contingency plans available to allow for the restore from archives during the migration process.

Obviously, there are many more considerations to archival beyond the scope of what has been described here, and a full coverage of electronic archival is beyond the scope of this book.

* The reason for this may not be immediately apparent — however, consider what might happen after an extended period of time if a recovery from the archive is required. Will the same backup software be in use? Will the databases within the backup software for the archive still be online and available? Even if the backup software used to generate the archive is no longer in use, this information will at least allow media to be located for recovery while a server is prepared. If the company has entirely replaced its system administration department three times and its backup software five times during that period, without this information available someone may have the rather odious task of installing all the previously used backup software as well as regenerating indices and media database information before the recovery takes place.

Chapter 9

Problem Analysis

9.1 Introduction

While every backup product will have its own mechanisms for debugging problems that occur within the environment, there are a variety of techniques for isolating faults that are common across all backup products.

At the end of this chapter it should be possible to perform preliminary diagnosis of backup failures, and have an understanding of the basic types of information typically required by backup vendors and support providers when evaluating backup problems.

Remember when working through a debugging/validation exercise that it's as much about eliminating items that aren't broken as it is about finding something that is broken. If not sure of what might be the problem, moving through a process of elimination at least allows the narrowing down of the possibilities.

When complicated recoveries are being performed, the status of the recovery should be tracked. In the same way, when performing problem diagnosis it is important to keep records of where the diagnosis is up to, what has been tried, and, where pertinent, what the results were. This not only helps others if they have to assist in the diagnosis process, but also helps in avoiding back-tracking work and needlessly repeating tests.

9.2 Network

Network tests should not be underestimated in their usefulness to provide valuable data for the resolution of backup system problems. Time and time again, support staff have spent considerable periods of time debugging problems only to find that basic connectivity tests failed — i.e., while looking for a more complex problem, a simple problem lay out in the open, unobserved.

Network tests that should be performed fall into two broad categories — basic connectivity and basic configuration.

9.2.1 Basic Configuration

9.2.1.1 Switch/NIC Settings

Take the time to check switch and NIC settings if problems manifest as any of the following:

- Intermittent backup failures
- Intermittent timeouts
- Slower than usual backups

Even in well-running environments with rigorous change management procedures it is not uncommon to see unexpected switch or NIC changes causing backups to fail intermittently. These have been caused by anything from faulty switch ports to unexpected consequences of operating system patches, and even overly curious staff who accidentally click "yes" instead of "no" after experimenting with configuration changes.

9.2.1.2 Hostname Resolution

Few backup products allow the use of only IP-address details in their configuration for the server or client, and this means in turn that resolution becomes an important component in debugging failures. While this may seem as an inconvenience, it improves the legibility of the configuration and also helps to avoid security issues caused by IP address spoofing.

Typically it is possible to determine fairly quickly from backup or recovery errors whether hostname resolution is a reason behind a failure — however, in some cases the error message may be somewhat vague. When faced with an indecipherable error message, always try to keep in mind "this error message will at least make sense to a programmer at the backup company," i.e., don't just ignore/discount an error message that is not immediately understood.

In a DNS-based environment, it is necessary to ensure that both forward and reverse resolution succeeds. Forward resolution refers to resolution of an IP address from a hostname, whereas reverse resolution refers to the resolution of a hostname from an IP address. For example:

```
# nslookup nox.anywebdb.com
Server: asgard.anywebdb.com
Address: 192.168.100.99
Name: nox.anywebdb.com
Address: 192.168.100.4
```

This an example of the type of output that should be expected from a forward resolution check, whereas the following output is indicative of a reverse resolution attempt:

```
# nslookup 192.168.100.4
Server:        asgard.anywebdb.com
Address:       192.168.100.99
4.100.168.192.in-addr.arpa        name=nox.anywebdb.com
```

At the bare minimum, the following name resolution attempts should succeed

- The backup server can properly resolve itself.
- The backup server can properly resolve the client and any intermediate hosts.
- The client should be able to resolve itself.
- The client should be able to resolve the backup server and any intermediate hosts.

By intermediate hosts we typically refer to hosts that write backups to storage or read them back — i.e., storage nodes, media servers, or slave servers, depending on the backup software nomenclature.

In a hosts file-only environment, it is important to ensure that all host files have matching entries for the hosts involved in the backup process.

When environments have a combination of hosts file entries and DNS entries, there is one simple rule to follow in addition to the previously discussed DNS and hosts requirements — there should be no "dispute" between hosts and DNS on the addresses in use. (A dispute is where a particular host can resolve another machine (or itself) by both hosts file entries and DNS, but the two methods return different results.) Frequently hosts/DNS disputes are quite problematic to diagnose, and therefore wherever possible it is strongly encouraged to stick to one or the other resolution method.

Where there is a multi-tier environment (for example, storage nodes/media servers as well as clients and the backup server) there is even more need to keep these records synchronized. For instance, a client backup may fail, but fails to indicate that the problem is not with the client or the server, but that the storage node the client would use resolves the client as, say, "nox.anywebdb.com" although its hosts file has a typo of "nox.anywedbd.com."

Some organizations will run public and private networks, with the public network being the one visible to end users accessing the system and the private network being used exclusively by the backup product. It is important in public/private network environments to ensure that the hostnames do not get mixed up between the two networks. For example, many public/private networks see DNS used for the public network and hosts files used for the private network — particularly when the private network only covers some hosts as opposed to all hosts (e.g., the hosts with the largest amounts of data may be connected via a higher-speed network to help streamline the backup, but this network is not available to regular systems).

In these types of situations it is important to have clarity between the two networks. For instance, common failures include (1) not using hosts files on the client systems to describe the private address of the client and the backup server/intermediate hosts, leaving clients unable to resolve the private network; and (2) defining the public name of the client on the backup server in the private address space on the backup server. For example, the host "nox.anywebdb.com" might be defined in DNS via its public IP address 192.168.100.4, but is also available to the backup server via a private network with a hosts entry of "10.168.100.4 nox.anywebdb.com" — this will almost guarantee confusion in the backup software. Where a private network is used there should be alternate hostnames between the public and private addresses — e.g., "10.168.1.105 nox-prv.anywebdb.com."

Note that with name resolution tests complete and successful, subsequent tests should avoid using IP addresses, so as to continue to test the environment in the same way the backup server accesses it.

9.2.2 Basic Connectivity

9.2.2.1 Ping Test

Unless there is a firewall that prevents the use of ping, connectivity tests should in most cases start with simple ping operations. Can the backup server ping the backup client? Can the backup client ping the backup server?

If the client sends its data to a third host for backup and recovery, then the tests should be extended to include the additional host(s) involved in the backup and recovery process.

If a ping test fails when ping traffic is enabled, it should be clear that there is a basic network connectivity failure that must be resolved before any further diagnosis can take place.

9.2.2.2 Port Test

Various backup products will communicate via specific ports or ranges of ports. In some cases the product will come with a tool that will probe the port(s) required to determine whether the ports are actually available, and if the product does include such a tool, consider using it before moving on to a generic test such as that described below.

If such a tool is not available, in some cases basic connectivity can be usually confirmed via telnet tests. For example, consider a backup product that requires, say, port 7938 open. In this case it is possible to test using telnet's port function. By default, telnet is typically invoked to open an insecure login session with a particular host, via the "telnet hostname" command syntax. However, if the hostname is followed with a number, telnet interprets that to mean that it should make the connection attempt on the given port.

If telnet attempts to connect to a port that is not listening, an error such as the following will occur

```
# telnet nox 7938
Trying 192.168.100.4
telnet: connect to address 192.168.100.4: Connection refused
```

Alternatively, if the host is unreachable (which would typically be established by a ping test), then there should be a connection timeout error message after a few minutes from telnet. However, if connecting to a port that is listening, a response such as the following will be received

```
# telnet nox 7938
Trying 192.168.100.4...
Connected to nox.
Escape character is '^]'
```

If the backup software uses port-based connectivity between the server and client (or the server, client, and other associated hosts), then performing port-connectivity tests will be vital in determining where a problem exists.

9.2.3 Backup Software Connectivity

As stated previously, the extent of the failure can sometimes be worked out by determining what isn't failing. Therefore in the event of connectivity problems not being related to basic network testing/functionality, confirm the following:

- Do scheduled backups initiated by the server succeed or fail?
- Do ad-hoc backups initiated by the server succeed or fail?
- Do ad-hoc backups initiated by the client succeed or fail?
- Do ad-hoc recovery attempts initiated by the client succeed or fail?
- Do ad-hoc recovery attempts initiated by the backup server succeed or fail?

The combination of success and failure results to these questions can make a considerable impact on what may need to be done to resolve the problem. For instance, if server-initiated activities fail, but client-initiated activities succeed, it may indicate a failure with the agent installed on the client (e.g., it may not even be running). For some backup products, even with the client-server communications agent not running the client can "reach out" to the backup server and initiate a manual operation itself, but the server can't initiate any client activities itself.

If using a support provider, note that it will be necessary to report the combination of success and failure statuses from the above list if needing to escalate, as it will often make for a quicker diagnosis by the vendor.

9.3 Hardware Validation

Hardware validation is all about confirming that the hardware is working as it should be. This can in some cases come down to something as simple as "power cable unplugged," but it can frequently be a deeper-level problem than an unscheduled, unauthorized, and unnotified power loss.

Two key types of hardware validation must be performed — backup device validation and system hardware validation. Deciding which should come first in a discussion is analogous to the chicken and the egg conundrum, so the following validation methods shouldn't necessarily be followed in a fixed order.

9.3.1 Backup Device Validation

Keep in mind that the host attached to a backup device will only warn about events which it is aware of, or it is able to glean from devices, but this will not cover all possible diagnosis avenues available. The simplest avenue of investigation is a visual inspection, though this requires physical access to the location of the backup devices. This may not be readily available for reasons such as the following:

- Equipment is held in a secure site for which access is not available.
- Equipment belongs to a customer that remote support is provided for, but access is not available.
- It may be the middle of the night and the administrator performing the diagnosis doesn't particularly feel like heading into the office to examine the equipment.

9.3.1.1 Physical Inspection

Things to check for when confirming functioning hardware (or media) include

- Are there any blinking lights on the backup devices that shouldn't be there?

  - For tape-based backup units, it may indicate a dirty tape drive or an error state that a robot cannot solve. (Many drives blink their lights in a particular sequence or at a particular speed to indicate a specific type of fault, as opposed to just blinking erratically. Watch carefully to see the sequence of blinking — sometimes it's almost like working with Morse code — e.g., three fast blinks, three slow blinks and three fast blinks in succession might indicate that the tape has wound off its spool.)
  - For disk-based backup units, it may indicate a failed drive in a RAID backup unit.
- Are all the cables plugged in properly? Although we'd all like to have perfect computer rooms where there is plenty of access space and nothing is out of place, many of us are used to computer rooms that have "pinch points" at various areas of access, or have not been cabled in a well-ordered fashion. In these environments it is not uncommon to have a "backup" failure caused by a bumped cable.
- Is the device powered on? It may not necessarily be that someone has powered the device off (intentionally or unintentionally), but it could be that a power supply has failed, or a main power unit has tripped.
- What is the state of the tape library? For instance, after working through a problem where a tape wouldn't unmount, and trying just about every trick possible to reset the library, a physical inspection revealed to a customer that a tape was stuck in the robot arm of the library, which quickly explained why no other tapes could be unloaded.
- Has anyone been manually opening and rearranging/altering the contents of the tape library? Some products (e.g., EMC NetWorker) maintain an "internal map" of tape libraries to reduce the amount of state-querying they have to do, thereby increasing the speed of library operations. The downside of this is that the backup software expects and needs to be the only mechanism used to manipulate the physical contents of the library. (A customer in a training course, for instance, remarked at how much more stable backups had become when the tape library had been moved out of the development area and into a locked computer room that programmers did not have access to. Not knowing any better, the programmers had been "speeding up" the replacement of media in the library by opening the door and replacing media rather than using the CAP.)

9.3.1.2 Operability Validation

Common factors to investigate when diagnosing backup device issues:

- Does the operating system even see the device any longer? Sometimes if a device cannot be accessed from within the backup product, the reason can be that the operating system has lost connectivity to the device. At this point it doesn't really matter what is done within the backup product, the underlying operating system/hardware issue must be resolved.
- Does the operating system see the device (or library) at a different SCSI address? Some operating systems may exhibit issues whereby a device that temporarily "disappears" is reattached, but at a different SCSI address — e.g., instead of SCSI Bus 3 Target 2 LUN 1, it might suddenly appear to be at SCSI Bus 4 Target 2 LUN 1. (Of course, the issue here is that even if the backup software is reconfigured to work with the new address, it may really need to be rebooted to confirm whether the unit will be mapped back or remain on the new mapping.)

- Are there any base operating system tools that can be used to test operability? Sometimes the best way of eliminating a problem is to remove the backup software from the tests. Via UNIX, this can usually be done by basic read/write access to tape devices via the "dd," "tar," or "cpio." For Windows systems, it may be possible to use the "Windows backup" or "NT backup" tool, though there are some ported versions of the UNIX tools available. If a simple operating system tool can't access the backup device, then the backup server won't be able to.

9.3.2 Media Validation

Sometimes the problem isn't with the hardware itself, but with the media in use. Particularly in single-spool tape systems (i.e., where the second spool is inside the tape drive rather than being on the tape), small defects such as a tape spool sitting slightly off center may contribute to problems. Again, particularly with single-spool tape systems, a useful and easy check is to confirm that the tape leader is present. This is a small loop/hoop attached to the start of the tape, and is "grabbed" by the tape drive after it opens the tape to start unreeling it. If the leader is not there, there's a good chance that (1) it has previously snapped off inside a drive, and (2) with the leader not there, there's no chance a drive can take hold of the tape and start de-spooling it.

It is also important to remember that different types of media will have different tolerances to the distance they may be dropped, i.e., some media is forgiving to a certain level of poor handling, and others are very unforgiving. Although staff that handle media should always treat it with respect, accidents will always happen, so staff need to know how media should be handled after such accidents. For example, if a DDS or AIT tape is dropped from a height of a couple of feet, this may present no problem. Having considerably more fragile spooling mechanisms though, DLT tapes should instead, in this scenario, only be picked up to be disposed of, rather than re-used.

Another aspect of media handling not always considered is the risk involved in turning a tape drive off while there is a tape in the drive. This should always be considered a last resort when trying to diagnose a problem, and as such it should only be done after exhausting every other possibility of getting the tape out of the drive (including holding down the eject button for at least 60 seconds, which for most drives is the upper limit on triggering a forced unload).

9.3.3 Firmware Validation

Although not suggesting that the latest version of any firmware available for backup devices should be applied whenever problems occur, it is still necessary to consider it. It is therefore important to have a clear line of communication with the library vendor(s) to obtain release notes for firmware updates. In particular, if access to the release notes of device firmware updates can be provided, it may be found upon review that the firmware upgrade addresses a sporadic problem being experienced that has not yet been flagged as something for investigation.

Sometimes firmware can have a significant impact on the backup environment, and just because the backup environment has been working for some time doesn't meant that firmware won't suddenly become a problem.

> **Firmware Problems Don't Manifest on Every Tape, and May Not Cause Problems in Isolation.** Sometimes a firmware problem is not a permanent issue, but is an

incompatibility with individual units of media. Some modern tape formats rely on electronic/magnetic markers to indicate the physical end of tape, and to warn a tape drive to slow down. Normally this works fine.

For a while a popular media manufacturer experienced a problem whereby in specific batches of a type of media, the end of tape marker was not "fully" recorded on the media as part of the media construction process. Presumably because these tapes were deemed production capable, there must be some redundancy built into the end-of-tape marker mechanism.

Murphy's law, as previously stated, plays a part in IT. Around the same time a tape drive manufacturer had released a version of firmware that did not react "too well" to this situation. On normal tapes, with the end-of-tape markers fully and properly recorded, this did not present a problem, and so even on a single batch of tapes most media worked without a flaw. However, when a faulty tape was encountered, the drive would not halt the rewind process and physically de-spool the cartridge contents onto the internal drive spool.

9.4 System Hardware Validation

As discussed in section 2.3.3, "Service Component Layers," a backup system should provide protection in the event of the failure of any part of a host, but can't be guaranteed to function successfully in the event of ongoing system failures — e.g., hardware faults or operating system failures. In these instances it is necessary either to repair the hardware or recover the operating system. Backup software can't work miracles with faulty tools, and therefore as part of the diagnosis of backup problems, it is necessary to confirm that hardware — both on the client and on the server or storage node — is functional.

9.4.1 Server/Storage Node

Although much of the validation to be conducted on the backup server or storage node resolves around the backup hardware itself, sometimes other hardware can get in the way of a good backup. Factors to be considered here include

- Disks housing the filesystems that backup configuration and databases are stored on. If these disks completely fail, the problem will be noticed almost immediately. However, if the disks are intermittently failing, backups may behave very strangely.
- Memory or CPU stability of the server. Some backup problems only occur when the backup server is "swamped" — i.e., running out of CPU or memory capacity. When hardware is stretched to the limit here, minor fabrication faults that would otherwise be largely unnoticed can start to play a factor. It's not unknown to solve a backup problem by replacing the physical memory on a backup server, or swapping its host hardware with another machine.
- Other hardware chained to the backup devices. Most system administrators are reluctant to chain differing SCSI devices — in particular, linking disk and tape on the same SCSI chain is frequently fraught with issues. Sometimes when budget is limited, however, there may be no choice but to chain devices together. In these cases if problems occur, the following must be investigated

  - Are the other devices malfunctioning? If a device receives (or generates) a SCSI reset it may cause problems for everything else on the chain.
  - Do problems go away when the other devices are powered off? Even if a device is not actually reporting that it is malfunctioning, it may be intermittently causing problems that are difficult to catch.
  - Do problems go away if the other devices are temporarily unchained? Regardless of budgetary constraints, there may be an incompatibility that is not physically possible to be overcome.
- Sometimes problems come down to physical faults on NICs, HBAs, or cables (with cables being the more usual of the three). Poor management of cables — particularly fiber cables, which are very sensitive to sharp bends, may result in intermittent or complete faults.

9.4.2 *Client*

For hardware diagnosis on the client side, areas to check commonly include

- Disk status. Failed or failing disks can make the task of the backup agent difficult if not impossible — both reading from or writing to faulty disk is not a simple nor a reliable activity.
- NICs. Intermittent network connectivity failures can be evidence of a faulty network interface card in an individual machine rather than a faulty switch port or network cable.
- Memory and CPU status. As per the server and storage nodes, if a client is doing a significant amount of processing during the backup, it may be "tickling" a problem that would otherwise not manifest on the client.

9.5 Software Validation

9.5.1 *Log Review*

The importance of reviewing log files while trying to determine the nature of a problem cannot be overstated. At the software layer, the first step in determining what may be going wrong is to conduct a comprehensive review of the log files available on a system.

There are two primary sources of logs that should be reviewed

1. Backup software logs — these may not be limited to one file, and it will therefore be necessary to compare against multiple files. For instance, when diagnosing problems with backup agents for databases, it may be required to review log files on both the server and the client where the agent is running. (If installing a new backup product, confirm prior to it entering production mode that all possible locations of log files are known, or whatever must be done to enable logging. If working with an existing product, this should be already known, but if not known, the support vendor should be contacted for details of where the file(s) are to be found.)
2. Operating system logs — these can be used to correlate system events and backup system events. For instance, at the time that a tape wouldn't unload, did the event logs show a SCSI reset occurring on an HBA? At the time the backup logs show all backups failing, do the system logs show the disk space on the backup server temporarily filling? Correlations

between log files are rarely random coincidences — there is typically a strong cause-and-effect relationship.

When reviewing system and backup logs, be prepared to investigate logs on any of the following devices that may be in the environment:

- Tape libraries — for instance, is there a drive failure registered in the library at the time a tape unload failure occurred?
- Fiber-channel switches — in a SAN-based environment, are there any issues reported with the SAN around the time of a failure? Take into account that SAN and SCSI failures may take a while to time out — e.g., if an LIP occurs on a port approximately five minutes after the last recorded successful tape library operation, there may be a relationship between the two events.
- Fiber-channel bridges — when using fiber-channel bridges (or any other interconnectivity devices), it's very important to cross-reference device problems with events on the bridge.
- Network switches — does the log on the switch show a port re-negotiation occurring during backup performance issues? If connectivity is lost during the backup process, it may be due to mundane factors such as client software failures, but it may also be due to a faulty switch port, an unreliable cable, or a network load issue (e.g., failures might only occur when the network link between the server and a client is more than 90 percent loaded).

To be able to correlate logs properly between such a diverse range of systems, it's vitally important that time synchronization exists between the systems. Many fiber-channel and network switches have the capability of synchronizing time from an NTP time server, and although this is not common in tape libraries, the time can still be periodically checked, and if necessary, reset to closely match the system time of the host attached to it.

9.5.2 Version Compatibility Validation

In section 2.3.3, "Service Component Layers," we introduced the notion that backup software needs to become part of corporate change control so that upgrades of system components (e.g., operating systems or applications such as databases) don't create a situation where backups are being attempted of a configuration that is not supported. Unfortunately, not all companies implement change control, and even in those that do, change control does not 100 percent guarantee success at mitigating all risk. Therefore when trying to diagnose a backup issue, it may be necessary to confirm that all versions of software in use are known to be compatible.

Most vendors provide version compatibility guides, and this information should be readily available when working on the backup environment. Regardless of which backup product is being used, several common guidelines should be followed

- Whenever preparing to deploy a new operating system or database, confirm via the backup software compatibility guide one of the following:
  - All versions are compatible and it is safe to go ahead.
  - The proposed version is not registered as being compatible without upgrades to the environment.
  - The proposed version is not registered as being compatible, and with no clear compatibility guideline, the vendors have to be approached to certify compatibility.

- Don't use a backup client version newer than the backup server version unless there is explicit documentation or vendor release notes approving it.
- Keep storage node versions at the same version of the backup software.
- If planning a basic backup software version upgrade, confirm that it is possible to upgrade just the backup server and any storage nodes first. The clients should then be upgraded following confirmation of successful core server upgrades. (It would be preferable in most situations not to have to upgrade all clients at the same time.)
- Keep an eye on version end-of-life announcements from vendors. Most vendors will provide at least one version EOL announcement per year, sometimes more.
- Read release notes when they come out. Just like the release notes for backup device firmware, it could be there's a problem affecting the environment that has not yet been traceable, but has now been fixed in the latest release of the software.

9.6 Error Review

Although it can be argued that the error messages produced by backup software are frequently cryptic, they are often a valuable source of information in determining what the nature of the problem is, and as such should not be dismissed simply because they do not appear to be relevant.

Coming from a programming background and having worked with many programmers at backup companies in diagnosing complex issues, I have learned that even the most esoteric and seemingly meaningless error message can actually be vital in determining what segment of program code is exhibiting problems. For example, an error message that may appear to be completely nonsensical or useless can be of particular use to a programmer who wants to search the source code to find the part of the program that generated that particular error. Of course, many errors that users get are more simply diagnosed at an earlier level than involving programmers at the vendor; nevertheless this highlights the importance of accurate error message reporting.

A key requirement when reviewing errors is that they are noted exactly. This has a fundamental effect on the way in which a problem can be attacked and solved. Unfortunately, some users tend to "panic" when problems are encountered and do not necessarily gather all the details — this simply delays the determination of a solution (often by a significant period of time) while all the data and logs are gathered.

For instance, in backup support it is not uncommon to get support calls logged with descriptions such as:

- "Backups failed"
- "Please tell me why my recovery didn't work"
- "Jukebox broken"

The first step is always to find out what errors were produced. If the errors are not recorded, the process will often start by asking the users to repeat the activities so the error message can be properly retrieved. (Contrary to popular opinion, good support consultants do not ask for error logs and configuration files just to "delay" the work!) Errors should preferably be captured in their original state rather than re-typed to avoid errors — or if they are re-typed, they should be very carefully checked to ensure the spelling, grammar, punctuation, and spacing are exactly the same.

Following from this, it is just as important to note when error messages change. For instance, it is not uncommon when diagnosing faults to go through a series of steps to try to resolve the problem. It may be after one particular step that the "initial" problem is solved, but a failure still occurs. Failing to notice a change in the error message(s) can result in expending time chasing a problem that technically no longer exists.

> **Debugging a Recovery.** When diagnosing a particular recovery problem for a customer we started with a message indicating that communication was lost during the recovery between the backup client and the server. After checking basic network functionality and ensuring that there was no underlying message, we went on to test a different recovery to find that the other recovery worked. This seemed to indicate a faulty tape, and as the recovery was not urgent (being performed only for periodic testing) the customer decided to re-run the test the following week after the next full backup. However, the next test failed in the recovery at exactly the same location.
>
> Checking the data on the original server ensured that the underlying disk/filesystem was not corrupt. Although it was unlikely to see two tapes fail in the same location we checked the tapes and found that they were OK as well.
>
> Finally, we decided to upgrade the client software in use (which was a little older than the backup server software), and the customer reported that the recovery still failed.
>
> After another few hours of diagnosis with changes being made to the backup server and the customer being asked to run the recovery, the recovery was performed with the support staff present, and it was at this point that we noted that while the recovery was still failing, the error message being produced now was considerably different. Instead of simply reporting a loss of connectivity between the server and the client, the error message was now providing details of a "permission denied" problem. With this knowledge in hand we quickly determined that the virus-scanning software being used was attempting to scan the recovered file and aborting when it didn't have permission to do so. With the virus scanner disabled, the recovery was completed.

When reviewing errors, always note the following:

- What leads to the generation of the error — what was being done, and how was it being done? Are any documented steps being skipped?
- The exact text of the error message, including all punctuation and correct quoting characters. (For example, there may be considerable difference as to what causes the errors between "Recovery failed, `host' reported communications lost" and "Recovery failed: 'host' reported communications lost.")
- If working in GUI environments, get a screenshot of the error.
- Compare system event logs/messages files on both the backup server and the client where the recovery is failing to determine if there are any other errors being logged in association with the failure.
- Can it be reproduced? Can the failure be reproduced on another system? The ability (or failure) to reproduce a problem makes a significant impact on how to go about diagnosing the fault. For instance:

- If the problem can't be reproduced on the system where the error originally occurred, it could be that it was a one-off problem (which, although concerning, may reduce the severity of the issue), or it could be that there were additional circumstances leading up to the error (e.g., other activities occurring on the system), which were not known at the time.
- If the problem is reproducible every time a certain sequence of steps are repeated on the system, this means that the problem can be demonstrated, and that logging can be increased in verbosity, or a trace execution could be executed to highlight the exact spot the error occurs.
- If there are multiple hosts of the same type, and the error only occurs on one of those hosts when stepping through the sequence of steps, it is most likely to have a host-specific error. This doesn't mean that the fault is actually with the host the error occurs on — it may still be caused by the backup product or some other product, but it may also be caused by an interaction unexpected by the backup product vendor. (For instance, one problem took three months to resolve until it was determined that although it didn't happen frequently, every time it did happen, it was exactly midnight. This turned out to be caused by a system cronjob that did a forced date synchronization at midnight. When it forced the date backwards by too much, the backup management software lost communication with its database. Thus the error was host specific, and unlikely to be reproducible in a lab without a server built exactly the same way.)
- If there are multiple hosts of the same type and the error occurs on all of the hosts under the same circumstances, then it is almost certainly a bug (though there is still some chance of an environmental factor influencing the system, particularly when all hosts are built using the same SOE). At this point, check the release notes to confirm whether the issue being experienced is a known issue (or at least a publicly reported known issue).

9.7 Tracking Failures

In an enterprise backup environment, be prepared to track failures when they occur. This is useful not only in isolating problems that have occurred previously, but also allows tracking the repetitive failures that, if examined in isolation, may appear to be "one-off" failures. When trying to isolate the nature of a problem, there are significant changes in what may be investigated between a problem that:

- Has only ever occurred once
- Occurs every day
- Occurs every Friday at 9 p.m.
- Occurs every time more than 12 hosts are being simultaneously backed up
- Occurs every time the backup administrator goes on leave for more than a week

It is not always easy to determine exactly what should be tracked, and unfortunately backup products typically do not provide the level of database functionality required to record failures over an extended period of time in a way that can be queried. Nevertheless tracking failures can help to identify the root cause of a problem.

A failure log should be maintained to keep track of failures and detect recurring issues. The format of this log is entirely company dependent. It may be that a company already has a generic issues register that can be used for this. Alternatively, if a company uses a case tracking system, this would be an appropriate environment to act as the failure log. In this scenario, each new failure that occurs in the backup system gets logged as an internal support case, assigned to the appropriate administrative or operational group, with the group tasked (1) to resolve the problem, and (2) to note the resolution as part of case closure.

At bare minimum a failure log should be used to track the following:

- Date and time that the failure has occurred.
- System(s) the failure occurred on, including hostnames, operating system versions, backup product versions, and additional products involved in the failure — names and versions.
- The exact text of error message(s) produced during the failure.
- Type and implication of the failure — in particular, did the failure impact the enterprise; was it a major issue, a "regular" problem, a minor issue, or simply a logged message that doesn't appear to be a failure but requires investigation?
- If there were any particular steps taken during the investigation of the issue that are relevant to the solution, these steps should be noted.
- If the issue is escalated to vendor(s), the date and time it was escalated, the priority at which it was escalated, and the responses from the vendor should be noted.
- If the issue is resolved, the description of the resolution that was achieved should be noted. If the issue was a serious one, an analysis of what caused the issue, and what can be done to prevent the issue from occurring in future should also be noted.
- If the issue is not yet resolved, who is responsible for resolving the issue? An ongoing status report should be required from that person or those persons as well as an estimated time on when it should be resolved.
- If there were any "patches" or "hot-fixes" applied to resolve the problem, what versions of the product are they for? Where has a separate copy of the patches been stored? (A common problem observed is when companies receive and apply a patch for their backup system, but don't store another copy anywhere. This may not be an issue in regular operations, but where problems can occur is during operations such as failed upgrades. If the software is upgraded, but it is later decided to downgrade due to issues, what happened to those previously installed patches? Usually they'll be deleted or over-written as part of the upgrade process.)

Failure logs work for both IT staff and for management. For management, a failure log becomes a feedback mechanism into the corporate reporting. For IT staff, it becomes part of the overall IT environment knowledge base, becoming a valuable tool in the monitoring, diagnosing, and correcting of failures.

Chapter 10

Backup Reporting

10.1 Introduction

Backup reporting is always a controversial topic, as backup software vendors are frequently torn between user demands for better reporting within the core product, and their desire to upsell additional reporting tools to customers. In this section we will review the types of backup reports that must be retrievable from a backup product, regardless of whether those reports come for free with the backup product, come from data that is retrieved from the backup product and processed, or are provided by a third-party reporting tool.

When evaluating backup software for report functionality, it is important not to look necessarily for the specific reports required, but confirmation that any data required can be retrieved from the product, so that reports can, if necessary, be constructed. As long as this capability exists, the report can also exist. It is also important never to assume that just because a particular report seems logical as being in the core product, it should be. Always check.

> **SNMP.** The Simple Network Management Protocol is designed to allow devices to report their status to monitoring units that can centrally report that state. When choosing backup products, many organizations "get stuck" on whether or not the backup product supports SNMP. Although a complete discussion on SNMP is outside the scope of this book, it should be noted that another acronym for SNMP could equally be Simply Not My Problem. Some people swear by SNMP, but it should be noted that SNMP does not guarantee message delivery. When considering absolutes of "guaranteed message delivery" versus "non-guaranteed message delivery," SNMP is at best as reliable as e-mail.
>
> If the backup system doesn't support SNMP, but it supports e-mail or even custom notifications, there is no cause for alarm. If it only supports e-mail, then e-mail can be sent and automatically converted by a short script into an SNMP alert. If it supports custom notifications as a result of (reasonably) arbitrary events, then an external SNMP alerter can be installed on the host, thus allowing the backup system still to report into the SNMP system.

10.2 Reporting Options

At a bare minimum, for each backup that runs, backup software should provide details of whether the backup was successful, and any errors that may have occurred. However, this is barely the tip of the iceberg in what can be gleaned from a backup system.

The first challenge when looking at reporting options is to differentiate the following types of reports:

- Automated status reports
- Performance/capacity/trending reports
- Diagnosis reports
- Frivolous reports

The last point is somewhat controversial. People in one department may consider a particular report to be frivolous while others in another department consider it to be critical. For instance, reports requiring a complete list of all files backed up in the most-recent backup could be considered frivolous. However, although this report provides questionable value as a daily report in an enterprise environment, it may actually be very important when diagnosing backup issues, backtracking changes to a system, or responding to auditors.

Therefore, when asked whether a backup system can provide a particular kind of report, it is not necessarily important to understand whether or not the backup system can generate the report; it is much more important to understand why the report is required.

It is entirely unreasonable to expect that a backup software company will think of every possible report that users may ever want to run against their software, and although the provision of pre-created reports is useful, the more useful feature of backup software for long-term integration into an enterprise environment is the ability to perform "data mining" — i.e., retrieving from the backup software and its database(s) details of backups that have been performed. This applies not only to the product's database, but also to its log files; for instance, are the log files generated in such a way that someone could write a parser for them if necessary? Or are they written in a sufficiently ad-hoc manner that they are useful only to a human reader?

Data mining in itself is typically not enough, so there may be a requirement not only to make use of data retrieved from the product's databases, but also from the data that can be extracted from log files. The reason for this is simple — typically the backup databases concern themselves with successful backups. Equally importantly, however, are the unsuccessful backups — for instance, how does a database designed to store information about the files backed up for a particular client store seven days worth of failures?

This brings us to a fundamental reporting requirement. Not only do successful backups have to be tracked, but also the unsuccessful ones. Indeed, some would argue that of the two, tracking the unsuccessful backups is more important.

10.3 Automated Reports

As part of routine automated backup monitoring, it should be possible to receive or automatically generate information about the following:

- Enterprise backup software typically supports multiple "collections" of clients that share a common start time among other potentially common features. Three common terms for these collections are "group," "policy," and "class." A status report should be retrievable for each collection that automatically runs. Preferably this should provide as components to the report at least:
  - Number of hosts in the collection that were successfully backed up
  - Number of hosts in the collection that failed to backup (including those that experienced a runtime failure and those that failed to run)
  - Details of the successful backups
  - Details of the unsuccessful backups
  - Details of the backups that generated warnings
- Volumes that need to be removed from the system for off-site storage.
- Volumes that are eligible for return for re-use by the system.
- Notifications of media requirements (e.g., needing tapes for a complete backup).
- Notifications of backup errors or faults (e.g., tape drives going offline due to hardware errors).

10.3.1 Automated Report Parsing

A common requirement in larger organizations is the ability to parse backup reports and generate a notification or alert only when errors need to be investigated. The end goal of this is to reduce considerably the amount of checking that needs to be performed by backup, system, and application administrators while still ensuring that errors are caught and investigated.

Although this is an admirable goal, it is fraught with potential for errors to go unseen and unnoticed for an extended period of time. If intending to implement automated report parsing, strongly consider the following rules to avoid the extremely unpleasant scenario of attempting a recovery only to find out the backup hasn't worked for some time:

- Even if there are no errors, there should be a notification — in this case a notification that there are no errors. Otherwise, what is the difference between not receiving a notification because there were no errors or not receiving a notification because the parsing utility crashed? (Or to put it another way, who watches the watcher?) This is a very common cause of problems in automated parsing systems.
- Any unexpected output should be handled as if it were an error, and a report should be generated, forcing review. Otherwise new, unanticipated errors may occur without notification. Although this may result in additional work during times when new systems, software, or processes are introduced, it ensures that any new output from the backup system is properly captured into the parser without delay.
- The raw information produced from the backup product that is used to generate the automatically parsed reports should be stored in an accessible location for the retention period of the backups, preferably alongside the parsed report for ease of reference. Thus if a problem occurs, the original data can be referred to.
- The accuracy of automated reports should be periodically and randomly checked to ensure that no errors are slipping in. If the automated parsing has been written locally, the checking should preferably be performed by someone who wasn't responsible for the parser. Additionally, the raw information from which the parsed reports are generated should be used

to act as additional validation during the checking process. For example, when comparing the parsed report(s) for a day against the raw reports generated by the backup system, there should be no discrepancies.

This may seem to suggest that automated parsing could be more effort than is worthwhile, but it should help to highlight that there needs to be considerable thought put into an automated backup report parser. This ensures it fulfills the requirement for simple reports while also making sure that errors are still properly tracked. In general, only implement automated parsing if all of the above steps are also undertaken. When implemented without these considerations, automated reporting too often results in untracked failures and, in the case of backup software, data loss.

10.4 Zero-Failure Policy

At all times, a zero-failure policy must be the goal for backup reports. This is not to say that errors will not occur, but rather, it reflects the nature of a normal report. Many companies receive a daily backup report that includes expected errors. For example, errors might be explained by one of the following:

"That host was decommissioned a while ago, but I haven't got around to removing it from the backup system."
"Those files are always open so we always get errors about not being able to back them up."
"We back up those database files using an agent, so it doesn't matter that we get an error during the operating system backup about them changing."
"That's a slow system that always has network problems during incremental backups ..."

No repetitive error should be tolerated if it is not being actively worked towards resolution. The reason for this is simple. Consider a backup report that cites ten errors, of which nine are errors routinely disregarded as being repetitive. The chances of actually spotting the one "important" error is considerably more difficult when there are a plethora of errors that are routinely ignored. (Remember the story of the little boy who cried wolf?) Even worse, while the normal backup administrators may be adept at picking out the expected errors from the regular errors, another administrator asked to fill in while staff are on holiday may be able to make no such distinction, and therefore may spend considerable time debugging "errors," all the while wondering why the system is suddenly encountering so many problems.

By aiming for a zero-failure policy in backup reports, such scenarios are avoided. In essence, the backup reports should reach the point where any error message is a flag to start investigating immediately to determine what can be done to fix the problem.

Achieving a zero-failure policy is actually much easier than it sounds, and typically requires only some sensible management backing for it to succeed.

Eliminate the Problem, Not the Error. A company providing backup services for its customers established a zero error policy towards backups, promising customers that their backups would be error free. Unfortunately, the way in which "error free" was achieved was less than desirable. Instead of determining the nature of each error, steps were taken to simply eliminate the error. For example, whenever a file was reported as being inaccessible during backup due to it being opened, the administrator simply added that file to the list of files to be excluded during backups. For at least one server this was a disaster, as the host was a Web server that kept files opened for a period of time after they had been accessed by users. This resulted in a server that could not be restored when it failed, as critical files were deliberately excluded from the backup process as a means of reducing the errors involved in backup.

This sort of situation goes to prove the need to address the core problem in backups rather than the symptoms when resolving errors. Clearly in this case a backup strategy was required that would allow open files to be backed up or snapshots to be generated, which could then be backed up.

All backup environments — no matter how small — benefit from the adoption of a zero-failure policy, as long as that policy is properly implemented. True errors are noticed and corrected considerably more easily when there are no false positives in the reports.

The adoption of a zero-failure policy is frequently seen as a daunting task, but in reality is not necessarily difficult; rather, it is an activity that staff experience difficulty scheduling into their daily activities. However, management should recognize that by providing staff the time to eliminate "non-critical" failures, a more-stable backup system is available where failures are responded to with greater ease.

Chapter 11

Choosing a Backup Product

11.1 Introduction

At the conclusion to this section, we should have established a clear understanding of the checklists that should be built when evaluating and determining which backup product is most suited to a particular organization.

One thing to keep in mind is that depending on the complexity of an environment, it may not be possible to find any one product that provides everything required. For all but the smallest of organizations, there may be some compromises to make in the selection of a backup product, and alternatives may need to be found to achieve what is required without immediately dismissing a particular product, simply because it fails to natively perform a particular function that is required.

When considering what to put into a backup environment, consider the following:

> There are old backup environments, and there are bold backup environments, but there are no old, bold backup environments.

What does this mean? This is a warning: more so than any other part of an environment, backups are not the place to "go bleeding edge." Backup is all about recovery, and recovery is all about stability and protection. The ability to protect systems should not be jeopardized by deploying a system that is so bleeding edge that untested components are in use, or combinations of equipment not certified by vendors have been deployed, and so on. In some senses this is akin to pharmaceutical drugs not being available to the general public until they have been comprehensively tested. Going "bleeding edge" with drugs may address an immediate concern, but without measured tests it may also result in worse problems than those solved. This is the same with backups — going "bleeding edge" may appear to solve a particular aspect of the backup requirements, but it may turn around to create a much more unpleasant situation at a later date.

This doesn't mean an organization can't be leading edge, where the latest in developed technology known to work is used. At all times, however, with a backup system the aim should be to avoid a situation whereby when the question "has anyone else had this problem?" is asked of a vendor, the reply is, "no one else has done it before." Remember "no one else has done it before" can also mean any of the following:

- This is not certified.
- We've never tested this, but it should work.
- We've never supported this configuration before.

Should recoverability of an environment be trusted to a system where any of the above statements are true?

11.2 Coverage

11.2.1 Value Products That Value Protection

Although this seems an odd thing to suggest in regards to a backup product (that is explicitly designed for protection), it is worthwhile understanding that different products approach backup protection in different ways. Making such a recommendation means looking for:

- Products that use dependency tracking for backup life cycles
- Products that use an exclusive data selection model rather than an inclusive data protection model
- Products that don't use "gimmick" features such as antivirus scanning or "full once, incrementals always"
- Products that don't place arbitrary restrictions on what can and can't be done ("this product supports a maximum of three copies of a backup, and only the primary copy can be recovered from") — even if those restrictions are considered workable initially, remember that the system being purchased may be used for a decade or more depending on its capabilities and growth
- Products that allow customized backup scripts or actions to be run so that additional products can be integrated with the system
- Products that provide backup catalogues and media databases to allow for rapid access to backups

These types of features are indicative of products that value protection over cost reduction rather than products that try to save the user money regardless of whether it compromises recoverability protection.

11.2.2 Value Frameworks, Not Monoliths

Two fundamental design models can be applied to backup and recovery products — frameworks and monoliths. Obviously, both provide core backup and recovery services, but it's what they do after this point that determines whether the product is a framework or a monolith.

A backup framework is a product that is designed for extensibility. If a feature doesn't exist, the vendor can either add it at a later date or a company can develop its own solution that "plugs in" to offer that feature. To be a framework, a backup product must at least:

- Allow for the arbitrary execution of commands before, as part of, and after the backup process
- Allow for data mining and automated log review for the construction of arbitrary reports
- Feature a fully qualified command line that can be used to do anything the GUI can be used for, and more

Without these features, a backup product is stagnant and not able to grow within an environment.

Contrary to the framework model, a monolithic backup product is designed on the principle that the designers have thought of every possible activity a user would want to do, and therefore doesn't need to provide extensibility. (The obvious conclusion to this line of thought is that, clearly, if the user wants to do something that the backup product doesn't do, the user shouldn't be trying to do it!) Although this may be appropriate for SOHO environments that require simplicity, the "one size fits all" approach doesn't really fit all, and isn't appropriate to enterprise environments.

To ensure maximum coverage, the backup system must be provided as a framework rather than a monolithic system. Although this may in itself require a little more setup time than a monolithic system, the benefit is that over time as the environment grows and changes, the backup system can similarly grow and adapt to suit the environment.

11.2.3 Operating Systems

The goal in deploying a new enterprise backup environment is to reduce to an absolute minimum the number of different backup products that need to be implemented to protect all the operating systems in use.

Note that we have not said that only those products that provide coverage for all operating systems in the environment should be considered. There is an important reason for this — some products are better at particular operating systems than others. For instance, it may be that a product is found that backs up all the mid-range systems with ease, but cannot perform backups of legacy mainframe systems. In this case, better backup results may be achieved by using two different backup products — one that focuses on the mainframe, and the other system does all the remaining operating systems. It could be that there is a product for the mainframe that also backs up mid-range systems, but with considerably less functionality than other products that are dedicated to mid-range systems (or vice versa). In this case, don't shoe-horn a "barely functional" system into place that slightly reduces management overhead, but in doing so reduces the ability to deal with a wider variety of systems or types of failures. This applies even if all the systems in an environment are mid-range — for instance, it could be that a particular product is most suitable to NetWare hosts, but another product is more suitable for all the UNIX, Linux, and Windows hosts.

Depending on the circumstances, some consolidation can still be achieved using this approach if hardware consolidation is looked at instead. For example, rather than configuring and installing two separate tape libraries — one for each of the backup products deployed, it may be possible to deploy a single, larger-tape library and use library virtualization or partitioning software (e.g., StorageTek ACSLS) to "present" partitioned, independent virtual libraries to each backup product.

A common approach to watch out for, used by backup vendors when their own software doesn't work with a particular operating system, is to recommend partner or alliance backup software for those systems. To foster a belief that the systems "integrate," they recommend something along the lines of the following: "We don't support operating system X, but backup product Y does. We recommend you back up system X using product Y, writing the backup images to disk. You can then back up the backup images using our backup software. That way, all backups will be stored and managed together on tape."

This strategy works almost as effectively as using shavings of ice to cool down a volcano. It can be very easily shown that this form of "support" is not useful, and can result in data loss. If one considers the implications of this recommendation, it rapidly becomes apparent how much of a marketing vaporware comment it is.

Using the "secondary" backup product Y, backups are generated for multiple hosts, storing them to a common disk area. Once these backups are complete, the primary vendor's backup software then backs up all those backup images to tape. Over time the disk backup area used by product Y starts to fill, and it will be necessary to delete older backup images. These backup images are typically stored in esoteric filenames that give no clue to their original host. Therefore, some of the older files are deleted. Using backup software Y at a later date, an attempt is made to restore from some old backups — backups that have been deleted from disk. This is where everything falls apart. Unless backup product Y has been designed to integrate with the primary vendor's backup software, how does it know that its data has been backed up to tape using another backup product? It will inspect the disk backup unit, find that its backup is not on disk and fail the recovery.

Step by Step — Why This Strategy Doesn't Work. Say, for example that backups are stored on disk with a filename that is signed, 32-bit number, starting from zero and working their way upwards, thus supporting up to 2,147,483,648 backups on disk. When the backup product was on file 13,742, disk spaces had started to fill, so knowing that the older files were backed up by the "primary" backup product, all files numbered 5,000 or lower are deleted. This frees up disk space and the "secondary" backup server is able to continue to write backups to disk to be picked up by the other server.

Let's assume that a week passes and then a recovery is required. This recovery makes use of a variety of backup files, including several files that were deleted. However, because the secondary backup system is written on the basis that the backup file(s) it needs to retrieve data from will be online, it doesn't produce a message saying, "Backup set 4,934 missing, please restore" — it will typically just abort the restore or, even worse, crash. It may not provide sufficient error messages to state what was missing.

As such the only way to accomplish the restore is to restore all files that might be associated with the recovery — e.g., every file created between now and the time that the first client file to be restored was backed up.

Therefore such "solutions" should be avoided. Under exceptional circumstances, a company should be prepared to deploy two backup products into the environment if necessary. Deploying two separate products that are definitely not integrated can often be far simpler than trying to force integration between two products that only work together in marketing documentation.

11.2.4 Databases

For each database that is used, find out:

- Does the backup product provide an agent for that product?

- If it does provide an agent, can it be afforded? (This is a controversial but important question.)
- If it does provide an agent, are there any limitations on how the agent can be used that might affect how the databases are currently being operated? (This might include such items as how the database can be restored — e.g., complete restores only, point-in-time restores, or both, as well as partial restores.)

- Regardless of whether or not an agent is used, are there any special pre- or post-processing activities required in relation to the backup of the database?
- If there is no agent, does the vendor have an alternative method for backing up the database?
- Does the database agent support all forms of backup and recovery needed for the environment? For example, does it support incremental and differential backup levels? Does it support recoveries relocated to another host?

Make sure clearly explained answers (and workarounds or alternative scenarios) to these questions are available for any backup product being evaluated.

This similarly creates a requirement that after having chosen and implemented a backup product, any time there is need to plan for the installation of a new database, these questions must be revisited, and the appropriate method of backing up the new database must be determined before it is deployed. Also evaluate whether a particular database really should be used if an acceptable way of backing it up can't be found. (Obviously an acceptable answer to this consideration is "yes, the database is really needed," as long as an alternative backup method can be determined.)

11.2.5 Applications

For each primary application that a company uses, its backup requirements should be carefully mapped out, and it should be determined whether the intended backup product can back up that application. For example, consider the following questions:

- Does the application run on a system that performs exclusive file locking when files are opened for writing? If so, how can this be handled so that the application can still be properly backed up along with its data files?
- Are there any special pre- or post-processing activities required in relation to the backup of the application?
- What happens if the application maintains data files on two or more hosts that must be backed up consistently?
- What limitations are in place in relation to recoveries?
- Are there licenses associated with the application that only users with particular permissions (not normally available to a "backup" user) can access them?

Be aware of the backup requirements for each application, and to what extent a new backup product meets them, to ensure that systems can be recovered without corruption.

11.2.6 Clustering

Clusters are now a common feature in many computing environments, and they have their own special backup requirements that must be considered.

- Does the backup product support clusters?
- If it does:
  - What are the licensing requirements? For instance:
    - Are licenses required for all nodes, regardless of whether they are active or passive, or are they just required for active nodes?
    - How are databases handled? Is one database agent license required per active node, or for every node in the cluster?
    - Is it necessary to have a license for the backups of the regular host associated with the cluster nodes as well, or are these combined licenses?
  - Can the backup performed on a particular cluster node be restored to another cluster node (assuming a failover has occurred)?
  - Is it required to remember which cluster node (in an active/passive arrangement) hosted the cluster backups to do a recovery?
- If the product does not support clusters, what plan can be put in place to achieve reliable backups?

An important factor to consider when evaluating a backup product with clustering is to ensure that tests are not only performed against a working cluster, but also a cluster that has experienced failover and failback. That is, ensure administrators are comfortable not only with how the backup system works when running in the normal configuration, but also after an application has switched nodes, and after that same application has switched back.

11.2.7 Hardware

When planning a backup environment, ensure the planned hardware configuration is compatible with the backup software. While often assumed to be something that can be banked on, hardware compatibility is not actually guaranteed, and a lack thereof has been known to cause even large implementations to either fail or be re-evaluated.

Items to consider are:

- Does the backup software support the backup devices that are going to be used? If so, does it require any additional licenses depending on the type of device that will be used?
- Does the backup vendor offer a certification program for devices and autochangers? If so, does the equipment to be used appear on the list? If not, is there a procedure to get the proposed equipment certified, or does it literally mean that the equipment is indeed physically incompatible with the proposed backup software?

Particularly in regards to automated media changers (e.g., tape libraries), it will be necessary to confirm how licenses are priced based on the types of hardware the system will be implemented with. For instance, some products license media changers based on the number of drives in the changer, whereas others license media changers based on the number of physical slots available.

This difference could make a considerable impact on the amount of money that will need to be spent on the backup software, and may even impact the choice of tape media to be used in the system.

As almost all systems experience growth over time, be certain to confirm what sort of costs may be involved in upgrading library licenses over time. (If the growth percentages aren't known — assume a 50 percent data volume growth per annum for three years.)

It is also vital to confirm that the hardware that has been proposed will not have its warrantable usage time or activities exceeded by the backup windows and plans that will be established. For instance:

- Some tape drives are not warranted for 24/7 usage, and instead have a maximum number of hours that they can be run in any one day, e.g., 16 hours a day.
- Tape media will often come with a stated maximum number of passes or a maximum number of mounts — ensure that any tape choice made is compatible with the intended use — in particular, for instance, remember that there can be considerable differences between tape media suitable for general backups, hierarchical storage and archival. (Different types of media, particularly linear serpentine models such as LTO Ultrium-1, DLT, and Super DLT, will have many tracks. For instance, LTO Ultrium-2 has 512 tracks, and so a single complete tape read or complete tape write means 512 passes, not 1.)
- Certain hardware vendors have been as cheeky as to release hard disks for disk backup arrays that have a maximum mean-usage-hours per day over the life span of the drives before warranty is voided. (This would be somewhat akin to purchasing a computer that is warranted for use only between 2 p.m. and 11 p.m.) Ensure if planning to make use of disk backup units that the vendor warrants the drives for 24/7 operations.

There has been more than one occasion where a company has purchased hardware from one vendor and backup software from another, ending with two working individual components that just don't happen to work together, sometimes with the end result that neither hardware nor software vendor will refund the purchase on account of their product not being "broken." To avoid that, even if the hardware and software are being purchased from different vendors, be sure to keep both vendors informed as to what is required, making compatibility a condition of purchase, so that it is their responsibility to check compatibility.

11.2.8 Functionality Checklist

When evaluating potential new backup products, it is necessary to evaluate the core functionality offered by the products and determine which offerings most suit the required environment.

It's worthwhile to record how different backup products compare against one another when evaluating the feature set of each product. This allows the most informed decision about which product is to be deployed, or whether multiple products must be deployed.

Obviously it may not be possible to literally install and deploy multiple backup products (and potentially multiple sets of hardware) and therefore the goal in this respect should be to assemble a comprehensive check list of functionality requirements and "nice to haves." These should then be put to different backup vendors or system integrators so they can explain what each product can and can't do.* However, always be prepared to provide vendors with an opportunity to either rebut a requirement or provide a functional alternative. For instance, if a particular feature is stated as required, and the vendor knows that implementing that feature will cause problems, they should be able to make note of this. Being willing to advise what not to do can often be the sign of a vendor who has as much interest in their customers' backups as their customers' money. Also, vendors (and particularly system integrators) may know ways around limitations in backup software — for instance, "we can't do X, but we can do Y and Z, that essentially provides X, just via a different mechanism." It may not necessarily be as good a solution for one particular feature, but in total, by considering alternate solutions, it is possible to end up with a system that still meets or maybe even exceeds requirements.

One rule to consider when evaluating new backup products that cannot be stressed enough:

> **Never, Ever Assume Anything about a Backup Product That Is Under Evaluation.** Backup consultants occasionally encounter situations where customers purchase a backup product after a reasonably comprehensive analysis period. After it is deployed, they state they don't particularly like it because it doesn't perform a particular function that they believed was a logical requirement of a backup product. Unfortunately this isn't always the case — particularly when moving from workgroup to enterprise backup products, which frequently have different operational criteria. As such it is always best to outline everything desired in the product, regardless of how "obvious" it is.

This rule of course can be applied to a lot of areas other than just backup, but it is vital that this is kept in mind when looking at backup products. Don't assume that feature X will be included by default in the backup software — ask the vendor whether the backup product supports that feature.

When comparing multiple backup products, there will always be discrepancies between the various functionality offered versus the functionality actually required. To avoid being overwhelmed by the possible options, it must be clearly understood what features are required and what features are desired prior to starting the comparison.

Invariably the choice of a backup product will be a compromise-based decision — e.g., "product A supports 90 percent of the mandatory functions, but only 60 percent of the desired functions. Product B, which supports only 75 percent of the mandatory functions supports 85 percent of the desired functions." Which product should be chosen in such a situation? There should only be one answer: the product that provides the most protection!

For the most part, the checklist will need to be assembled based on the overall requirements and desires of an individual organization. However, a sample checklist might resemble Table 11.1 (and serve as a starting point). [Remember if using this particular checklist, the products must still be evaluated against their required functions, so in a comprehensive checklist it may be acceptable to fill in a lot of "N/A" (not applicable) entries.] A copy of the checklist in Table 11.1 may be found on the Web site.

* When doing this, avoid specifying which items are "requirements" and which are "nice to haves," but instead keep this information private while getting a full functionality checklist provided.

Table 11.1 Sample Backup Software Functionality Checklist

Functionality	*Product*		
	A	*B*	C
Control and management			
Centralized			
Decentralized			
Supports remote administration			
Supports centralized administration of multiple servers if required			
Backup levels			
Full			
Incremental			
Differential (simple)			
Differential (complex)			
Consolidated/synthetic full			
Manual			
Data availability options during backup			
Offline			
Online			
Snapshot backups			
Virtual machine backups			
Data selection methodology			
Exclusive (disregard products that fail to offer this!)			
Inclusive			
Backup retention strategies			
Dependency-based retention			
Simple retention (be cautious of using products that only offer simple retention strategies)			
Media pool support			
Support data separation for different intended locations			
Support data segregation for legal requirements			
Support retention-based media pools			
Enterprise features			
Support for pre- and post- backup processing commands			
Support for client collections (usually called groups, classes, or policies)			
Allows backup schedule overrides ("set once and forget" schedules)			

(continued)

Table 11.1 Sample Backup Software Functionality Checklist (Continued)

Functionality	*Product*		
	A	*B*	*C*
Recovery options			
Coherent filesystem view			
Point-in-time recovery			
Complete filesystem overwrite			
Non-index recovery			
Incremental recovery			
Server impact			
Supports serverless backups			
Supports server-based backups			
Supports snapshot backups			
Database backup types supported			
Offline			
Online			
Hot backup without an agent			
Hot backup with an agent (note supported databases)			
Export backups			
Snapshot backups			
Backup initiation methods supported			
Server initiated			
Client initiated			
External scheduling system initiated			
Tiers available in the backup environment			
Server/client only (be wary of products that only offer a two-tier "enterprise" backup model)			
Storage nodes/media servers supported			
SAN (dynamic) storage nodes/media servers supported			
Dynamic reallocation of SAN shared backup devices supported			
Backup devices supported			
Tape (focusing on type required, if known)			
Backup to disk			
Virtual tape libraries (VTL; confirm brands)			
NDMP backup devices (confirm brands)			
Magneto-optical devices			

Table 11.1 Sample Backup Software Functionality Checklist (Continued)

Functionality	*Product*		
	A	*B*	*C*
Confirm whether a backup product requires its own device drivers, or whether it works with vendor/operating system device drivers; products that require their own drivers typically take longer to work with new devices			
Maintenance functions			
Can backup its catalogue/index data			
Can backup its catalogue/index data while other backup and recovery operations are running			
Can re-index backup media if original index/catalogue information is lost			
Can import backup media from other servers of the same product			
Can purge unnecessary records automatically			
Storage options			
Supports SAN storage			
Supports NAS storage (check versions and platforms)			
Allows NDMP backup (note restrictions and versions available)			
Supports integration with SAN/NAS snapshots			
Supports integration with filesystem snapshots			
Bandwidth options			
Supports client side compression			
Supports bandwidth limiting			
Supports block-level backup			
Supports file-level restore (from block-level backup) — note restrictions			
Supports file consolidation			
Supports data deduplication			
Command Line Interface (CLI)			
Supports CLI for volume management			
Supports CLI for media and backup reporting			
Supports CLI for alteration of configuration			
Supports CLI for backup activities (e.g., stopping, starting, and restarting backups)			
Operating system support			
Note each required operating system			
Bare metal recovery options for each operating system required			

(continued)

Table 11.1 Sample Backup Software Functionality Checklist (Continued)

Functionality	*Product*		
	A	*B*	*C*
Cluster support			
Supports active/passive <cluster>			
Supports active/active <cluster>			
Supports n-way <cluster>, where n > 2			
Application support			
Note required application support			
Note applications that require multi-host consistency in backup and recovery operations			

11.3 Administrative Considerations

This primarily deals with the non-operational aspects of running the backup environment.

11.3.1 Training

Remember that the hardware/software solution already installed or that is to be installed may actually be quite complex, and therefore some form of training will be required. This is sometimes difficult to explain to the business — even though they'll typically approve formal training for database administrators, application administrators, and system administrators. Although staff may be able to configure rudimentary backups without training, some form of training may give them the "big picture" understanding of the backup product that allows them to get the full power out of the product or to understand why they have to configure the product in a particular way.

In section 5.3, the general guidelines for training were discussed. Ensure that each different group within the organization that requires training can receive the appropriate level for their activities, whether this be through formal vendor training, formal integrator training, or custom in-house training/tutoring. Also, training should not be a one-off activity, but should be periodically repeated

- To ensure that there is always a particular number of trained staff, as staff come and go.
- If major new functionality is introduced into the product.
- If hardware or software is significantly altered. For example, just because administrators have been trained in product X it doesn't mean that they'll be able to pick up product Y immediately. Although many of the core concepts may be the same, the nomenclature and methodology will most likely be sufficiently different as to leave the system administrators or backup administrators feeling as if they're wading through treacle while learning the product.

As such, confirm that there are training courses available for staff on the products purchased and installed. This may be training provided directly by the vendor, by a training partner, or by a third-party integrator. Don't discount the training offered by third-party integrators, and certainly don't assume that the training offered by the vendors is the most appropriate for their products, or the most relevant to an actual running environment.

In particular, if a system integrator is engaged for the actual installation and configuration work, it may very well be the case that they can deliver training targeted for the installed systems at site, and thus the course may be shorter but more complete than the equivalent backup vendor course.

11.3.2 Support

11.3.2.1 Maintenance

Always be cognizant of the fact that for the most part, like many enterprise products, backup software will typically have both maintenance and support fees, which may be priced out as separate line items. When they are priced separately it is important that the difference between the two options is understood.

Maintenance typically refers to a yearly payment (usually a certain percentage of the current off-the-shelf prices of the software licenses) that entitles the receipt of patches and hot-fixes, minor updates (e.g., to move from backup software version 7.1.2 to backup software version 7.1.3), and major updates (e.g., to move from backup software version 4.5 to backup software version 5.1). However, this is normally the total extent of the services provided as part of a maintenance contract.

Before purchasing a backup product, confirm the following:

- How much maintenance comes for free with the initial purchase? (Typically the first 12 months of maintenance is included for free, but some companies offer more.)
- What is an indicative maintenance cost for the backup software based on current market rates over a period of two to three years following the end of free maintenance? (This often forms part of a "total cost of ownership" calculation.)
- Are there any exclusions in the maintenance contract? For example, check
  - Are major updates covered, or do they require an additional fee?
  - Is it necessary to pay additional fees to transfer the backup software from one host to another? (For instance, it might be already planned to upgrade the backup host from a two-processor machine to a four-processor machine in the next budgetary cycle.)
  - Are additional fees required in the event of transferring the backup product to another platform?

11.3.2.2 Technical Support

The backup software must always have current technical support. Again, this is akin to ensuring that an insurance company has an underwriter. Obviously the requirements for support will vary on a company-by-company basis, and therefore the requirements of the service level agreements (both internal to the business and any customer service level agreements) must be met by the support agreement. The following questions should be asked

- Does the intended support vendor have an escalation plan that ensures there will always be someone to contact?

- What support times are needed — 24/7, 9/7, 15/5, or 9/5? Keep in mind associated questions such as:
  - If 24/7 support is not chosen, will there be the option of engaging out-of-hours support in the event of a critical problem?
  - If there is the option of engaging out-of-(contracted)-hours support, what will be the associated cost of that engagement? Will the support issue be dealt with at the same severity level as a customer with the same issue but with 24/7 support?
  - If 24/7 support is offered, is it offered by a "follow the sun" support system or a 24/7 help desk?
- Is on-site support required, or is telephone/e-mail support sufficient? If choosing to engage only telephone/e-mail support, check for indicative pricing of receiving on-site support in an emergency.
- Does the support vendor require staff to have a particular minimum set of skills or training to log support calls?
- Will any staff member be able to log a call, or will the vendor only accept calls from named personnel?
- Does the vendor have any testimonials from businesses in a similar field, or the same geographic region?
- Is the support local, or remote — i.e., are the vendor's support staff in the same city, state, or country?
- Does the vendor provide service level guarantees regarding how quickly support issues are accepted and assigned? [Vendors who provide absolute resolution-time guarantees should be treated as suspect, as not all problems can be anticipated; however, percentages of absolute resolution time are more realistic (e.g., "90 percent of severity-1 issues will be solved in a 24-hour period pending customer availability and system access.")]
- Does the vendor provide any remote monitoring service?
- If opening up a security/firewall for individual activities is an option, does the vendor's support plan include their staff logging onto systems remotely to observe or participate in the debugging of a particular problem?
- If a backup environment is being installed by a system integrator, do they offer a support plan? One of the advantages of working with system integrators is that it is often the case that the staff who install the system are also the staff who helped to architect the system, and also will support it if a support contract is taken out. This represents a considerable amount of site knowledge and expertise that should not be readily discounted.
- Does the purchase of a support contract include maintenance, or is it necessary to buy that separately? (If there is the option to buy support but not maintenance, never do this, as it means that a vendor may be able to diagnose the fault as requiring a patch that can't be provided!)

As much as any other component, support must be considered prior to the purchase of a backup system, not after the backup system is in place, and particularly not after the first error occurs.

Chapter 12

Best Practices

12.1 Introduction

Proposing activities and procedures as being best practices can be controversial, as there will always be exceptions to a rule, and there will always be sites and companies that need to perform backups a different way to what is proposed here. What remains true, though, is that following these guidelines is a good starting point in achieving a stable, optimum backup environment.

Although many of these topics will have been discussed previously, this chapter should serve as a single point of reference when determining what should be aimed for in an optimally designed backup system.

12.2 Backup to Recover

There is really only one reason we perform backup — to recover. All other potential reasons to backup are secondary when it comes to needing to perform a recovery. As such this means that backup systems must be designed with recovery performance in mind rather than simply focusing on the amount of time the backup will take. In environments with service level agreements (SLAs), the design of a backup environment should actually start with determining what the recovery SLAs are, and then working backwards to a backup system that can deliver such performance, rather than assuming that the backup system designed will be able to meet the recovery requirements.

As backups are done to recover, by implication it also means that there must be adequate testing, monitoring, and protection of backups performed.

12.3 Documentation

Always document as much as possible in a system, and always remember that backups do not negate the need for system recovery documentation (or any other form of system or application documentation).

Have readily available backup and recovery procedures for each system protected by the backup environment. This should include disaster recovery procedures that cover activities beyond the computer-related steps to a recovery, such as whatever other corporate procedures or references to external documentation and support systems may be potentially required during a recovery.

The documentation for each system should additionally include contact details for the owners, key users, and administrators of the system. This is useful not only in recovery situations, but also for general administrative actions such as:

- Notification of failed backups
- Confirming that planned changes in the backup procedure will be acceptable
- Confirming whether to re-run failed backups
- Confirming whether a new contact is authorized to make backup/recovery requests regarding the system (inadequate vetting of requests from previously unknown contacts may result in a security breach)

12.4 What to Backup

Everything — or rather, always follow the axiom that it is better to back up more than not enough. Don't be miserly with the backup system by pruning out items from protection that may be necessary during a recovery. Ensure that any decision not to backup particular files, data, or applications is done either at the request of the system owners or, at worst, are made with the system owners understanding and acknowledging consent. Verbal agreements after all aren't worth the paper they're written on when it comes to discussing why a system wasn't recoverable due to files not being backed up in the first place.

12.5 Protect the Backups

Backups should not represent a single point of failure within an organization, and therefore they also require protection — typically through duplication, so that if any one piece of backup media fails, the backups can be retrieved from another piece of media. This creates obvious implications in how a backup system should be designed — not only does the system need to be designed in such a way that recoveries and backups can be completed in a timely manner, but the duplication of backups also needs to be completed within a timely manner as well.

There is typically a lot more to protecting backups, however, than just duplicating. Questions such as the following also need to be considered

- If there is a logical or functional difference between duplicates and originals, which copy is sent off site?
- Are the off-site backups stored at a location that is sufficiently remote from the primary site so as to not be affected by the most-likely causes of failure or disaster that could occur at the primary site?
- Do backups get tested periodically to ensure they can be recovered from? If so:
  - What is done if a backup is tested and failed to be recovered from successfully?
  - Does the recovery documentation reflect the procedures used to perform the test recoveries?

  - Is a log taken of backups that have been tested?
- If backups are not tested periodically, why not?
- When backup media are moved from location to location (e.g., offsiting backup tapes), are the media properly protected from environmental factors such as humidity, extreme temperature variations, etc.?

Using a backup system that enforces backup dependencies can make a considerable improvement in the protection of backups. Remember that the backups are only as stable as the operating systems and hardware that they are running on, and can't perform miracles if the underlying hardware and operating system are experiencing problems.

12.6 Results Checking and Reporting

Always design a system with a goal of zero failures during normal operations. That way, true failures are easily detected without needing to winnow through false-positives on a daily basis. This assists in day-to-day operations for the backup environment, but also ensures that new staff can easily adapt to the system and need not be trained in what is and is not an acceptable error.

If backup results are not being checked, assume 100 percent failure. As this is obviously not a desired result, it should highlight the need to check the backup results. Backups are not performed to be able to tick a few boxes on a daily report of duties undertaken, but have a serious place in ensuring corporate continuance. As such, they need to be treated seriously and monitored properly, just like any other key system in an environment.

12.7 Core Design Considerations

Particularly when planning a new backup system from scratch, always aim to meet the following core design practices:

- Centralize wherever possible — management of enterprise backup systems is considerably easier when a minimum number of master servers are in use.
- When choosing technology, software, and practices, remember that leading edge is perfectly fine for a backup environment, but bleeding edge should be avoided. (If the decision is made to go bleeding edge, do try to remember when a failure occurs that this choice was made — i.e., document, and get sign-off.)
- Keep as much of the shortest retention cycle as possible in the automated media handling units (typically tape libraries). For example, if daily backups are kept for six weeks, aim to have sufficiently sized online storage to hold this at minimum. However, more than this capacity is required; there should be room for blank volumes to be used for duplication, spares, recovery volumes, and a suitable number of monthly/yearly volumes online as well. This will ensure that recoveries are easier to facilitate.
- Ensure everyone understands that backup is another form of insurance — particularly when budgets come up for renewal.
- In a backup environment with ongoing data growth, new media should typically be seen as operational expenses as opposed to capital expenditure. It is very important to remember that media prices almost always come down. If it is predicted that the system will require, say,

4000 tapes over the course of three years, it may be a costly mistake to buy them all at the very start of the implementation. Instead, wherever possibly, buy media to cover periods of three to six months at most so that advantage can be taken of falling media prices. (If providing backup services for multiple departments, divisions, or customers, it will be necessary to cross-charge media requirements accurately.)

- In large organizations, give careful consideration towards a storage and backup administration group rather than leaving such considerations with individual operating system administration teams. This allows a further reduction in systems management costs, and provides more consistency in protection regimes across the organization.
- Avoid "fancy" extras such as integrated virus scanning that distracts from core backup requirements.

12.8 Track Failures

For the best long-term management of a backup system, tracking failures as they occur over time is critical, as it provides the best possible chances of successful problem diagnosis. Track (i.e., record), at bare minimum, the following information about failures:

- The date and time the failure occurred
- The host(s) associated, differentiating between server, client, and remote backup node as appropriate
- The exact error message noted in the failure
- What the resolution to the problem was, if the problem was resolved
- Any activities occurring outside of the backup software (e.g., system outages, hardware failures, etc.) that may have had an impact on the backup system and therefore may have played a part in the failure

This tracking list should at least be able to be sorted by:

- The date and time of the failure(s)
- The host(s) associated with the failure
- The error message(s) associated with the failure

12.9 Clearly Delineate Roles and Responsibilities

Every system will have various roles and responsibilities, and as discussed at the start of the book, a backup system will involve a large number of different personnel in a company in one way or another. Two of the most crippling personnel issues that can occur with backup systems are domain disputes (where different people believe that their "territory" is being encroached on) and activity disconnects. A domain dispute, as discussed, is where two teams disagree over who is responsible for a particular activity, and as a result friction occurs whenever that activity is performed. An activity disconnect is where everyone assumed that a particular task was the responsibility of another person or another group, and therefore it wasn't performed.

The most appropriate way to avoid these scenarios, and thus increase the effectiveness of the backup system, is to ensure that everyone is formally aware of their roles and responsibilities in relation to the backup system. (If this means having a formal delegations document, so be it.)

12.10 Network, Not Netwon't

The importance of a fully functioning network in an enterprise backup environment can never be over emphasized, and thus this subject deserves special consideration in best practices. By "fully functioning," we are referring to:

- Complete and correct name resolution between all hosts, regardless of what name resolution method is used.
- Use of forced network speed and duplex settings where supported by the network to reduce impact of autonegotation under high backup load.
- Although not directly related to the network per sé, having functioning time synchronization between all hosts involved in the backup network will result in a more properly integrated environment that can be fully relied on and more readily debugged.

(Often deployment of centralized backup systems has an unanticipated benefit of finally fixing all those annoying little network problems that have been impacting business for a long period of time but in themselves never were sufficient to warrant spending time to track down.)

12.11 Ensure the System Is Supported

It is almost guaranteed that no matter whom a company employs, they won't have an answer to every problem. Further, not every problem is going to be solved by a debugging exercise — some problems turn out to be bugs in software or failures in hardware. When these types of problems do arise, or regular problems become too difficult to diagnose, it is important to refer the problem to someone else. Remember that a backup system is in many ways the keystone to the environment. Not having support and maintenance contracts in place for a backup server could result in any, all, or even more than the following scenarios:

- Getting hardware serviced without a support or maintenance contract can result in a higher cost for a single service activity than the entire contract for a single year — for example, a customer once decided not to spend $3000 per annum on hardware maintenance for a stand-alone tape drive. When it failed nine months later it cost $3300 for a one-off service of the drive.
- Staff might exhaust all avenues of analyzing a problem occurring with the backups and still not necessarily find a solution. It makes little sense for a company to pay hundreds of thousands of dollars in support for primary production servers, providing 24/7 platinum support with one hour response times, but leave such systems unrecoverable because of a problem in the backup environment that can't be escalated.
- Worse than the above, staff may determine that there is a known fix for the backup software that addresses the problems being encountered, but maintenance for the backup software

was not purchased, and therefore the backup software company chooses to charge the full cost of the licenses to get access to the patch (effectively charging for new licenses).

A backup server, its operating system, hardware, software, and associated remote backup devices must be considered to have the same level of production criticality as the most important machines they protect.

Appendix A

Technical Asides

A.1 Introduction

Discussions in this area focus on providing additional information on concepts raised in the main document. In some cases it is worthwhile to provide some background information, but that information is not relevant in the main context of the document.

A.2 Transactional Logging

The section on hot database backups mentioned the role of transactional logs. These maintain details of what is going to be done (future perspective) or what has been done (past perspective). Sometimes known as intent logs, they play a vital role in database recoveries.

Figure A.1 represents a chunk of a database just before a backup has been started. The database is running in transactional log mode. Each square at the bottom represents a single "bit" of data. (In actual fact a typical database with blocking mechanisms will be significantly more complex than this, but I've simplified for the sake of explaining transactional logging.)

Assume that a backup starts. In an offline backup, this would mean that the database can't change until the end of the backup. This can only be guaranteed by shutting down the database. Obviously for a database that is required in a 24/7 environment, this is not acceptable. In hot

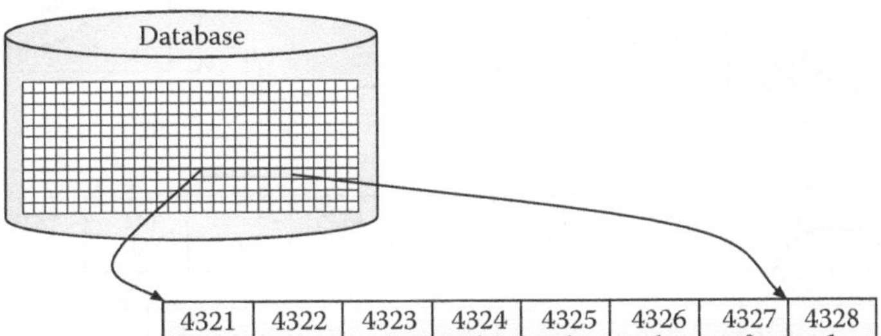

Figure A.1 Database content

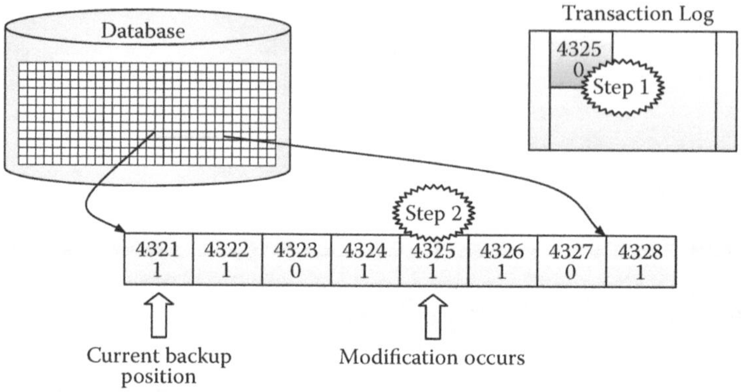

Figure A.2 Changes to a database during a hot backup

backup environments, a transaction log is used as a "change journal" to record changes that are to be committed. This can be "replayed" following a recovery so that even if an inconsistent database file was backed up, it can be restored to full usefulness.

While the backup is in progress, modifications may continue to occur to the database. When a request comes through to modify a part of the database, the modification is first written to the transaction log, then written to the database itself. (See Step 1 and Step 2 in Figure A.2.) This means that when a recovery occurs, the file is recovered, then the "pending" modifications in the transaction log (backed up later) are applied. It doesn't matter where the modification to the database occurs — i.e., it can occur to a point of the database that has already been backed up. It is still recorded in the transaction log. In Figure A.3, a part of the database already backed up has been modified (4321 changed from "1" to "0"). This means that the backup of the database file is inconsistent, but with the transaction logs available, consistency can be restored.

Transaction logs are typically only allowed to grow to a particular size before the database moves on to a new log. However, depending on the level of database activity, this may not take place for some time, possibly hours after a backup has completed. Therefore, databases support "flushing" transaction logs, i.e., forcing the start of a new transaction log.

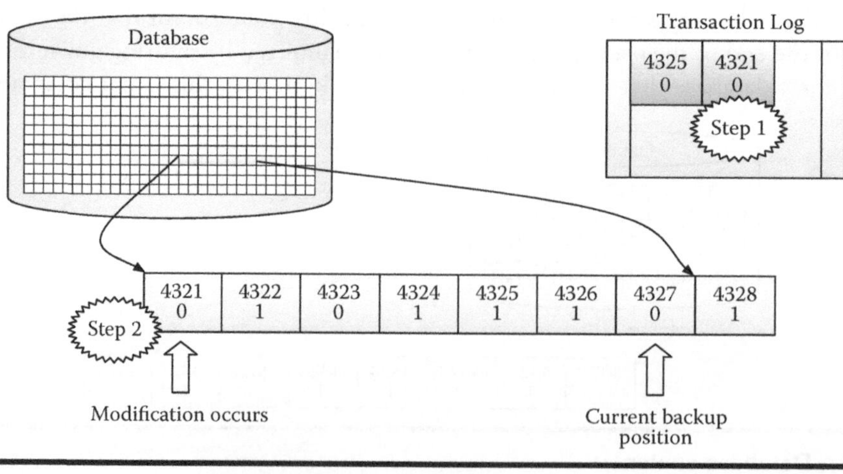

Figure A.3 Applying transaction logs during recovery

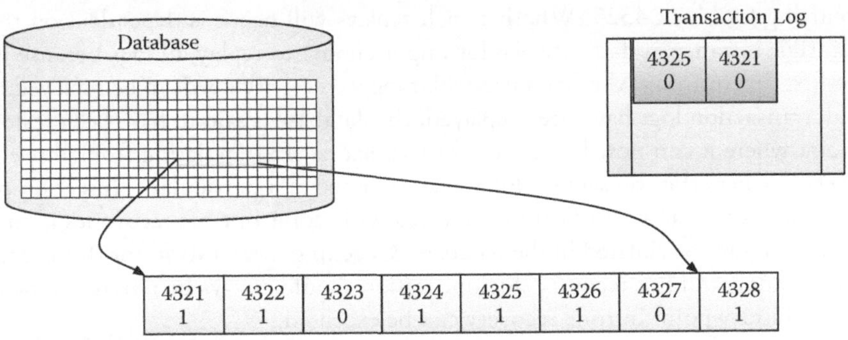

Figure A.4 Recovered database files and transaction logs

A hot database backup using transaction logs typically means the following sequence occurs:

- Notify database that a hot backup is going to be performed
- Backup database files
- Notify database that the hot backup is complete
- Force a new transaction log to be started
- Backup (and possibly trim) all currently unused transaction log files

It is when using transactional logging that we start to see a separation between the terms recover and restore. In these situations, we term the two activities as recover (retrieve from the backup media the database files and transaction logs) and restore (reapply database consistency based on the transaction logs). If we continue with our current example and look at the restore process, we will recover inconsistent database files and completed transaction logs. Our recovered files will resemble the configuration shown in Figure A.4.

Once the files have been recovered from backup media the restore process will commence. At this point, all transaction logs generated between the start of the backup and the end of the backup (recorded as part of the backup process) will be "replayed," over-writing the contents of the nominated database blocks, as shown in Figure A.5. Note that an "unnecessary" log replay is

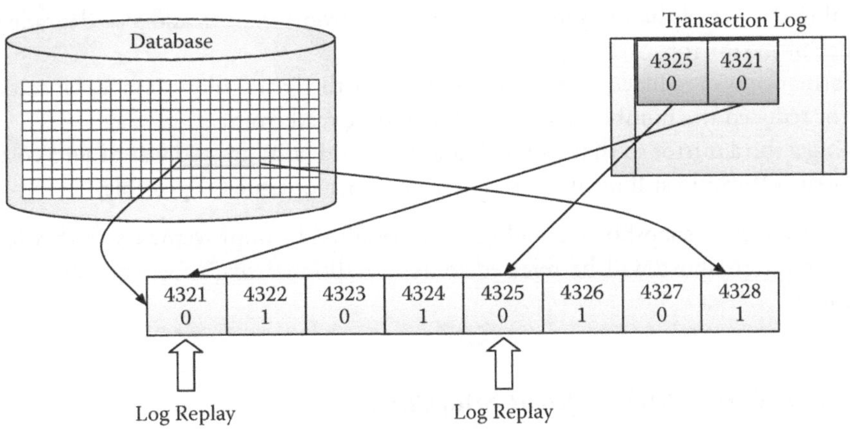

Figure A.5 Database restore process via log replay

shown occurring for block 4325. Whether such replays will occur is dependent on the database being used. (For instance, a database vendor might choose to replay all logs because it would be faster than first determining whether a particular logged activity needs to be replayed.)

Once all transaction logs have been replayed, the database is said to have been restored — i.e., it is at a point where it can now be opened for user access. Extrapolating from above, a point in time recovery is where the transaction log replay is halted at a particular transaction prior to the last transaction. Note that a significant issue faced with point in time recoveries is ensuring that referential integrity is not violated in the database. Checking mechanisms for this is dependent on the database vendor, and hot recovery documentation should always be referred to before assuming that any arbitrary point in time recovery can be executed.

A.3 Snapshots

Five main types of snapshots are currently in use:

1. Traditional
2. Fast resynchronization
3. Copy-on-write
4. Cache
5. Apply-deferred

Each technique has its own features and benefits, discussed briefly in the following sections.

A.3.1 *Traditional Snapshots*

Traditional snapshots have been controversial during their history. A traditional snapshot consisted of "breaking off" a mirror and mounting that mirror in another location for the purposes of backup. This created several issues:

1. Unless three-way mirroring was performed, redundancy was lost for the duration of the backup.
2. The resynchronization time for the mirror could be quite high, as it was directly proportional to the size of the filesystem — such resynchronization would also degrade the performance of the mirror.
3. Performance was reduced during the backup on the "real" filesystem because the loss of a mirror reduced the number of disks that could be read from.
4. Adding a third mirror so that issues (1) and (3) could be addressed was often a costly activity, and issue (2) would still occur, with a reduced form of issue (3) possible.

Recent advances in snapshot technology have resulted in improvements to this scenario; the snapshot description above will be referred to as a traditional snapshot when comparing to the latest snapshots.

A.3.2 *Fast Resynchronization Snapshots*

Fast resynchronization is based on the principle of a bitmap dirty log region for a particular disk or filesystem. Bitmaps were developed in this area first to allow fast resynchronization of mirrors

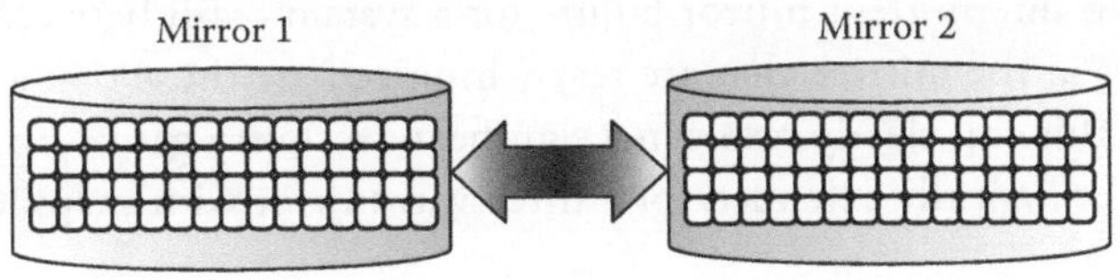

Figure A.6 Normal mirrors

in the event of a temporary service outage, but were quickly recognized as having applicability for snapshots as well.

Consider normal mirrors, such as those shown in Figure A.6. In the event of the path to the second half of the mirror being lost, the system must rebuild the dirty mirror from the clean one. For a traditional mirror this works along the lines of:

- Copy Mirror-1 Block-1 to Mirror-2 Block-1
- Copy Mirror-1 Block-2 to Mirror-2 Block-2
- Copy Mirror-1 Block-3 to Mirror-2 Block-3
- and so on...
- Copy Mirror-1 Block-n to Mirror-2 Block-n

Therefore the re-mirror time takes at least as long as a complete end-to-end read of the clean mirror and an end-to-end write of the dirty mirror, assuming that no other activity is occurring at the same time.

A bitmap is utilized to record the intent to update the mirror with data and can be used to track what blocks need to be resynchronized in the event of mirror failure. Each "pixel" in the bitmap represents a block of disk, and this process can be represented as shown in Figure A.7. In this case the mirror write sequence becomes

- Intend to write to block 1 of mirror
- Write to pixel 1 of bitmap to indicate that it is now "dirty"
- Write to block 1 of mirror 1
- Write to block 1 of mirror 2; at a certain point after this, the bitmap pixel 1 will be updated (reset) to indicate that block 1 is no longer "dirty"

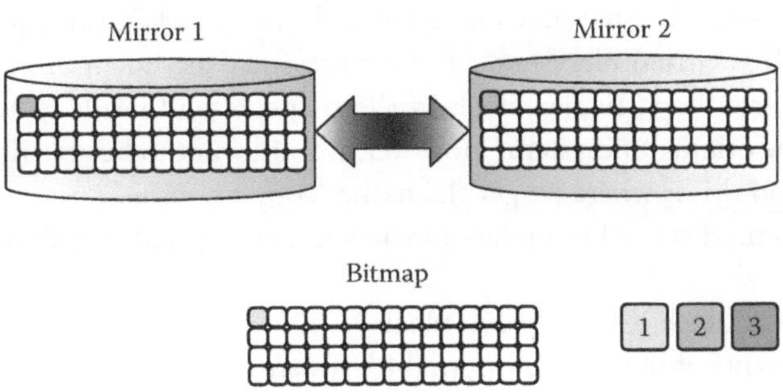

Figure A.7 Mirrors with bitmaps

In the event of an intermittent mirror failure (or a system crash between mirror-side writes), the only components of the mirrors that are resynchronized are those that are marked in the bitmap as being dirty. This can clearly result in a significant recovery gain.

The bitmap can be logically extended for a three-way mirror with snapshot as follows:

- During normal operations all three sides of the mirror are attached and operational.
- When a snapshot is required, a new bitmap is created to handle the resynchronization of the tertiary mirror.
- The tertiary mirror is detached.
- Operations are performed on the tertiary mirror (read or read/write).
- When operations are complete, the tertiary mirror is reattached using the snapshot bitmap for a fast resynchronization.

Note that using only two mirrors with fast resynchronization snapshots is still not recommended — while the performance impact for resynchronization will be significantly lower, the loss of redundancy during backup remains a real problem.

A.3.3 Copy-On-Write Snapshots

To do traditional snapshots or fast resynchronization snapshots without impacting system redundancy, a minimum of three-way mirrors must be used, which many organizations may find to be cost prohibitive. Although some organizations perform traditional snapshots or fast resynchronization snapshots using only two-way mirrors, this is a foolish and dangerous activity.

The aptly named copy-on-write snapshot overcomes this limitation, and is based on the principle that whenever a snapshot is created for short-term access or backup, it is not likely that there will be a large amount of change to the original filesystem during that period. Therefore, copy-on-write techniques can be used.

When a copy-on-write snapshot is first created, the following will result:

- The original filesystem will continue to function "as is."
- A "virtual" filesystem will be created that contains no data, with all blocks referring back to the original filesystem for its data.

This relies on the idea that if there is a requirement to read from block X of the snapshot, and that block hasn't changed since the snapshot was generated, then block X can equally be read from the original filesystem. This virtual filesystem can be represented as shown in Figure A.8. In this case any attempt to read from a particular block in the snapshot will result in a read from the corresponding block in the original filesystem. However, we still want to be able to make updates to our original filesystem and this is where we get the name "copy-on-write."

The following method is used to update block X in the original snapshot:

- Copy contents of block X to snapshot block X
- Write new contents of block X to original filesystem

This can be represented as shown in Figure A.9.

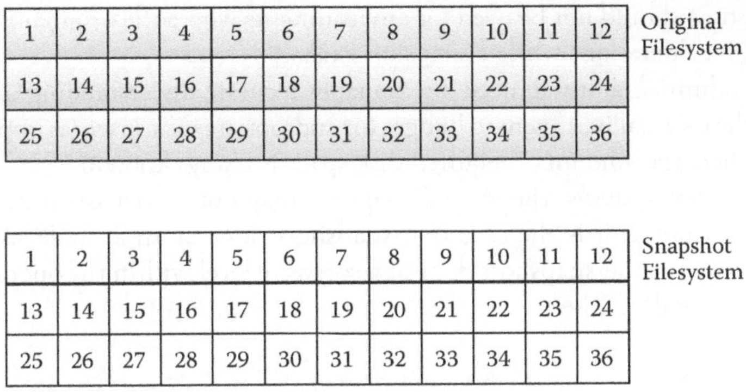

Figure A.8 Copy-on-write snapshot with new snapshot

So in this case we have a snapshot filesystem now that still mostly refers back to the original filesystem, but one block has changed, which means that the snapshot now takes one block of disk space (other than any other metadata required).

A few caveats with copy-on-write filesystems must be considered

- Many systems that provide copy-on-write snapshots do not allow the snapshot to be available read-write.
- Reading from the snapshot filesystem can result in a performance degradation on the original filesystem, which will increase the risk of backups impacting the production system.
- The write speed of the original filesystem becomes limited to the write speed of the snapshot filesystem. This becomes critical in environments where fast disk is snapped to slower disk — e.g., filesystem provided by 15,000 RPM fiber channel drives being snapped to 5,400 RPM IDE drives. In these cases it is imperative to snap only in situations where there will be either (1) absolute minimum write activities or (2) little need for write performance during the lifetime of the snapshot. (However, more correctly, slow disk should not be used as snapshot regions for high-speed disk.)
- A logical extension to the above — these snapshots should have short life spans. Extended life spans will result in lengthy amounts of copy-on-write operations or large snapshots.

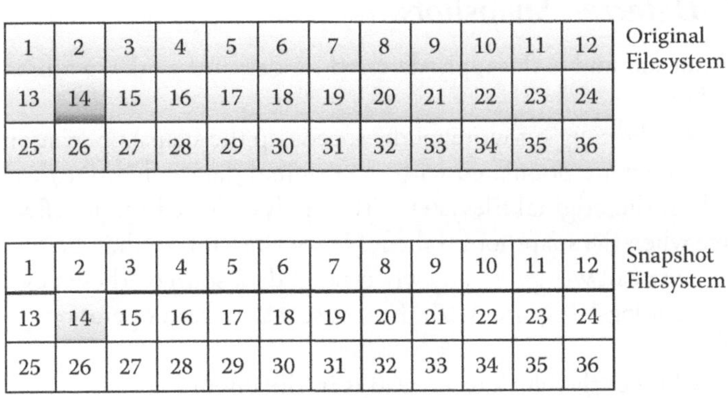

Figure A.9 Copy-on-write snapshot with updates to the original filesystem

- These snapshots should not be used for environments where the original filesystem will have write-intensive operations while a snapshot exists.
- The system administrator will need a reasonably accurate understanding of the percentage of change on the original filesystem to budget for appropriate disk space (as opposed to traditional snapshots where the amount of required disk space is always known).
- In some snapshot systems, the virtual snapshot may not be persistent across reboots. (Frequently, for instance, it is the case that snapshots done at an array level will be persistent across host reboots, but snapshots done at a software level within the operating system on an individual host will not be.)

A.3.4 Cache Snapshots

A cache snapshot is similar to a copy-on-write snapshot, with the proviso that cache snapshots refer to multiple filesystems that all perform snapshots while sharing a common pool of space from where the space allocated for their snapshots are generated. That is, in non-cache snapshot environments, each filesystem will have its own snapshot filesystem associated with it if snapping is done at the operating system level, or in an array each LUN will have its own snapshot LUN associated with it.

In cache snapshot environments, a single volume or LUN exists from where all the snapshot filesystems draw their space. This is designed to take advantage of the fact that there may be a (potentially) large number of filesystems on a host that all need to be snapped simultaneously, but across all of them the write activity during the lifetime of the snapshot is quite low. For example, depending on the environment, a 1-GB snapshot cache may be sufficient for ten or more filesystems that receive few writes during backup.

This obviously creates the advantage of minimizing the total amount of disk space that must be allocated for snapshots with respect to backups. This in turn can result in reduced budgetary requirements for an environment. The disadvantage of this is that it effectively places all the snapshot eggs in the one basket — if a single filesystem encounters unexpected growth while snapshots exist, then snapshots may be lost for multiple filesystems — every filesystem that snapped from the allocated cache. Therefore if even one disk area that receives cache snapshots "overflows," all snapshots may be lost.

A.3.5 Apply-Deferred Snapshots

An alternate snapshot method is the apply-deferred model, and works in almost the reverse of the copy-on-write model.

As will be recalled, the copy-on-write model speeds up the snapshot creation process by having "blank" snapshots, which are populated with the original data only prior to a write occurring to an individual block in the original filesystem. The apply-deferred model effectively "freezes" the original data source when the snapshot is taken. New writes, rather than being written to the original data source, are instead written to a newly created data source. These new data sources could be referred to as "intent logs" (Figure A.10). In this scenario, read operations work as follows:

- Check to see whether the block to be read is in the intent log.
- If the block to be read is in the intent log, read it from there.
- If the block to be read is not in the intent log, read it from the original data source.

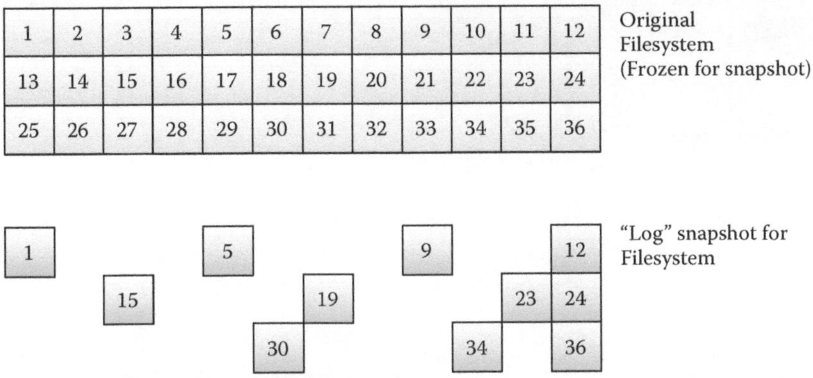

Figure A.10 Apply-deferred snapshots

An obvious advantage of apply-deferred snapshots is that the "double write" does not occur while the snapshot is active, thus increasing performance. Proponents of this model argue that with the double-write eliminated, an unlimited number of snapshots can be taken without impacting data access performance.

While the snapshots are active at least, this is relatively true. It is reasonably trivial to avoid a double-read operation by maintaining a simple bitmap in memory indicating which blocks belong to which data sources.

However, a key downside of this method is the performance impact that can occur when the intent log is applied to the original data source at the end of the snapshot (assuming it is decided that the updates should be kept). If a large number of writes have occurred during the period of the snapshot, both the original data source and the snapshot intent log will be highly active for write and read operations, respectively. Indeed, for data integrity reasons it is highly likely that updates during snapshot intent log application will be suspended. (Apply-deferred snapshots are used in several of the primary x86 virtualization systems, and can cause virtual machines to "freeze" while snapshots are released and rolled into the primary image if the number of changes were high.)

Appendix B

Sample Recovery Request Form

Obviously every company will need its own procedures, but when no system has previously existed to allow users to request recoveries formally, any form is a good starting place. The following might be considered a template for what users would fill in when requesting a recovery:

Your name	
Login name	
Contact phone number	
E-mail address	
Preferred recovery time	
File(s) to recover (including folder names)[a]	
Recover to[b]	
Signed (you)	
Signed (your manager)	
Completion date	
Recovery operator	
File(s) recovered to	
Completed by (signed)	
Recovery complete (signed by you)	

[a] If the full path to the file(s) is(are) not provided, the recovery time will take longer.
[b] If the file(s) cannot be recovered to the nominated location, you will be notified.

A sample recovery form document may be found on the Web site.

Appendix C

Sample Test Form

If formal test forms are not available, the following might be a useful template for an organization attempting to document the results of acceptance testing for a backup and recovery system. (Note this is not meant to be a comprehensive test plan, merely a sample.)

TEST (*number*): Windows 2003 file and directory recovery		
DATE:		
DESCRIPTION: This test is to confirm that files and directories previously backed up by <product> can be successfully recovered.		
REQUIREMENTS: The following requirements must be satisfied before this test can be conducted.		
1.	A successful full backup must have been reported as having taken place.	
2.	Files must have been added to the filesystem in the regions outlined in the "Test Procedure" below.	
3.	A successful incremental backup must have been reported as having taken place.	
4.	Staff conducting the test must have completed basic product familiarization.	
TEST PROCEDURE:		
1.	Delete the directory "D:\User Documents"	
2.	Following the instructions outlined in the product user manual, complete a recovery of the files and directories below:	
	a.	(Test 1) "D:\User Documents" to its original location, choosing to overwrite existing files
	b.	(Test 2) "D:\User Documents" to "E:\Recovery"
	c.	(Test 3) "D:\User Documents" to its original location, choosing not to overwrite existing files

REQUIRED RESULTS	
1.	Test 1 should succeed without errors or warnings.
2.	Test 2 should succeed without errors or warnings.
3.	Test 3 should show no files recovered, as all files should have been recovered by Test 1.
ACHIEVED RESULTS (*note "Success" or "Failure" only*)	
Test 1:	
Test 2:	
Test 3:	
THE FOLLOWING ACTIONS MUST BE UNDERTAKEN AS A RESULT OF THIS TEST	
STAFF WITNESSES	
Staff Name:	
Signature:	
Staff Name:	
Signature:	

A sample acceptance suite may be found on the Web site.

Appendix D

Glossary of Terms

ACL (access control list): Advanced file access permissions system found in several operating systems. The term "ACL" is generic and thus two competing operating systems that implement ACLs will not necessarily have the same ACLs. ACLs go beyond the traditional "user," "group," and "world" access models found in simple UNIX systems, offering more advanced customization of access.

Administrator (backup): A person tasked with responsibility for the configuration, monitoring, and accuracy of a backup system or systems.

API: Application Programming Interface. A set of libraries, tools or functions made available by a piece of software to facilitate being called by, or extended by a third party program, utility, etc.

BLOB (binary large object): This is the generic term for very large rows or tuples within databases and is typically associated with use of a database to store archival files or multimedia files.

BMR (bare metal recovery): This is the common term for restoring an entire machine and all its data from a fresh install (or no install at all).

CAP (cartridge access port): Used in tape libraries to facilitate the insertion of new media into the library, or removal of existing media from the library, without needing to interrupt any other operations occurring; e.g., pause the library to open the main doors. Where libraries have CAPs, they should be used exclusively in comparison to opening the front doors of the library.

CDP (continuous data protection): Refers to a backup activity that remains ongoing, updating a backup image or destination volume with real-time updates of any changes made to the source filesystem.

Centralized backup: An environment where at least control of the backup configuration, scheduling, media management, and monitoring is coordinated by a single host in the environment. Centralized backups will typically also see backup data stored on only a few hosts in the environment.

Cold backup: Typically used in database environments for offline backup.

Consolidated backup: A special backup action where a previously executed full backup is "merged" intelligently by the backup software with a new incremental or differential to create a new full backup. This avoids having to run a full backup explicitly after initial commissioning/backup.

DAS (direct attach storage): Refers to storage that is physically plugged into the host and can only be relocated to another host through physically moving the storage.

Decentralized backup: Refers to an environment where each machine is responsible for its own backup. Administrators must work on each individual host to configure, schedule, manage media, and monitor backups.

Differential: A backup that encompasses changes made over a series of one or more backups, designed to reduce the number of overall backup sets required for a recovery.

Disaster recovery: Complete restoration of a machine or an environment. This is often synonymous with BMR.

Full: Refers to a complete backup of all items, regardless of when they have changed.

HBA: Host Bus Adapter. Usually refers to a PCI-card (or other variant) that allows either SCSI or Fibre-Channel connectivity.

Hot backup: Typically used in database environments for online backup.

HSM (hierarchical storage management): Refers to a system whereby less frequently used data is migrated from disk to tape, leaving behind a "stub" file in place of the real file. When someone attempts to open the stub, the HSM software automatically initiates a tape-based restore of the file, copying the file back into place for access. This allows for the appearance of considerably more storage than might be economically feasible to deploy.

ILM: Information Lifecycle Management.

ILP: Information Lifecycle Protection.

Incremental: Refers to a backup of all items that have changed since the last backup.

Index: In backup parlance, an index typically refers to a database or other structure that contains details of the files that have been backed up (or sometimes more generally, simply the backups that have been performed).

JBOD (just a bunch of disks): Refers to a "dumb" disk pack that may either present the disks inside it individually or, at best, in a simple stripe/concatenation. Sometimes JBOD is used to describe more intelligent RAID-based systems, which nonetheless are not full SAN arrays.

LUN (logical unit number): A SCSI term referring to a particular device on a bus, but extended in many SAN environments to refer to a physical slice from a RAID structure presented to a host for access. (Typically, each processor on the array capable of presenting storage is seen as a different SCSI target by the operating system, with individual data units presented by the processor visible as LUNs for that particular target.)

Mail Slot: *See* CAP.

Murphy's law: If something can go wrong, it usually will.

NAS (network attached storage): Refers to a disk storage system attached to the TCP/IP network and provides "shares" to hosts as required. Hosts with NAS attached recognize the storage as network-presented.

NDMP (Network Data Management Protocol): Typically refers to the backup of filesystems and other data attached to a host that does not run a traditional operating system and therefore needs a mechanism other than a backup agent/client to be able to protect its data successfully.

NTP: Network Time Protocol.

Offline backup: A backup that is taken where the data being copied/protected is inaccessible to other applications, users, and sometimes even the operating system for the duration.

Operator (backup): Typically a person tasked with day-to-day activities to ensure the backup system continues to operate in its configured capacity; most normally this refers to media management.

Online backup: Refers to the generation of a backup where the data being backed up is not "quiesced" before the backup; i.e., access (reads and writes) may still be occurring during the backup.

Race condition: In computer science, a race condition is where a check is made to ensure something is safe to occur, but then it becomes unsafe between the time that the check is run and the action occurs. For example, if an application checks to confirm that a file using a particular name does not exist before it writes the file, then that same named file is written by another process before the original application writes its file, data corruption or application instability can ensue. Avoiding race conditions is a difficult and challenging task, depending on the application or operating system.

RAID (redundant array of inexpensive disks): Two or more disks are presented as a single storage unit to a host.

RAID 0: Depending on the RAID processor, this may be either concatenated or striped storage. This provides no redundancy. In a concatenation, x disks are written to one after the other, with disk $x + 1$ only being written to after disk x is physically full. In a stripe, x disks are written to simultaneously, based on the stripe width. For example, if two disks are provided in a 64-KB stripe, then a write of 128 KB will write the first 64 KB to one disk, and the next 64 KB to the next disk.

RAID 0+1: This is where a set of stripes (or concatenations) are mirrored. For example, with six disks there would be 2 × (3 disk-stripes) mirrored.

RAID 1: Mirrored storage. Two or more disks of the same size act as "mirrors" of each other, holding identical copies of the data. For a write to be considered successful, both mirrors must be written to. This uses the most space out of all redundancy techniques, as x disks will provide at most the capacity of $x/2$ disks.

RAID 1+0: This is where a set of mirrors are striped. For example, with six disks, three mirrored pairs would be constructed, and then the mirrored pairs would be striped. This is often advocated as a mechanism of protecting against more than one disk failure, but in actuality two disk failures can still result in a total filesystem loss. Consider the following:

S1-M1 ↔ S1-M2

S2-M1 ↔ S2-M2

S3-M1 ↔ S3-M2

where S-x refers to stripe component x, and M-y refers to the mirror number. RAID 1+0 allows for multiple disks to fail as long as the failures do not occur on the same "row" as in the above. For example, it is possible to lose all M1 disks, or a combination such as S1-M1, S2-M2, S3-M2, and not lose the system. However, it does not actually guarantee any higher availability than regular RAID 1, and thus should only be considered for the performance gains it offers.

RAID 3: Striped storage with redundancy. This requires a minimum of three disks (with best performance typically provided by five disks) and for *n* disks gives a capacity equivalent to *n*-1 disks. Any write to the storage will have the data striped across *n*-1 disks, with the final disk writing a "parity checksum," which can be used to reconstruct the data in the event of one of the data disks failing.

RAID 5: Striped storage with redundancy. This works in the same way as RAID 3, with the exception that the parity write staggers across all disks, rather than being written to a dedicated disk as it is for RAID 3.

RAID 6: Striped storage with dual redundancy. Not an "official" RAID standard but the common term for either a RAID-5 environment (where the parity is either striped across two disks or the parity is mirrored) or a RAID-3 environment (where the parity disk is mirrored).

Raw device: A disk or partition that is written to without any filesystem in place. That is, the application responsible for the data is responsible for all disk writes, data organization, etc. In some high-performance environments, this can yield additional speed and capacity.

Restore (database): Database vendors often make a point of difference between a restore and a recovery. Typically, the difference is that a recovery is seen as a retrieval of backup data from the backup medium, whereas a restore is what is performed on the recovered data to reinstate consistency in the database following the file recovery.

SAN (storage area network): Refers to storage provided by a disk array over a fiber network. Storage is mapped to hosts on an as-needs basis, allocated out of a central pool. Hosts with SAN attached storage typically consider the storage to be "locally attached."

SLA (service level agreement): Typically a formal contract indicating the maximum amount of data loss that can occur within a system or the maximum amount of time that can elapse before either (1) the system recovery starts or (2) the system is actually recovered.

Snapshot: Generation of an "image" of an existing filesystem or LUN that can be used to perform fast restores, maintenance, and backup/recovery operations without impacting the data on the "original," or to provide read-only access to the data for another purpose. Unlike mirrors, snapshots are designed for rapid generation.

SNMP (Simple Network Management Protocol): A UDP-based alerting protocol intended to allow for centralized systems management and event reporting.

SOE (standard operating environment): A documented OS or application configuration which is mandated for use or ever automatically installed.

Stripe: Typically used to indicate a RAID set where data is written in discrete "column widths" across multiple disks. For example, if the stripe width is set to 32 KB and there are four disks, and 128 KB of data is to be written, the first 32 KB is written to the first disk, the second 32 KB is written to the second disk, the third 32 KB is written to the third disk, and the fourth 32 KB is written to the final disk. Stripes may be used in conjunction with RAID protection (e.g., RAID 3 or RAID 5), or may refer to a non-fault-tolerant group of disks.

Synthetic full: *See* Consolidated backup.

WWN (Worldwide Name): A unique string associated with any fiber-channel device to ensure that communications can be directed accurately to and from the device, and which allows for access control mechanisms to be used.

Index

C

D

E

F

G

H

N

O

P

Q

R

S

T

U

V

W

Z

For Product Safety Concerns and Information please contact our EU representative GPSR@taylorandfrancis.com Taylor & Francis Verlag GmbH, Kaufingerstraße 24, 80331 München, Germany